WORKING IN SILICON VALLEY

ISSUES IN WORK AND HUMAN RESOURCES

Daniel J.B. Mitchell, Series Editor

WORKING IN SILICON VALLEY

Economic and Legal Analysis of a High-Velocity Labor Market

ALAN HYDE

M.E.Sharpe
Armonk, New York
London, England

Library of Congress Cataloging-in-Publication Data

Hyde, Alan, 1951–
    Working in Silicon valley : economic and legal analysis of a high-velocity labor market /
Alan Hyde.
        p. cm. — (Issues in work and human resources)
    Includes bibliographical references and index.
    ISBN 0-7656-0750-6 (alk. paper)
        1. Labor market—California—Santa Clara Valley (Santa Clara County) 2. Manpower
policy—California—Santa Clara Valley (Santa Clara County) 3. High technology
industries—Employees—Supply and demand—California—Santa Clara Valley (Santa
Clara County) I. Title. II. Series.

HD5725.C2 H93 2003
331.12′09794′73—dc21   2002036970

CONTENTS

FOREWORD

During its boom phase, the Silicon Valley was a center of attention for many reasons, but especially for its labor market arrangements. With the dot-com/high-tech stock market bust of 2000 and beyond, many will be tempted to view the institutions that surrounded the Silicon Valley as yesterday's news. But they would be wrong to do so.

Job-market mobility—what Alan Hyde in this volume terms "high velocity"—was and is a key characteristic of the Silicon Valley's labor market. As such, an understanding of Silicon Valley employment practices provides an understanding of labor market practices in *any* industry where mobility is high and the employment relationship is loose. A key finding is that labor markets characterized by inherently high job mobility require institutions to function properly. Flexibility does not imply a free-for-all with no constraints. For example, if employees move from job to job, what obligation do they have to former employers with regard to confidential information? Exactly who does a temp work for? The agency supplying his/her service to some employer? Or the employer that uses the service? Answers to these questions are needed to guide both employers and employees toward appropriate behavior.

Moreover, public policies can assist the operation of such high-velocity labor markets—or can hinder them. Hyde's conclusion that flexible labor markets may well require more elaborate social safety nets is an important one. Employer functions, such as the provision of health insurance and pensions, that developed by the middle of the twentieth century are difficult to implement in the context of constant job changing. Hyde notes that in some older industries, for example, construction, these functions are mediated through labor unions. But he finds that unions and union-type organizations in the Silicon Valley are unlikely to develop anytime soon to the point where they can handle these social welfare tasks. This conclusion suggests that some external source is required to provide for such needs.

Generally, the Silicon Valley's labor market faces issues that are found in more traditional sectors of employment. Hyde notes, for example, the issue of race, sex, or ethnic discrimination is not avoided simply by pointing to high mobility and meritocracy. Options for skill development and training are intertwined with the issue of discrimination. Questions of incentives and incentive design, epitomized by stock options in the Silicon Valley, are common to all industries. The Silicon Valley—especially in view of the boom/bust cycle it has exhibited—has not settled into a fixed pattern. Its labor market continues to evolve. And Hyde provides us with a road map for that evolution.

Daniel J.B. Mitchell
Series Editor

ACKNOWLEDGMENTS

Earlier versions of chapters 2 through 4 were delivered at a Cardozo School of Law faculty colloquium (February 17, 1994); Rutgers School of Law faculty colloquium (October 17, 1996); Columbia School of Law "Make or Buy: The Boundaries of the Firm" pre-conference (February 7, 1997); and Columbia School of Law Sloan Project on Corporate Governance Conference, Corporate Governance Today (May 21–22, 1998). That version was published in the conference proceedings. Thanks particularly to Jeffrey Gordon, Mark Roe, Bernard Black, John Coffee, David Charny, Saul Levmore, and Ronald Gilson. A later version was presented at the "Contracts with Highly Skilled Workers" conference, John M. Olin Law and Economics Program, Georgetown University Law Center (November 3–4, 2000; thanks to Warren Schwartz, Eric Talley, Eric Posner, George Triantis, Rachel Arnow-Richman).

An earlier version of chapter 9 was presented at the 50th Annual New York University Conference on Labor (May 29, 1997). Thanks to Sam Estreicher for making NYU such an exciting center for labor law scholarship, his help in letting me try out ideas at the conferences, and his blanket permission for later publication of his conference's preliminary efforts. A later version was presented at "The Role of Unions in the 21st Century" conference, University of Pennsylvania Law School (January 26, 2001), was later published in *University of Pennsylvania Journal of Labor and Employment Law* 4, no. 3 (2002): 493–527, and appears in this book with their permission.

Chapter 12 was presented at the "Behavioral Science Implications for Employment Discrimination Law" conference, New York University School of Law, April 19, 2002. Thank you to Mitu Gulati and Michael Yelnosky for organizing it; Sam Estreicher for hosting it; and Christine Jolls, Linda Hamilton Krieger, Deborah Malamud, Vicki Schultz, and Susan Sturm for helpful comments.

Presentations of the overall project took place at the International Network on Transformative Employment and Labor Law (INTELL) in Kent, England (July 1996) and again at Cape Town, South Africa (March 18–20,1999). I am grateful to all my Intell colleagues for supporting work that is so different from most of theirs and particularly recall the support and criticism of Karl Klare, Joann Conaghan, Michael Fischl, Harry Arthurs, Jim Atleson, Guy Mundlak, and Brian Langille.

Other presentations of the basic economic model took place at the 52nd Annual New York University Conference on Labor (May 20,1999); Institute of Industrial Relations, University of California at Los Angeles (October 19, 1999; thanks to Gillian Lester and Dan Mitchell); "Reflexive Labour Law: The Next Step" conference, Hugo Sinzheimer Institute, University of Amsterdam (December 13, 2001; thanks to Ton Wilthagen and Rolf Ragowski); Boalt School of Law, University of California at Berkeley (October 17, 2002; thanks to Linda Hamilton Krieger); and was the keynote address at XII Inter-American Conference of Ministers of Labour, Montréal, Canada (October 2, 2002).

A grant from the Sloan Project on Corporate Governance at Columbia Law School permitted me to spend a week in Silicon Valley in March 1996. This was the only financial support that I received in writing this book. Many of the ideas of this book were tried out in my seminar, "Legal Issues in High-Technology Employment," given at New York University School of Law, Spring 2000. Thanks once again to Sam Estreicher for allowing me do that, and to all the students in that seminar, particularly Matthew Bodie, whose paper I draw on in chapter 10. At Rutgers, Steven Hari-Das, Megan Roberts, and A. Hyun Rich checked citations at various points. At M.E. Sharpe, thanks to Lynn Taylor and Susan Rescigno.

Special thanks to Anna Lee Saxenian, whose book made me see how differently Silicon Valley people, economists, and lawyers think about information; Tim Clark, Mia Clark, Deborah Satten, and Boris Feldman, who introduced me to their friends and colleagues; Paul Schachter, who brought a case into my class in Employment Law that first got me thinking about employer-employee disputes about intellectual property; Kenneth Arrow, Paul Romer, James Baron, and Edward Lazear, who generously gave their time to a total stranger and helped me think that there were really problems here that might interest economists; Ian Ayres, Joe Bankman, Yochai Benkler, Robert Bone, Ronald Gilson, Wendy Gordon, Henry Hansman, Al Klevorick, Mark Roe, Roberta Romano, Chuck Sabel, and Alan Schwartz, for crucial conversations at crucial times; Gillian Lester, Cynthia Estlund, Steven Willborn, and Stuart Schwab, for guidance, support, and encouragement; Paul Gewirtz, for telling me that the next book had better be on employment or labor law; Tony Kronman, for demanding a new paradigm. Always, and above all, Ellen Gesmer, Toby Hyde, and Laura Hyde, for everything.

Every page in this book reflects conversations with the late David Charny, who provided not only intellectual guidance, but also support, encouragement, and advice at a difficult time. I am so grateful for the chance to have known David in his tragically short life and dedicate the book to his memory.

INTRODUCTION

Frisbee games in the halls. Refrigerators stocked with soft drinks and junk food. Engineers sleeping under desks. Teams of employees skipping nimbly to competitors, or start-ups. The labor market institutions associated with high technology in Silicon Valley, California, have passed into popular culture without ever having been the subject of academic examination.

This book won't have much to say about those refrigerators. It will, however, examine the following list of labor market features commonly associated with high-technology employers or districts, like those in Silicon Valley, the southern San Francisco Bay area stretching between and beyond Stanford University and the city of San Jose:

- rapid job mobility;
- short job tenures;
- heavy use of temporary labor, independent contracting, and other contingent labor;
- weak internal labor markets;
- weak loyalty to individual firms;
- career paths that often involve starting a business or joining a start-up;
- hiring for specific skills (as opposed to hiring that contemplates future training);
- labor market intermediaries that facilitate such short-term hiring as temporary help agencies and Internet job boards;
- flexible compensation involving heavy use of bonuses and stock options; and
- strong inequality in earnings and labor market participation.

This list of aspects of high-technology employment has a kind of paradoxical status. To human relations professionals, it is almost a cliché. The list began appearing in the human relations literature about fifteen years ago (Kleingartner and Anderson 1987; Colclough and Tolbert 1992). It has been fairly stable since then. (The only three additions one might make since the early 1980s—important ones—associate [1] immigrant scientists and engineers, some on short-term visas; [2] participation in global production networks; and [3] the Internet.) To breathless boosters of the new, wired economy and its "free agents" or "fast company," the entire list seems self-evidently cool (e.g., Gould et al. 1997). To critics on the left, such as Richard Sennett (1998), it represents a "corrosion of character." Yet there has been surprisingly little sober analysis of such a labor market from an economic or policy point of view, to determine its actual structure, dynamics, benefits, and costs; to what extent it represents the future of the entire labor market; how its components do (or do not) contribute to rapid technological and economic growth; and which of its components represents a model for the larger economy.

This book aims to be that analysis, or at least a preliminary attempt at one. It focuses precisely on the high-technology industries of Silicon Valley and tries to gather academic knowledge concerning its distinctive labor market, which I call "high-velocity": what keeps it going, how it is distinct, what benefits and problems it brings to society.

It is shaped by the fact that both legal and economic scholars normally analyze such labor markets using concepts that last made sense in an older labor market. This book will sketch out the beginnings of an alternative economics of employment, one in which problems of the economics of information play the central role—specifically, the economics of endogenous growth through the creation and diffusion of valuable information.

Law has the potential to disrupt the distinct labor market institutions developed in high-velocity labor markets, without necessarily intending to do so. The law of labor and employment carries, embedded in its concepts, many assumptions about employment, formed in an era when a typical contract of employment lasted a long time and was full of implicit, unwritten promises. These assumptions reflect the prevailing economic analysis of employment relations. They may yield strange results when applied to today's high-velocity labor markets. Law is certainly not the best perspective from which to view a high-velocity labor market, but it does alert us to points of conflict and uncertainty. We can use these legal problems to highlight the assumptions, common to both law and economics, that often disable understanding of today's labor markets.

Consider four legal problems that we will spend much time on. A team of engineers leaves its employer to form a start-up that will make products that compete with their old employer's. An executive is wrongfully terminated, and argues that his principal economic loss was in stock options that had yet to vest, or even issue. (Or, in a variation on this problem, former employees of a bankrupt company say they were induced to accept stock options through fraudulent representations.) Production employees nominally referred by a temporary help agency claim that they are legally employees of the original equipment manufacturer. An engineer is fired, and seeks to send e-mails to company employees, enlisting their support for his lawsuit.

These four problems have nothing to do with each other. They arise in different doctrinal areas of law. The answer to one has nothing to do with the answers to the others. Yet they share a number of structural similarities. All arise from ordinary, everyday aspects of working in Silicon Valley. All nevertheless raise issues that are extraordinarily difficult to analyze under existing employment and labor law. A court deciding any of these lawsuits will have to employ legal concepts that "don't fit," because they were shaped through an implicit assumption that employment is stable and long-lived. The court's decision, on start-ups, stock options, temporary employment, or e-mail systems, will make high-velocity labor markets easier or more difficult to maintain. Finally, if the court wants to employ economic analysis to understand the employment contract before it, it will not be able to find that analysis.

When the engineers start a company, the court will have to decide if they are violating their old "employer's" "trade secrets." The stock options of the terminated executive or disappointed employees might be analogized to "wages," "pensions," or "investment securities," none of which they resemble well. The production workers might be "employees" of the temp agency instead of the manufacturer, or "jointly employed," or even "independent contractors." The fired employee's e-mails might be "trespass" on the "employer's" e-mail system, or "protected concerted activity" of "employees."

All of these legal concepts, and others we will examine, have taken traditional life by assuming stable communities of employees, working a long time for a particular employer. This image of stable employment tells us who is and is not an "employee" with duties of loyalty toward an "employer" and rights to communicate with other "employees." The image similarly tells us whether the piece of paper in the "employee's" hand represents an investment, wage, or pension. If that individual, however, is a high-technology employee in a high-velocity labor market, who moves rapidly among competing firms and may start his or her own firm, the image will give a misleading picture of that individual's community, organizations, relations (implicit and explicit) to employers and others, and compensation. This book will discuss all these and other issues, at some loss of the detail that lawyers might prefer. Its goal, however, is to put a new image in place of the old prototype of employment. It will try to put together what we know about the implicit and explicit contract of employment in high-velocity labor markets, its economic analysis, and social and policy implications.

Throughout this book, I will be contrasting Silicon Valley's "high-velocity" labor market with a stylized portrait of a "traditional" employer. A traditional or "old economy" employer has a well-developed internal labor market where employees make a lifetime career. Compensation and benefits are backloaded to encourage lifetime commitment. For example, the firm will pay pensions and for health insurance (worth more to senior employees). Managerial ranks are open only to those who "worked their way up" in that company or "won" a job "tournament." The firm provides significant training in "firm-specific human capital" to these long-term employees, even to employees who had few skills and little experience at hiring. Employment contracts are unwritten and contain many "implicit promises." The concepts used by economists and lawyers to describe such companies—which obviously have not disappeared from America, though they do not employ as many people as they used to—will map poorly onto Silicon Valley's start-up culture, compensation arrangements, employee contracts, and organizations.

It is no exaggeration to describe the entire structure of U.S. labor and employment law as assuming such traditional careers in traditional companies. The right of employees even to communicate with each other, let along form unions or organizations, depends entirely on their being "employees" together at a single company. This creates strange results when employees are frequently laid off and rehired and seek (like the engineer) to communicate with former coworkers. The structure of benefits protection focuses not on incentives to provide them, but on making such promises completely nonforfeitable after five or ten years, vesting schedules that are increasingly irrelevant in a country in which the median private-sector employee has been with his or her current employer for 3.3 years. The discrimination laws, without anyone specifically intending this, apply as a practical matter only to late-career employees who are dismissed (or sometimes not promoted), losing substantial salaries and benefits and unable to obtain new jobs. (They also apply to victims of particularly offensive individual harassment, particularly sexual harassment.) They do not effectively reach failures to hire, and thus have little relevance in industries with few such late-career employees. Thus, Silicon Valley employers can maintain workforces that are genuinely meritocratic in most ways, yet have few African-American or Latino/Latina employees. Similar is the idea that employees have obligations to preserve "trade secrets" that are the "property" of their "employer," or have a "duty of loyalty" to that employer (who has no reciprocal duty of loyalty to them). It, too, made more sense under an assumption of implicit contracts for lifetime employment, than against Silicon Valley's constant churning of employees. Some of the institutions that supposedly address these problems will turn out to be worse than the disease. This is true of 401(k) stock purchase plans, often touted as ideal for today's mobile workforce, but turn out to be no such thing.

Suppose the court is unusually sophisticated, senses these legal anomalies, and wants to ask some serious policy and economic questions. Is society better off when employees can easily leave to form start-ups, or does this diminish incentives for employers to invest in the creation of information? Is society better off when compensation arrangements are as flexible as stock options, or would all be better off if law encouraged stable compensation and made such aleatory compensation more difficult to arrange? What would be the economic consequence of requiring employers to treat their temps as if they were employees? What would happen if employers could not employ so many programmers on five-year nonimmigrant visas? Should employee organization be made easier in a high-velocity labor market, or does the economic success of such markets depend importantly on impediments to employee organization? I will try to address these questions in this book, but must admit at the outset that the answer to none of them is clear. Analyses of any under traditional economics of employment and labor often embeds in its concepts assumptions about the stability of employment that do not reflect high-velocity labor markets. Moreover, such conventional analyses will not incorporate the more relevant economics of information creation and diffusion.

Academic literature on the work practices associated with a high-velocity labor market advances four general, and contradictory, premises about the relationship between such practices and economic growth. It is possible to combine elements of these four propositions; but in their pure form, although all seem plausible, they cannot all be true.

First, the work practices may play no role in encouraging growth. They may merely reflect it. If new firms start up, some employees will switch to them. They will thus have job changes and short tenures at their current employer. I haven't found anyone who argues this, but Daniel Mitchell made this point to me (heuristically).

Second, a high-velocity labor market may be good for employers, but bad for workers. It may simply shift risk and uncertainty from capital to labor. Or, in Richard Sennett's (1998) deeper critique, it may represent "The Corrosion of Character." This seems to assume that high-velocity work practices are imposed by strong employers on workers without bargaining power. As we shall see, such practices are instead associated with employers who have little bargaining power and are enthusiastically accepted by employees with much.

Third, it might be bad for both employers and workers. Employers may lose because their employees are not loyal to them, do not put their efforts into the firm, or withhold information. Employees may lose because of constant anxiety and uncertainty. Classical economists may have a hard time understanding how a particular contract could exist if it were not beneficial to each party. Economists of labor and employment, however, understand how often these markets reflect fads and conventions: employees wanting what everyone else has, employers feeling compelled to offer it. This kind of critique is associated with Baron (2000) and Pfeffer (2001). It would seem to suggest that Silicon Valley firms will abandon high-velocity practices as they mature. We shall see instead that such practices are growing.

Finally, high-velocity practices might benefit both employers and workers by contributing to economic growth. This is the thesis whose strongest academic support is Saxenian (1994) and Mendelson and Pillai (1999), though it is also associated with journalism on Silicon Valley, particularly in the years of its biggest boom, as well as the literature on what Michael Arthur and Denise Rousseau (1996) evocatively call "boundaryless careers." As Almeida and Kogut (1999) found, mobility of engineers has a significant and positive effect on the practice of a given patent's building on other patents issued to engineers in that very region. It is this thesis I hope to develop and generalize in this book, trying to show how high-velocity work practices contribute to economic growth, not only anecdotally, but in theory as well.

In general, I have become more of an advocate for such high-velocity labor markets as my research proceeded. Let me just assert here briefly what the rest of this book will try to show in detail. There is a kind of rapid technological and economic growth that can probably be achieved only in a high-velocity labor market. Of course, any society might choose to forgo this kind of growth, and prefer slower growth and more stability. But if people want to unleash scientific and technological imagination or increase wealth, they will find this difficult without permitting most of the defining features of a high-velocity labor market found on the list above. These labor market institutions are not the key to Silicon Valley, or sufficient for its replication. Venture capital, ties to universities, and collaboration among businesses are all probably more important. This book addresses only the labor market institutions, which are long overdue for specific analysis. It is not a book on how your state, province, or country can create its own Silicon Valley.

High-velocity labor supports rapid technological growth in two general ways, one quite a bit more obvious than the other: "flexibility" and "information diffusion." The "flexibility" paradigm is well known, but there is much truth to it and we will both refine and apply it. By contrast, the "information market" perspective on labor markets is the more original contribution of this book.

First, flexibility. A high-velocity labor market is obviously a flexible labor market, and this contributes to technological and economic growth specifically by facilitating start-up companies. A culture of small firms, networked with others, turns out to be better than a culture of large employers with internal labor markets for seeing opportunities, bringing new products to market, and creating new jobs and wealth. Such start-ups, however, face tremendous market uncertainty, and must be able to hire (and shed) labor without making crippling long-term commitments. This is why start-ups are associated with temporary and self-employed labor, employment at will, rapid turnover, unusual labor market intermediaries, and flexible compensation such as stock options. It is also why some European labor codes that prohibit these kinds of employment contracts will impede new business and new job creation. This is fairly familiar, although it is wrong to think that economists have a generally accepted model of the relationship. This book, however, will present numerous examples of how the relationship works in practices that inform our law and policy toward self-employment, temporary employment, and compensation.

The most important point is that a *flexible* labor market is not a *deregulated* or *unregulated* labor market. A flexible labor market requires some severe restrictions on freedom of contract. In a flexible labor market, employers are *not* free to require employees to promise not to compete with them. Nor may employers enter into trade secrets agreements that are as broad as they might like. These are serious restrictions on freedom of contract. A flexible labor market also requires vigorous antitrust policies. Silicon Valley could never have developed had IBM and AT&T been permitted to monopolize computers, telecommunications, or transistors.

Even more important, however, is the analysis of labor markets as markets for the information that is the chief input into endogenous growth. Thinking of labor as an intellectual input, contributing information to production, and linked across firm lines with other workers contributing such information is the real theoretical breakthrough of this book. When employees leave one Silicon Valley firm to start another, bringing in engineers, programmers, and executives from other firms, information diffuses without formal contracting other than the employment contracts. When the workforce is mobile, people know what is happening in other shops. Even temporary employees know useful things about how other firms in the industry do things. Firms can make effective use of patented information that in theory is available to all, but in practice may be utilized effectively only in regions. Software programs and hardware products can be designed to be compatible with other programs and products not even on the market. Costly duplicative research can be avoided. New firms can quickly assemble knowledge that was once produced only inside established firms (or universities) with large staffs of varying productivity, all in stable contracts.

This is not exactly news either. It is roughly the thesis of Saxenian (1994), the biggest intellectual influence on this book, and much other writing on Silicon Valley (e.g., Langlois 1992; Almeida and Kogut 1999; Lee et al. 2000). But, as we shall see, it too represents an enormous challenge to disparate areas of economics and of law. Indeed, I have described this book sometimes as "the law and economics behind AnnaLee Saxenian."

Briefly, economists of information and economists of labor and employment have been going their separate ways, and neither has come to grips well with the role of employment contracts in the diffusion of technological information. Economists who write about the economics of information normally employ the metaphor of "information spillover" without concerning themselves with the "mechanisms" of such spillover. In this approach, labor mobility is no different from technology licensing, or reading an article in a professional journal. They are all "externalities" created when innovation creates information that cannot be monopolized. Often, in this literature, such a "spillover" is a kind of problem, something that nobody would create if he or she could avoid doing so. Economists of labor and employment, by contrast, employ a different metaphor for the information in employees' heads. They may describe it either as "human capital" or, perhaps, a "public good," two powerful metaphors for many purposes that mislead when applied to the problem of shared information in a high-velocity labor market. Law conceptualizes much of that crucial information as the "trade secret" of the former employer, and has difficulty modifying that conception to fit the kind of shared information that is crucial to technological advance.

When seen through the lens of the economics of information, many of the labor contracts and market institutions characteristic of high-technology districts turn out to be devices for lowering information costs. In one way or another, most of the unique institutions that typify Silicon Valley's labor market may be understood as ways of providing information, and, in most cases, their information functions are much more important than their contribution to "flexibility." People hired short term, like consultants or temporary workers, provide information about themselves that is not attainable any other way. Networks of former colleagues, chat groups, list serves, Web sites, temporary help agencies, Internet job boards, and ethnic organizations—the "employee organizations" found in high technology—provide employees and employers with information about job and market opportunities. Labor market intermediaries like these are not necessary to create "flexibility," something that American employers may create without use of an intermediary. Rather, they convey information. Short-term visas do not create a pool of competent, cheap programmers. That pool is a creature of Asian educational institutions and labor market conditions. Rather, short-term visas permit Silicon Valley employers to make those programmers more productive, by locating them physically in California. Stock options provide outside investors with information about managers' and employees' sense of the value of their firm. New employees provide information about other places they have worked.

Since a high-technology labor market is also an information market, its analysis must supplement conventional labor economics with aspects of the economics of information: multiple equilibria, network effects, unexpected incentives for the production of information, weak property rights. In understanding why a given engineer is worth more in Silicon Valley than in Bangalore, examining his "human capital" will mislead. He has the same knowledge in his head in Bangalore as in San Jose. "Capital" is not usually worth more where it is plentiful than where it is scarce. To understand why people migrate from areas of low human capital to high human capital, models of network effects in information markets are much more valuable than invocations of "human capital." Similarly, protecting the kind of technological and economic growth that comes from shared information requires that law reevaluate its concepts of unfair competition, trade secrets, and employee organization.

Finally, this theme, of employees valuable for their minds as well as their "labor power," for the information they create and carry, and their links to counterparts in other firms, will be an important philosophic challenge to the way economists and lawyers usually think of labor: as units of input into a production process. A high-velocity labor market is not the only way to organize a labor market, and it is not for everybody. It is no part of my argument that there is some inevitable historic force destroying (either for good or evil) regulated labor standards and replacing them with "neoliberal" labor markets. High-velocity labor markets can be encouraged or destroyed by political and legal choices, and rational societies might choose to forgo them, though I think they should rather encourage them. High-velocity labor markets, like other markets, create winners and losers. By studying some of the ways that winners win—the networks they turn to for information and support, the attitudes they carry toward risk, the careers that transcend boundaries of a single employer—we can make life better for the janitors and production workers, not just the engineers. Much current and proposed law and policy toward independent contractors, temporary employees, trade secrets and intellectual property, equal employment opportunity, employee compensation, and immigration law looks different when viewed through the lens of the high-velocity labor market.

On the other hand, while I have become more of a booster of high-velocity labor markets while researching this book, I have also developed new respect for publicly funded national health insurance and retirement savings. I had originally thought that Silicon Valley's well-compensated mobile workers would create a market for the innovative marketing of health insurance and retirement savings, tailored to their needs, through innovative employee organizations and other labor market intermediaries. I had thought that these employee organizations and benefits plans could become the model for new institutions to protect comparatively unskilled temporary labor. As we shall see in chapters 9 through 11, even in the boom years of the late 1990s, the Valley failed to develop such institutions. I think therefore that we may declare the debate on private health insurance and retirement savings for a mobile workforce to be closed, though of course many Americans disagree. If the wealthy managers and engineers of the 1990s did not develop such private institutions, who will? Providing retirement savings and health insurance to mobile employees, who lack lifetime commitment to a single employer, will have to be a public function.

This book will argue finally that today's high-velocity labor markets offer the hope, not of the "corrosion of character," but a new era of work in which workers have freedom and power never before experienced. Of course, this too is a cliché of the breathless "wired economy" school of journalism, but I hope to demonstrate its credibility as an empirical and economic matter. The new high-velocity labor market arises from the ashes of all those schemes of work reorganization that start from the assumption that too many people experience work as a site of degradation and oppression, while too many others who want to work cannot. There is no magic bullet to the transformation of work.

Throughout my career, I have studied democratizing collective bargaining, transformative labor statutes of the European type, workplace reorganization, employee ownership, making employees stakeholders. None of these activities is worthless, and all merit further study, implementation, refinement. Yet all have their limits and my personal sense is that those limits have been scraped-down-to and now loom before us, daring us to butt our heads against them again. Refashioning labor and employment law and economics toward flexibility, risk, entrepreneurship, and, most important, employees' knowledge, information, and creativity, is no panacea, as I have said already several times. It may in the end require bigger social safety nets and new protections for employees who lose in the market. It certainly requires legal regulation of a particular kind. As we shall see, an effective high-velocity labor market is not a deregulated market. However, for the first time in my career, I feel I am studying labor market institutions whose limits lie on the horizon, not in our face; that create wealth and jobs, not destroy them; that reward maturity, not dependence.

Even if I am wrong about this, high-velocity labor markets are now part of life. Even if they never grow into a larger part of the general labor market, there is still much to be learned about how they work, and how they could work better.

The chapters that follow will observe a characteristic pattern. They will start with a real legal dispute or anecdote that illuminates genuine conflict over work relations in the new economy, and possible legal interventions for good or ill. They will show why the dispute is essentially not resolvable under existing employment, labor, or intellectual property law, normally because that law embeds concepts of employment that are at odds with the facts before it. The same defect will often inflict economic analyses of employment that rely on concepts like "implicit contract," "human capital," "job tournaments," and the like. The book will try to show the potential gains from an analysis that makes problems of information and endogenous growth central to the analysis. I am a consumer, not a producer, of economics, and I am well aware that these economic discussions will not satisfy economists. My biggest regret about this book is my inability to find an economist coauthor. However, I hope the analyses will provoke economists into rethinking some of their models of employment, growth, and information, to emphasize their important, and not well understood, interrelation. I am also aware of the oversimplifications inherent in my approach. But while there are other sources for information on stock options or immigration, there is no book that tries to put them together, let alone to try, as I will here, to illuminate both with a common economic paradigm of endogenous growth and informational asymmetry.

Indeed, this is my aspiration for the entire book: to provoke and inspire more detailed future studies by scholars trained in economics, ethnography, sociology, and human relations, as well as law. In David Lodge's academic satire *Small World,* Morris Zapp plans (but never finishes) "a commentary on the works of Jane Austen, the aim of which was to be utterly exhaustive, to examine the novels from every conceivable angle—historical, biographical, rhetorical, mythical, structural, Freudian, Jungian, Marxist, existentialist, Christian, allegorical, ethical, phenomenological, archetypal, you name it. So that when each commentary was written, there would be *nothing further to say* about the novel in question" (1984: 24) Any academic recognizes the ego, but mine is of the opposite type. In fifteen years, no one will read this book. Silicon Valley will have changed many times in many ways; there will be better ethnographies of the lives of mobile workers, statistical information on their savings and compensation, economic models of their implicit employment contracts, legal cases to analyze. There are many, many further things to say about workers in the new economy. I hope, however, that some of that work will reflect, even where it does not remember, the questions raised in this book.

WORKING IN SILICON VALLEY

1

THE DEVELOPMENT OF SILICON VALLEY'S HIGH-VELOCITY LABOR MARKET

Silicon Valley, the nickname for the region of high-tech industries clustered around Stanford University at the south end of San Francisco Bay, has now given rise to a small library exploring the ecology, management, and psychology of high-technology businesses and districts (Saxenian 1994; Kenney 2000; Lee et al. 2000). This book focuses entirely on its distinctive labor market, in particular the way Silicon Valley represents a "high-velocity" labor market in which job changes are frequent and employees do not expect ever to make careers inside a single employer. In this book, Silicon Valley means its high-technology industries, from CEOs and engineers to janitors and manufacturing workers. I will not discuss Santa Clara County's work force outside high technology, for example the Mexican-American agricultural workers whose history is told in Pitti (2003).

The Valley's labor market has not been a neglected topic either. There are excellent studies of many subgroups of workers on which I will draw. However, the economic and legal analysis of these distinct ways of working has lagged behind the sociological and management literatures. We know little about the causes and consequences of rapid employee turnover and short job tenure. While turnover and short tenure are closely associated with high-technology employment, and with Silicon Valley more so than other high-technology districts, they are becoming more important throughout the U.S. labor market. So our gaps in their understanding are increasingly important.

This chapter is a brief history of Silicon Valley, describing its changing industrial base, and summarizing what little we actually know about job tenures and turnover at different stages of the Valley's history. This draws on the research of others. It is here partly for the convenience of readers who may associate the Valley merely with computers, or the Internet, and to provide context for the following chapters, many of which present research that represents a particular point in time.

The Silicon Valley analyzed in this book has a nearly century-long tradition of scientific and technological innovation. During at least the latter half of that period, its labor market has been characterized by frequent mobility, short tenures, career paths that journey through entrepreneurialism and consulting, and flexible compensation—a high-velocity labor market. This book is not particularly focused on the immediate past five or ten years.

A Brief Historical Outline of Silicon Valley

For purposes of this book, I will employ a fairly conventional stylized history that divides the history of Silicon Valley into seven phases: Pre–World War II Radio and Electronics; the Defense Period (1941–59); Semiconductors and Other Components for Large Computers (1959–80); Consolidation and Slump in Semiconductors (1980–86); Revival Built Around Microcomputers (1983–present); Internet and Other Communications Boom (1984–present); and Slowdown (2000–present).

Before World War II

Guglielmo Marconi's first radiotelegraph signals were in 1895, but by 1909 practical applications were scant. Few homes had receivers, so when the first radio station in the United States with regularly scheduled programming was set up in San Jose, California (later the metropolitan hub of Silicon Valley), in 1909, it gave away crystal receivers to listeners within its range. Communication with ships was limited by the difficulties of generating radio waves from sparks passing between poles.

In 1908 a recent Stanford University graduate named Cyril Elwell realized that an arc transmitter that he had seen demonstrated at an exhibition in Paris in 1900 would generate waves that would be more practical for long-distance voice transmission. He negotiated the rights from the European developers, and, on returning to Palo Alto in 1909, proceeded in ways that will come to be identified with "Silicon Valley": the best technology; ties between Stanford and industry; venture capital; mobility of key scientific personnel to start-ups; and the role of intellectual property law in shaping high-technology enterprise. (Sturgeon 2000, the source for this entire section, gets the credit for tracing Silicon Valley back to 1909.)

Elwell turned to David Starr Jordan, president of Stanford, and C.D. Marx, head of its civil engineering department, to finance a new company to provide wireless telephone and telegraph services using arc technology. A small system was built to transmit between Stockton and Sacramento, and financing was obtained from a group of San Francisco financiers including the Crocker family. In 1912 Elwell demonstrated the Federal Telegraph Company's (FTC) system to the Navy. As it was superior to the competition, FTC became "the navy's darling of the World War I period" (Howeth 1963, as quoted in Sturgeon 2000). Technical improvements in the system were made in the Stanford High Voltage Laboratory, where Stanford professors worked with FTC employees (including the son of Stanford professor and FTC investor C.D. Marx). In return, FTC donated an arc to Stanford where it was used for other investigations. Around the same time at the FTC laboratory in Palo Alto, Lee de Forest in 1912 perfected a vacuum tube that could amplify faint radio signals.

By 1913 Elwell and de Forest had both left FTC, Elwell for Universal Radio Syndicate (UK), holder of European rights to the arc technology; de Forest to start Radio Telegraph and Telephone company, destined to fail in the Bronx. Under intellectual property law, FTC retained "shop rights" (a nontransferable license) in inventions that Elwell and de Forest had made while they were its employees. Between 1910 and 1932, other groups of FTC employees left to found, successively, Magnavox, Fisher Research Laboratories, and Litton Industries.

> Perhaps the strongest thread that runs through the Valley's past and present is the drive to "play" with novel technology, which, when bolstered by an advanced engineering degree and channeled by astute management, has done much to create the industrial powerhouse we see in the Valley today. Indeed, the caricature of the "ham" radio enthusiast—the shy but intelligent teenage boy who, bent over his homemade radio set in his bedroom late at night, taps into a secret world known only to him and his far-flung community of fellow hams—bears a striking resemblance to that of the "computer geek," "code hacker," and "web surfer" of more recent vintage. (Sturgeon 2000: 44)

A more typical dating of Silicon Valley's origins is the founding of Hewlett-Packard Company (HP) in 1937 in a Palo Alto garage that is now a historic landmark. Hewlett had developed an audio-oscillator as a Stanford graduate student. His professor Frederick Terman encouraged Hewlett and his fellow graduate student David Packard to commercialize the device, lent them $538 to start the business, and arranged for a further loan from a Palo Alto bank (Packard 1995; Saxenian 1994: 20). Saxenian quite correctly notes, however, that the scale of industrial activity in the Valley before World War II was "insignificant compared to that of the Boston area" (Saxenian 1994: 21) and that both firms and individuals commonly migrated east.

Defense Period (1941–1959)

Firms like HP, Litton, and the Varian brothers' early operations (also supported by use of Stanford laboratories and equipment in exchange for half their patent royalties) prospered during World War II. Terman spent the war years at Harvard. When he returned to Stanford in 1946 as dean of the School of Engineering, he had a particular vision of expanding partnerships between Stanford and industry. Stanford, wrote Terman, "had not been significantly involved in any of the exciting engineering and scientific activities associated with the war" (quoted in Saxenian 1994: 22). Terman helped found the Stanford Research Institute to conduct defense-related research, the Stanford Industrial Park, and other institutional ties between Stanford and electronics and aerospace companies. Research was funded mainly by federal defense funds during this period (Leslie 1993, 2000; Henton 2000), and initially continued to focus mainly on radio and microwave technology (Lécuyer 2001: 668).

The most powerful and enduring industry proved to be semiconductors. Their chief ingredient was to give the Valley its name in the 1970s (Hoefler 1971). Some histories date the origin of Silicon Valley to the founding of Shockley Transistor in Palo Alto in 1955. Shockley, a Stanford graduate and one of the inventors of the transistor, left AT&T's Bell Laboratories to commercialize the invention. He attracted outstanding engineering talent but was an impossible person, and two years after the firm's founding, eight of its leading engineers—later known as the "traitorous eight"—left to form Fairchild Semiconductor, a competitor. Fairchild produced silicon transistors for military markets. Its departing personnel—ten spin-offs in its first eight years—eventually founded numerous technology companies (including Intel, National Semiconductor, and Advanced Micro Devices) and venture capital firms (including Kleiner Perkins) (Saxenian 1994: 25–26; Kenney and von Burg 1999: 81–85; Kvamme 2000).

Semiconductors and Other Components for Large Computers (1950–1980)

The integrated circuit was invented in 1959. During the 1960s, over thirty semiconductor manufacturers, nearly all the U.S. firms, were started in the Valley. From one perspective, this was a quite undiversified industrial base that would suffer severe recession in the early 1980s. An observer of these electronics manufacturers would hardly have noticed much difference from such other centers of electronics as Boston or southern California, or at least few observers at the time did.

Nevertheless, with hindsight, this is the period in which Silicon Valley developed some distinctive features that would later distinguish it, even though most of these features became clearer in retrospect than they were in the 1970s. They include the culture of start-ups, high labor mobility, informal ties across firm boundaries, nonhierarchical management practices associated with HP, and venture capital. All of these continue to characterize Silicon Valley to this day, though all have evolved since the 1970s. Saxenian (1994), the best source on these innovations, is quite clear that their importance lies in the way they facilitated a very different kind of growth in the late 1980s. Less careful celebrations (or critiques) of Silicon Valley sometimes treat these as if they had survived intact (e.g., Putnam 2000: 324–25; Storper and Salais 1997: 174–88).

Culture of Start-ups

Crucial to Saxenian's entire contrast of Silicon Valley with Boston's Route 128 is the Valley's culture of start-ups. Engineers in the Valley dream of founding their own firms, and often do, while their counterparts back East are likelier to spend careers inside one large corporation. This was true for the period of Saxenian's research (the late 1980s), true, as we have seen, for 1909; probably true today, although there are signs that Route 128 has become more receptive to start-ups since Saxenian's research. This culture of start-ups alters employee incentive structures and career planning and is the key influence on every other item on the list that follows.

Its precise origins, however, remain somewhat mysterious, and do not become clearer when we trace the Valley's origins back to 1909, rather than 1937 or 1955. The answer must lie in some combination of a young region with few established industrial corporations and the active role played by private investors, and Stanford University, in encouraging start-ups. Once start-up culture reaches some critical stage of development, it can sustain itself through the accumulated institutional expertise that facilitates newer start-ups, such as venture capital and specialized law firms (e.g., Lee et al. 2000: 3–15).

Fortunately it is not necessary for purposes of this book to pin down the origins of start-up culture more precisely, although it is the crucial mystery for planners who seek to replicate the Valley elsewhere. Kenney and von Burg (1999) emphasize semiconductor technology; this can hardly be taken seriously since the Valley's start-up culture long predates that technology and extends to other technologies. Indeed, semiconductor production actually became quite concentrated for a time in the late 1970s. Bankman and Gilson (1999) note that employers should normally be able to outbid outside investors for the services of particular employees—an important point, to which we shall return in chapters 3 and 4. This suggests to them that start-ups will be found where employers would incur particularly heavy costs to their compensation arrangements by engaging in such bidding. It is not clear how this model applies to real-world examples, such as the traitorous eight's departure from Shockley, or later departures from Fairchild. What costs would Fairchild have incurred that prevented it from outbidding the investors who funded Intel? Nor does it distinguish among regions. Hellmann (2002) models employee and firm decisions whether to develop innovations inside the firm or in a start-up. The crucial variable is the hospitability of the environment to start-ups, when that is just what one wanted to have explained. Perhaps if there were data on propensity of employees to leave and start-up, such propensity could be associated with firms of particular size, market position, R&D expenditure, and the like.

High Labor Mobility

If new firms start up and draw their employees from existing firms, tenures will be short and mobility high. This began to be observed in the 1970s. People familiar with technology firms in the Valley and back East observed that Valley engineers frequently changed employers (e.g., Parden 1981). There is no reason to doubt this observation—no reason to assume bias in the observation, for example—though hard data on turnover rates are not available either for this period or subsequent periods (see estimates in Hayes 1989: 49). Saxenian (1994: 34–35) notes:

> Silicon Valley was quickly distinguished by unusually high levels of job hopping. During the 1970s, average annual employee turnover exceeded 35 percent in local electronics firms and was as high as 59 percent in small firms. It was rare for a technical professional in Silicon Valley to have a career in a single company. An anthropologist studying the career paths of the region's computer professionals [quoting Gregory 1984: 216] concluded that job tenures in Silicon Valley averaged two years. One engineer explained: "Two or three years is about max (at a job) for the Valley because there's always something more interesting across the street. You don't see someone staying twenty years at a job here. If they've been in a small company with 200 to 300 people for 10 or 11 years you tend to wonder about them. We see those types coming in from the East Coast."

I have found no evidence that any Silicon Valley employer in the 1970s consciously encouraged short job tenures. Hewlett-Packard was one of the few companies whose executives had much to say about management in the 1970s ("the HP Way"). Their relaxed, creative management style became a national cult after popularization in Peters and Waterman (1982). HP's preference, then and for many years thereafter, was to encourage loyalty (through encouraging creativity, delegating to teams). Layoffs were avoided by the practice, rare in U.S. companies, of shared pay cuts in slow times (Peters and Waterman 1982: 244). Not as many Valley employers followed HP as the number that respected it, but I have not found any articulated rejection of HP's emphasis on loyalty during this period. The short job tenures observed in the 1970s reflected, rather, the natural statistical result of start-ups (if firms start up, tenures will be short and employees will change employers); employee choices; and employer decisions not to impede this process (by, e.g., aggressively suing departing employees for violation of trade secrets). Silicon Valley's heavy conscious use of temporary help agencies or outsourced production, for example, still lay in the future.

Ties Across Firms

If people move from firm to firm, any individual will know others at rival firms with whom they previously worked. "Competitors consulted one another on technical matters with a frequency unheard of in other areas of the country" (Saxenian 1994: 33; see also Sitkin 1986). Crucially, these questions were normally answered. "As a result, Silicon Valley's engineers developed stronger commitments to one another and to the cause of advancing technology than to individual companies or industries" (Saxenian 1994: 36).

Other ties linked individuals across firms in the 1960s and 1970s, but they were never as important as networks among friends and former coworkers, and became less important over the next two decades. In the 1950s and 1960s, when the "Fairchildren" who had worked together at Fairchild founded companies, "The wives all know each other, and remain on the friendliest terms. The men eat at the same restaurants, drink at the same bars, and go to the same parties" (Saxenian 1994: 32, quoting Hoefler 1971). This is important, because it sent the signal to employees at the time that ties across firm lines were good, not bad things. But after the 1960s, the Fairchild tie as such necessarily weakened, and one rarely finds references to the importance of particular circles who worked at particular companies. There are no similar stories about close-knit alumni of Apple or HP, for example, and former Intel employees will figure as such in this book only through their lawsuits concerning their departure. Nor, given the changing role of women in the labor market, will "wives" ever have that same role.

Similarly, the few formal organizations that linked engineers and scientists may have received disproportionate attention. I am thinking of the Homebrew Computer Club, founded in 1975, where young computer enthusiasts exchanged hardware and software to help create cheap computers. Its alumni eventually founded over twenty computer companies, including Apple

(Saxenian 1994: 34). This is an important chapter in the history of the personal or microcomputer, although Apple was the only important microcomputing manufacturer associated with the Valley until the recent HP-Compaq merger. However, it is a somewhat misleading example of interaction across firm lines, which rarely involves an organization with a name (see chapter 9 for some counterexamples). In any case, the Club is long gone.

Nonhierarchical Management

Few Valley employers published much about their managerial styles during these years, but the exception has been influential. Hewlett-Packard popularized concepts such as top executives' (including Bill Hewlett and David Packard) "managing by wandering around," autonomous teams, encouraging active participation from all levels of the organization, breaking up large entities to keep them mobile and responsive (Peters and Waterman 1982; Packard 1995; Wilms 1996; Zell 1997; Shockley-Zalabak and Burmester 2001). HP's success helped vindicate these unconventional ideas, which served the Valley well in the 1980s, though no longer characterize much Valley industry, including HP itself (Poletti 2001). Lécuyer (2001: 669) attributes the growth of independent teams, autonomous engineers, and financial incentives such as profit sharing, stock ownership, and stock options, to managerial efforts (not merely at HP) to fight organizing efforts by San Francisco unions, as well as to a streak of utopian and socialist yearnings in the microwave (but not semiconductor) community.

Venture Capital

Sometime in the 1970s, venture capital supplanted federal defense spending as the largest source of financing in the Valley. Xerox founded its legendary Palo Alto Research Center (PARC), subsequently the birthplace of so many innovations, in 1970 (Smith and Alexander 1988; Hiltzik 1999).

Consolidation and Slump in Semiconductors (1980–1986)

The institutions described in the previous section (start-ups, labor mobility, ties across firms, informal management, and venture capital financing) did not strike all Silicon Valley executives as essential to their success at the time. Instead, the trend during the 1970s was toward consolidation into large companies and mass production of what Intel cofounder Andy Grove called "high technology jelly beans" (Saxenian 1994: 86). Of the thirty-five semiconductor manufacturers started between 1966 and 1975, only seven remained independent by 1980 (Chandler 2001: 127). Their mass-production processes are described by Hossfeld (1990), Katz and Kemnitzer (1983), and Green (1983): assembly lines of foreign-born women supervised by white men, repetitive, unsafe, and poorly paid. The transition into a mature, mass-production industry is normal enough in the U.S. economy (Chandler 1990). Observers concluded that the same was happening in Silicon Valley, and that the era of start-ups was over.

Disaster struck when large Japanese manufacturers began producing some of the same mass-produced semiconductor memory products in 1984, quickly underselling Valley manufacturers and capturing most of the world market for memory. Valley firms were unable to compete (Chandler 2001: 117–31). Journalism of this gloomy period (Hayes 1989) portrayed a Silicon Valley of alienated if not psychotic loners. (Rereading this literature for this study reminded me of the extraordinary gloom of the late 1980s and early 1990s, when so many believed that Japan had replaced American economic power and saw no role for the U.S. economy.) Academic observers (e.g., Florida and Kenney 1990) concluded that the Valley's practice of forming new firms had prevented large firms from making the "necessary" transformation to efficient mass production.

Revival Built Around Microcomputers (1983–Present)

The truth was just the opposite. Silicon Valley revived from the slump of 1985–86 by capitalizing on three exogenous opportunities. First, the development and popularity of personal (micro) computers. Second, the breakup of AT&T, creating demand for sophisticated, modular communications and networking equipment for the ensuing decentralized voice and data networks. Third, the opening of the Internet for commercial use (the latter two discussed in the next subsection). Silicon Valley was able to seize these opportunities by reviving its older structure of cooperating smaller firms with rapid labor turnover, and largely abandoning mass production. Interestingly, all three of these exogenous opportunities reflected federal government decisions taken long before. The Internet originated as a research project of the Department of Defense (Newman 2002). The modern software and telecommunications industries reflect earlier antitrust suits against IBM and AT&T, formerly dominant in each industry.

First came the microcomputer revolution, effectively created by IBM's decisions to create a personal computer (a field previously occupied only by hobbyists' machines like those from Commodore, Tandy, and Apple), and— fearing antitrust liability— to give up its historic monopolies over software. This created markets for such new entities as pure software firms (above all,

Microsoft) and components manufacturers (above all, Intel), as the number of microcomputers shipped to business rose from 344,000 in 1981 to 3,290,000 in 1985 (Chandler 2001: 139). The microcomputer revived the U.S. computer industry just as Japanese competition had shut memory plants.

Saxenian's basic story is how the Valley was better equipped than Route 128 to take advantage of developments in computers, particularly micro-computers and work stations, in the 1980s (1994: 2–3):

> Silicon Valley has a regional network-based industrial system that promotes collective learning and flexible adjustment among specialist producers of a complex of related technologies. The region's dense social networks and open labor markets encourage experimentation and entrepreneurship. Companies compete intensely while at the same time learning from one another about changing markets and technologies through informal communication and collaborative practices; and loosely linked team structures encourage horizontal communication among firm divisions and with outside suppliers and customers. The functional boundaries between firms are porous in a network system, as are the boundaries between firms themselves and between firms and local institutions such as trade associations and universities.

Of 176 start-ups formed in the world's semiconductor industry between 1977 and 1989, 88 percent were in the United States, 55 percent in Silicon Valley (Almeida and Kogut 1999: 909, citing Dataquest 1990). Start-up software and components firms were able to hire top labor forces without fear of legal or practical restriction. The Valley's tradition of short tenures and frequent job changes continued, if not intensified. Almeida and Kogut (1999: 913) traced through patent citations the careers of 438 semiconductor engineers holding major patents, from 1974 to 1994. Silicon Valley was "clearly unique" among regions. Its engineers moved more frequently, normally within Silicon Valley. It had more than twice as many intraregional job moves as any other region. A different small national survey of semiconductor engineers covering 1980–86 also showed much higher mobility among engineers in Silicon Valley. Indeed, over half of all job changes recorded by the survey were moves in which both the old and new employers were located in Silicon Valley (Angel 1989: 106; 1991: 134–37).

The Valley came to dominate the production of semiconductors, particularly for personal computers (Intel, Advanced Micro Devices, Cypress Semiconductor, Cirrus Logic, Maxim Integrated); semiconductor manufacturing equipment and processes (Applied Materials, Varian, Lam Research, KLA/Tencor); hard disk drives (Seagate, Maxtor, Conner Peripherals, Quantum); other, mostly high-end, computer-related products like work stations (HP,

Sun Microsystems, Silicon Graphics); and some key application software companies (Oracle, Novell). These employers, and others in computer and electronic product manufacturing, still employed the largest share of Santa Clara County high-technology workers, and 40 percent of all employment in the county, in the 1997 Economic Census (Cortright and Mayer 2001). (I should mention that statistics of this kind in the book from governmental sources usually refer either to Santa Clara County or metropolitan San Jose, which includes nearly all of the area usually included in Silicon Valley. Statistics from the private research group Joint Venture Silicon Valley include adjacent communities in Alameda and San Mateo counties. The distinction does not seem to matter for any issue discussed in this book.)

Valley firms do not make, or even outsource, many microcomputers themselves. Apart from Apple, the big computer manufacturers (IBM, Compaq, Gateway, Dell, Packard-Bell, AST) are not Valley firms, although Compaq has just merged with HP.

By contrast, Valley firms continue to dominate the world production of hard disk drives—exactly the sort of product that, it was predicted, would be most efficiently produced by Japanese firms using mass-production methods at which they excel. This is an important supplement to Saxenian's story about regional agglomeration economies. Hard disk drive manufacture involves global production networks that link regional agglomeration economies (Saxenian briefly mentions global production networks, 1994: 156–59).

Silicon Valley firms continue to dominate the production of hard disk drives by moving physical production to Asia, particularly Singapore, and exporting, and exploiting, the same regional agglomeration effects of small networked production units. The firms moving to Singapore were largely new firms that entered the industry from 1980 to 1985, when forty companies entered the hard disk drive industry, most founded by personnel departing industry leaders, mostly IBM (McKendrick, Doner, and Haggard 2000: 94). The California production pattern had been for the manufacturer to do its own assembly—few firms use contract manufacturers—purchasing components such as heads, media, and spindle motors from outside manufacturers. The new manufacturers founded in the 1980s, starting with Seagate, reproduced exactly this pattern in Singapore. While retaining R&D and product development in the United States, actual manufacture takes place in Singapore, where firms assemble components purchased from over a hundred local suppliers (McKendrick, Doner, and Haggard 2000: 159). "All of the most successful companies of the period [late 1980s] employed ex-Seagate people in their top engineering teams. . . . Almost everybody we interviewed had worked for more than one HDD [hard disk drive] assembler or recording head company in their careers. . . ." McKendrick, Doner, and Haggard 2000: 179).

"Everybody had information about the production and product plans of their competitors because assemblers needed to share that information with their suppliers, who served multiple customers" (McKendrick, Doner, and Haggard 2000: 180). By 1990, Singapore manufactured 55 percent of the world's hard disk drives, substantially all by U.S. companies.

Communications and Internet Boom (1985–2000—and Beyond?)

Silicon Valley is, however, the most diversified high-technology district in the United States, indeed, the only such district that may really be described as diversified. It is also the largest, with the most jobs in high technology at the close of the century of any district (Cortright and Mayer 2001; Lüthje 1997). Sixty-one of the nation's 500 fastest growing technology companies were based in Silicon Valley (Joint Venture 2000). For example, biological science firms will figure little in this book, as the largest employers in the San Francisco Bay Area (Genentech, Chiron, and Bayer) lie a little outside the usual boundaries of Silicon Valley (in South San Francisco, Emeryville, and Berkeley, respectively). However, it is rarely appreciated that these and other Bay Area biotech firms have a market capitalization that exceeds their counterparts in San Diego, New England, and New Jersey *combined* (Joint Venture 2001: 16).

Since the publication of Saxenian's book, and as if to provide further confirmation of her thesis, the Valley has become a leader in networking and communications technology, and has exploited the Internet—a word that (not surprisingly) does not appear in her 1994 book. The breakup of AT&T in 1984 created demand for communications and networking technology that would work across different telephone networks, sparking the growth of local area networks. (We will observe repeatedly in this book that a flexible labor market is not a deregulated one; it requires vigorous antitrust and other procompetition policies, of which the breakup of AT&T is but one example.) The spread of access to the Internet, including its commercialization in 1994, created enormous opportunities for companies that could provide search software and technology (Netscape, Yahoo, Google), help businesses relocate on line, design Web operations, and so on: the so-called dot-coms.

Both the telephone and Internet developments contributed to the growth of manufacturers of ethernet technology like 3Com; routing and serving equipment like Cisco, Bay Networks, and Juniper; networking software like Novell and Adobe; and many firms involved in fiber optic and other networking technology. These large Valley firms, and their many smaller associates, were able to capitalize on the microcomputer, communications, and Internet revolutions because they had abandoned (or never attempted) mass production (at which they weren't much good). They returned to the production networks described by Saxenian, often now making them more high velocity in ways that became more important after her book. Production networks became more global; employing short-term labor became a conscious part of firm strategy; and compensation increasingly revolved around stock options. (Some of the software firms mentioned, such as Netscape and Novell, later stumbled, were targeted for extinction by Microsoft, or both.)

Elements of a Twenty-First-Century High-Velocity Labor Market: Start-ups, Turnover, Stock Options, Outsourcing, Global Production Networks

Start-ups. Start-ups continued to be crucial to this process of networked production. New firms started up to bring single products to the market, sometimes expecting ultimately to be purchased by a large firm such as Microsoft, Intel, or Cisco. Start-ups are almost invariably started by staff departing an existing firm, in order to create and market a product that will either compete with the former employer's or work with it. Launching a start-up requires functions that will not recur, and thus a labor market infrastructure that permits start-ups to find and employ people without having to create jobs that cannot later be eliminated. This "high-velocity" labor market is the subject of this book. The start-ups knew that they would be able to hire top talent in the Valley from existing firms, often hiring entire teams. Talent could be identified by the start-up's founders, among people they had known on past jobs. Many of the functions necessary to start the company could be outsourced to other firms in the production network, or to independent contractors or consultants. The best account of the process that I have read, by a founder of a software start-up eventually sold to Microsoft, is Ferguson (1999).

Turnover. Start-ups were particularly prone to employee turnover. The Stanford Project on Emerging Companies (SPEC) collected data on the personnel practices of around 200 start-ups in 1994 and 1995 (Baron, Burton, and Hannan 1996, 1999; Baron, Hannan, and Burton 1999, 2001; Baron, Hannan, Hsu, and Kocak, 2002; Hannan, Burton, and Baron 1996). Overall turnover rate was around 13 percent (Baron, Hannan, and Burton 2001) but varied among firms depending on their initial founding vision and subsequent history. Turnover was between 27 and 28 percent for firms that changed from their original model, for example by going public or bringing in a nonfounder CEO.

By 1995–97, high-tech workers nationally turned over at 19.2 percent annually, while workers outside the high-tech sector turned over at 11.7 percent a year (National Research Council 2001: 95, analyzing data from the National Science Foundation). Silicon Valley was often said (for e.g., in publications of the private research group Joint Venture Silicon Valley) to experience turnover at twice this national rate, but this figure cannot be documented. The Radford Surveys used by human resource managers often showed turnover rates for high-tech firms in Silicon Valley of 25 percent, according to Darby Siempelkamp, Vice President for Human Resources at Tibco Software. Another estimate frequently encountered was that the average length of stay at any single high-tech job in Silicon Valley was eighteen months (U.S. Department of Commerce, Office of Technology Policy 1999: 13). All published figures on employee turnover are somewhat subjective. Ann Moncus of Andersen Business Consulting told me that her first client when she moved to the Valley in 1995 was Sun Microsystems, which at the time didn't keep head counts.

Start-ups in the Stanford study clustered at the time of their founding into five basic visions of personnel practices. The *engineering* model is the most common, in which employees are selected because they already hold quite specific task abilities. Commitment is attained through challenging work ("cool technology") and peer group control. About 34 percent of the firms in the sample started life under the engineering model. Engineering model firms have few formal personnel practices in their early years other than meetings, and only half as many managers as would a comparable bureaucratic firm.

Hiring employees with specific skill sets is crucial to understanding these modal start-ups, and information technology more generally. It reflects the demand on firms to meet rapid schedules, imposed either by clients or market opportunities. As *Information Week* reported: "The vast majority of companies do little to train people to fill IT positions or reassign senior people—they treat filling IT jobs like buying PCs, looking to fill a specific spec sheet for the lowest price" (quoted in U.S. Department of Commerce, Office of Technology Policy 1999: 11). Firms that followed this strategy complained about difficulties in hiring the personnel they needed (National Research Council 2001: 92). Nevertheless, none seemed to feel the need (or see the ability) to compromise at the hiring stage and then undertake extensive training—contrasting with the stereotyped internal labor markets of earlier generations, in which individuals had fewer specific skills at hiring but were trained by firms. This successful demand for specific skills shapes the kind of labor market intermediaries used in Silicon Valley (chapter 8) and strongly shapes disparate labor market outcomes by race and age (chapter 12).

The Stanford study identified four less common models of personnel practices in Silicon Valley start-ups. The *star* model (11 percent), found mainly in medical technology or research, is built around a star, often academic or scientist; it seeks a longer term commitment by rewarding professional autonomy, among elite employees, in addition to providing challenging work. This model is "widely perceived in Silicon Valley as turnover-prone, due to perceived inequities it can foster, the high mobility of scientific and technical 'stars' to whom the model is targeted, and the tendency of star-oriented firms to rely more on stock options (which either stay underwater or else vest and are exercised, in either case making the firm vulnerable to turnover)" (Baron, Hannan, and Burton 2001). Star firms are particularly likely in their first two years to adopt stock option compensation, mission or values statements, formal intellectual property and trade secrets agreements, performance evaluations, and affirmative action plans. The *commitment* model (13 percent), patterned on HP, seeks to build emotional and familial attachments. It spends more time in the first year on organization building (company social events, orientation programs), but thereafter adopts formal personnel practices at a slower rate. It has the lowest proportion of managers of any pattern, only about 37 percent of the number of a comparable bureaucracy. The overmanaged *bureaucracy* model (less than 6 percent of start-ups), familiar from outside high tech, is an engineering model with more layers of formalized control, less reliance on peer group control. Finally, the *autocracy* model (7 percent) selects employees to perform predefined tasks, motivates them entirely with money, and supervises them closely. It is also associated with, indeed fosters, high employee turnover.

The models are not static. They develop in predictable ways, and personnel practices, including turnover, reflect these developments rather than merely the model prevailing at a particular moment. The star, commitment, and autocracy models are unstable. They are hard to "scale" in Valley parlance (increase the volume while holding everything else constant) and often turn into the default engineering model or bureaucracies. By contrast, firms that start as something else never turn into star, commitment, or autocracy models. Changing from one model to another, hiring a CEO, or an initial public offering (IPO) of stock all increased employee turnover. On the other hand, stable bureaucracies had the lowest turnover, after first losing employees, often the old guard from the earlier era, who left at the time of the changeover to bureaucracy (Baron, Hannan, and Burton 2001).

In other words, Silicon Valley employers who complain about employee turnover have the means to reduce it. For example, they can turn into bureaucracies. They typically choose not to do so, in order to maintain employee autonomy or flexible organization. We will return to this fact repeatedly throughout the book.

High turnover, and careers spanning multiple firms, are not limited to engineers and scientists. Neither of my two closest friends in Silicon Valley is an engineer, but careers like theirs shape the legal problems, analysis of which has given rise to this book.

Debbie was interested in new ways of designing fulfilling jobs even when we were undergraduates together, and she worked on a book on the subject as an undergraduate. After she graduated, she taught in Asia for a few years, and attended business school, focusing on problems of job design. Since graduating from business school, she has worked on various teams as an employee of Apple Computer, Netscape (before and after its purchase by America Online), and most recently the Net subsidiary of a large retailer. I expected her to be typed as a specialist on Asian markets, or job design. This is exactly what did not happen in Silicon Valley. Her projects have been even more varied than her employers, and call on her range of exposure to problems.

Tim wanted to be a journalist, and started on a small-town paper. Once in Silicon Valley, at different newspapers, he initially covered local news but eventually was switched to business journalism. This was a lucky break for him. Eventually he left print journalism to write for an exclusively online journal for a portion of the Internet marketing industry. Tim's next move was from journalism to business consulting. He insists that the skills he uses in preparing reports for clients, advising them how to use the Net, are the same skills he used as a journalist, except better compensated. He continues to be employed during the post-2000 slump, with of course more focus on cost-effective uses of the Net. He has moved among several consulting firms and now is a principal in his own.

Neither of my friends is a millionaire or drives a BMW. Both, and others I knew or met researching this book, have had interesting, rewarding, remunerative careers, full of new challenges that they have been able to exploit only by a willingness to change jobs and consider options in consulting.

Labor markets also became even more high velocity at the low end in the 1990s. This low-end contingency reflected conscious choice by employers. It had not featured in Saxenian's book. Temporary help agencies were a small and unremarkable part of the Silicon Valley labor market until the 1985 slowdown, probably used, as they were anywhere else at that time, to provide a secretary or receptionist if a regular employee was unavailable. Today, as we shall see in chapters 5 and 8, they are employed at twice the national rate. As the local president of a major national temp agency told Chris Benner in 1996, temp agencies began to expand in

> the economic downturn of 1985, when many Valley companies, led by AMD, which had said it would never lay people off, began laying people off. Companies re-evaluated and recognized the need to maintain flexibility to be competitive. Many companies are now keeping a 20–25% buffer,

some lower, some higher, so they can develop new products quicker, ramp up for production at a greater speed, etc. (Benner 2000: ch. 4)

Flexible Compensation. The obsession with stock option compensation is another high-velocity feature that grew in the years since Saxenian's book. When I returned to the Valley in 1998 after an absence of two years, my friends assured me that things had changed—meaning, it turned out, a universal obsession with making money through stock options. Stock options had long been common in the Valley (Lécuyer 2001: 669; Stephen C. Smith 1988; Balkin and Gomez-Mejia 1986), as incentives for employees and possibly as a way of retaining them. By 1998 retaining employees seemed neither feasible nor desirable in most cases (e.g., Shreve 2000), and stock options were understood almost entirely as incentives, particularly to induce employees to leave established companies and join start-ups. The core group of founding employees would be compensated largely in stock options, anticipating the start-up's eventually going public. In some cases the stock options would supplement generous base pay; in others, substitute for it. Silicon Valley came to signify not just a place that produced cool technology and brought it to market, as it had for me as late as 1996. It was now seen as a place where people could become very rich. Popular literature (much of it very good) celebrated the Valley's culture of innovation and wealth, not necessarily distinguishing the two (Lewis 2000; Bronson 1999; Kaplan 1999; Finn 2001).

Networked Production. Another innovation was the rise of contract manufacturers like Flextronics, Solectron, Celestica, Jabil Circuit, Sanmina, and SCI Systems, who would take on all the manufacturing responsibilities (Markoff 2001; Lüthje 1997). Most manufacturing migrated to Asia or Latin America (Ernst 2000, 1997; Lüthje 2001), often replicating, as mentioned above, Silicon Valley's structure of small networked firms with significant interchange of information and personnel (McKendrick, Doner, and Haggard 2000: 94). Surviving manufacturing in the Valley would be done by employees of temporary help agencies, another conscious choice to create highly contingent employment (Carnoy, Castells, and Benner 1997; Hayes 1989: 50–54; see chapters 5 and 8). Internationally, success came to "information age organizations in computers and elections that are decentralized, networked, and share information" (Mendelson and Pillai 1998). Some 20 percent of large European software companies moved their corporate headquarters to Silicon Valley (Audretsch 1996: 124).

The word "networking" came into vogue to describe the ever-changing interrelation of multiple firms. (It will be used in many other senses in the course of this book.) Silicon Valley in the 1990s certainly demonstrated the strength of this kind of business networking. Employment grew 20 percent over the decade (as the population grew 14.5 percent); value added per employee was twice the national average. In the single year from 1999 to 2000, Santa Clara County, by then among the fastest growing counties in the United States, saw employment increase 6.2 percent and payroll increase an astonishing 36.7 percent (U.S. Department of Commerce, Census 2002). By the end of that year, 1.3 million people worked in Silicon Valley, and the unemployment rate was around 1.8 percent. Average pay was $76,500, more than double the national median of $35,300 (U.S. Department of Commerce, Census 2000b: 3; Joint Venture 2002: 8–9). Metropolitan San Jose has the highest percentage of residents with bachelor's degrees of any U.S. metropolitan area (U.S. Census 2000a: Table 15).

Yet at the same time, other kinds of networking atrophied or failed to develop. In general, the U.S. economy in the 1990s saw increases in inequality, in which real incomes rose very slowly for the bottom deciles and astronomically at the top. In Silicon Valley, the trend was even more extreme. Indeed, the 2000 Census showed it to be one of the few U.S. regions in which real income actually declined for the lowest 20 percent of the population (Koch et al. 2001: 8 [from Current Population Survey]). This predominantly represented the influx of immigrants earning very low wages, rather than actual declines in any individual family's income. Santa Clara County had more foreign-born residents than San Francisco County, and while many of these are scientists and engineers, many others clean the floors or stuff the circuit boards.

Complaints were common about the low development of community and civic participation, apparently confirmed in the Social Capital Community Benchmark Survey coordinated from Harvard's Kennedy School of Government. Silicon Valley was below the national average on all indicators of social capital. Its index of "civic leadership" (serving as officer or committee member in a local organization, or attending any public or club meeting) was the lowest of any community in the study. People in the Valley do not volunteer to help the poor or elderly, for a health or disease cause, or to assist in neighborhood, civic, or congregational groups. All these volunteering indices were also at the bottom nationally. Giving of time or resources is 31 percent less than the national average. Valley people may still know former colleagues at other Valley firms, but are less likely than people elsewhere to socialize with coworkers outside of work (so much for the world of the "Fairchildren," whose wives "knew all the other wives"). Some of these low indexes reflect the heavy immigration into the county: all the civic engagement indexes were particularly low for Hispanics. Yet for all groups, labor market demands were at war with civic engagement. Fifty-six percent of respondents said that work demands kept them from civic engagement (as compared to 42 percent in the national sample). Only 25 percent identified any other obstacle to community involvement (Koch et al. 2001).

Slump (2000–Present). Of course, Silicon Valley's economy has been one of booms and busts, driven by technological and organizational developments, for decades. Too much venture capital flowed into technology companies in the 1990s, particularly, in the final years, the "dot-coms" that were supposed to exploit the Internet in ways that made little sense, except to investors hoping the stock price would rise and they could cash in. Correction set in during 2000. Between December 2000 and the following October 2001, the Valley lost 3.7 percent of its jobs (Joint Venture 2001). By April 2002, unemployment in metropolitan San Jose was up to 7.4 percent (U.S. Bureau of Labor Statistics). Friends suggested that I call this book *Not Working in Silicon Valley.* The "dot-coms" themselves had employed relatively few people, but the withdrawal of venture capital from them soon spread to reduced investment even in larger companies in information and communication technology. Cisco, 3Com, and even HP (Poletti 2001) undertook layoffs for the first time in their histories. Venture capital investment, which had amounted to $21 billion during 2000, shrank to $6 billion during 2001. Initial public offerings shrank from 82 to 14 (Joint Venture 2002).

As this book is written, many things about the future of Silicon Valley are unclear. Will the Valley reinvent itself around some new technology, as it has so many times before? Will the next big technology be mobile Internet services, or software for business applications, or biological or genetic information, or nanotechnology (Joint Venture 2001; Markoff and Richtel 2002)? Or is this really the end, and are we in for a revival of the *schadenfreude* of the late 1980s? Certainly many aspects of business in Silicon Valley in the 1990s are being rethought, a good example being the merger of HP and Compaq, apparently seeking to realize a conventional manufacturer's economies of scope and scale.

I see no sign, however, that the Valley's distinctive ways of working are undergoing the same kind of rethinking. If anything, the slowdown of 2001 added impetus to the kinds of high-velocity work practices that are the subject of this book.

I spent some weeks in the summer of 2001 searching for a Valley company to exemplify a "return to basics" in personnel organization. My example might, I thought, be trying to reinstitute an internal labor market, offering implicit contracts for lifetime employment, with benefits backloaded in the later years. It might even bring back pensions, maybe even defined benefit pensions. At least, it would be reducing or eliminating the role of stock options in its compensation package. It might relocate activities from the Valley to remote areas in which employees would be unable to change to other employers without substantial geographic relocation. A literature has begun to appear on companies (not in Silicon Valley) that "went too far" in the 1990s in outsourcing production or hiring temps (e.g., Moss, Salzman, and Tilly 2000). Perhaps Silicon Valley had such companies, too. I interviewed management consultants, law firm partners, and human resources directors.

I do not believe that this mythical company exists. While there was rather little hiring of any kind in the summer of 2001, the hiring that I could trace *all* involved stock options. A 2002 private survey of Western high-technology firms (of which about one-quarter were in northern California) found 28 percent *increasing* the number of stock option awards, only 19 percent decreasing them (William M. Mercer Inc. 2002).

No firm seemed to see a market opportunity that it could exploit by offering, instead, traditional personnel practices or benefits packages. (Professor James Baron of Stanford Business School, a knowledgeable observer of the Valley whose writings have already been cited, told a Brookings conference in 1998 of a Valley company that had decided to redefine itself "as a place that, in contrast to competitors, offers *careers*" [Baron 2000: 98]. This message must have been muted in the explosive growth of 1999–2000. In any case, one doubts that this company ever instituted pensions or restricted managerial positions to internal candidates, for example.)

Intel may come closest. Ann Moncus, who has worked on their personnel practices from Andersen Business Consulting, told me that they regard much of their wealth creation as over, so increasingly they offer employees below-market compensation in less-expensive areas like Folsom, Albuquerque, Salt Lake City, and Hillsborough, Oregon. (The association of traditional work practices with inability to create wealth is quite telling.) Valley folklore has always described Intel and HP as the two firms in which individuals might be able to make careers, Cisco perhaps being a third, though all reduced workforces in 2001. Even so, Intel never hesitates to hire managers from outside its own operation, and has neither pensions nor traditional job ladders.

By contrast, Cisco, for example, seems to be looking for ways not to become a traditional company. It has always had low turnover rates by Silicon Valley standards, 2 or 3 percent a year. Its main facilities are all in areas of high-tech concentration: San Jose; Chelmsford, Massachusetts; and Raleigh-Durham, North Carolina. It benefits from the concentrations of talent in these places, and has never needed or wanted to relocate any projects to areas with lower labor turnover. It has acquired companies with facilities in remote areas and has problems recruiting to those facilities and with designing career paths for their personnel, according to Vice President Mark Chandler.

Accompanying its unprecedented downsizing in 2001, Cisco announced *more* stock options: new, quicker vesting stock options, offered as a goodwill gesture to the remaining workforce and to mark a new beginning, according to Michael La Bianca, the Cisco attorney handling its personnel matters. (I was not making any effort to gather information on Silicon Valley downsizing practices, a novel experience for most companies that, according to press reports, spanned the range from caring to brutal. A book on downsizing Silicon Valley, if it is ever written, is several years away. Cisco's however were justly famous. It paid one-third of salary for laid-off employees doing community service, and kept them on Cisco's generous benefit plans.)

Predicting the future of Silicon Valley is hazardous. Based on my 2001 interviews and press reports, however, it appears that short job tenures, rapid turnover, weak internal labor markets, and heavy use of flexible labor and compensation are well established and will endure there, whether or not they spread further throughout the economy. They will continue to generate legal and policy issues (such as the definitions of "trade secret," "employer," "employee," "employee organization," and "discrimination," and the correct treatment of stock options) that are difficult to analyze within the existing law and economics of employment. High-velocity work practices represent a substantial challenge to the concepts through which economists and lawyers normally make sense of labor markets.

In seeking to understand them, I have found the most helpful economic literature to be that on endogenous growth, economics of information (particularly information spillover), and network effects. In my model, firms hire employees on short contracts in order to realize gains from information transmitted from other firms, provide incentives for employee performance, and realize gains from flexible deployment of labor. Employees accept these arrangements because they are well compensated for doing so, and benefit from new implicit contracts, not to impede their progress across firm boundaries or into start-ups of their own.

Part I

The Information Story

2

MOBILE EMPLOYEES, INFORMATION SPILLOVER, AND TRADE SECRETS

Gigabit ethernet over copper was in the summer of 1999, depending on whom you talked to, either the next sort-of cool thing, or a headache in the making. The case for "really cool thing"—well, by now it practically made itself. Most local area networks (LANs) already used copper wiring. The progression from 10BaseT Ethernet (ten megabits per second) to Fast Ethernet (100 BaseT) to Gigabit Ethernet (1,000 BaseT) was just the usual development from fast to faster. Is there not always a market for doing the same thing faster? Many people thought that gigabit ethernet could rival or surpass infinite bandwidth. The headaches? First, the future might lie with fiber, not copper. Second, the physical layer (PHY) chip technology might be delivered either as discrete chips or integrated into other chips, the way Texas Instruments and Philips were already doing with technology licensed from an Israeli company called MystiCom. Finally, if you decided that the discrete PHY chip was the way to go, the only company actually shipping them was Broadcom. Intel had bought a company called Level One in March 1999 that was working on PHY chips. But Intel bought a dozen companies making communications and Net hardware that year, trying to ensure itself a life after personal computers. And while Intel had paid $2.2 billion for Level One, its product was not ready to ship; production delays were going to turn out to be worse than anyone expected; and the technology was different from Broadcom's, with more analog mixed in with the digital. Nobody could be sure which would be the winning technology, or whether Lucent or somebody else was not going to wipe them both out (E. Clark 2000; Kubes 1999; La Pedus 1999; Strauss 2000).

Intel had no gigabit ethernet chips ready to ship by fall 1999. It began negotiating to purchase chips from Broadcom to work with Intel chips known as MACs. At the same time, three of Intel's top people in Fast or Gigabit Ethernet, frustrated at Intel's inability to produce a working PHY chip, went to work at Broadcom: Greg Young, the product manager for Fast Ethernet and gigabit MAC products, Steven Lindsay, who Intel later described as the "chief architect" of the software for its gigabit MAC products, and a midlevel

Danish engineering manager named Martin Lund. By March 2000, Intel's negotiations to purchase Broadcom PHY chips had gone nowhere, and a fourth Intel employee, Brad Gunther, interviewed for a job at Broadcom and was asked some very specific questions about Intel's business plans for chip sets. At that point, Intel did something that, while not routine in Silicon Valley, is not unusual either. It sued under trade secrets law to enjoin any of the four former employees from working on Broadcom's gigabit ethernet products, where, Intel claimed, they would "inevitably disclose" Intel's trade secrets.

The court's decision had something for each side. Young, Lindsay, and Lund could keep their jobs at Broadcom and would not be enjoined from working on any particular projects. They had been working at Broadcom for some months, and Intel could not show that any had actually disclosed any of its trade secrets. Each insisted he could succeed at Broadcom without misappropriating any Intel secrets, and each seemed "credible" and "trustworthy" to the judge. Each had moved to California to take the Broadcom job and an injunction would be a "significant hardship" for each. Moreover, the judge found that California has a "strong public policy against limitations on employment mobility." This probably referred to California's unusual statutory prohibition on "covenants not to compete," employment contracts in which employees promise not to compete with their employer after leaving employment. A psychologist had testified how difficult it is for any individual to tell whether information, which he or she is supposed to hold secret, is influencing his work. The judge turned that around, saying that if this "testimony were carried to its logical conclusion, no employee (possessed of trade secret information) could freely move to a competitor in the same arena."

However, Broadcom's interviews with Brad Gunther about Intel's business plans went over the line. Intel secrets were probably misappropriated. Broadcom's approach to protecting Intel secrets was "extremely cavalier." Broadcom's CEO was "unpersuasive and not credible," and Gunther "not trustworthy." The court enjoined Gunther from working for Broadcom in any capacity pending trial and required Broadcom to demonstrate to the court an adequate training and educational program on the obligation to protect trade secrets (*Intel Corp. v. Broadcom Corp.*). The case then settled.

The Unresolvable Problem of Trade Secrets

I have started with this story because it meets, rather spectacularly, the three criteria for inclusion in this book. First, a personnel practice that is typical of working in Silicon Valley: mobility of technical personnel. Second, a legal dispute raised by that personnel practice that cannot be avoided yet is essentially unresolvable under current law: the definition of trade secret and other doctrines of trade secret law. Third, the need for fresh economic analysis, focusing on the economics of information, to help resolve the legal and policy problems raised by high technology's new ways of working.

Personnel Mobility and the Spreading of Technical Information

When people are hired in Silicon Valley, they take information with them that they learned at former employers, and it is hoped and expected that they will use that information on the new job. It may be convenient for law to assume that this is not true. But a realistic analysis of the problem must start from the assumption that the flow of such information happens every day in the Valley. Examples exist in histories of the Valley, earlier research, and my own interviews.

Start with the story that is a kind of primal myth of the origins of Silicon Valley as a high-technology district. The earliest crucial technology was the transistor, developed principally at AT&T's Bell Laboratories by William Shockley. In 1954 Shockley left Bell to attempt to establish a transistor firm in Massachusetts under Raytheon, but soon returned to Palo Alto to start Shockley Transistor Corporation. Two years after its founding, eight of his leading engineers (the "traitorous eight") went into competition with him as Fairchild Semiconductor. By 1968 all of the eight had left Fairchild to found other technology firms (of which the best known is Intel, plaintiff in the Broadcom suit!) or venture capital firms (Lécuyer 2000; Saxenian 1994: 25–26). Note that the traitorous eight took the very technology at the center of Shockley Transistor, founded a new firm, competed directly with their old employer, and went on to repeat the pattern. Sturgeon (2000) and Bahrami and Evans (1995) show that such departures to form start-ups have characterized the electronics industry in the Bay Area since World War I.

AnnaLee Saxenian's book, as mentioned, attributes the rise of Silicon Valley, and its triumph over Route 128, precisely to the rapid exchange of information across firm boundaries. Most of Saxenian's accounts of information-sharing among firms involve either close vendor-customer relations, or formal technology licensing. However, her book also includes examples of information spread informally by mobile employees. All these modes of knowledge spillover underlie comments like that of the venture capitalist who told her in 1990: "In Silicon Valley, I learn that my buddy is designing a new chip, so I develop a system to use it and have a big lead on the competition. Likewise, I can design a new Conner Peripherals disk drive into my product before my competitors elsewhere have even heard of Conner" (Saxenian 1994: 114). The engineers in Sitkin (1986) are constantly asked by friends, housemates, and former associates at rival firms for software or equipment. Firms often share that information, though guard themselves as well, perhaps by sharing only an outmoded version.

I found employers to be quite open in discussing the way mobile employees carry information. They agree that this process has been crucial to the success of the Valley. Cisco, for example, takes a relaxed view of employee mobility and claims never to have sued a departing employee under a theory of "inevitable disclosure" of trade secrets. Juniper and Redback are two rival manufacturers of routers, founded by former Cisco employees without legal challenge from Cisco. Cisco does maintain a policy that current employees who move to Juniper or Redback will not be rehired at Cisco, but I was told in interviews in July 2001 that exceptions have been made to this policy. When I asked when, I was told frankly: "When we think they've learned something."

Trade Secrets Law and the Conflict with Ordinary Personnel Practices

As *Intel v. Broadcom* shows, law conceptualizes information quite differently than employers like Cisco or Fairchild, or their employees. It seems pretty clear that the traitorous eight who founded Fairchild (then left it), or the Cisco employees who founded Juniper and Redback, might have been sued for violation of trade secrets. Of course, there is no reason for public concern if Shockley, Fairchild, or Cisco simply choose, for their own purposes, not to insist on their legal rights. The problem arises because other employers, like Intel, will sue departing employees. Law must ultimately decide whether such suits serve the public interest.

Trade Secrets Law and Its Potential to Harm Silicon Valley

Every American jurisdiction imposes on employees a legally enforceable obligation not to disclose their employer's trade secrets. The obligation is not limited to employees, but by far the bulk of trade secrets litigation is brought by employers against departing employees. The duty to protect trade secrets was created by judges as a matter of the common (i.e., judge-made) law of property and torts. In nine or so northeastern states, trade secrets law is still entirely common law. This list includes such important technology states as Massachusetts, New York, and New Jersey. Most states, including California, have adopted the Uniform Trade Secrets Act. The adoption of the statute has not made any significant change in the law. Courts read it as if it simply codified their state's common law. When they apply the statute, they frequently cite their earlier common law, and do not look for ways in which the statute's language might be said to change the law. They do not make any effort to make the law uniform among the states that have adopted the Uniform Act. Finally, a federal statute, applicable in all states, makes misappropriation of trade secrets a federal criminal offense (Economic Espionage Act of 1996).

Nevertheless, the law of trade secrets is fairly similar in all states. (At least, the law "on the books" is similar. It is likely that there are some significant differences in judicial attitude toward that law, but this is a difficult thing to show.) A trade secret is information, not generally known, that derives value from not being generally known. It is used by someone to make money, and that person must make reasonable efforts to keep it a secret. If these criteria are met, the owner of the trade secret may seek an injunction or damages against anyone who acquires it by improper means.

Trade secrets law is weaker protection than that provided by patent or copyright law. If I have a patent on a machine, I can keep you from making a copy by taking apart one of my machines and "reverse engineering" it. By and large, however, "reverse engineering" is a proper means for learning a trade secret (Friedman, Landes, and Posner 1991). Learning a trade secret from your rival's former employee, however, is not.

Silicon Valley therefore owes its existence to the reticence of employers to enforce their rights under trade secrets law. Start-ups are the strength of the Valley. Most start-ups are founded by employees of existing firms. Sometimes the start-up will compete directly with the founders' former firm. Examples are the many firms making knock-offs of Intel and other chips. Sometimes the start-up will make products, software or hardware, designed to be compatible with the products of the former firm. In either of these homey examples—everyday practice in the Valley—the start-up will make use of some piece of information that is a trade secret of the former employer.

Hard drive manufacturing, mostly by firms headquartered in Silicon Valley, was studied by the Federal Reserve Bank of Minneapolis (Franco and Filson 2000). Successful firms are founded by departing employees of existing firms. Of sixty-eight firms entering that industry over a twenty-year period (1977–97), forty were started by former employees of existing firms, and those forty included all but four of the start-ups that generated revenue, accounting for 99.4 percent of the total revenues of the start-up group. (Of course, many of the "established" firms that gave birth to employee start-ups had themselves been spun out of even older firms). The more valuable a company's technology, the more its employees will leave to start new, successful firms. It does not matter how big the old firm is. The greater its technological know-how (measured by the range and capacities of its products), the greater the likelihood of employees leaving to develop a start-up, and the longer the start-up will survive. Start-ups included both innovators and firms that basically imitated the older firm. The result was that the price of disk drives fell while firm profits increased. There are no reported lawsuits during this period by hard drive manufacturers against departing employees.

As mentioned in the previous chapter, hard disk drive manufacturers succeeded by exporting Silicon Valley's culture of employee mobility, shared information, and ties across firm lines to their new assembly plants in Singapore. The Singapore plants learned how to assemble hard disk drives by hiring employees of, and otherwise copying, competitors (McKendrick, Doner, and Haggard 2000: 178–81). The Japanese firms that had been expected to dominate the manufacture of hard disk drives (as they had memory chips) missed this opportunity for years. "No Japanese incumbent had spun off a new HDD firm, nor did employees job-hop among companies. A senior manager in Fujitsu's disk drive operations could not remember a single engineer who was hired from a competitor; instead, the company preferred to hire new university graduates" (McKendrick, Doner, and Haggard 200: 105).

How California Law Somewhat—But Not Totally—Tames the Litigation Threat Against Departing Employees

While most Silicon Valley employers do not sue departing employees—they are like Cisco—occasionally, one does—like Intel. These occasional cases expose the uncertainties and current issues in trade secrets law. By and large, as is obvious, law supports the practice of Silicon Valley start-ups. Most litigation against departing employees is unsuccessful, as was true, for the most part, of *Intel v. Broadcom.* Some of the devices used to bring about this result are unstable, however. If courts became convinced, through some economic or policy analysis, that the public would be better served if more employers could enjoin departing employees, they could achieve this result without major doctrinal change. Similarly, if courts became convinced, by this book or another, that the public is best served by permitting the rapid employee turnover of Silicon Valley, they could facilitate that result more effectively than they do now.

This section will summarize the current law affecting employee mobility, emphasizing the pressure points and uncertainties that will define whether law will reinforce, or restrict, employee mobility. The following section will summarize how employers see trade secrets suits against departing employees, drawing on journalistic coverage, and my own interviews. Chapter 3 will offer an economic analysis, drawing on the economics of information, which supports the courts' general support for free employee mobility.

California Does Not Enforce "Covenants Not to Compete." Outside of California, employers have a different way of preventing an employee's departure, where they feel this would damage them. Employees may be required to agree that, on leaving the company, they will not compete with it for a certain limited time. Even in California, many employees are asked to sign such "covenants not to compete." Young, Lindsay, and Lund may well have been asked to sign such covenants, since none of them worked in California when he worked for Intel. In most of the United States, such covenants are enforceable if reasonable in duration and geographic scope. In California, they are not, under a century-old California statute that reflects accidents of nineteenth-century codification, not policy on high-technology districts (Gilson 1999).

Gilson argues that California's old ban on covenants not to compete is the crucial factor explaining Silicon Valley's triumph over Route 128. Massachusetts, like most states, enforces such covenants, and Gilson argues that the threat of litigation dissuades start-ups. Certainly the law of covenants is the single clearest difference between California's law and other states'. Certainly any jurisdiction trying to create a high-technology district, or improve its high-technology growth, should experiment with limiting or denying the enforceability of covenants not to compete. States that do not enforce such covenants tend to see unusual growth in computer employment (Valletta 2002).

Nevertheless, it is hardly plausible that this single statute could by itself really explain the Valley's supposed triumph over the Route 128 district in Massachusetts (Wood 2000). For one thing, other western states like Montana and Oklahoma adopted the same code as California, with the same ban on restrictive covenants, yet their courts read the statute as if it merely enacted the common law's ban on "unreasonable" covenants (Malsberger 1996). So there is a larger cultural story involved in understanding why the same statute in California was not narrowed but was read literally, that is, broadly, and then (in *Intel v. Broadcom*) as a source of "policy" that can be applied to the different problem of trade secrets.

In particular, the California Supreme Court held many years ago that trade secrets agreements fall completely outside the statute (*Gordon v. Landau*). So it is not enough to point to the statutory ban on noncompete covenants in order to explain Silicon Valley. One must also explain why trade secrets law has not developed into an effective substitute.

California Has Neither Accepted Nor Rejected the Doctrine of "Inevitable Disclosure of Trade Secrets." Plaintiffs in trade secret cases must normally identify the precise trade secret that the employee and his new employer are allegedly infringing. Only by plaintiff's identifying the precise secret can the court determine whether it really is a trade secret, whether the plaintiff took reasonable efforts to keep it secret, whether the defendants will infringe it, and so on. This requirement is itself a significant impediment to litigation. Holders of trade secrets complain that in order to protect their trade secrets, they must partially disclose them to the court, and some aspect of the secret— its existence, if not its details—will be secret no longer.

Plaintiffs who do not wish to disclose the existence of a particular trade secret sometimes allege that a particular employee, departing for a rival, will "inevitably disclose" some trade secret or another, that they need not identify. Most such attempts have been unsuccessful, and only two appellate courts have squarely adopted the doctrine of "inevitable disclosure." The best known is *PepsiCo v. Redmond* in the federal appeals court in Chicago (assertedly applying Illinois law, that is, the Uniform Trade Secrets Act). The decision is criticized in Bui-Eve (1997), Gilson (1999), Hyde (1998), Merges (1999), and Whaley (1999).

In the early 1990s, PepsiCo and Quaker Oats each manufactured a sports drink, All Sport and Gatorade respectively. When Quaker wanted a new vice president of field operations for Gatorade, the president of its Gatorade division offered the job to William Redmond, Jr. Redmond was then serving his first weeks as general manager of Pepsi-Cola's California operations, having just been promoted from general manager of its northern California operations.

What else was Gatorade supposed to do? Either they promote from within, or go outside. Promoting from within may not make sense if the brand is underperforming. Even if the brand is doing well, however, it is supposed these days that promotion from within has lost its former resonance, not merely in Silicon Valley, but throughout the economy (Osterman 1996; Arthur and Rousseau 1996; Chan 1996). If Gatorade does not promote from within, or hire a novice, it must by definition be looking at experienced sports drink managers with rival firms.

Nevertheless, Redmond was preliminarily enjoined under the Uniform Trade Secrets Act, which Illinois (like California) has adopted, from taking any position at Quaker for a year; from ever assuming any duties at Quaker relating to beverage marketing, pricing, or distribution; and from ever divulging PepsiCo trade secrets or confidential information. On remand, the district court narrowed the injunction, permitting Redmond to take the job at Quaker (which he did), but merely enjoining disclosure of confidential information or trade secrets. This is a true "inevitable disclosure" case. PepsiCo never identified any specific piece of information that Redmond had and Quaker wanted. PepsiCo did not show that Redmond knew the recipe for All Sport, or new flavors being worked on secretly, or which athletes had been approached for endorsements, or anything of that sort.

What *did* Redmond know? He was far from the key figure in All Sport. He was one of many regional general managers. He had access, said PepsiCo, to its "Strategic Plan" and "Annual Operating Plan" covering "financial goals, marketing plans, promotional event calendars, growth expectations, and operational changes." He knew which markets Pepsi would focus on, and some aspects of a new delivery system. In other words, he knew what any manager knows.

The *PepsiCo* decision is unusually proplaintiff, not typical. It inhabits a world in which all managers on distribution lists for "strategic plans" and "annual operating plans" serve for life, and may have their departures to work in the area they know enjoined at the option of their employer. It seems not to relate at all to today's world of corporate downsizing and managerial layoffs. It does not rest on any economic analysis of the efficiency advantages of letting Redmond go as against letting PepsiCo enjoin him, even though the Court of Appeals for the Seventh Circuit is famous for its law-and-economics approach. Nor does it reinforce employment-at-will, to which, in other cases, that court has paid homage. Employees with other options, such as competent managers, may choose not to accept employment at will if, following involuntary termination, they will be unable to work in their area of expertise.

In particular, the *PepsiCo* decision is unusual in its lonely forthright adoption of the theory of "inevitable disclosure." Although the phrase is sometimes used for other purposes, such as defining the scope of injunctive relief, a true "inevitable disclosure" case in my usage is one in which employment is enjoined because the employee would "inevitably disclose" *some* trade secret, but the old employer does not identify one. Only one state's appellate court has squarely adopted this kind of "inevitable disclosure": New Jersey (*National Starch & Chemical Corp. v. Parker Chemical Corp.*).

The status of the doctrine is open in California. One intermediate appellate court (*Schlage Lock Co. v. Whyte*), and some trial courts (like *Intel v. Broadcom; Bayer Corp. v. Roche Molecular Systems*) reject it. Lawyers to whom I spoke expect the *Broadcom* decision to be influential. However, other trial courts have adopted it, in unreported opinions (*Advanced Micro Devices, Inc. v. Hyundai Electronics America;* Ballon 1998; Feinberg 1998). One intermediate court of appeal allegedly adopted the doctrine, though its actual decision carefully examined each purported secret and decided that none of the claimed secrets was really a secret, a method that is really the opposite of the doctrine of "inevitable disclosure." Then, to top off that already-ambiguous case, the Supreme Court of California ordered that it is not to be cited as authority, a mysterious local custom in which the Supreme Court liquidates a lower court decision without giving any reason why (*Electro*

Optical Industries v. White). The situation then is highly fluid. If courts became convinced that the public interest would be served by limitations on employee mobility, they could, without legislative action, adopt the doctrine of "inevitable disclosure." This would make it very difficult for the typical start-up, in which managers leave one firm and start another that makes products that compete with, or are compatible with, their old employer's.

California Does Not Give Independent Weight to Negotiated Trade Secrets Agreements. It is common in Silicon Valley and elsewhere to have employees sign agreements in which they agree not to disclose trade secrets or confidential information. Everybody I talked to uses them. Such agreements have the symbolic effect of educating employees in the employer's trade secrets policy. However, they do not appear to have any legal effect. A respected California judge stated in *dictum* many years ago that a trade secrets agreement must be limited to information that the law already considered a trade secret. A trade secrets agreement that purported to make secret, what the law did not consider a trade secret, would be a covenant not to compete and as such unenforceable in California (*State Farm Mut. Auto Ins. Co. v. Dempster*). However, the statutory definition of trade secret is very broad, covering any information not generally known that gains value from being secret. Courts in California have declared to be "trade secrets" an employee's knowledge of how his former employer set up standard, commercially available manufacturing equipment (*By-Buk Co. v. Printed Cellophane Tape Co.*), or Jedediah T. Steele's using a reserve to sweeten chardonnay, practiced for centuries (Fisher 1992). A court in Massachusetts, home to many high-technology businesses, enjoined a cookie bakery from making use of the "trade secret," brought by an employee from his old employer, of incorporating the nut dust into the chocolate chip cookie batter (*Peggy Lawton Kitchens Inc. v. Hogan*). If knowledge like this is really an employer trade secret, it is hard to see how agreements could broaden the definition.

I have not located any cases giving any independent effect to a negotiated trade secrets agreement. This may represent another aspect of California law that favors employee mobility, like the statutory ban on covenants not to compete, although it is not clear that California law is really any different from other states' on this issue.

In Other Respects, California Trade Secrets Law "on the Books" Is Like Other States'. It is sometimes claimed (e.g., Liebeskind 1997) that trade secrets laws do not protect "inchoate" or noncodified knowledge, or cannot be applied to all proprietary knowledge of a given employee. Case law, in California and elsewhere, does not support these statements as a statement of formal law. The portion of *Intel v. Broadcom* dealing with Brad Gunther applied to all his proprietary knowledge, including inchoate and negative information.

Statements that refer to a restricted definition of "trade secret" may be true as a matter of practical application. Trade secrets suits are indeed hard to win in practice. Juries at the damages phase, and many judges at the preliminary injunction phase, hate them. Juries throughout the Bay Area increasingly reflect exposure to Silicon Valley's high-velocity labor practices, as lawyers note and as we shall observe again. They are aware that people change jobs frequently and do not believe that either employer or employees owe each other anything.

However, the low success rate does not reflect a narrow legal definition of "trade secrets" for, on the contrary, that definition is very broad (how the machines were set up, chardonnay reserves, nut dust). California's definition of "trade secret" is as broad as any. It includes "negative information" such as potential customers who did not place orders (*Morton v. Rank America; Courtesy Temporary Service v. Camacho*). It may reach all unspecified trade secrets held by an employee (the portion of *Intel v. Broadcom* dealing with Brad Gunther). A trade secret need not be written down. Practical know-how is included (*By-Buk Co. v. Printed Cellophane Tape Co.*). The last case involved exceptionally harsh relief, in which Employer 2, who learned from a new Employee how Employer 1 had set up the machines, was ordered to dismantle the machines, account for all sales, and pay punitive damages. While the case has not been cited in many years, it has never been overruled. If it were still good law in California, there could hardly be a start-up in the Valley.

In California, as in other states, trade secrets suits rarely turn on the *definition* of trade secret, for that definition is quite malleable. Remember the Massachusetts court that thought that adding nut dust to chocolate chip cookie batter was a trade secret? The same court had found four years earlier that the design of "technical information retrieval and analysis systems" for satellites was not a trade secret but "general skill and knowledge" (*Dynamics Research Corp. v. Analytic Sciences Corp.*) Apparently all the ingredients of such systems had been published in journals. The court chose to ignore any difference between published information and the practical know-how to put it together. In real life, however, this difference is often crucial. For example, a device called the TEA laser had been described in every detail in published articles. Yet it was successfully built only in laboratories that employed someone who had seen one built (Collins 1974).

Instead, trade secrets litigation is usually quite moralistic. *Intel v. Broadcom* is typical in its emphasis on which employees were "trustworthy." Focusing on employee morality permits the judge to duck hard issues. In *Intel v. Broadcom,* the judge did not make findings about Intel's trade secrets in its ethernet technology. Intel put all its eggs into the basket of "inevitable disclosure." But surely Intel had some trade secrets in its MAC chip technology or the informal know-how that goes into the chips' design or manufacture. Surely the three employees knew at least some of these secrets. Surely situations will arise at Broadcom in which their knowledge of these secrets will guide their action. So when the judge found that the employees were "trustworthy," he must have meant that they were trustworthy not to disclose legally protected secrets that they actually knew.

Lawyers who litigate trade secrets cases are quite open about this moralistic approach, which makes trade secrets litigation so different from patent litigation. "I just have to show something was taken improperly. That is very different from an infringement analysis that is so very technical," says the chair of the technology group at a large New York firm (Slind-Flor 1993).

Trade Secrets Suits Are Difficult to Win and Harm the Companies That Bring Them. The main reason that start-ups are rarely sued by the former employers of their founders is not because the law forbids such suits, but because they are difficult to win, rarely accomplish much, and harm the company that brings them. Many firms (like Cisco) choose not to sue departing employees; firms that do sue departing employees are criticized in the industry and have trouble recruiting; and firms that sue departing employees (like Intel) rarely accomplish anything by doing so. Another famous Silicon Valley trade secrets suit illustrates the vagaries of trade secret law, the moralism of current litigation, and the need for a newer, economically sophisticated approach.

Intel was the plaintiff here, too. This is not a coincidence. In the late 1980s, Intel took an aggressive approach toward protecting the specifications of the basic chips that became the 286 and 386. This just implemented their CEO Andy Grove's philosophy as stated in the title of his book *Only the Paranoid Survive* (Grove 1996). A technology exchange agreement, in which rival Advanced Micro Devices was supposed to be the second source for the 386, collapsed when Intel refused to share its technology, which an arbitrator later found to be in bad faith and a breach of the contract (*Advanced Micro Devices v. Intel*). Intel cultivated an image as an aggressive litigant against those using its alleged secrets, including departing employees (D. Clark 1993).

Alfred Chan was an engineer who had worked on Intel's popular 80387 math coprocessor. In 1989 he left to join ULSI Technology, a start-up chip manufacturer, to help develop a math coprocessor that would work with the basic Intel 386 chip and compete directly with Intel's math coprocessor. Manufacturing Intel knockoffs is not unusual. In this case, though, Chan

showed his boss, ULSI's President George Hwang, an early target specification for the 387, marked "Intel proprietary." (Other ULSI employees besides
Chan had worked or were still moonlighting at Intel, and the source of the
document was never identified.) The specification had been superseded by
the version that went into manufacturing, and its key information had been
published in a trade magazine. Hwang nevertheless called Intel and offered
to open his databases and computers to Intel experts to show that he had no
Intel proprietary information. Intel declined the offer and instead persuaded
the Santa Clara County District Attorney to prosecute Chan and Hwang for
criminal theft of trade secrets. This included a search of the ULSI offices for
evidence, in which many ULSI documents were taken. The prosecutor assigned to the case had previously worked for Intel's law firm and Intel paid
the cost of investigation, an arrangement used in several trade secrets cases
but later criticized by the Supreme Court of California in a different case
(*People v. Eubanks*).

The criminal and civil litigation lasted four years. The preliminary investigation in the criminal matter alone took up two and a half. Each side
had a morality tale for the media and the eventual criminal and civil juries.
Intel focused on the documents. When we get to the economic analysis in
the next chapter, I will want to question whether the economic analysis of
a company document is any different from the information in an employee's
head. In litigation, however, lawyers all report that juries and judges are
more impressed when plaintiff can show documents or diskettes or computer files taken.

Intel portrayed sneaky and ungrateful thieves biting the hand that fed them.
The defendants portrayed an overbearing gorilla, interested only in insulat-
ing itself from the market competition to which the rest of us are subject and
heedless of the individual lives it crushes in that pursuit (Bennet 1994; Slind-
Flor 1993).

In this case, Intel lost all the legal battles. The criminal case ended in jury
acquittals. In the civil case, the jury found that the documents did not contain
Intel trade secrets, presumably because of the trade magazine publication. A
federal injunction against ULSI for patent infringement was reversed on appeal. Nevertheless, a low-cost competitor was prevented from coming onto
the market for four years (Jackson 1997; Fuller 1993).

A high Intel official, who spoke to me under strict promise that I not identify the source, told me in March 1996 that the ULSI litigation and similar
litigation at the time had been a disaster for Intel's recruiting. "Chat groups
lit up all over the Valley," I was told, and job applicants frequently asked
about the chance of being sued when they left Intel. Intel did not sue any
departing employees between the ULSI litigation and Broadcom. When I

asked my Intel source in 2000 why it sued Broadcom, however, the answer reflected more anger at Broadcom's interviewing techniques than real estimate of economic harm to Intel.

The Intel-ULSI litigation, and similar litigation at the time, was closely watched in the Valley. My interviewees normally draw three conclusions from it. First, companies that sue departing employees will suffer harm to their reputation. Cadence Design Systems is a rare successful trade secrets plaintiff (*Cadence Design Systems, Inc. v. Avant! Corp.*). It was able to prove its allegations that rival Avant! was built on technology stolen from it, leading to criminal convictions and prison terms for some of Avant!'s founders (Mintz 2001). Cadence's CEO, Joseph B. Costello, nevertheless "was lambasted in the media as a bully and his board, customers, and friends urged him to give up the chase" (Burrows 1997). Publicly traded companies that report criminal theft of trade secrets are normally punished by the market with a drop in share value. The higher the value of the missing trade secrets, the greater the decrease in stock price (Carr and Gorman 2001).

Second, this reputational harm will directly affect recruiting—as my Intel source told me. All Valley firms recruit constantly. Potential recruits always think about the next move. They want to be able to move to the next job able to trade on what they learned on the last. They do not want to be sued when—not if, but when—they move.

Third, trade secret suits rarely accomplish anything. They are hard to win. Rivals will arise. Trade secrets will leak out. Gerry Keeler is the partner in Arthur Andersen's Palo Alto office who handles intellectual asset management and has consulted on litigation. In his opinion, companies that sue departing employees are trying to "prove a point" and keep a threat potent. They have little hope of accomplishing anything else.

The question of the legal infrastructure of Silicon Valley's high-velocity labor market is thus a complex one, even in this brief treatment. By and large, law has facilitated the culture of start-ups and labor mobility. Some unusual (though not unique) aspects of California law have reinforced a general employment law that is favorable to labor flexibility. The law does not cry out for reform, and one should be careful about changing it.

Nevertheless, the intellectual foundations of current law are somewhat weak. Courts could easily stumble into adoption of the doctrine of "inevitable disclosure," or give independent weight to negotiated trade secrets agreements, or subtly change attitudes in ways that could impede the formation of start-ups, or employees switching to rival firms. It is long past time to examine the economics of current legal arrangements.

3

A NEW ECONOMIC ANALYSIS OF TRADE SECRETS LAW FROM AN ECONOMICS OF INFORMATION PERSPECTIVE

Suppose that a legislator, or judge, wanted the law of trade secrets and covenants not to compete to reflect an economic analysis of what is best for society as a whole. He or she might want to foster the maximum creation of useful information and the most rapid diffusion of such information to users. These goals might conflict. Property rights in information might provide incentives for its creation, yet inhibit its diffusion. In this case, our hypothetical legislator or judge would want to know how to trade off these two goals so as to serve each as efficiently as possible.

A policymaker with such a consumer's perspective on economics will learn two things immediately. First, he or she will learn that economists cannot at the moment answer the policy question definitively, or even very well. Kenneth Arrow said to me in conversation in 1996 that economists are nowhere near "even a sort-of-good theory."

James Boyle, a law professor who writes brilliantly about information, wittily (if unfairly) summed up much economic writing about information as infected with what he modestly named "Boyle's Paradox." Information is treated simultaneously as "perfect": "free, complete, instantaneous, and universally available" and as a commodity ("costly, partial, and deliberately restricted in its availability") (1996: 35). Boyle's gibe is unfair. Many economists write with penetrating understanding of the problems of information. Some have even won Nobel prizes for this work. I will spend most of this and the next chapter summarizing their work and applying it to the legal problem. Nevertheless, as we shall see, Boyle's gibe isn't *totally* unfair, for we will also observe Boyle's Paradox, sometimes in unexpected places.

Second, he or she will learn that many of the dominant frameworks, employed by economists to answer the question, incorporate assumptions at odds with the stylized empirical picture in the previous chapter. Economists may assume that information has value only insofar as it is somebody's property, and fail to model the wealth effects of shared information. (A leading and quite brilliant textbook on the economics of innovation, Aghion and Howitt [1998], contains, as nearly as I can see, not a single reference to information that is shared by multiple users and therefore nobody's property.) Or they assume that information is produced as "spillover" from some more fundamental economic activity, and fail to model the actual production of the information. Some see that information has "spillover" value—that is, creates an externality. But they may assume that the value is the same whether held by employers or employees. This ignores the fundamental asymmetry under which employees must disclose the information that they hold, in order to get hired (or their start-up funded), while employers may effectively keep it secret. Or they may assume that only employers, not employees, need incentives to produce information. No doubt for each one's economic analysis, such a simplifying assumption is essential. However, for our policymaker's purpose, all assume what should be open for analysis at this point. That is, the legal and policy question is defining the proper standards for trade secrets and covenant not to compete suits. That analysis must include accounts of how information is created, who needs incentives to produce it, and what value it will have if widely shared, or in employees' hands.

Of course other viewpoints than the economist's are possible. The lawyer or policymaker might choose other ways to defend intellectually the results in cases, like the Intel cases, that permit employees to leave Intel to join or start competitors.

First, an argument from fairness, not welfare. One might think that "trade secret" should reflect a certain reciprocity in the underlying employment agreement. "Trade secret" meant something to an employer in the 1950s or 1960s that implicitly offered its technical staff lifetime employment contracts. It must necessarily mean something different when both employer and employee know that the employee will be back on the job market when his or her current project comes to an end. Employers that don't offer long-term employment can hardly insist on long-term confidentiality. I find this argument appealing, and so do many other people. It is argued particularly strongly in Stone (2001). However, it apparently has never been the articulated grounds of a legal decision. (I should note that this argument does not have clear results in either of the Intel cases I've mentioned. Intel, like Hewlett-Packard, is an unusual Silicon Valley employer that does enter into implicit contracts for stable employment.)

Second, some people have argued that employees like Steven Lindsay, the chief software architect for Intel's gigabit ethernet products before departing for Broadcom, have some kind of moral right to exploit their own inventions (e.g., Cherensky 1993). Third, some European systems of employment law have as an articulate norm the "protection of the weaker party" which probably means the employee.

Fourth, this book breathes the same atmosphere as other recent investigations by legal academics of a "commons" of information shared by all to the benefit of all (e.g., Gordon 1993; Boyle 1996; Benkler 1999; Lessig 2001). This book seeks to establish that commons as an economic, not merely political or legal, concept (see also Benkler 2002).

In this book, however, I want to set aside all these moral arguments and consider, as coldly as possible, what economics can tell us about the underlying question: the welfare trade-off between knowledge that is held as private property and knowledge that diffuses with employee mobility.

I want to make clear from the outset that there is no way to be certain which outcome in these trade secrets cases maximizes social benefit. There is no standard economic way of modeling the trade-off involved. Nevertheless, we can use economics to improve policy in the area and develop better ways of having law and economics enrich each other in the future. Moreover, although we will not be able to state definitively whether society is better off with broad or narrow trade secrets protection, we know enough to be skeptical of the alleged advantages of broad trade secrets protection. In California, employees are normally free to change jobs without a lawsuit alleging either breach of a covenant not to compete or theft of trade secrets. There is no evidence of any social harm from this. In particular, there is no evidence that firms lack incentives to invest in the production of information. On the other side, there is considerable evidence that weak trade secrets protection, like California's, decreases the cost of diffusing information, decreases costs to firms when they hire labor, increases joint product, and increases incentives to employees.

I will outline an economic framework for analyzing the problem, deriving from recent developments in New Growth Theory and the economics of information. This is an important economic approach that will be applied throughout the book to a variety of legal problems. However, there are alternative approaches that have been applied or might be applied to the problem of modeling information spillover and employee mobility, approaches deriving from the economics of contract, human capital, industrial organization and models of competition, and an older psychological approach associated with Fritz Machlup. I will take those up in chapter 4.

It is a cliché that the economy of Silicon Valley, or perhaps the entire modern economy, is an economy of information. Yet the implications of this cliché for the law and economics of labor and employment remain largely unexplored. Markets for information have many unusual features: difficulty in measuring units, multiple equilibria, signaling, increasing returns, and network effects, among others we will encounter. Yet a labor market that is, at least in part, a market for information has not yet been analyzed in these terms.

As applied to the problem of modeling property rights in trade secrets carried by mobile employees, we can distinguish three different questions. The first involves the economic analysis of information that is shared by many users, specifically, incentives for its production and diffusion. This literature is extensive but divergent. We will be able to use it to show that shared technical information plays an important role in economic growth that is not reflected in most legal and policy discussions, and that no special property rights are required as incentives for the production of such shared technical information. Sharing such information cannot, surprisingly, be shown to reduce incentives for its creation or production. And since institutions for sharing information (such as a weak law of trade secrets) increase incentives for diffusing information and lower costs considerably, these seem to offset, if not overwhelm, any tendency (itself not easy to demonstrate) for shared information to reduce incentives for its creation. So as a general rule, society will not suffer from weak residual property rights in information and strong institutions encouraging its diffusion. This has been confirmed by all the relevant empirical research. It provides strong support for a generally weak law of trade secrets, such as the rejection of the doctrine of "inevitable disclosure" and a narrow definition of protected information.

The second question involves applying the literature on the economics of information to the employment of particular individual human beings, who are neither commodities nor public goods. The information transferred by employee mobility includes tacit knowledge or know-how that is important for economic growth. Knowledge transfer through employee mobility is particularly effective in distinct geographic districts (which may be another way of saying labor markets). This too supports a narrow version of trade secrets law.

The third level of complexity involves the role of private contract in markets for information, a question barely explored in the economic literature. Showing that society and individuals benefit generally from shared information is not the same thing as showing that any particular private contract, which purports to restrict such information transfer, reduces social welfare. I will try to answer this question by reference to the new implicit employment contract in high-tech employment.

The Importance of Nonrivalrous, Nonexcludable Information

If Information Spreads, Will It Still Be Produced?

Information is different from other economic goods. This much, at least, is an old idea. Information is expensive to produce but cheap to copy and, unlike other economic goods, does not necessarily decline in value when held in common. Unlike other commons, information doesn't get overfarmed or overfished. In Thomas Jefferson's elegant formulation: "He who receives an idea from me, receives instruction himself without lessening mine; as he who lights his taper at mine, receives light without darkening me" (Jefferson 1813).

In this way of thinking, there will be a social tendency toward the under-production of information, since producers will not be able to realize the full market value of their creations. The social benefit of information thus exceeds any private benefit. Without special incentives, such as patents and copyrights (the subject of Jefferson's letter), for the production of information, there will be underproduction of information. This insight can justify such eighteenth-century solutions as legal property rights in information, or twentieth-century public subsidies or research boards (Arrow 1962b; Romer 1993). (Not all economists agree that there is any tendency toward underproduction of information; I will come to that momentarily.)

It would seem that the economic case for strong trade secrets protection against departing employees would surely start here. Before expending public funds to subsidize technological research, it might seem that employers like Intel should be given property rights that would ensure that their innovations not be carried immediately to competitors. But while some have supposed that opposition to all information spillover is implicit in the concern of Kenneth Arrow and Paul Romer for incentives for production of information (e.g., Langlois and Robertson 1996), neither Arrow nor Romer has advocated restrictions on employee mobility. (Arrow in fact has appeared as an expert witness on behalf of the defendant employee in trade secrets litigation.) The reasons are instructive.

In Romer's New Growth Theory, technical information is the single most important factor in economic growth. Information becomes more important when shared among many users, than when held as private property, for example by Intel.

> To see why extremely strong property rights might be a problem, imagine that Bell Labs had been given a nonexpiring, ironclad patent on the discovery of the transistor. Or even worse, imagine that such a patent had gone to an organization such as IBM or General Motors. Think of how different the digital electronics and consumer electronics industries would be if every inventor who improved on the design of the transistor and every person who applied the transistor in a new setting had to negotiate with one of these large, bureaucratic organizations for permission to proceed. (Romer 1993: 358)

Under Romer's model, Intel will have adequate incentives to innovate without special devices permitting it to keep those innovations secret, while society will be better off the quicker such technical information diffuses. Romer's theory is limited to information that is nonrivalrous and nonexcludable.

> Rivalry is a purely technological attribute. A purely rival good has the property that its use by one firm or person precludes its use by another; a purely nonrival good has the property that its use by one firm or person in no way limits its use by another. Excludability is a function of both the technology and the legal system. A good is excludable if the owner can prevent others from using it. (Romer 1990b: S73–74)

Examples of nonrivalrous information include formulas, algorithms, bit streams. If none of these qualifies for patent, copyright, or trade secrets protection, they are all both nonrivalrous and nonexcludable.

Limiting the theory to this kind of information heightens the contrast with conventional economic goods (which are both rivalrous and excludable) and opens up an economic analysis in which such information can be accumulated without bound or convexity. We will not, however, be able simply to apply Romer's New Growth Theory to the labor market. A labor market may be a kind of information market, but it is not a market in purely nonrivalrous information. An employee like Steven Lindsay or Alfred Chan would rarely be hired simply as a way of obtaining nonrivalrous information. Once we turn to information in a human head, the information will become rivalrous to some extent: a person can only be in one place at one time. Even Cisco's hiring back its former employees who "learned something" at Juniper or Redback means that Cisco is acquiring both nonrivalrous and rivalrous information. We will soon examine other theorists who have looked more closely at just this kind of rivalrous or embodied information, sometimes called "knowledge" or "tacit information" or "know-how" to distinguish it from the kind of pure information that Romer models. However, each employee hired also can transmit Romer's kind of nonrivalrous information, so we will need to examine economic analysis of both kinds of information.

Romer's model is based on three premises, each of which sounds plausible. First, technological change—information about new things to do with the same raw materials—accounts for most economic growth. Second, technological change results from the intentional actions of people responding to market incentives. Third, technological change, as information, can be used over and over at no additional cost.

If these three premises are accepted, there can be no equilibrium with price taking. Given any set of production inputs, there must always be another, investment in which would yield a greater return, than would the production of information with a marginal revenue of zero. So how is information produced in markets?

Romer reviews earlier attempts to deal with the paradox, which normally involve dropping one of the three premises. I will group these into five basic accounts.

First, in some accounts, nonrivalrous information is treated as exogenous and publicly provided (Solow 1956; Shell 1966, 1967). This drops premise (2), market provision of information. Much information useful in the production process is indeed exogenously provided, such as schools teaching principles of mathematics or physics. If the crucial knowledge to economic growth was the mathematics and science taught in schools, the United States would have no advantage over many Asian and European countries (if you believe the studies on the comparative scientific knowledge of schoolchildren)—unless, of course, immigration of foreign engineers was facilitated.

However, much of the information crucial to the growth of Silicon Valley is not of this type. Consider, for example, the very example (quoted in the previous chapter) that Saxenian's informant uses to show Silicon Valley's superiority over Boston, but that also gives rise to litigation: "In Silicon Valley, I learn that my buddy is designing a new chip, so I develop a system to use it and have a big lead on the competition. Likewise, I can design a new Conner Peripherals disk drive into my product before my competitors elsewhere have even heard of Conner" (1994: 114).

Intel's suits against Broadcom and ULSI, discussed in the previous chapter, involved just this kind of technical information: specifications of Intel products in development—the easiest kind of case, on might think, for trade secrets protection. Romer's model is more realistic than its predecessors and rivals by modeling just this kind of information produced by firms.

Second, in other accounts, nonrivalrous information is the unintentional side effect of the production of a conventional good. "The appearance of a product on the market automatically conveys information; if nothing else, the information that the product can be produced" (Arrow 1996b: 649). This is true, too. Much of the information spread by mobile employees from firm to firm is indeed the inevitable side effect of normal production. I think that even temps and other "unskilled" employees contribute to increases in productivity in contemporary America because they can (if they choose) tell the employer, for whom they currently work, what other employers do (cf. Juravich 1985; Kusterer 1978 on the information that "unskilled" workers have and managers lack). I will return to this point later. However, the "side effect" model of information cannot explain the kind of information involved in trade secrets cases like *Intel v. Broadcom* or *Intel v. ULSI*. That information is intentionally produced, through research and development efforts. Specifications, of chips or other products, are again a good example.

A third approach models nonrivalrous information as privately produced and compensated out of rents (Shell 1973; Griliches 1979; Romer 1986). Romer discusses technical difficulties with this solution. For my purposes, I will observe (as Romer also does) that it doesn't address our problem. Rents or quasi rents will accrue to whatever aspects of production we are treating as fixed, but the question will still remain why they would be used to produce information that will not earn its marginal product (as opposed to some other investment).

Fourth, human capital theorists sometimes assume away the distinction Romer draws, by treating knowledge as "human capital" that is rivalrous (my use precludes yours). This kind of information is important too, perhaps ultimately more important to labor market analysis than nonrivalrous information. The typical trade secret case, though, also involves nonrivalrous information, not all of which is the human capital of the employee (or employer, for that matter). The "human capital" approach also seems to overemphasize the knowledge that comes from schooling and underemphasize the knowledge that is produced by firms.

Finally, the only way all three premises can be maintained is to assume that the producer of the information is some kind of monopolist. Romer cites Schumpeter (1942); in the next chapter I'll discuss some work of Fritz Machlup (1952) in this tradition. Romer discusses some of the technical economic problems with all these assumptions. I will observe only that none well describes the kind of information involved in trade secrets disputes in Silicon Valley, information that is privately not publicly created, by firms that are almost never monopolies in a price-setting sense, and, given high job turnover, cannot be kept from competitors.

In Romer's model, production has four basic inputs: capital, labor, rivalrous human capital, and nonrivalrous information to which everyone has equal access. Capital is assumed to grow by the amount of foregone consumption, and labor and rivalrous human capital are assumed for simplicity to be fixed. (Rivalrous human capital obviously does grow as nonrivalrous knowledge grows, but for Romer the embodied kind of human capital has limits: individuals die and their embodied knowledge dies with them).

Under these assumptions, Romer derives a solution in which nonrivalrous information can grow without bound and becomes the most important factor of production for growth. Obviously, as in any economic model, this is an assumption and not a finding; the interest lies in its implications. The limitless growth of nonrivalrous information is crucial and what distinguishes it from other factors of production. Raw materials, water, and workers' bodies can be overfished, used up, particularly if held in common without strong property rights. Information is not a common pond that can be overfished. It never wears out and private actors use it over and over again.

Firms nevertheless invest in research, even though they will not be able to exclude rivals from the information produced, because they can nonetheless charge more for their products than the costs of production. However, the equilibrium will be socially suboptimum: additional gains may be had if the government directly subsidizes research (Romer 1990b, 1993). A companion paper reviews cross-country data on economic growth and finds that such growth is indeed better correlated with increased investment in human capital devoted to research, than with increased investment in physical capital (Romer 1990a, 1994).

Romer's appears to be the economic theory that explains much of the difference between Silicon Valley and Route 128 observed by AnnaLee Saxenian. Saxenian is not able to compare direct investment in the production of information by California and Massachusetts employers during the years of her study, but there is little reason to think that the differences, if any, could account for Silicon Valley's much greater growth. Silicon Valley produces more growth from employer investment in information, because more of that information is nonexcludable. As Ed McCracken, former CEO of Silicon Graphics, put it: "Some secrets are more valuable when shared" (Lee et al. 2000: 10). Rapid employee turnover turns information, which firms and lawyers might consider proprietary (such as specifications of forthcoming products), into Romer-like nonrivalrous, nonexcludable information. Yet firms do not, in general, stop investing in the production of technological change, merely because they know, in a high-velocity labor market, that this information will soon pass to competitors or even enable employees to start their own competitor.

Romer does not discuss issues of labor contracting or labor economics. He develops his model against a background of literature on economic growth. The student of labor contracting will instantly spot three important assumptions that the model makes about labor contracts.

First, in Romer's model, new technological innovations are produced by firms and increase directly with investment. But in the real world, innovations are produced by human beings. Their contracts of employment may give them more or less incentive to produce valuable information, yet this relationship is not easy to model (e.g., Nalbantian 1987).

Second, in Romer's model, information is assumed to be nonrivalrous and nonexcludable by its nature and by law, respectively. Yet this, too, is not always true. It is closest to true in Silicon Valley, where California law does not enforce covenants not to compete and courts have followed by restricting the application of the law of trade secrets.

Third, in Romer's model, firms make equal use of nonrivalrous information. In the real world, a firm's ability to use information that is unquestionably nonrivalrous and nonexcludable may reflect its ability to hire someone experienced in the use of just that information (e.g., Collins 1974; Almeida and Kogut 1999).

The thesis of this book in a sentence is that the contracts and labor market intermediaries characteristic of Silicon Valley's high-velocity labor market exist in order to realize the endogenous economic growth that comes from the production and diffusion of valuable information. Its contracts and careers provide maximum incentives for employee production of information; maximum diffusion of that information; and maximum absorptive capacity in firms. One can imagine costs to the adoption of such contracts, but so far these have not appeared. They might include reduced incentives in firms to produce information; employee resistance to the uncertainty of high-velocity labor markets; or reduced information flows within firms. The rest of this book will show how firms realize growth from high-velocity labor markets while not yet experiencing costs.

Let me deal first with what might appear to be the most telling objection to the thesis, the possibility that firms in high-velocity labor markets will reduce their investment in the production of information. Obviously this does not appear to be happening in Silicon Valley, and there are good reasons in economic theory for thinking this observation to be more than anecdotal.

In Romer's model, firms continue to produce technological information *despite* the fact that rivals cannot be excluded from it. Why might this be? At least six reasons seem to me possible explanations of any particular case.

First, the firm can make so much money from technological change that it is still its best investment. Romer's model is of this type. Models of employee training are directly parallel. People used to say that firms would never train employees in general skills and information, because other firms would just snap them up. The observation goes back to A.C. Pigou, but became canonical in the "human capital" school, which posited that firms would pay only for "firm-specific" training, while employees would have to pay for their own general training, typically through reduced wages. Now "human capital" as a concept-metaphor makes us think about information precisely as somebody's property, and directs our attention away from the ways in which information has value even if it is shared with others. It turns out, of course, that firms *do* pay for general training (Acemoglu and Pischke 1999; Chang and Wang 1996; Katz and Ziderman 1990). Even temporary help agencies train temps in computer skills (Autor 2001a). The investment in training is worth it to firms, even if some of that training spills over and becomes the "human capital" of employees and rival firms.

Second, access by firms to each other's information can reduce their costs. We will let Michael Spence stand in for the second point. In Spence's model (1984), increased information spillover indeed reduces firm incentive to invest in research and development. However, it also reduces the level of R&D necessary to achieve a given level of cost reduction. What Romer has written of free trade is equally true of free labor markets with high amounts of nonexcludable information: "With free trade it is possible to put to better use human capital that might otherwise be used to redesign the wheel" (Romer 1990a: 351). Cooper (1999, 2001) is also a model of this type, in which the firm's gains, from hiring other firms' employees, always exceed the "losses," if any, when its monopolies over information become duopolies. Sharing information among firms, to reduce costs, is actually fairly common. Von Hippel (1988) studied "informal know-how sharing," engineers asking their counterparts at rival firms questions. Such questions are usually answered unless the answer is both secret and crucial to the firm. The phenomenon has been observed in Silicon Valley semiconductor firms (Sitkin 1986, with many stories of employees asked to share products of their current employer with friends, former coworkers, roommates, and others in their networks, now employed at rival firms) and biotechnological research (Powell 1996).

Third, access by firms to each other's information may increase joint profit, for example, if the rival, to which the information spills over, does not compete directly with the first employer. A famous example might be 3Com's developing networking capabilities for emerging microcomputers, at a time when its rivals continued to focus on larger computers (Kenney and von Burg 1999: 91–95). Fosfuri, Motta, and Rønde (2001) is a model of this third type. They model the decision by a multinational enterprise to manufacture in a developing country, where this involves training a local in its technology and the risk that the local will depart for a competitor. In their model, the company makes the investment when both it and the new firm will together make profits. This is one of the few models of technology transfer I have found that focuses specifically on technology transfer through employee mobility. There is no reason to think its application is limited to multinationals in developing countries. In the new economic literature on "networks" (e.g., White 2002), the economic actor is often the network, not the firm, so gains to the network will justify the investment.

A fourth reason firms might produce technical information, despite its spillover to rivals, was proposed by Kenneth Arrow (1996a): information inside firms is embedded in firm-specific, path-dependent codes and thus simply not as valuable to rivals. This may be true of much information but does not seem to capture the kind of information usually litigated in Silicon Valley, which often seems just as valuable to rivals as to originators.

Fifth, firms let employees depart with valuable information because this is necessary either to recruit those employees or induce them to accept high-velocity employment. For example, in the model of Lewis and Yao (2001), engineers with high bargaining power negotiate at hiring for an "open" firm environment. In such an "open" environment, employees may exchange information with employees at other firms and universities, and depart without litigation. Engineer bargaining power in turn reflects the supply of engineers, the efficiency with which engineers may find competing offers, and also the firm's ability to use the law to control intellectual property. While these factors are certainly important, I think our ultimate model will not be able to model open research environments as simply something that powerful engineers impose on unwilling firms. It will have to understand the advantages *to firms,* apart from recruitment of personnel, to such open arrangements. In Silicon Valley, as we have shown, firms rarely assert the intellectual property rights that the law gives them. While firms, strong and weak, do bargain for trade secrets protection, the strongest intellectual property protection given them by California law, they rarely sue on these contracts and have done no lobbying or test litigation designed to strengthen this protection. We still have to explain why firms like Cisco identify their success with open environments, and do not simply regard these as second-best bargains necessitated simultaneously by worker negotiating power and resource constraint.

Finally, incentive effects might explain firm investment in information that it cannot keep. *Employees* may have maximum incentives to produce valuable information in a high-velocity labor market like Silicon Valley's. Employees know they may be on the job market soon. They may produce even more technological change, if they will be able to trade on technological developments in which they participated, by taking them to future employers or their own start-ups. Firms benefit so much from these increased incentives for employees that they continue to invest in their projects. Motta and Rønde (2002) model these incentives. They point out that if employees' compensation cannot be adjusted and they are bound not to compete with their employers, they have no incentive to innovate. Even in the more realistic case in which employees may be given a bonus for innovation, the prospect of employment at a rival is still a better incentive for those employees. Lester and Talley (2000) also attempt to model incentives for employees under different regimes of intellectual property. Franco and Filson (2000) show that employees earn more by virtue of having previously been employed at firms with valuable patents and other intellectual property.

In Møen (2000), employees in R&D-intensive enterprises in Norway partly pay for that R&D in reduced wages early in their career. They make more later, because they formerly worked at an R&D-intensive firm. Some Silicon Valley firms may work this way. For example, Cisco claims to pay low base salaries (65 percent of industry average) (Osterman et al. 2001: 69). Presumably these employees expect to make more later, either at Cisco or on their next job. However, Cisco also claims to acquire rather than produce most of its new technology (Lee 2000: 114). A Silicon Valley start-up normally must pay market wages and must also produce technology. For the start-up, and perhaps for Cisco, too, potentially mobile employees are worth more to the firm, but not because they may be underpaid at the beginning of their careers. Rather, the presence, as live options, of moving to another employer or starting one's own company, are more powerful incentives for employee production of valuable information, than is the prospect of promotion up a career ladder in an internal labor market.

Relaxing the Assumption of Underinvestment in Information

I mentioned above that some economists have always questioned any supposed tendency to underinvest in the production of information, merely because others cannot be excluded from the final product. We will let Jack Hirshleifer represent this view.

Hirshleifer (1971; Hirshleifer and Riley 1992) has long sought to supplement the traditional Arrow story, of underinvestment in information, with an equal and opposite account of overinvestment, specifically duplicative research efforts to locate or produce the same information. These arise partly because undiscovered ideas are a sort of commons in which many will fish, and, even more so, because of the speculative advantage gained by the first discoverer or developer of valuable information. The first to know of an important development (Hirshleifer's example is the cotton gin) is in a position to reap gains in other markets (cotton futures, slaves, cotton-bearing land) irrespective of whether he or she holds property rights in the gin itself. When this story applies—and this depends on "the externalities causing discrepancies between private and social valuations" (Hirshleifer and Riley 1992: 263)—there need be no special concern about special property rights for the firms investing in technological information. As first movers, they should be amply compensated for their early knowledge of information even if it then spills to rivals. (Boldrin and Levine [2002], Hellwig and Irmen [2001], and Cohen and Levinthal [1989] similarly model the advantages of being the first developer of information even if it will spill over, so there is no monopoly to the innovator.)

If you worry about multiple firms duplicating each other's research, in such a "race to invent," you may no longer worry about incentives to research. You may worry instead about waste. The social advantage in having multiple firms, like Intel, Broadcom, and Lucent, all competing to produce PHY chips, is of course the normal benefit of competition, including incentives to invent and lower costs to consumers. But there is no social advantage in having all these firms independently spending to discover (for example) the same flaw in the production process. A hypothetical, suggested to me by the New York lawyer Evan Chesler, will show what I mean.

Suppose that, while one or more of the employees involved in *Intel v. Broadcom* was at Intel's subsidiary Level One, the firm invested millions of dollars in an unsuccessful attempt to improve a particular production process, only to learn that the process could not be improved in that way. Such "negative information" is, legally, a trade secret of Intel's. Intel paid for this information, and it is not generally known. Two California cases have stated that negative information (such as customers who never ordered a product) might be a trade secret (*Morton v. Rank America; Courtesy Temporary Service v. Camacho*), though neither seems to turn on the point. Now, after the court's holding in *Intel v. Broadcom,* those employees are free to join Broadcom. One implication of this holding is that those employees may be faced with a difficult dilemma if, for example, a consultant hired by Broadcom should happen to recommend a similar investment in its production process. If the employees stay silent and watch Broadcom pour millions down the rat hole that Intel fed, they have violated their obligations to their employer Broadcom. If they explain how they know that production cannot be improved in the way the consultant suggests, they may disclose a trade secret of Intel's. I do not believe that faith in their "trustworthiness" can solve this dilemma. For me, trade secret cannot extend so far. There is no *social* advantage in having every producer of ethernet chips throw money down the same rat hole. The history of Silicon Valley is that, as soon as chip makers converge on the correct diagnosis of their production problems, a market for solutions will arise, whether the solutions involve new technology or consultants (Saxenian 1994: 164).

Under Romer's, Spence's, or Hirshleifer's models, firms continue to invest in the production of technological information *despite* the fact that they cannot exclude rivals from it (so we need not necessarily be concerned that their property rights in that information are far from perfect). It is time to consider an even more intriguing possibility: that firms invest in the production of technological information in part *because* it will diffuse to rivals. This involves the literature on "agglomeration effects": information spillovers in geographic districts.

The Importance of Information Spillovers in Industrial Districts

Network Effects and Increasing Returns

Unlike conventional economic goods, information is sometimes more valuable the more widely it is known. These are sometimes called "network effects." Network effects in information-labor markets may be illustrated by the hypothetical example in the previous section. Suppose Intel discovers that defects in chip manufacture stem from production process B, rather than production process A. This might be a trade secret. Intel, by being the first firm to identify production process B, may indeed realize economic gain from this information, if it can correct the process and outperform its rivals.

But it might be the case that the first firm won't be able to realize any advantage from being the first to target production process B. Perhaps it won't be able to do anything with that information. Perhaps a market in "process B improvement" will arise only when numerous manufacturers converge on the diagnosis that process B is causing the high failure rate in chip manufacture, and that only at that point will technology manufacturers and engineering consultants begin producing improvements in process B.

Other models of "increasing returns" show the gains to be made from producing software or hardware for particular equipment once users converge on particular standards or protocols (W.B. Arthur 1994; David 1985). In cases of increasing returns to information, the firm needs no special property rights in order to create incentives to improve its production or make its products standard. Instead this information becomes more valuable when shared. Open-source software or Sun Microsystems' open architecture are common illustrations.

Of course, these cases of increasing returns won't usually produce difficult legal problems. In these cases the law doesn't have to provide special incentives for information sharing. The firm should be able to see that its interests lie in convergence on diagnoses or protocols. It should choose to disclose or share information, for example at trade conventions or in professional journals or through von Hippel's informal know-how sharing.

A legal problem might arise if the firm changed its strategy as its technology matured. The underlying implicit employment contract might incorporate the firm's original strategy of increasing returns. For example, the firm *ex ante* might have encouraged employee mobility, the better to diffuse its own protocols throughout the industry in the hopes of creating an industry standard. Cisco, with its well-publicized refusal to sue departing employees, may be an example. Employees hired on that basis might justly complain if the firm *ex post* sought to limit their mobility by now claiming that the same information was a trade secret. I do not personally believe that labor mobility normally is an important part of a conscious strategy to increase demand for one's products, but this may be an important research area for the future.

Industrial Districts

A more important clue to the correct legal result in cases like *Intel v. Broadcom* and similar cases starts from examining the features of industrial districts, like Silicon Valley, and the role of information in their growth. This will require setting aside (momentarily) the economic literature (like Romer's) on nonrivalrous information, and examining the literature on the inchoate, embodied know-how or knowledge of individuals.

If you think only about nonrivalrous information—information reducible to bit streams—it is not easy to explain industrial districts like Silicon Valley's. *That* kind of information may be put into code instantly and transmitted everywhere. Romer's models try to capture just that feature of that kind of information. People who think only about this bit-stream-type of information used to predict that geography would cease to matter in the new age of (that kind of) information, that any given worker would be as effective in front of his or her computer anywhere in the world.

The chief lesson of Silicon Valley, however, is that geography still matters, a lot (see generally Drennan 2002). Firms vary in their "absorptive ability" with respect to information (Cohen and Levinthal 1989). One way of putting the point is to distinguish "information" of the coded, bit-stream type, from "knowledge" embodied in individuals, not fully reducible to code, often more practical, often vaguer and harder to recognize. This is an old distinction in both philosophy (Polanyi 1962: 87–91 on "ineffable knowledge"; Winch 1958: 58 on people following rules that they can't formulate; Ryle 1949: 25, distinguishing "knowing that" from "knowing how"), and economics (Arrow 1962a; Lucas 1993). I introduce it here in order to bring the embodied kind of knowledge back into the picture, and to introduce the "new economic geography" literature on the economics of districts.

Cowan, David, and Foray (2000) are quite correct to observe that the alleged distinction between "information" and "knowledge" has been vastly overstated in much recent managerial writing. Such a sharp distinction is poison for explaining Silicon Valley's labor market. There is no operation for distinguishing them. The typical hiring of an employee involves a firm's acquiring *both* some coded information, which I do not want to deny, along with embodied know-how. Another problem with the distinction is that it leaves me without a "neutral" word to include both types. I will normally use "information" and "knowledge" to include some mix of the coded type and the noncoded type, unless I'm quoting from someone who distinguishes the two. The construction of economic models that combine economic analysis of rivalrous and nonrivalrous information will surely be one of the important projects of the next decades.

"Knowledge" of the tacit, embodied type is not equally valuable anywhere in the world. Even recognizing it as "knowledge" may presuppose interaction with others. Certainly its transfer (being nonreducible to code) normally requires personal contact and hence geographical proximity (Audretsch 1998; Drennan 2002; Baptista 1998; Swann et al. 1998; Langlois and Robertson 1996; Collins 1974). Alfred Marshall (1961 [1920]: I: 271 [iv.x: 527]) was the first to both write about such districts and identify their workings with the diffusion (and perhaps production) of embodied, tacit knowledge. In such agglomeration districts, he wrote, in a phrase that has appeared in dozens of articles on Silicon Valley (e.g., Brown and Duguid 2000): the "mysteries of the trade become no mysteries; but are as it were in the air, and children learn many of them unconsciously." As discussed in chapter 1, Silicon Valley well illustrates Marshall's model of "external" or "agglomeration" economies. None of its leading firms succeeded because of the kind of vertical integration or internal economies associated with the work of Alfred Chandler (1990). As Richard N. Langlois (1992) has shown, technology and markets moved too quickly for large enterprises to benefit, and the decentralized structure of vendors and purchasers maximized trial-and-error learning (see also Saxenian 1994). Knowledge spillover through employee mobility solves the problem of how small firms, which spend little on research and development, acquire the knowledge that enables them to produce disproportionate numbers of new products and innovations (Audretsch 1998).

"Knowledge spillover" is a broader concept than Marshall's "agglomeration effects." "Knowledge spillover" includes any gain or externality realized by somebody other than the originator of knowledge or information. It is not a technical term (Griliches 1992: S43). Both the nonrivalrous kind of codable information discussed in the previous section, and embodied, rivalrous know-how, can spill over in this sense.

The mechanisms of knowledge acquisition are broader than labor mobility. Formal technology licensing is another (e.g., Zucker et al. 1998; Arora, Fosfuri, and Gambardella 2001). Acquiring a company is another. Some people might not want to call these knowledge "spillovers," preferring to reserve that term for externalities created as a by-product of such transactions in information. I prefer to keep the term "spillovers" broad and nontechnical, because my focus is precisely on the firm's decision to acquire information. At least in theory, the firm might do this by licensing technology, acquiring or investing in another firm, hiring employees, conducting internal R&D, or funding R&D at an external location, such as a university.

In fact, we know very little about how firms make such knowledge-acquisition decisions. Some research has emphasized the choice among them. For example, in the U.S. electronics and electrical equipment industries, there is a strong negative correlation between expenditure on internal R&D and propensity to acquire other firms (Blonigen and Taylor 2000). This may suggest a developmental process under which the firm matures, grows larger, and does less R&D. However, low direct spending on R&D may also be found among technology leaders. As Don Listwin of Cisco Systems has said, "We don't do R&D, we do A&D: acquire and develop" (Lee 2000: 114).

More recent models, however, have emphasized complementarity among the strategies *other than* hiring, finding correlation among internal R&D, research partnerships, and acquiring other firms (Arora and Gambardella 1990; Cassiman and Veugelers 2002). This sounds more like some other Silicon Valley firms. None of this research, and no other research to date, has focused on hiring employees as a distinct mode of acquiring information, or how it relates to internal R&D, acquiring firms, or licensing technology. My remarks are therefore somewhat speculative.

One thing that obviously differentiates knowledge spillover through hiring employees or acquiring a company, from knowledge acquisition through licensing technology or R&D, is that knowledge in employees is lodged in bodies in physical, geographic space. By contrast, when knowledge is reducible to code, or "spills over" through a formal market in technology, geographical proximity probably doesn't matter very much. For example, Irwin and Klenow (1994) found semiconductor manufacturing firms learning rapidly, when their rivals introduced new chips, how to improve their own. It did not seem to matter whether the chip manufacturers were in joint ventures, across the road, or on different continents. In other words, while this book focuses on the economic and legal consequences of employee mobility, and finds it positive for economic growth and knowledge diffusion, there is much to be learned about precisely what kind of knowledge is actually transmitted by mobile employees, or alternative means of spreading that knowledge. (Irwin and Klenow raise the question of whether in Japan, government-sponsored cooperative research and other formal and informal ties among firms play the role in knowledge spillover that employee mobility plays in Silicon Valley.)

In other studies, the transfer of knowledge depends directly on geography and physical contact. One example is Collins's (1974) famous tale of the TEA laser, where all its technical aspects were published, yet no one succeeded in making one without employing someone who had developed one someplace else. Almeida and Kogut (1999) studied patent citations in semiconductor technology, and found location to be very much more important than Irwin and Klenow did. In regions dominated by one semiconductor manufacturer, such as IBM in New York State or Texas Instruments in Texas, that firm's patents cite mainly its other patents (Almeida and Kogut 1999: 915). Silicon Valley is at the other extreme, the only region in which firms significantly cite the patents of other firms—mostly, other Silicon Valley firms (pp. 911–12). They attribute this building on other firms' knowledge precisely to Silicon Valley's uniquely high employee mobility. "Even after controlling for agglomeration and unobserved localization captured through the control variable, mobility still has a significant and positive effect on the probability that a patent will build upon a major patent from the same region" (p. 915).

Hiring employees (or acquiring companies) is thus likely to be crucial for acquiring practical knowledge as opposed to coded information, keeping in mind my caution, expressed earlier in this chapter, that this distinction is hard to operationalize and is frequently overstated. As an effective mode of acquiring information, it requires that knowledgeable employees actually be available to firms, available in geographic space, and unconstrained by legal restriction on employment. Research focused on this narrow topic, of that subset of knowledge spillover, carried by mobile employees, in geographic districts, is just beginning. (See, e.g., Audretsch 1996; Audretsch and Feldman 1996; Audretsch and Stephan 1996.) So far, however, the knowledge spread by mobile employees seems to have, in fact, the importance given it in Silicon Valley folklore.

For example, consider the story a Cisco insider told Lee (2000: 116). "Cisco's acquisition of Precept Software was not the complete failure outsiders assume it to be, because it brought the company an outstanding CTO [Chief Technology Officer]." Acquiring a company must be one of the more expensive and difficult ways of hiring talent, but at bottom that may be just what is going on. Again, because we do not have models of knowledge acquisition through hiring, we may assume that a corporate buyout is the unusual case, and hiring a team is uninteresting. Perhaps it is just the reverse: buying a company should just be regarded as a more-or-less efficient way of hiring many people—meaning, under our new models of hiring in high-velocity labor markets, acquiring information. Consider Cisco's 1999 purchase of a switch maker for fiber optic networks, Cerent. Cisco paid $6.9 billion—$26 million per employee—for a company that had posted less than $10 million in sales in the first six months of that year (Laberis 1999). This may represent a recent high point for price-per-employee of an acquisition; acquisitions in 2001 came in at closer to $1.3 million per employee (Lashinsky 2001). Yet Cisco acquired some extremely successful technology, now widely sold to AT&T and others, and has apparently done very well by acquiring

Cerent. One can only speculate whether hiring a smaller team of Cerent employees would have been feasible or as successful.

Another example of the importance of employee mobility to knowledge acquisition is the Franco and Filson study, discussed in the previous chapter, showing that essentially all successful manufacture of hard drives takes place in firms founded by employees departing other manufacturers of hard drives. If trade secrets suits could have prevented such start-ups, we would all be paying more for hard drives. If hard drives were made by only a few large manufacturers, improvements would be slower to arise. Franco and Filson point out that in this model (like Romer's), the arrival of new technology is endogenous and depends on actions by agents in the economy; but (unlike Romer's) there is no tendency toward underproduction of information and no need for government policy to increase innovation. Another implication, that they were not able to test empirically, is that firms with the best technology should be able to pay lower wages, if employees will be able to imitate that technology at their next job. (Møen [2000] finds that technical staff, in Norwegian R&D-intensive firms, pay for their knowledge by receiving reduced earnings during the first twenty years of experience, and reap the benefit later.) Of course, employees will accept low wages, anticipating future mobility, only if they are actually able to depart without a lawsuit, which I have shown is normally true but not always true.

To sum up, the experience of Silicon Valley confirms the economic theory that high employee mobility creates no tendency to underproduce technical information. On the contrary, such information will continue to be produced despite the fact, and perhaps sometimes because of the fact, that employees will be back in the job market soon and may share that information with rivals. Information is produced because the firm can make more money from the production even of nonrivalrous information than from other investments; because mobile information lowers the firm's costs; and because such a labor market provides maximum incentives for employees to produce information. If this is correct, our legal default rules—that is, the Uniform Trade Secrets Act or its common law analog in ten or so Eastern states—should normally permit such mobility absent some very specific showing of harm by employers.

Legal and Policy Implications of the Literature on Endogenous Growth and Information Spillover

The economic literature discussed is suggestive, but a long way from proving that public policy should really abolish the concept of trade secrets as applied to employee mobility. In particular, it doesn't tell us what employers and society lose when employees depart with the information in their heads. There is still much to be learned about what kinds of information will be produced, even if it cannot be kept secret, and what kinds will not.

I think the combined literature on endogenous growth and geographic districts may settle two legal points, and thereafter suggests a new kind of inquiry for trade secrets cases. First, it deals a death blow to the casual assumption that information can have value only when it is somebody's property. I have not seen this said in so many words in a trade secrets case. It is fair to say though that *Intel v. Broadcom,* as prodefendant as it is, still illustrates the usual approach to trade secrets litigation, like covenant-not-to-compete litigation outside California. Both are seen as calling for a balance between the employer's interest in its secrets and contracts, and the employee's interest in making a living. Courts sometimes claim to weigh in a public interest, but rarely identify any public interest other than a fairly abstract interest in competition. We have seen now that there is a public interest in employee mobility: the interest in economic competition, a culture of start-ups, technological growth, product competition, lower prices. The interest may be more or less strong in particular cases and possibly outweighed by a particular employer's interest in secrets, but it should not · be ignored any more.

Second, a trade secrets case might interpret the Uniform Act (or common law) in light of the implicit employment contract. The economic literature reinforces the argument that the real employment contract, certainly in Silicon Valley, often assumes employee mobility, including freedom to form a start-up or go to a rival. This may be true if, for example, the employee was hired for a very short term, or in general was not offered a stable career in an internal labor market. It may also be true if the firm is located in an industry in which spin-outs are common, or in which mobility to such a spin-out was built into the recruiting or reward structure, or in which employees accepted lower income precisely to expose themselves to the best technology, which they would then use in their next career step. Again, any of these might or might not be true in a particular case. The economic literature gives us a way of asking whether they are implicitly part of the contract or not. Courts should be alert to the possibility that a trade secrets suit against a departing employee is an *ex post* repudiation by an employer of an employment contract, *ex ante* efficient, in which free employee mobility was a term of employment.

None of this suggests that trade secrets litigation against departing employees has been abolished, just that it must be understood in a social and economic context. I would suggest the following inquiry in trade secrets suits that rest generally on the Uniform Act or common law. The plaintiff-employer should bear the burden of identifying a particular trade secret that the employee would be likely to disclose on his new job. The doctrine of "inevitable disclosure" is indeed tantamount to giving every employer an enforceable covenant not to compete, contrary to California law. As part of the definition of "trade secret," the plaintiff employer should have to demonstrate that the information in question would not have been created unless it could have been kept secret. A court might ask directly, "Would this information have been created if it had to be published in a trade journal?" This redirects the inquiry toward the question of incentives for information creation, and away from moralism. Finally, the court should consider any public interest in either trade secrecy or employee mobility.

Under this approach, the litigation involving Intel and ULSI, Chan, and Hwang, discussed in the previous chapter, was correctly decided and should have been decided much earlier. The details of the Intel product had already been published, and the public benefits strongly from products that compete with, or are compatible with, Intel's basic processors. The hypothetical about negative information—the engineer whose current employer proposes to waste money in a way that his former employer already did—is also easy. The first employer developed the information, that Process A could not be improved, for its own purposes. It would have had to develop this information even if there were no such legal concept as trade secrets. That negative information having been produced, there is no social advantage in keeping it secret, and considerable social advantage in its diffusion.

Intel v. Broadcom cannot be evaluated under this standard, since Intel put all its eggs into the basket of inevitable disclosure, while the defendants won by demonstrating their trustworthiness. Under my proposed standard, a court should not be able to skip inquiry into the nature of the alleged secrets held by an employee and the precise harm their disclosure would cause the employer.

A plaintiff's victory under existing law that would still be a victory under my standard might be *Salsbury Laboratories v. Merieux Laboratories*. In that case, two employees left the company that dominated the market for a particular poultry vaccine, and enabled a rival to enter the market by replicating the former employer's production process. The court found that the production process was a trade secret because it was not generally known, though individual parts of it were, and awarded the first employer an injunction and damages. Under my approach, the analysis is a little more complicated though the result may stay the same. There is a public interest in competition among manufacturers, lower-priced knockoffs, employee mobility, and diffusion of knowledge. Perhaps the decision should have given this more recognition. However, the first employer might be able to show that it would never have created this vaccine in the first place if the information had to be shared. In such a case, society is better off for the existence of the vaccine. My proposed approach does not guarantee better results, but at least it refocuses attention on the basic problem of the public interest in knowledge creation. If lawyers had to litigate under this standard, courts would develop a repertoire of examples of information diffusion that in turn would enrich further economic analysis.

Of course I am sympathetic to Silicon Valley's labor market and its high labor mobility. I wouldn't have written this book if I weren't. Silicon Valley's new ways of working have contributed directly to one of the greatest explosions of technological and economic growth in history. Still, we have no way of knowing what costs were paid for this. The economic literature sometimes suggests that firms with inadequate intellectual property protection may divide up information so no individual employee is well enough informed to harm it by departing (Friedman, Landes, and Posner 1991: 67; Liebeskind 1997; Demski et al. 1999; Rønde 2001), or so that each employee is redundant (Feinstein and Stein 1988). These actions do not seem feasible in the typical Silicon Valley high-technology firm, with heavy use of teams and flat hierarchies (cf. Milgrom and Roberts 1990), and despite some searching I have been unable to find any anecdotes illustrating them.

The more realistic cost that firms (and society) may pay for weak intellectual property protection is the failure to invest at all in certain types of project. The point was made vividly for me by the vice president of one of the Valley's best-known companies, the individual who debriefed departing employees and explained the company's practices to me, but then said that departing employees weren't the real problem around there and offered an opinion about what was.

> We don't have a single person in this building who gives a damn about anything we make. In the old days, GM had Chevy engineers who lived and breathed, thinking about how to make better Chevies. You don't have to tell me what was wrong with that system. I know why it fell apart. But around here, we've gone to the other extreme. We don't have anybody who gives a damn about what we make.

One need not grieve for this company (which has had its ups and downs). If it really wanted the benefits of a stable workforce committed to the company for long careers, it could presumably offer implicit or explicit employment contracts, with steadily increasing wages, and benefits like pensions and health insurance backloaded for the benefit of older employees. (It might want to relocate its facility away from the Valley.) No doubt the advantages it gains from location in the Valley outweigh the potential gains from reverting to implicit contracts for lifetime employment.

Still, there is a trade-off here. One cannot have everything, not even in California. Neither this company, nor society as a whole, knows what kinds of projects were not undertaken—were not even imaginable—because the company knew its personnel turnover would be high, and loyalty therefore low. It is possible that this fear is exaggerated. I have asked many people to identify a project that was not undertaken because of fears that mobile employees would carry its secrets to rivals, and nobody has been able to come up with a specific example. However, this is not a definitive proof that the problem doesn't exist.

Perhaps in a few years, people will think these foregone projects a serious loss to society, and will want to refigure employment law so as to encourage lifetime commitments and discourage job-hopping. I don't think this is likely. At the same time, I don't think the particular firm, with a case to be made for trade secrets and against employee mobility, should be prohibited from making that case. The case should be made, however, in economic terms that address directly the public interest in incentives for the creation and diffusion of technical information.

Short job tenures, however positive for information flows among firms, may be negative for information flows *within* firms. At least that is what Laura Castaneda (2001) found. She studied temporary employees working at the Santa Clara facility of Applied Materials, a manufacturer of processes and technology used by nearly all chip manufacturers. Temps were hired for terms. If it became clear at the end of the term that the temp would not be converted to permanent employment, the temp was likely to withhold information from coworkers, and spend a lot of time looking for his or her next job. Of course, this doesn't represent a legal problem. In fact, it reinforces the point we have been making that firms have resources to prevent information loss, namely to offer more stable employment contracts—and not just to star engineers, but, perhaps, to temps. Still, this research suggests that it would be a mistake, given our current state of knowledge, to identify short job tenures with endogenous growth. It might be less of a mistake to enforce actual employment contracts. If employers offer only short-term employment contracts, they may expect legal protection only of short-term information.

Default Rule or Restriction on Negotiated Contract?

Law and economics distinguish between default rules, the rules that apply in the absence of a contrary contract, and strong prohibitions on negotiated contracts. As we have seen, California's law of employee mobility and intellectual property combines both. It flatly prohibits covenants not to compete, and gives no independent weight to negotiated trade secrets agreements that reserve to the employer more than its rights under statute. These flat prohibitions on freedom of contract are normally thought in the law and economics literature to require extraordinary justification. They show, by the way, how misleading the concept of "flexibility" can be when applied to understand U.S. high-velocity labor markets like Silicon Valley's. Silicon Valley's is in some ways a very flexible labor market, particularly by European standards, when it comes to short job tenures, use of temporary employees, and flexible compensation (such as stock options). However, its restrictions on freedom of contract aren't flexible at all.

At the same time, California law includes default rules on trade secrets. As every other U.S. jurisdiction, it makes employee knowledge about the job the trade secrets of the employer, if not generally known. This is a default rule, in the sense that employers and employees are legally free to negotiate transfers of information, which would otherwise be the property of the employer, to the employee. This possibility seems strictly theoretical. I have asked numerous human resources professionals and employment lawyers representing employers if they can think of any negotiations between an individual employee and employer in Silicon Valley over ownership of intellectual property. I have not been able to find a single example. Star employees negotiate over stock options. They don't negotiate over ownership of intellectual property—perhaps because they think, with good reason given the Valley's history, that they will eventually be free to move on and take information with them.

Economists normally find default rules to be more justifiable than flat prohibitions on freedom of contract. A default rule is often assumed to be a small matter, where parties are free to negotiate its reallocation, and transaction costs are not so high as to prevent this. A restriction on freedom of contract is a more serious matter, requiring different justification. Proving that many firms, or most firms, benefit from a high-velocity labor market in which employees and information flow among firms, does not prove that every firm in such a market receives the same benefit.

An economist might say, even if this chapter showed that a good default rule would be one that permitted employees to depart for rivals without fear of litigation, that was a long way from showing that contrary agreements should be prohibited. What would be wrong with this approach? In other words, does this fragmentary economic analysis go further, to justify a prohibition on negotiated trade secrets agreements—like California's statutory ban on covenants not to compete? If an approach like my suggested approach became common, we can predict an increase in such express trade secrets contracts. Should California courts rethink their historic unwillingness to give any weight to negotiated trade secrets agreements that favor employers?

I think not, unless somebody can identify some actual harm that Silicon Valley employers suffer from California's restriction on their freedom of contract. To understand why a default rule would not work as well, it is necessary to explain some asymmetries in the operation of default rules in labor markets, where legal default rules are often "sticky," in an asymmetrical way. If law allocates a right to employees, it is easy for employers to buy it back, essentially without transaction costs. For example, law gives employees the right to go to court to complain about discrimination, but it is essentially cost-free for employers to require employees to agree to arbitrate these claims instead. By contrast, if law allocates a right to employers, it is essentially impossible for individual employees to purchase it back.

In fact, most employees in the Valley probably already sign promises to protect an employer's trade secrets in form contracts of employment. When I first started interviewing employees and employers, I asked about individual negotiations about such clauses, thinking that certain star employees, such as academics, might negotiate specifically for control of intellectual property (say in biotech). I couldn't discover any such stories. I also wondered if particular firms cultivated a reputation for letting employees hold intellectual property. The last empirical survey of such employment contracts was over thirty years old and found all employers using substantially the same contracts, assigning all employee inventions to the company and (outside California) forbidding employment by, or advice to, competitors. However, it also reported that Polaroid granted all requests to modify this formal contract (Neumeyer 1971). I did not discover any Silicon Valley employers with Polaroid-like reputations. They all seem to use roughly the same contracts.

After an earlier version of this chapter was posted on my Web page, a completely nonrandom sample of engineers began sending me copies of the technology assignment contracts they had been required to sign at hiring. The differences appeared to me to be minor. In any case, no California case in which employers and employees disputed the ownership of intellectual property has turned on a close parsing of the language of these agreements. Gerry Keeler is the partner at Arthur Andersen's Palo Alto office who deals with intellectual asset management. He has never heard of negotiations with employees over ownership of intellectual property. Employees who expect to develop valuable products may negotiate incentives, or of course generous pay. They don't negotiate to hold intellectual property rights but sign the same invention and nondisclosure agreements as everybody else.

The practice in California, as mentioned in the previous chapter, has been to give little or no weight to negotiated trade secrets clauses in contracts of employment. Judge Mathew Tobriner, a respected judge, stated in dicta many years ago that the set of trade secrets agreements, exempt from California's statutory ban on covenants not to compete, was limited to agreements that govern secrets that are already trade secrets under law. Employers and employees are not authorized to enter a contract, making confidential something that would not otherwise be a trade secret. Such a contract would be a covenant not to compete, and could not be enforced (*State Farm Mutual Insurance Co. v. Dempster*). I haven't found any subsequent California cases that speak to this issue. Frankly, given the breadth of the statutory definition of "trade secret," it would be hard for this situation to arise. In any case, California cases do not give any independent weight to a negotiated trade secrets contract.

If the statutory definition of trade secret were narrowed as I have suggested, to information that would not have been produced if its passage to rivals was unforeseeable, these issues would reemerge. Employers would attempt to have courts give independent weight to negotiated trade secrets clauses.

With some hesitation, I think that these are just covenants not to compete, by a different name, and should also be unenforceable under section 16600. Employers who have a special need for secrecy, exempting them from the benefits of the open labor market, should have to demonstrate that need to get an injunction under the statute, and should not be able to substitute a form employment contract in order to avoid making that demonstration. I might feel differently if there really were an effective market on this issue at the *ex ante* (hiring) stage, so that new hires chose among employers on the basis of their different intellectual property schemes or frequently negotiated over the terms of trade secret agreements. However, as nearly as I can determine, neither of these is true. (As we will see in the next chapter, the important negotiations between employers and employees over intellectual property occur *ex post,* at the time of separation.)

I am convinced by economic theory and Silicon Valley reality that social advantage is normally maximized by free labor mobility, that free labor mobility does not diminish the incentives to invest in technical information, at least not in the aggregate, and may increase such incentives. I also think that employers seeking exemption from this general rule should have to put their case in economic terms, by showing the specific disincentive to the creation of information that free mobility would bring. The point of this proposed legal requirement is to lead to more economically sound legal decisions, by opening a dialog between law and economics. This goal would be defeated if a form employment contract could eliminate the dialog.

Put another way, this book aims to sketch out the implicit contract in high-technology employment. In this contract, employees willingly accept a great deal of insecurity in tenure and compensation, and not only because they are paid well now. They are also implicitly promised that, though they will be out on the job market again very soon, they will be more valuable at that time, because of the problems to which they were exposed while at the previous employer. Neither I nor anyone else has a comprehensive database of employer and employee descriptions of this implicit contract, and there is no value in a lawyer attempting to synthesize it by staring into the sky. However, my unsystematic interviews often turned up surprisingly precise accounts of its terms.

When I interviewed Will Poole in 1996, he had just joined eShop, one of the new companies developing use of the Internet for marketing. He had already worked for Sun Microsystems in Massachusetts and Silicon Valley and Pen Computer Solutions, and thought there was "something wrong" with a resume that showed five years at the same place. I told Will about the economists' concept of an "implicit contract" (chapter 4), and asked him whether he thought there was a similar implicit contract for Silicon Valley professionals like himself who changed jobs frequently. He understood that being hired by Sun or Pen or eShop involved absolutely no implicit or explicit promise not to be let go. Nevertheless, he thought there was an implicit contract, very different from the economists'. "I normally get a year to show what I can do; I get a month's notice before I'm let go; and I will be more marketable when I leave this job than I was when I got here." If Will is correct about the last term he mentioned, his implicit contract must therefore contain an implicit promise by the employer not to interfere with Will's mobility. His employers implicitly promise not to sue him for theft of trade secrets, unless perhaps the trade secret belongs to a much smaller set than the total, expansive set of trade secrets recognized by law. This is the only way in which an employee could enforce a promise that he or she will be worth more on leaving Sun or Pen than he or she was when hired.

Implicit contracts like Will's are normal in Silicon Valley, and most employers both enter into them and abide by them. Of course, the law forbids them from enforcing covenants not to compete. However, few Valley employers sue to enforce trade secret rights, and this reflects some combination of their sense of self-interest (Cisco) and the prevailing culture. Since the relative absence of trade secrets suits is cultural not legal, it creates possible free-riders. These companies benefit from Silicon Valley's high-velocity labor market, for example when they hire. When they seek to restrict mobility in ways that may seem to benefit them in the short run, they risk harming the entire system of free mobility. They threaten to make employees unwilling to accept the contracts that are their basis. To eliminate free riders, courts are justified in enforcing the implicit *ex ante* contract under which employees are normally free to join, or start, rivals. This requires making the statutory ban on covenants not to compete truly effective, by extending its logic to trade secrets.

Conclusion: When Labor Markets Act Like Information Markets

Before looking at alternative economic approaches to trade secrets and employee mobility (next chapter), let me point out some implications of this chapter that will guide the rest of this book.

The debate about short-term or "contingent" labor is both familiar and narrow. It is usually linked with the idea of "flexibility." Its usual justifications are to permit employers to operate in the face of genuine uncertainty about their markets and costs, and to permit way-stations out of recession or job loss. The usual criticism is that such short-term labor moves the risks of uncertainty from employers who bear them with difficulty to individuals who bear them even less well. I do not want to criticize any part of this story. We will see examples in this book of Silicon Valley's high-velocity labor market doing all these things: permitting flexible responses to uncertainty; rapid adjustment to recession or downsizing; high levels of uncertainty for employees.

This book means to supplement the flexibility story with another, a story about the economics of information. What do employers hire when they hire for short terms without implicit promises? At least some of the time, they must be hiring information. They do not have anyone in-house who knows how to develop this project or produce this kind of program and they need to hire someone with the information, and knowledge, to do it. We do not need to decide which story explains the popularity of high-velocity labor; both are consistent with it.

The possibility opened up is to treat the labor market as in part a market for information. Markets for information face particular technical problems in economics, stemming from the fact that information is expensive to produce, easy to copy, and hard to use up. Markets for information may have nonconvexities (they do not experience decreasing returns to scale). Information, unlike other property, may be used by others, even though the original "owner" "possesses" it. Even more interestingly, information may be even more valuable when shared by competitors (sometimes called "network effects," see generally Shapiro and Varian 1999). Markets for information may have multiple equilibria, and interesting market failures.

What would it mean to describe a labor market as in part a market for information? This is only a metaphor. In a labor market, unlike a market for information, the marginal cost of reproducing another unit never equals zero. However, I think that imagining a labor market as a market for information could turn out to be as useful a metaphor as "human capital" once was.

We would expect to see a lot of short-term hiring. Firms have incentives to acquire through hiring the information that rivals have produced. They have less incentive to invest in long-term employment contracts: the information that can be obtained from any individual human being is limited; the information that can be obtained in a market is limitless. There need be no convexities in the hiring of labor, when that labor is hired in repeated short-term hires, of different individuals, who bring different information to firms.

We would also be alert for the benefits that firms get when their information is shared with rivals. Lawyers who represent plaintiffs in trade secrets cases always analogize trade secrets to tangible assets, asserting that defendants have "stolen their property." We can now say exactly what is incomplete about this analogy. I do not propose to address whether a trade secret is property purely as a way of promoting a larger social good, or whether the employer may have any kind of natural right to any or all of its intellectual property (cf. Gordon 1993). Rather, I want to focus on the fact that all the firm's technical property has life only in the minds and bodies of its employees and is realized in labor markets. This may be true even for some technical data and formulas that may not be realizable without know-how (Collins 1974). Unless firms can own their employees, they simply can never own intellectual property just as they own factories or tools. At least, they enter labor markets as hirers as well as firers, benefit from labor mobility, and thus must accept some restrictions on their abilities to own intellectual property. Even more tantalizingly, they may reap specific *benefits* from the departure of their own employees. Such departure was contemplated when the short-term employment contract was entered into, a contract that enabled the firm to hire the labor it wanted. The firm benefits from its location in a high-velocity labor market. It may benefit from seeing its own products and protocols become standard in the industry.

These remarks will remain speculative until more economists model labor markets as the information markets that they partly are. Much less controversial, however, is the observation that high-velocity labor markets involve massive asymmetries—better, deficiencies—in information about the individuals being hired or the positions to which they are hired. When firms hire unknown employees in markets, rather than promote known employees from within, they must be achieving benefits (or they would not do it). But they certainly encounter problems. They may know little about the people they are hiring and little about their own future needs. These help shape the kinds of labor contracts, labor market intermediaries, and compensation schemes characteristic of high-velocity labor markets. We will take those up in later chapters.

4

INFORMATION OWNERSHIP AND TRANSMISSION
BY MOBILE EMPLOYEES: ALTERNATIVE
ECONOMIC APPROACHES

Silicon Valley's new ways of working require new economic analyses. This book will be devoted primarily to approaches from the economics of information, modeling a high-velocity labor market as a kind of market for information. In the previous chapter, I showed how this analysis supports weak property rights in information, narrow definitions of trade secrets, and non-enforcement of covenants not to compete. Later in this book, the concepts of asymmetric information, search costs, signaling, and so forth will be applied to legal issues arising from the use of independent contractors (chapter 6), temporary employees (chapters 5 and 8), immigration law (chapter 7), and compensation (chapter 10).

Before leaving the issue of trade secrets and other intellectual property disputes between employers and employees, we should examine some alternative economic approaches that have been applied or might be applied. As mentioned, there are no trade secrets cases or (outside California) covenant-not-to-compete cases that employ any economic analysis, so almost anything would be an improvement. I will review some alternative approaches. None has yet been applied to trade secrets, though they have been applied to other problems in intellectual property. They are: (a) the "property rights" or "transaction costs" or "economics of contracting" school that models likely contracts under various allocations of property rights; (b) "human capital" approaches that treat information as the result of investment in training and education; (c) industrial organization approaches that make the allocation of intellectual property turn on the kind of market competition faced by the employers; and (d) older, psychological theories of monopoly put forward by Fritz Machlup a half-century ago.

Contracting, Property Rights, and Transaction Costs

While the work of Paul Romer and other New Growth Theorists is rarely if ever cited in law reviews, legal audiences are quite familiar with the branch of economics that models the likelihood of contract under various assumptions concerning information and other transaction costs. This is an important change from the law and economics approach of the 1980s, which often assumed low transaction costs, thus markets that would reach all Pareto-optimal trades until equilibrium was achieved.

A particular transaction cost that has received searching analysis is the allocation of property rights. In the work of Oliver Hart, property rights have been applied to problems of industrial organization and the nature and boundaries of firms (Grossman and Hart 1986; Hart and Moore 1990; Hart 1995). This work is a more elaborate model of Ronald Coase's basic insight that firms and other hierarchies arise when individual contracts are too costly (Coase 1937). The Grossman-Hart-Moore approach might be described as a considerably more elaborate version of the difficulties of contracting. A particular insight of this school is that all contracts are incomplete, so the background law of control over assets, that is, property rights, will continue to be salient even when contacts are actually negotiated.

Several recent articles apply this approach to contracts between inventive employees and employing firms, asking what kinds of bargaining equilibria could result from various allocations of intellectual or other property. This work is a useful supplement to the "information market" approach of the last chapter, and I will review some of the competing models in this section.

The "property rights" approach is at best a supplement to chapter 3, because it begs the most important question I have tried to answer: whether there should be any property at all. Analyses in the Grossman-Hart-Moore approach start by assuming some kind of property right, whether tangible or intangible—an asset, a patent, the right to terminate a contract—then ask what kind of equilibrium would result from various allocations of the property right. This approach obviously best translates into legal and policy applications for a class of problems where law, too, unambiguously creates that property right—a patent, for example. In such cases, it surely makes sense to ask what kind of bargain will result depending whether patents are held by employers or employees. However, it is simply not possible within the property rights approach to ask whether there ought to be property at all. Yet that is the precise legal question posed by cases that ask whether chip specifications, or configurations of machines, are a "trade secret" or "general knowledge" in the "public domain." Exactly the same problem bedevils the few analyses in a "human capital" framework that address intellectual property disputes between employers and employees: human capital by definition can belong only to the employer or employee, and cannot be nonrivalrous information (Møen 2000; Rubin and Shedd 1981).

These bargaining models may also fail to address two important aspects of the analysis of the chapter 3: incentives and welfare. As we shall see, they typically assume away the difficult question of comparative incentive effect of intellectual property in the hands of the employee or employer. They also normally assume the First Theorem of Welfare Economics, under which strong property rights and free contract will necessarily maximize public welfare. This precise assumption is challenged, for rights in information, by the economists of information discussed in chapter 3.

A final problem with property rights approaches, typical though not inherent, has been identified by the legal scholar James Boyle (1996). Economists, he writes, often simplify analyses of information by simultaneously treating information as "perfect" ("free, complete, instantaneous, and universally available") and as a commodity ("costly, partial, and deliberately restricted in its availability"). He modestly names this "Boyle's Paradox." I do not think this critique applies to Arrow, Hirshleifer, Romer, Spence, Stiglitz, and others discussed in the previous chapter, who are quite sensitive to these competing aspects to information. However, as we shall see, articles in the economics of contracting school are often guilty of Boyle's Paradox.

Still, one welcomes any sort of economic approach to the difficult legal issues arising from high-velocity labor markets. No doubt some day a convincing metatheory will combine an analysis of the question Property versus Nonexcludable Information with an analysis of the different question, Whose Property?

The published bargaining models so far turn out to be, not surprisingly, highly responsive to their underlying assumptions. One may choose among bargaining models that assume efficient Pareto-optimal contracting between employers and employees; bargains that assume imbalances in bargaining power that result in suboptimum investment in production of ideas; or a model that assumes such high transaction costs that efficiency demands employer ownership of all intellectual property. These different results stem largely from the simplifying assumptions of each model. I summarize them in chronological order of publication.

Pakes and Nitzan: Pareto-optimal Negotiations at Employee Departure

Pakes and Nitzan (1983) model an optimum labor contract to hire scientists for a project "when one takes explicit account of the fact that the scientist may be able to use the information acquired during the project in a rival enterprise" (p. 345). They focus on negotiations as the employee departs, which they assume will reach a Pareto-optimal outcome, in which the employer will or will not make an offer to the employee that will induce him or her to stay. Under this assumption, the optimal hiring policy is thus one that permits the scientist to depart at any time, free to trade on information acquired on the previous job.

This is the oldest article I have been able to find addressing the question of employer-employee disputes over the ownership of ideas. It long predates the Grossman-Hart-Moore approach and takes a cheerful approach to negotiations between the employer and the departing scientist. Today's models, as we shall see, are much likelier to hypothesize numerous inefficiencies in this contracting process. I think, however, that there is much realism in the Pakes-Nitzan analysis. A central assumption of their model is that Employer 1 should always be able to outbid either a second employer or a start-up. Whatever information Steven Lindsay has, Intel should be able to exploit more efficiently than a new employer or new enterprise. Employer 1 (Intel) knows more about Lindsay's information (and about Lindsay). A rival has start-up costs (Bankman and Gilson 1999; Bankman 1994b). If, prior to the scientist's departure, Employer 1 is a monopolist over this information, its bargaining position is even stronger. Competition will divert to consumers some of the gains that would otherwise accrue to Employer 1, the monopolist. Thus, to any employee threatening to defect, Employer 1 should be able to offer a bonus that would offset the amounts that would be made by moving to a rival or start-up. One form of such a bonus discussed, with considerable prescience, by Pakes and Nitzan, is to offer the favored employee stock options. They note that these were common in Silicon Valley when they wrote; they are considerably more common now. Pakes and Nitzan conclude that there "will always exist a particularly simple labor contract consisting of a flat rate and a profit-sharing scheme which satisfies" (p. 353) the following conditions: maximize expected profit; ensure no rivals appear; and compensate the employee at no less than his or her alternative wage.

Thus, when employees leave, it must be because their employers didn't bid to keep them. This might be because it is easy for new firms to enter the market (low start-up costs, venture capital), so any monopoly held by Employer 1 was ending anyway. Or the information may not have been secret. For example, reverse engineering may be feasible. Under conditions like these, Employer 1 will not offer a bonus and the scientist will depart. The optimum labor contract is thus one that permits such departures. "Provided the firm is free to choose among alternative labor contracts, it can provide an incentive structure which controls the mobility of the scientist—only inducing him to leave and set up a rival when it is in the firm's interest for him to do so" (p. 361). This can be true simply because it was not worth it to Employer 1 to pay the bonus that would have kept the scientists. But it can also be true, as Pakes and Nitzan note, because "the establishment of a rival [may] increase the sum of the returns accruing to the two agents involved" (p. 359).

In Romer's, Spence's, and other models of increasing returns to endogenous technological change, this is precisely what characterizes Silicon Valley.

We will turn in a moment to more recent analyses with gloomier assumptions about the efficiency of negotiations between employers and departing employees. I must say my sense, based on my interviews, is that the Pakes and Nitzan picture is quite realistic. The key negotiations do occur at the time of proposed departure, not the time of hiring. It is not that big a deal to decide whether or not to try to hold the employee. Firms have a great deal of discretion in fashioning employment offers. They are not simple price takers (Card and Krueger 1995).

What would cause the contracting process, at the time the employee proposes to depart, to fail? The popularity of Oliver Williamson's (e.g., 1985) work has perhaps oversensitized us to problems of firm-specific human capital, fixed investments, hold-ups, and endgame bargaining. The genius of Silicon Valley's high-velocity labor market is that none of these is likely to be present. Rival firms and venture capitalists are available to provide accurate information about the employee's alternative earnings. There is little information asymmetry. If Employer 1 chooses not to outbid this value, it has probably concluded that what this employee knows is easily replaceable, or that the firm itself would benefit from increasing returns (such as Intel employees moving to other manufacturers and designing chips that would increase demand for compatible Intel products). Employer 1's actions in letting the employee go often speak louder than the words of its trade secrets suit. In short, *courts in trade secrets cases should be alert to firms attempting to use the courts to impede employee mobility that the firm itself could easily have purchased from the employee, but chose not to.*

I must point out three possible critiques of Pakes and Nitzan. First, they expressly do not model issues of incentives. By contrast, they assume "that the effort the scientist devotes to the project is independent of the terms of the contract" (p. 347). We will have to look elsewhere (e.g. Motta and Rønde 2002; Baccara and Razin 2002; Lester and Talley 2000) for the really difficult trade-off: do the gains from having employees able to market all they know outweigh the losses from diminished firm incentives (if any) to invest in the production of information? Moreover, it seems likely to me that the incentives issue is related to the issue of whether Employer 1 can really always outbid Employer 2. In particular, I think that the chief reason employees dream of their own firm is that they anticipate they would gain more working for themselves than for another (Hyde 1991; Bankman and Gilson 1999). Second, Pakes and Nitzan seem to me guilty of Boyle's Paradox: information for them is simultaneously a commodity that Employer 1 monopolizes, and something the market evaluates efficiently (because it is known to all). Third, they assume property rights in information that are so weak that the employee can plausibly depart the firm without being sued (but see *Intel v. Broadcom*) and without being forced to disclose ideas in his head (but see *Brown v. DSC Communications Corp.,* ordering an engineer to disclose algorithms to his former employer. I will discuss this case further later in this chapter).

Anton and Yao: Contract in the Absence of Property Rights

Anton and Yao (1994) model the contract of an inventor whose invention is not protected by any property right: it is too closely related to prior art to receive a patent, or just too conceptual to protect. He cannot develop the idea himself, yet any buyer or employer to whom he reveals the idea might steal it. Is a contract possible? Yes, they say, and even if the inventor has no wealth. The inventor reveals the idea to one investor, who then negotiates with the inventor in order to preserve its new monopoly position. Their 1995 article analyzes the situation when the inventor is already an employee, deciding whether to disclose his idea (also unprotected by property) to his current employer, or depart. The principal difference between the two situations is that noted by Pakes and Nitzan and sources cited there: because of the asymmetry of information between the current employer and other investors, the current employer should be able to outbid them. The current employer, however, will never pay more than the added value of monopoly over duopoly, so there will be a set of cases where the employee will leave to start a firm even though the joint profit potential of a spin-off from his old employer is greater.

These articles are important early efforts to model contracting in the absence of property. The First Theorem of Welfare Economics is such a standard support for strong property rights that many people have trouble seeing how there could ever be efficient contracting in the absence of property—which, I have been trying to show, happens in Silicon Valley every day. So I must applaud any effort to show how efficient contracting, particularly for information (or employment that amounts to information), does not necessarily require property.

That having been said, two unrealistic assumptions of these models limit their applicability to the legal and policy issues I have been addressing. The more basic is the problem of why any employer or investor will price the invention as a monopoly (or duopoly), if it is unprotected by any intellectual property and already known to one inventor in a high-velocity labor market. Any monopoly in the idea lasts only until the next employee leaves. The investor may well buy the idea or employ, or back financially, the inventor, on the theory that it thereby would obtain first-mover advantages with respect to the intellectual property (the sort of advantages discussed by Hirshleifer in chapter 3). But the price of an idea that gives the investor only first-mover advantages is presumably less than a real monopoly. The kinds of information that form the basis of Silicon Valley employment contracts— and trade secrets suits—are more like ideas open to first movers than they are monopolies. This is necessarily true when rapid employee turnover threatens all informational monopolies. In other words, Anton and Yao seem guilty of Boyle's Paradox, where the same idea is unprotected by property, may be copied at will, yet will be priced by investors as a monopoly. The second questionable assumption, also made by Pakes and Nitzan, is that employers lack legal recourse against employees who leave before disclosing ideas they developed on the last job. I think this would be desirable but is by no means always the case.

Aghion and Tirole: Incentives to Create Value and the Problem of Bargaining Power

Aghion and Tirole (1994) model ownership of intellectual property as a question of an initial contract assigning property rights. Unlike Pakes and Nitzan, and Anton and Yao, they do not focus on negotiations at the stage at which the employee departs. They seek to allocate property rights so as to create incentives to produce value.

They assume a research unit RU (who may be an employee) performing research for a customer C (who may be an employer). They also assume that the probability of discovery depends on the effort by the research unit, which cannot be specified ("noncontractible") and the investment by the customer. Crucially, the research unit has no initial cash endowment and therefore cannot pay the customer anything; also its income cannot be negative. These last two assumptions suggest to me that the research unit has been defined to be a human being, whether employee or independent contractor.

Aghion and Tirole show that, under these assumptions, "whether C or RU should own the innovation hinges on two basic considerations: (a) the *marginal efficiency* of RU's effort compared with the marginal efficiency of C's investment; (b) the *ex ante bargaining power* of the two parties" (p. 1190). That is, if bargaining power were equal, the parties would efficiently contract to place the property right in order to provide incentive for the more marginally productive extra investment, be it RU's effort, or C's capital. They analyze a number of common or legally implied contracts as split incentives for further effort and investment, such as trailer clauses and shop rights. However, observable contracts may not enact this efficient result, for two reasons. First, since RU cannot compensate C for extra investment, C will hold some property in ideas even where ownership by *RU* would have resulted in higher total surplus. Second, unequal bargaining power may also result in suboptimum contracts for property rights. A recent empirical study of Aghion and Tirole's thesis suggests that this last observation has serious observable consequences. Lerner and Merges (1998) studied the allocation of intellectual property rights in technology alliances between biotechnology firms, and found that bargaining power seemed to explain these allocations better than the incentive or wealth-creating effects stressed by Aghion and Tirole.

I argued in chapter 3 that courts in trade secrets cases would do well to ask precisely the question that we may now call Aghion and Tirole's: namely, which allocation of property rights would provide the best incentives for further productive investments of effort and capital. This may not be the only question, but it is certainly an important one. It is not conceivable that the parties would want to allocate property rights so as to *diminish* the surplus they will divide.

While Aghion and Tirole's analysis is most valuable to the policymaker, it is incomplete for at least three reasons that have already been mentioned. First, and most important, they assume the point that has been at issue: namely, whether information is to be property at all, or rather nonrivalrous information diffusing among firms. Theirs is a fair enough assumption in a typical patent case, where the issue is likely to be whether the employer or employee owns a patent. The question this book has been addressing is, however, unavoidable in the typical Silicon Valley suit against a departing employee, where the legal question is whether a given employee's knowledge is a "trade secret" (employer property) or "general knowledge" (nobody's property).

Second, the wealth of shared information informs even their set of problems, yet goes without express recognition by them. For even in the class of genuine choices between employer property and employee property, we have seen that employee property is unlikely to remain secret long. Employees must disclose it to live; it will move among firms with the employee and contribute to the kind of endogenous growth that we have discussed. These third-party effects are not reflected in their model. Presumably their model can accommodate this by treating these third-party effects as giving *RU*'s additional comparative advantage in creating value. However, we do not really have good estimates of this comparative advantage, so incorporating it into Aghion and Tirole's model may just destroy its utility. Similarly, they assume convexities in modeling C's return on investment, ignoring the difficult features of investments in information, namely social returns that may be much higher than private returns. Anand and Galetovic (2000) do incorporate these third-party effects into their more realistic model, in which venture capitalists and corporate employers make competing offers to finance innovation. In their model, weak property rights do indeed lead to venture capitalists' outbidding employers. However, they treat the strength of property as inherent in each project and thus exogenously given. One could not take their analysis, fine as it is, to a court trying to decide precisely how to define particular property rights.

Third, if applied to legal problems (like *Intel v. Broadcom*), their analysis is a good starting point in analyzing the implicit employment contract. However, it must be supplemented by additional assumptions. How is a court to determine whether Intel or Steven Lindsay, or Kendall-Jackson winery, or winemaker Jedediah Steele has "comparative advantage in creating value" so as to determine implicit ownership of chip designs or chardonnay reserve techniques?

If applied to legal issues, a time value would have to be added. For example, for a long time in the development of the 386 chip, Intel surely had "comparative advantage in creating value." But, according to the California courts, at some time that advantage ended. After some specifications were published in a trade magazine, did its former employee Chan, or Chan's new employer ULSI, have as much or more advantage as Intel in using the specifications to design compatible math coprocessors? When it became clear that Intel was not living up in good faith to its contract making Advanced Micro Devices (AMD) the second source, the Supreme Court of California held (affirming an arbitrator), AMD became entitled to damages. However, its damages were limited because it should have "reverse engineered" the 386 (*Advanced Micro Devices v. Intel*). At that point, did AMD have "comparative advantage" over Intel? When did this happen? How could we know?

Merges: Sole Ownership Is Less Costly Than Shared Ownership

Merges's Argument

Merges (1999) argues that shared ownership of intellectual property between employers and employees would create such insuperable obstacles to efficient contracting as to call rather for strong judicial default rules lodging intellectual property in employers, and enforcing contracts that do the same. Merges analyzed invention assignment agreements, a subject, like Aghion and Tirole's, in which there will definitely be some property (typically a patent), and the question is, whose. As such, there is no direct conflict between Merges's analysis and mine. Merges of course recognizes that disputes over trade secrets raise the possibility that nobody has property in the relevant secret, and indeed calls for some narrowing of trade secrets protection along the lines of my proposals in chapter 3. I suggested, however, that if courts continue to limit trade secrets protection, employers will make greater use of explicit contracts transferring intellectual property to them. The judicial construction of such contracts would implicate the issues raised in Merges's article.

Merges's chief concern is the employee-owner of a patent on an invention that is complementary to his employer's assets, that is, each asset has value only when combined with the other. The employee-inventor of such a complementary asset, Merges argues, would be able to extract such a high price from the employer as to frustrate agreement, and research and development itself. He is also concerned about incentives to employees who can realize more gain by pursuing "their own" projects rather than the employer's (applying familiar models of multitask principal agent contracts; e.g., Holmström and Milgrom 1991). While such employer ownership of intellectual property may appear to disadvantage employees, Merges argues that this is not so since employees retain an "exit option" to become entrepreneurs of their own ideas without disclosing them to the employer (Anton and Yao 1994).

For independent consultants (as opposed to employees), Merges makes the contrary argument: they should normally own their own inventions, and purported assignments to the customer should normally be construed narrowly in favor of the consultant (pp. 41–43). This gives consultants maximum incentives to perform, and also functions as a "penalty default rule" as defined by Ayres and Gertner (1989). That is, it gives customers an incentive to disclose complementarities to the consultant in order to show him that his ideas will be more valuable if developed together with the customer.

Critique of Merges

Merges's discussion is subtle and valuable; I cannot discuss all its observations here. I do not disagree with any of the applications he discusses, where property has already been recognized by law and the issue is how to allocate that property to facilitate contract and create incentives for its further development. Courts should not lightly assume that parties have contractually allocated rights in information so as to diminish the value of that information. However, it is easy to imagine extensions of Merges's analysis, to the problems of this book, that would be harmful to Silicon Valley. Merges does not discuss any of the literature on endogenous economic growth, information spillover, nonrivalrous and nonexcludable information, or the application of his views to a high-velocity labor market. Particularly (but not exclusively) in that context, one might ask whether low transaction costs ought to be the only value; whether transaction costs are the problem that Merges claims; and whether law is really prepared to enforce the property rights that Merges advocates.

Costs of Firm Ownership of Intellectual Property. I have been developing a catalog of welfare costs to firm ownership of intellectual property that might have been shared. Corporate-owned intellectual property does not grow as rapidly as nonrivalrous information (Romer 1990b, 1993); does not spill over across networks that promote regional growth (Saxenian 1994); does not provide as powerful incentives to the individual (as Merges recognizes in his discussion of consultants; see also Motta and Rønde 2002); and dissipates rents in duplicative and delayed research (Cheung 1982; Romer 1993). Merges properly and correctly cautions courts not to presume that contracts have assigned intellectual property rights so as to minimize their value. By precisely the same token, courts may sometimes have to construe contracts in order to provide for technology sharing, informal know-how trading, or nonrivalrous information in the public domain, and by the same logic. If I am right, the employment contracts between Intel and its employees Young, Lund, and Lindsay, may be such a contract. Courts will assume, either as a default or perhaps nonnegotiable rule, that employers and employees have implicitly agreed to lodge property where it will increase joint wealth the most— that is, as nonrivalrous information that travels when employees do.

Is Contracting for Intellectual Property a Serious Problem? Much of the intellectual property valuable to any firm is held by people outside it, such as rival firms, suppliers, customers, consultants, and (occasionally) employees. This would be true even if courts employ all of Merges's presumptions to assist firm ownership. Thus, firms must contract for use of others' intellectual property. I have spoken to venture capitalists who have told me that intellectual property issues arise in every start-up. I know of no empirical literature that suggests that contracting for rights in intellectual property is a distinct social problem (as opposed to a formal assumption of Grossman-Hart-Moore models). (For arguments that most economic literature overstates the difficulty of contracting for technological information, see Arora, Fosfuri, and Gambardella 2001; Lamoreaux and Sokoloff 1999.)

When employees know things (secrets, know-how, protocols, inventions, conceptions), the key negotiation, as Pakes and Nitzan correctly supposed, is the exit negotiation. Employees are subject to an exit interview in Silicon Valley, whatever documents they signed at the time of employment. In Silicon Valley, as elsewhere, the employee almost surely signed an agreement assigning inventions to the employer, possibly lasting some period after the end of employment, and agreeing to the secrecy of proprietary and confidential information. Such agreements may strengthen the employer's negotiating position but do not obviate the negotiation problem.

The employer still has to evaluate what the employee has been working on, how valuable he is to the company, how damaging would be his working for a competitor. The employer still has to decide whether to match or beat the outside offer, sweeten it with stock options or some other compensation keyed to the new business that the employee wants to pursue. Such negotiations are as tricky and interesting as any other employment negotiations, but that is what personnel relations are all about, and Merges's proposals will not spare employers from them.

In that tiny subset of negotiations that comprise the world of Merges's article—the set in which the employee claims legal ownership of an asset that is complementary to firm assets in the sense that neither has value without the other—the firm should be able to put together the most attractive bid for the employee's invention. At least I don't know of any bargaining model that predicts the contrary. Employees are not stupid. If their invention really has more value when exploited by Intel than when exploited by the employee himself, the employee would be foolish to leave Intel. In any case, an employment market (free of covenants not to compete and accustomed to job mobility) and venture capital market should be able to provide highly accurate assessments of the value of the employee's invention in hands other than his employer's. Colorful talk of hold-ups simply begs the normative question of who is holding up whom; it assumes that the information is the employer's asset, when that is precisely what must be determined.

In other words, the problems that Merges fears are not such big problems. They are faced hundreds of times a day in Silicon Valley's high-velocity labor market, when employees (or consultants) want to leave (or the firm wants to change their status) and negotiations ensue. I know of no empirical evidence that such exit negotiations are a particular social problem and my interviews in Silicon Valley have not turned up any such evidence. In short, contracting at the exit stage is a theoretically efficient and socially common way of reaching optimal allocation of intellectual property, a conclusion not negated by the occasional lawsuit.

Are Ideas in Employees' Heads Property Like Any Other Property? Central to Merges's analysis, like that of Pakes and Nitzan and Anton and Yao, is the "exit option": the idea that an employee with a good idea, not yet in readable form, is normally free to leave the company and start his or her own or join a rival. Central to my analysis is the idea that this is efficient and normally true. However, the employee is not always free to leave. Unlike the supposed high transaction costs of exit negotiations, this is a real social problem.

Evan Brown is an engineer who was ordered by a Texas court to disclose to his former employer algorithms that he had never written down anywhere. Brown claims to have developed these to solve problems, of intellectual interest to him, in converting older software into newer codes. These are continuing problems for anyone working with older software, but not something for which DSC Communications Corp. markets programs. DSC claimed, successfully, that the algorithms were its property under the invention assignment agreement that Brown signed at hiring (*Brown v. DSC Communications*). The extensive press coverage seemed mostly sympathetic to the employee (e.g., Pratt and Dosik 1997; Rosenberg 1997). Following the dismissal of his appeal in 1998, Brown disclosed his algorithms to his former employer (now owned by Alcatel). The Texas courts have already ordered that 20 percent of the ideas' value belongs to the employer and will decide ownership of the remaining 80 percent (Bajaj 2000; Steffy 2000).

Professor Merges does not discuss the case. At least, the case casts doubt on the easy assumption that the employee with a good idea always retains an exit option. But I think the holding flows directly from talk of employer property in employee inventions. To be fair to Merges, DSC surely did not show that Brown's ideas had value only as complementary to its own assets, and Brown denied this. Even if Brown's ideas were more clearly the property of DSC than was true here, the "property" involved can never be the same kind of property as a machine or notebook. Brown's algorithm is classic nonrivalrous information that, once disclosed, can be used by many without losing its value. If Romer is correct that the production and diffusion of such nonrivalrous information is the most important factor in economic growth, accounts of such information as "property" must always be supplemented mentally by accounts of how it would function if nonexcludable.

Like most of the press coverage, I find the spectacle of a court ordering a human being to disclose his ideas to the employer that fired him to be barbaric. That is not the point of this book, however, which has tried as dispassionately as possible to examine the economic analysis of the legal issues that arise in labor markets for mobile employees. The success of Silicon Valley should caution those who cannot see the value of Brown's ideas as anything but employer property.

Implicit Contract and Human Capital Approaches

The economic concept that has been the most fruitful in applications to labor and employment law over the last two decades has been the model of the employment contract as an "implicit contract" in which employees are hired for a very long duration, perhaps for life until retirement. In this contract, employees receive predictable wage increases that are imperfectly related to individual productivity. Indeed, the wage increases will continue after the individual's productivity has begun to decline. Compensation will reflect this "back-loading" of benefits. It will include pensions and health benefits that are more valuable to older than younger employees. Downward wage adjustment is rarely feasible, so if the employee becomes really unproductive, the contract will be terminated rather than compensation adjusted. The implicit contract is normally self-enforcing (as opposed to legally enforceable). The main risk that such contracts place on employees is that of employer opportunistic termination of the contract during the period when compensation exceeds employee productivity.

This model of the employment contract was originally developed by Edward Lazear in order to explain the institution (once common, now typically illegal) of mandatory retirement (Lazear 1979). It first appeared in a legal publication in Wachter and Cohen (1988) to explain labor law's definitions of mandatory subjects of bargaining as devices to protect against employer opportunism. The model was a powerful lens before the eyes of legal scholars in the 1990s, bringing into focus many aspects of the law of labor and employment that now emerged as devices for protecting employees against opportunism in such implicit agreements. Such protection was said to characterize common law doctrines of wrongful termination (Weiler 1990; O'Connor 1991; Schwab 1993); the Age Discrimination in Employment Act (Issacharoff and Harris 1997; Worth 1995); insurance for employees against risk (Charny 1996); employee stock ownership plans (Hyde 1991); worker participation institutions (Howse and Trebilcock 1993); and the proposed doctrines, which never really got off the ground, making employees into stakeholders (Stone 1991).

"Implicit contract" models of labor contracting include other contracts that have nothing to do with "human capital"—for example, all kinds of "efficiency wage" contracts in which employers for whatever reason pay wages above the rate at which the market will clear (Akerlof and Yellen 1986). Employers may, for example, do this in order to reduce the cost of monitoring workers by increasing the cost to them of job loss (Shapiro and Stiglitz 1984), or to save on search costs by attracting "better" workers (Weiss 1980). However, I am unaware of any explanations why an employer should offer an implicit contract for *lifetime* employment, other than to realize gains from investing in the human capital of employees, particularly firm-specific human capital. So, while "efficiency wage" and "human capital" models sometimes compete, they are often hard to distinguish as explanations of the once-common corporate practice of employing managerial, professional, and sometimes even blue-collar employees until retirement.

Of course, just as law professors became entranced with the economic model of lifetime employment, its social basis began eroding rapidly (e.g., Ellwood et al. 2000; Cappelli 1999; Cappelli et al. 1997; Herzenberg, Alic, and Wial 1998; Lester 1998; Osterman 1996, 1999). Study after study has shown sharp decreases in tenure on the job, with particularly noticeable drops in very long tenures (over ten years) and particular groups (men with no education past high school) (Farber 1997, 2000; Swinnerton and Wial 1995; Rose 1995; Cappelli et al. 1997: 173–93). (Trends are less clear when tenures of one or two years are compared, e.g., Neumark [2000], but it seems clear to me that a focus on one- or two-year tenures completely misses the point.) This national erosion of lifetime jobs led impetus to this book's study of a labor market organized on completely different principles. Given labor markets in which absolutely any service may be obtained on a short-term contract, including the services of a chief executive or financial officer (Bradach 1997), it is harder and harder to say why firms ever thought that lifetime contracts were necessary.

Obviously Silicon Valley would never have been predicted by a model of employment as a series of implicit contracts for lifetime employment in which firms and employees invest in firm-specific human capital. However, the problems involved in applying this model to Silicon Valley are even deeper. Consider just our first problem, whether or when employers should be able to enforce covenants not to compete or trade secrets law against employees who depart for rivals or start-ups. There is no inherent harm in approaching this as a problem in efficient investment in human capital. However, invoking human capital carries with it some characteristic assumptions that will make solving our problem harder, not easier. First, like some of the transaction cost models already mentioned, human capital models assume that information is somebody's property, in this case the result of some investment. Human capital models rarely concern themselves with information that is widely shared except to see it as an externality to some other investment. They miss the crucial asymmetry under which employer human capital may be kept secret, while employee human capital will necessarily be disclosed, and rapidly so, in a high-velocity labor market.

A second aspect common (though not necessary) to human capital models is a somewhat factitious distinction between "general" and "firm-specific" human capital. Gary Becker (1993) hypothesized that firms would only provide training in "firm-specific" human capital, not in "general" knowledge that others might appropriate. Becker hypothesized that employees actually pay for training in general skills. If this were true, we could be confident that covenants not to compete performed no valid purpose, only an invalid anticompetitive purpose, since the employee had already paid for his or her general knowledge, while firm-specific human capital is plainly of no value to a competitor. Rubin and Shedd (1981) suggested by contrast that covenants not to compete should be enforceable to protect the employer's investment in an intermediate kind of knowledge, general knowledge that is too expensive for the worker to pay for. They also suggested that such covenants create incentives for each side to behave opportunistically: the employer by not providing the general training, and the worker by leaving and trading on the training. (Posner and Triantis [2001] also model covenants not to compete from a similar human capital perspective.)

Rubin and Shedd are certainly more realistic than Becker. Employers do indeed pay for general training (Acemoglu and Pischke 1999; Chang and Wang 1996; Katz and Ziderman 1990). Even temporary help agencies train temps in computer skills (Autor 2001a). However, the success of the California economy, despite its refusal to enforce covenants not to compete, directly raises the question whether such contracts provide any additional incentive, let alone an indispensable incentive, to employer training.

Employers have considerable power to define contracts of employment (Card and Krueger 1995). As we have seen, this is true even in a highly competitive, high-velocity labor market. It becomes even more true as employers become more monopsonistic. Any labor market imperfection may turn general training into firm-specific human capital (Acemoglu and Pischke 1999). An employer that needs incentives in order to invest in employee training may structure an employment contract that provides incentives for employees to stay, rather than depart. As we have observed repeatedly, it may locate facilities in areas where there is little competition from other employers, provide implicit contracts for lifetime employment, and back load compensation. Intel, Cisco, HP, and other large Silicon Valley employers do have facilities in remote areas, but, as we have seen, they do *not* use them for new, important projects that must be kept secret. Rather, they use them for older, less profitable products. Given the employer's freedom to structure employment contracts that will let it recoup, in most cases, the benefits of training, it is a most difficult issue to model any marginal advantage that it gains from adding an enforceable covenant not to compete, particularly given the costs that such covenants impose on the affected employees, and their anticompetitive effect.

Now it is true that Silicon Valley is no model of training. It is not possible to observe investment in training, but many kinds of training that may be observed elsewhere do not seem to exist in the Valley. Programmers are hired for actual experience in very specific applications of very specific programming language, as we have seen and will see again. Firms do not retrain older programmers trained in older languages, but expect such individuals not only to retrain themselves, but somehow to get experience themselves. Training for management positions also barely exists. There is no Silicon Valley equivalent to that old economy practice of selecting a promising young man (it always was a man) for management potential, circulating him for two years' duty at each of the company's locations (there was always a wife to move the children along at each location), finally bringing them back to headquarters. Firms' failure to train has created market opportunities. As we shall see in chapter 8, temporary help agencies provide some training to workers at the low end of the labor market, and have encouraged at least one union, Working Partnerships, to try to take that role itself (chapter 9). In short, the concerns of the human capital school are not foolish or misguided. It is certainly possible that, ten or twenty years from now, we will look back on Silicon Valley as a place that provided inadequate incentives for training, not merely because California does not enforce covenants not to compete, but because of the entire complex of high-velocity labor contracts. However, as with trade secrets law, there is little sign of this now. Instead, it is high-velocity labor contracting that seems to provide far better incentives than implicit contracting for the production of innovation, increasing firms' absorptive capacity, and diffusing valuable information. In any case, an analysis in terms of "human capital" does not add any additional perspective to those we have already examined.

Human capital models have other unattractive features that I will not belabor here. They do not, in fact, predict the levels at which firms or individuals will invest in education or training. Human capital models explain differences in income not by differences in jobs, but entirely by differences in the characteristics of employees (Lazear 1995). They are thus attractive primarily as ways of justifying unequal labor market incomes, which can always be attributed to "unobserved" differences in human capital. Obviously important advances in economics have been associated with human capital frameworks, but these models must be viewed with caution by the legal and policy communities.

Industrial Organization Approaches

In some models, an employer's contract with an employee concerning the latter's mobility depends on the kind of market in which the employer sells. Gersbach and Schmutzler (1999) argue that under price (tough or Bertrand) competition, firms have low incentives to acquire spillovers, high incentives to prevent them (so as to avoid entry by competitors), and high incentives to innovate that are not reduced by fear of spillovers. By contrast, in quantity (soft or Cournot) competition, endogenous spillovers are more likely to reduce incentives to innovate. Levels of competition are also central to Rønde (2000).

It is not easy to apply these models of competition to the Silicon Valley labor market, in which similar labor contracts are found among firms of different size and maturity that engage in different competition in very different markets. In particular, Silicon Valley has developed employment contracts and employment law to facilitate a very different kind of competition, being first to market with cool technology that may and will be copied, legally, so that the market winner will be the firm that gets there first and remains the most technologically advanced.

Future research will determine whether there is some deep intuition here about trade secrets and employee mobility in different product markets; if so, how it would apply to Silicon Valley; or whether this is just a working out of assumptions from the industrial organization literature.

Machlup on the Psychology of Intellectual Property

I do not suppose anybody reads Fritz Machlup (1952: 54–56) these days, or thinks about monopolies the way he did. However, his analysis of monopolies, including monopolies of information, written half a century ago, makes more sense to me as an explanation of contemporary Silicon Valley legal practice, than do most contemporary discussions.

In Machlup's models, the economic effect of a monopoly, specifically the incentives it provides for further investment by the monopolist, varies under different psychological assumptions. He specifically applies his analysis to monopolies over information, such as patents.

The worst case for society is to grant a monopoly to a pessimist who is wrongly convinced that new entrants' competition will arise at any moment to destroy his business. (If the monopolist is *correctly* convinced of imminent competition, Machlup points out, the monopoly will end and the case is of no social significance.) For such a pessimistic monopolist, "[i]nvestment in industrial research, development, and innovation will not appear promising in view of the supposedly imminent advent of competition." Granting such a monopoly may discourage competition yet achieve no gain in investment.

By contrast, Machlup hypothesized:

> the over-optimistic entrepreneur who underestimates the actual degree of pliopoly [ease of market entry] and overestimates the safe period. He need not be an actual monopolist, nor even imagine that he is one; it suffices that he believes it will take his competitors—imitators or makers of substitutes—

longer than it actually does to start competing with him. This optimism is the best promoter of technical progress. . . . [I]f imitation is rapid while the firms expect it to be slow, society will get the benefit of innovation as well as rapid imitation.

To buy innovation by paying with unnecessarily long delays of imitation is a poor bargain for society to make. Imitation always and necessarily lags behind innovation. It will be the best deal from the point of view of society if innovators optimistically overestimate this lag. If they expect the lag to be longer than it actually is, innovation will be enhanced and imitation will not be delayed. That it may create this socially wholesome illusion on the part of innovators is the strongest justification for a well-designed patent system. (Machlup 1952: 54–56)

Trade secrets law in Silicon Valley bears out the truth of Machlup's mordant analysis a half-century on. Law recognizes the concept of trade secrets. Every firm uses trade secrets agreements, and such agreements are exempt from California's statutory prohibition on covenants not to compete. Firms thus identify their assets with their secrets, and invest and innovate successfully. Yet in fact a secret is only as secure as an employee is happy. Innovations thus diffuse rapidly and are easily imitated, lowering costs to consumers. What more could anyone want from intellectual property law?

Part II

The Flexibility Story

5

HOW FLEXIBLE LABOR IS HIRED I: TEMPORARY HELP EMPLOYEES WHO WORK AT ONE CLIENT ("PERMATEMPS")

Silicon Valley is famous for all flavors of "flexible" labor contracting: employees referred from temporary help agencies, "permatemps" who work at one place but are nominally employees of a temporary agency, independent contractors and consultants. It seems therefore that the simplest and most obvious concept for understanding Silicon Valley's high-velocity labor market is that it is flexible (e.g., Carnoy, Castells, and Benner 1997). On this view, which is quite correct as far as it goes, its economic growth reflects the ease with which labor may be hired, fired, and directed to productive use, and contrasts with rigid, or regulated, labor markets, perhaps in traditional corporations with internal labor markets, or Western Europe. Everyone is familiar with the rhetoric that links "flexible" labor markets with high growth.

So far, I have been trying to complicate this view by developing an "information" paradigm of labor markets, along with the more familiar "flexibility" paradigm. The information spread by mobile workers is as important to include in our models of economic growth as are the efficiency gains from flexibility. Until we have more complete models of technological growth through hiring, it is anyone's guess whether the information aspect is more or less important than flexibility. In fact, contrasting a "flexibility" paradigm with an "information" paradigm is already somewhat misleading, since flexible relations themselves both create and spread information. Equally important, a high-velocity labor market is flexible, but not deregulated. A crucial lesson of chapters 2 through 4 is that a high-velocity labor market may require some quite specific and intrusive regulation, such as a ban on covenants not to compete, and a restricted definition of trade secret.

The flexibility story isn't wrong, however. Silicon Valley's high-velocity labor market reflects heavy use of some interesting institutions that facilitate hiring labor for short terms. The most important institution of "flexible" labor, though rarely appreciated as such, is the U.S. contract for employment.

Employment contracts in the United States generally do not require particular terms or benefits and may be terminated at will. Most flexible labor in the U.S. economy, certainly including Silicon Valley, is hired through relations of employment. That is, the individuals are classed as employees, their income is reported to the federal government on form W-2, and taxes are withheld.

This point is frequently misunderstood by commentators on today's assertedly contingent work force, and by nearly all commentators outside the United States. I greet a steady stream of graduate law students from outside the United States, who have come to the United States to study contingent labor, by which they mean self-employed individuals. I have to explain to them that most contingent jobs in the United States are held by statutory "employees," and the same is true of Silicon Valley. (This is why nationally "high technology" industries do not seem to make unusual use of "contingent or alternative" workers [Neumark and Reed 2002: 18]. Their contingent workers are mostly hired as employees and do not describe themselves as contingent. High-technology employers in their definition also include paints in New Jersey along with software in San Jose.) But, then, I have also been asked more than once to introduce European academic audiences to the "deregulation" of the U.S. labor market in the 1990s, that supposedly created a "neoliberal" and flexible labor market. I explain that there was no "deregulation" of the U.S. labor market in the 1990s or any other time. The only legal reforms of U.S. employment law in the 1990s increased regulation of employers on behalf of employees, namely the Civil Rights Act of 1991, increasing liability and remedies against discrimination, and the Family and Medical Leave Act. There is thus no "neoliberalism" in the United States, just the same old liberalism. Moreover, labor contracts in California are no more deregulated or flexible than anywhere else in the United States. If an American employer wants to create a job that will come to an end relatively soon and include no benefits beyond wages, it simply does so. It does not have to resort to subterfuges, so common in the rest of the world, like off-the-books employment or sham self-employment.

Silicon Valley employers make heavy use of temporary help agencies and independent contracting, but not simply as a device for "flexible" work relations, which (as just explained) could be achieved without them. Chapters 5 through 11 present a more rounded framework for the economic analysis of institutions of "flexible" labor: forms of hiring labor as needed; new labor market intermediaries; flexible compensation. Such institutions perform at least five different functions. Each presents a problem for economics, resolution of which would greatly improve debates over policy on flexible labor. They are: the different contributions of distinct institutions to "flexibility"; the role of information transmission across firm boundaries; other informational functions of flexible labor arrangements; enabling "precision hiring" for precise skill sets that eliminate firms' need to train (or even offer careers); and psychological aspects of flexible labor contracting, specifically the unequal treatment of workers at the same workplace.

First, all the institutions of flexible labor contracting do facilitate short tenures and easy discharge or job elimination—the flexibility story—though they are not necessary to achieve that purpose. Little needs to be said about the most familiar economic defense of short jobs. In any microeconomic model, gains are achieved by eliminating impediments to adjustment. Labor markets stand out for being slow to adjust. In the quip attributed to William Nordhaus, if auction markets adjust at the speed of light, labor markets adjust at 55 miles per hour. Labor markets characterized by internal labor markets, or wages above market-clearing levels (so-called "efficiency wages") are indeed slow to adjust, so anything that reduces those tendencies should achieve some gains through match.

While there is much truth to this familiar story, it would be wrong to suggest that there is an agreed-on economic model of the gains from permitting temporary employment, in a system of labor law that had previously taxed or forbidden it. Labor markets are full of idiosyncratic features: cultural traditions, specific wage comparisons, all the ways in which human beings are unlike other factors of production. It is thus by no means unusual for countries to shred safety nets or other "impediments" to "labor market adjustment" and achieve no measurable gains in job creation, wealth, or any other desired goal (Esping-Andersen and Regini 2000; Freeman 1994). If there were no more to the Silicon Valley job-creation story than increasing the speed of adjustment, there would be little reason for other countries to emulate it. The goal of this book is to move beyond this "flexibility" paradigm, limited to the speed of adjustment.

Still, flexibility is an important part of the Silicon Valley story. As we shall see repeatedly, its labor market institutions facilitate rapid hiring and shedding of labor, so crucial to firms in uncertain markets, particularly start-ups. Is there really an economic problem in understanding it? We obviously do not need to invent economics of flexible employment. That is what neoclassical labor economics is all about. The caricatured version of neoclassical labor economics is that it models the labor market as if the entire country formed a longshoremen's shape-up every morning. Much professional energy among economists of labor has gone, in recent decades, into modeling labor markets that supplement, or deviate from, neoclassical models, such as internal labor markets or efficiency wage models. It is sobering to find in Silicon Valley a labor market that is fairly classical, although, as we have just seen, not "deregulated."

The economic problem lies rather in understanding the different effects of the multiple devices available (i.e., temporary agency employment, in-house temps, consultants and contractors, H1-B visas, etc.) to facilitate flexible employment (see, e.g., Milner and Pinker 1997, 2001). If (for example) there were more legal regulation of temporary help agencies, can we assume that their employees would instead be hired as in-house temps, at essentially the same conditions of employment? Or do specific institutions associated with flexible labor have specific economic effects, perhaps associated with those institutions' informational or psychological aspects?

Second, building on chapters 2, 3, and 4, we will see that these institutions are, in part, devices for the flow of information across firm boundaries. The economics of information spillover through labor mobility are, as we have seen already, not well understood. They will be revisited throughout this book, not only in discussing knowledge spillovers, but also in discussing temporary help employees. For example, to return to the problem of the previous paragraph, if temporary help agencies capitalize on their ability to transmit information across firm boundaries, in-house temps would not be a complete substitute.

Third, some of these institutions perform other informational functions, necessary in labor markets that do a great deal of hiring on little information. We will consider these information problems in more depth in chapter 8 on for-profit labor market intermediaries, like temporary agencies and Internet job boards, chapter 9 on employee organization, and chapter 10 on stock options.

Fourth, Silicon Valley employers hire for very specific skill sets and experience. Unlike stereotyped older corporations with internal labor markets, they do not hire people leaving school or military service with no particular skills, intending to train them over time in their company's way. They are able to eliminate training, job ladders, tournaments, and mentoring because of specific labor market institutions that match specific skills with specific needs. This will prove to be important in chapter 12 when we discuss how such a meritocracy can generate disparate outcomes by race and age.

Finally, and most crucially in this chapter, these institutions reinforce traditional benefit structures by creating categories of employees who do not share them. Understanding how this works will require some understanding of the emerging field of behavioral economics of the employment relation.

Temporary employment and independent contracting are of course not unique to Silicon Valley and receive no special legal or policy support in California. Temporary help agencies play a larger role in Silicon Valley's labor market than they do nationally; rates of self-employment are completely unremarkable. Nevertheless there are some interesting aspects to their use. (Another form of hiring flexible labor, heavily used in Silicon Valley, is to hire immigrants on temporary, H1-B visas. This presents many economic and legal problems of its own and will be treated separately in chapter 7.)

The economic problem in the background of the next five chapters may now be stated in more detail. In Silicon Valley, as in the U.S. economy generally, we find a rich array of institutions by which flexible labor may be hired or shed, including employment contracts, temporary help agencies, self-employment, and outsourcing functions to other companies. Hiring computer programmers is a good example. A firm that needs programming for a particular project may readily hire programmers as:

- employees,
- self-employed independent contractors,
- employees of a temporary help agency, or
- outsource the programming to a contractor with its own employees (or independent contractors), perhaps in India (Arora, Arunachalam, Asundi, and Fernandes 2001; Sharpe 2001) or Ireland (Ó Riain 2001).

Programming is also the most common job for an immigrant on an H-1B visa. The same menu (except for the H-1B visa holder) is available for hiring low-skill manufacturing workers. Any of these may result in work relations that are flexible, stable, or anything in between. What drives the choice among them? It is not surprising that the answer to this question, too, involves primarily the economics of information, the economic effect of legal regulation, and the psychological consequences of worker classification.

In the remainder of this book, we will not be able to make use of the concept of a new psychological contract in which employers voluntarily limit their prerogatives. In chapters 2 through 4 on intellectual property my main focus was the welfare consequences of different labor contracts and restrictions on them. Nevertheless, there is some evidence of implied contracts under which employers promise not to interfere with the employability of departing employees. As we saw, Cisco makes such a promise explicitly; other employees told me in interviews that they believe they have such a contract. Thus, the analysis of those chapters was entirely compatible with Stone (2001), who argues the existence of such a new contract. By contrast, none of the different types of temporary employees discussed in the next few chapters can argue successfully for the existence of an implied contract of this type. Employees of temporary help agencies, and employees on nonimmigrant, H1-B visas, normally have express written agreements that under California law normally preclude any claims of implied contract (*Guz v. Bechtel Corp.*). I will suggest legal reforms that would improve the welfare of both those groups of employees without, I think, harming any legitimate interest of their employers. However, such suggestions will be based on an economic understanding of the welfare implications of the relevant employment contracts, and not on any hypothesized limits voluntarily, if silently, assumed by employers.

This chapter, after some introductory remarks on defining and counting "temporary" employees, looks at an institution closely associated with high-tech employment: employees who go to work every day at one high-tech company, yet are classified as if they were employees of a temporary help agency. Other modes of hiring "flexible" labor are discussed in later chapters.

Temporary Employees Defined and Counted

Silicon Valley uses temporary employees—that is, employees of temporary help agencies—at twice the national rate. About 3.53 percent of jobs in Santa Clara County are with temporary help agencies (Baru 2001: 31). In February 2002, around 14.4 percent of employees in the county worked in "business services," the two-digit industry category including personnel supply services, often used as a rough proxy for temporary help (author's calculation from Bureau of Labor Statistics [BLS] data). In high tech, temps do not just work as word processors and receptionists. They are programmers, manufacturing employees, group leaders, product testers, and executives, including CEOs (cf. Bradach 1997).

The term "temporary employee," though frequently used, has no legal or economic significance. The majority of U.S. employees might be considered "temporary" in the sense that they are employed "at will," and might be dismissed, or their job eliminated, at any time for any reason (or no reason at all). Thus, when economists or academics speak of "temporary" employees, they normally refer only to the narrower, countable group of employees of temporary help agencies.

There has been much concern in recent years over shorter job tenures and workforce uncertainty. This has motivated a search for a good statistical proxy for individuals facing high risk of job loss and uncertain futures. Because it is relatively easy (though, as we shall see, not without some difficulty) to count individuals employed by temporary help agencies, these individuals, though a small portion of the U.S. workforce, often stand in statistically for the larger group of temporary employees or perhaps contingent employees. Nationally, "on-call employees, direct-hire temporary employees, contract company employees, and independent contractor employment are all quantitatively as important or more important than temporary help agency employment" (Houseman and Polivka 2000). The number of "direct-hire temporary employees" hired by the employers for whom they work is believed (based on special surveys of the Current Population Survey) to be almost three times as large as the number of "temporary employees" who are employees of temporary help agencies (Houseman and Polivka 2000; Houseman 1999: 8–9).

We do not have any good alternative statistical measure for the larger group of temporary or contingent employees. During the 1990s, the U.S.

Current Population Survey attempted to develop a statistical measure of "contingent" employment. At two-year intervals, in 1995, 1997, 1999, and 2001, it asked people whether their jobs were contingent—specifically, whether their jobs were "temporary" or whether they could "continue to work for your current employer as long as you wish" (Cohany et al. 1998: 42). Under the broadest definitions, no more than 4 percent of the workforce describes itself as contingent under this definition (U.S. BLS 2001), and these few self-described contingent workers are disproportionately employed outside high technology (Neumark and Reed 2002: 18). Since about 15 percent of the U.S. workforce saw their jobs disappear forever just between the boom years 1993 and 1995 (Farber 1997), the Current Population Survey questions on "contingent" work tell us more about cognitive dissonance than about labor markets.

Even counting only the employees who work for temporary help agencies is no easy matter. There are two principal sources of information about such temporary help agency employees, both published by the Bureau of Labor Statistics, and they do not agree. The Current Employment Statistics (CES) series surveys business establishments, asking them to report their number of employees. It has a classification (873603) for the "personnel supply services" industry. The Current Population Survey (CPS) surveys households, and asks workers about their industry of employment. The business survey consistently shows twice as many temporary workers as the household survey. There are two reasons conventionally given for this. First, some individuals may work at different times in the month for different agencies and may be counted twice or more in the business survey. Second, many people tell the household survey that they are working in the industry to which they are assigned, rather than working in the "personnel supply services industry." In the 1995 CPS Supplement, 57 percent of agency temporaries incorrectly gave the client firm as their employer (Houseman and Polivka 2000). When we look at temporary employees in Silicon Valley, we will see more clearly how temporary employees identify with the client where they work, not the agency that signs their paycheck.

Nationally, about 2.2 percent of workers are reported in the business survey to be working for temporary help agencies. The figure is 2.39 percent for California and 3.53 percent for Santa Clara County (Baru 2001: 29–31). If direct-hire temps are 2.8 times the lower figure (as they are nationally), then almost 10 percent of the Silicon Valley workforce might be temps. (Of course, it is also possible, perhaps likely, that Silicon Valley's heavy use of agency temps substitutes directly for other regions' use of direct-hire temps. There are no data on direct-hire temps in Silicon Valley, and most of the ethnographies, as we shall see, describe temps who work for an agency.)

Under both surveys, the number of individuals who work for temporary help agencies grew rapidly in the 1990s, both nationally and in Silicon Valley. The Valley's pattern has been even more dependent on temporary help employees. The rapid national increase was first noticed in the early years of recovery from the first Bush recession of the early 1990s, and provoked concern about a "future of lousy jobs." Nationally (according to the business survey) the number of employees working in "help supply services" quintupled from 1982 (the first year the category was created) to 1997 (Houseman 1999: 10–11). It has been level since 1997 at around 2.2 percent of the workforce. In California, employment in the sector doubled from 1991 to 1998 (Baru 2001: 29). It subsequently emerged in national studies that many individuals passed through temporary help employment after either downsizing, or in the early stages of recovery, and soon found themselves in permanent employment. Relatively few individuals nationally were really trapped in that sector for a long time (Finegold et al. in progress; Farber 1999).

In Silicon Valley, however, temporary employment continued to grow even during the boom years 1999 and 2000, when unemployment in the region was below 3 percent. Temporary agency employment in Santa Clara County grew 62.35 percent from 1995 to 2002 (Baru 2001: 44). Temporary help jobs are not just transitional jobs in and out of booms, though they are that. In Silicon Valley they are also becoming a permanent way of life.

What accounts for the growth in temporary help jobs? Flexibility is not an answer by itself, since these workers might as easily have been hired as regular employees. Perhaps agencies are used to screen or train workers. We will see that when we look at labor market intermediaries in chapter 8. But let us start by looking at an institution closely associated with high technology and Silicon Valley: employees who work every day for a high-technology employer, yet are carried on the payroll of a temporary help agency. They are sometimes called "permatemps."

Studies of Permatemps in (and Around) Silicon Valley: Happy Temps, Hopeful Temps, Angry Temps

By far the best study of temporary agency employees at a northern California computer company actually looks at permatemps. Vicki Smith (2001: 90–119) studied the company she calls CompTech. While this particular facility was physically a little outside Silicon Valley, her picture seems consistent with large employers in the Valley, although the temps she interviewed were considerably more satisfied with their jobs than those in the few other published studies (Darrah 1999; Chun 2001). I did not interview temporary employees or managers at temporary help agencies. Smith's picture seems consistent with what I heard generally from human resources managers.

Smith interviewed forty-five employees (and observed others) in 1996–97 at CompTech, a leading manufacturer of computers and other information technology products. About a quarter of its workforce were called temporary employees and nominally employees of temporary help agencies, although they were what I am calling permatemps: they worked every day at CompTech and were not referred to other employers. (The precise institutional arrangements were complex.) The possible selection bias, which she admits, is that most firms had refused her request to interview temps. CompTech's personnel director welcomed the study, partly because of the firm's "open and progressive culture," and partly because some managers had complained to her about the mandate to use temporary workers, and she herself was interested in an in-depth study (Smith 2001: 17).

CompTech is a typical employer of temps in that it is a generous employer for permanent employees. This point is crucial and often misunderstood. CompTech, like other typical users of temps, offers its regular employees excellent benefits, training packages, and secure employment. CompTech also disperses management authority among self-governing teams that are rewarded for taking risks and assuming responsibilities (Smith 2001: 94).

Advocates for temporary workers, such as the labor movement, often associate the employment of temps with cutthroat employers out to minimize labor costs. While such employers exist, they are not the typical employers of temps. Rather, nationally, the likelihood of using flexible employees (of all types) varies directly with generosity of benefits for regular employees (Houseman 1997: viii). Firms use temps precisely because they want to preserve, for a core, generous benefits that they cannot or do not extend to the entire workforce.

Temps at CompTech understood this. As one told Smith:

> CompTech doesn't wanna go the way of IBM or Digital or any of those places where they, you know, where suddenly 14,000 people are lopped off the payroll. They're more responsible to their workforce than that. So, I mean, if you're going, if it's inevitable you're going to have some *pain*— where do you have it? With the people that you've had for twenty years? Do you want it to go there? Or is it to the people that you willingly and knowingly hired on a limited job? Now do you whack them or the other people? (Smith 2001:114–15)

Smith was surprised at how integrated the temps were into CompTech culture, and how much they liked their jobs. Some worked on an assembly line, configuring computers with particular equipment. While the work was not complex and the skill requirement low, temps, like other CompTech employees, were able to determine the pace of the line, helped each other when one station got backed up, and spent time evaluating problems in production. Other temps worked on far more complex, custom assembly, where they calculated schedules for filling orders, assigned tasks by team, and met with vendors when they encountered recurring defects in the vendor's product. Many of the temps spoke of situations in which they had been given responsibility for planning or other opportunities for learning. Everyone had been cross-trained for different positions. Temps are hired for eighteen-month periods, but many are hired back after a mandatory three-month hiatus. The median temp had worked at CompTech for twenty-seven months, close to the median tenure for U.S. service workers generally (2.4 years). Virtually all of them aspired to permanent employment at CompTech and believed with some justification that the temporary positions were their only vehicle for doing so. While CompTech did not keep statistics on conversion from temporary to permanent employment, managers interviewed by Smith estimated this likelihood at somewhere between 10 and 15 percent (Smith 2001: 107).

While all ostensibly were employed by a temporary help agency, many were unable to name that agency and insisted that they worked for CompTech. The vast majority had held a series of unstable jobs before coming to CompTech. For most, the temp job at CompTech was the best job they had ever had. Nevertheless, as Smith points out, "temps were earning lower wages than permanent workers for the same or similar jobs, . . . they weren't allowed to move up the job hierarchy, . . . they literally could not be certain that they would have their job from one day to the next" (Smith 2001: 103).

Smith was apparently unable to track down the management dissatisfaction with temps at CompTech. One wonders if, like the temps at Applied Materials studied by Laura Castaneda (2001), they spend the end of their terms holding back information and looking for their next job.

Permatemps doing manufacturing work at the contract manufacturer that Chun (2001) called FlexTech were also surprisingly satisfied. Although their work seemed far less desirable than the work that Smith observed at CompTech, these workers also felt it was better than other jobs they had had or might aspire to. Like the CompTech workers, they aspired to permanent positions with FlexTech, a more realistic aspiration, in their case.

FlexTech is a contract manufacturer, making printed circuit boards (PCBs) under contract to original equipment manufacturers. FlexTech uses surface mount technology (SMT) that builds boards through stamping and chemical fusion, rather than hand assembly. Chun worked there during the summer of

1997. Like most of the workers on her line, she was hired by a temporary help agency and thereafter received her paychecks from that agency. FlexTech itself does not recruit or hire. It outsources recruiting to several temporary agencies that operate an office at a local shopping center, exclusively for FlexTech.

Like CompTech and most U.S. employers of temporary employees (Dube and Kaplan 2003), FlexTech offers slightly higher wages, significantly higher bonuses, health insurance, paid sick days and vacation, and participation in the company's stock purchase plan as benefits to its "own" workers, but not to temporary workers. Temporary workers are told that "if they work hard and come to work on time, they will eventually become permanent" (Chun 2001: 143). Chun does not offer an estimate of how often this occurs. Becoming permanent is not a sure thing and "depends more on the profitability and productivity of a specific customer project than on an individual worker's performance." The promotion to permanent status that Chun observed came to fifteen workers on a different product line, the first group of temporary workers hired for that project eleven months earlier, now promoted, as a group, to permanent status. They celebrated by throwing themselves a party during the "lunch break" on their graveyard shift (2:30–3:00 A.M.).

Working at FlexTech is a far worse job than working at CompTech: intense, unstable, unsafe, and equally poorly paid. There are no eighteen-month terms, training for multiple positions, team self-governance, or opportunities for learning. FlexTech itself is entirely dependent on contracts. It has no internal product development capacity and produces nothing that bears its own name. "Just in time" manufacturing methods ensure that the line will be shut down and workers sent home without pay if parts do not arrive or machines break down. Production processes involve harsh chemicals to which many workers react badly. Chun was nevertheless surprised at workers' identification with FlexTech (and especially their team). They compared their job favorably to jobs that had no possibility of raises or bonuses.

Other, smaller-scale studies of temporary employment in Silicon Valley reveal more dissatisfaction. Certainly this emerges vividly in the film *Secrets of Silicon Valley,* directed by Alan Snitow and Deborah Kaufman. The film follows a young temporary worker, Raj Jayadev, manufacturing Hewlett-Packard products as a temporary employee nominally employed by Manpower and assigned to a company on Hewlett-Packard's property with the oxymoronic name Manufacturing Services Ltd. Jayadev complains about safety and other employees' short paychecks, without much success. He summarizes his experiences in Jayadev (2002). He has since gone on to found siliconvalleydebug.com, a Web site, newspaper, and organization advocating for the Valley's "young and temporary." (The manufacturing line has been moved to Mexico.) Interviews with a small sample of sixteen low-end temps revealed near-unanimity about the advantages of temp work (control of hours, low stress, and commitment) and disadvantages (lack of health benefits) (Darrah 1999). The psychological literature on contingent employees is remarkably thin, telling us what they must be feeling rather than what they actually are feeling (Beard and Edwards 1995; Sennett 1998). It is hardly surprising if unskilled workers are unhappy, yet few if any studies compare sets of employees similar except for contingent status.

Why Permatemps?

There is something troubling about employers using labor for which another employer is the legal employer, particularly when the jobs involved are not very good jobs. Before deciding whether law and policy should limit or eliminate this practice, we should ask why employers do it. It is surprisingly difficult to answer this question, but in general the answer must draw more on problems of behavioral economics than on "flexibility." We may reject three explanations for creating permatemp relations: they do not create general flexibility for employers; they do not result of their own force in exclusion of employees from benefits; and they do not solve information problems.

Ethnographies of temps or permatemps, like the extremely valuable studies of Vicki Smith and Jennifer Chun on which I have relied, often emphasize the risk and uncertainty that these workers experience, sometimes described as a transfer of risk from capital to labor. This does not explain why CompTech, or FlexTech, put employees on the payroll of a temp agency. There is considerable evidence of increased uncertainty in the worklife of all Americans (e.g., Bernhardt et al 2001; Bertrand 1999; Katz and Krueger 1999; Farber 1997; Lester 1998). Even employees who work for just one employer face increased risks of job loss, shorter job tenures, and compensation linked to market forces. If public policy wanted to address this uncertainty, it would have to do so for many workers, perhaps by developing national health insurance or revising unemployment insurance. It could not rationally target employees of temporary help agencies, whose job experience, as a group, does not clearly deviate from the experience of temporary workers hired directly by, or on call for, a single employer (Houseman and Polivka 1999: Tables 3 and 4). Presumably, if employment law made CompTech or FlexTech (or even FlexTech's client, the manufacturer) the legal employers of those employees, they would continue to be temporary employees without paid vacations or health insurance. So why didn't those companies set up the jobs that way in the first place?

Regular employees at CompTech and FlexTech have benefits like paid sick and vacation days, health insurance, and participation in a company stock purchase plan. Temps do not. Is that why the temps are temps? Perhaps it is psychologically easier for the workforce to accept unequal benefits if the workforce has unequal nominal employers. I will argue that this may be the case.

However, there is no legal impediment to granting such benefits only to a portion of one's employees. There is actually legal authority directly on this point, the universally misunderstood case of *Vizcaino v. Microsoft*. (A good journalistic account is Lieber 2000.) Microsoft, like CompTech and FlexTech, at one time had many "permatemps," nominally employees of temp agencies while working exclusively for Microsoft. (Microsoft classed some as employees of temp agencies and others as self-employed independent contractors.) The Internal Revenue Service (IRS) determined in an audit that many of these individuals were actually Microsoft employees, at least for tax purposes. (The next section of this chapter on legal and policy issues will argue that the same is probably true of CompTech and FlexTech "temps"; there do not appear to be any significant differences between the temps at those companies and the permatemps at Microsoft.)

The determination that Microsoft's "temps" were really its employees changed very little in the conditions of their employment. The IRS determination changed only Microsoft's obligation to withhold taxes, and the form on which it reported income to the IRS. Following the IRS determination, the "permatemps" sued, seeking inclusion in a wide range of Microsoft benefit programs, including health insurance, pensions, and the self-directed stock purchase plans known as 401(k) plans. It is rarely appreciated that they lost on every one of these claims but one. The federal court of appeals held that they had to be permitted to participate in one very unusual employee stock purchase plan that, by statute—unlike any other benefit plan—must be open to all employees. Stock purchase plans organized under this particular statute were rarely encountered in the years before *Vizcaino v. Microsoft*. Experienced benefits consultants have told me they had never seen one in their lives. They will presumably never be seen again, since Microsoft did eventually have to pay $97 million to settle claims of the employees excluded from this stock purchase plan. I will discuss this in chapter 10 on stock option compensation.

Lieber (2000) is unable to determine precisely why Microsoft set up its permatemping relations in the first place, and the same is true of such Silicon Valley employers as CompTech and FlexTech. Labor market intermediaries usually perform some informational function. We will see in chapter 8 that this is very much true of some temporary help agencies. However, like flexibility, information doesn't seem to explain the use of permatemps. The temp agency that CompTech temps can't even identify, or the temp agency recruiting exclusively for FlexTech in the shopping center, has no information about workers that CompTech and FlexTech lack. (They may have less information about the employers than the employers themselves!)

CompTech and FlexTech probably realize three advantages from having their workforce classed as employees of temporary help agencies. First, they may reduce liability, particularly under civil rights law, when they inevitably discharge employees. Second, FlexTech may realize some small cost savings in outsourcing hiring, as with any function that it outsources. Third, most speculatively, but in my opinion most importantly, it appears to be psychologically easier for a workforce to accept inequality in benefits if some of them are, even nominally, employees of another employer.

Reducing Civil Rights Liability

In general, there is little systematic legal advantage to a U.S. employer in classifying employees as independent contractors or employees of a temp agency. This is just another way of saying that the employment contract is very lightly regulated. The minimum wage, other labor standards, and the obligation to provide a safe workplace are the same for temps as for in-house employees. (There may be particular instances of tactical classification of workers, for example if the employer anticipates a union representation election. Influencing union elections, however, is never a factor in Silicon Valley, where there is little union activity, as I'll discuss in chapter 9.)

There appears to be one important exception to the generalization that use of alternative work arrangements is rarely driven by a desire to evade employment laws. Use of temporary help agencies appears nationally to have been spurred by legal doctrines permitting individuals to challenge their discharge. In 1991 the Civil Rights Act of 1964 was amended to increase damages for victims of discrimination and provide clearly for trial by jury. As discussed more fully in chapter 12, the act had already come to be applied almost exclusively to dismissal of employees (Donahue and Siegelman 1991), and it is dismissed employees who normally make use of the increased availability of lawyers, jury trials, and damages. It appears that this influenced the rapid growth of the temporary help sector over the next six years (leveling off nationally after 1997). Employers have candidly told researchers (e.g., Autor 2003) that they value the ability to have the agency get a particular individual out, without having to create a paper record or be vulnerable to a discrimination suit. Similarly, use of temporary help employees often jumps in the year following a particular state's adoption of legal grounds for challenging discharge (Autor 2003; Miles 2000). Many of the permatemps at

CompTech and FlexTech are members of minority groups (Asian or Hispanic), or women, who could plausibly threaten litigation if they were discharged and others were not. Discrimination by a temp agency, at the behest of its client, is equally illegal, but thought to be harder to prove. (We shall see in chapter 12 that there are essentially no successful discrimination suits against Silicon Valley employers.) The ease with which employers can thus refashion employment contracts places constraints on regulatory responses. Regulation of one kind of employment contract simply creates incentives for employers to use another.

Outsourcing Generally

Most high-tech manufacturers outsource significant aspects of production. For a typical personal computer, the ratio has been estimated as 80 percent of production costs (Ernst and O'Connor 1992: 34, 37), even higher for some manufacturers. Outsourcing personnel functions like hiring, payroll administration, or withholding does not require any fancier theory than cost reduction.

A recent study (Dube and Kaplan 2003) used national data from the Current Population Survey to compare janitors and guards working for business service contractors with those who worked directly for firms. The outsourced janitors were paid less despite equal educational attainment. They were also more heavily female, African-American, Latino, and Latina. They were half as likely to be unionized and about a third as likely to have health insurance. The relationship between outsourcing and low wages and benefits remains obscure. Why don't firms directly hire the same individuals? It is not obvious, however, what major savings are realized when low-skill, minimum-wage workers are recruited by a temp agency in a shopping center rather than by a FlexTech employee in FlexTech's human resources department (or physically in the same shopping center). I know of no data on this point. I suspect that the only saving is that the recruiter for the temp agency probably also receives no benefits, while an analogous recruiter who was a FlexTech employee probably would, for reasons I now explore.

Psychological Aspects of Workforce Division

The most pressing research agenda concerning temporary and contingent work involves its psychological effect on workplace morale. This probably cannot be researched without employer cooperation. Recent research in the economics of employment suggests, however, that employee morale has much more economic significance than has previously been thought. It leads me to think that the "permatemp" phenomenon has similar origins—particularly since it is otherwise difficult to think of any other reason to hire low-skill manufacturing labor as a permatemp, rather than an in-house temporary employee.

The importance of employee morale was the unexpected finding of Bewley (1999: 173). Bewley interviewed New England businesspeople in the Bush recession of the early 1990s to learn why firms normally lay off employees rather than cut wages (Hewlett-Packard was once an exception, but is so no longer). The interviews offer many rich insights deserving further study. Their main significance for our rather different problem was the importance of employee morale. Few employers had ever cut wages. All thought it would cause problems. The main anticipated problem was that employee reactions would cost more than the wage cuts would save. The two most anticipated reactions were low morale and increased turnover of the best employees. While managers had little direct experience with pay cuts, Bewley wrote (1999: 79): "I suspect that the principal cause of managers' preoccupation with morale is experience with inequities." "Managers claimed that internal equity was vital, since perceptions of inequity and favoritism embitter and antagonize employees." In laboratory games as in managers' perceptions, employees appear to be concerned with equity, and to take action other than that predicted by self-interested rationality in order to preserve equity (Fehr and Schmidt 1999; Fehr et al. 1998).

This literature suggests the following very tentative hypothesis. Suppose employers anticipate that certain jobs really are unstable, because of uncertain product demand, competition, or any other reason. They face a risk in hiring employees for those tasks, paying them minimum wage, excluding them from benefits, and laying them off without notice. They have no difficulty finding such workers, and there is no legal impediment to such contracts. However, such labor arrangements might lower morale among the permanent workforce, either because those workers have some commitment to equity, or because such arrangements would create anxiety about their own job security. For reasons that are completely hypothetical, classifying the temps as a different class of worker, employed by a different entity, has no legal, but intense psychological—hence, economic—effects. That is, hiring the disposable workforce as permatemps has less negative force on the morale of the core workforce. (Katz and Krueger [1999: 50] make a similar suggestion.)

I cannot prove this proposition. The only research that I have found seems to suggest the opposite. Core employees at a large aerospace company who worked with contract labor had *less* trust in the organization than those who worked in units consisting entirely of regular employees (Pearce 1993). As I said, I did not conduct interviews in Silicon Valley specifically on temporary employees or permatemps. It is not obvious that employees in Silicon Valley's high-velocity labor market would place the same importance on equity as Bewley's New England manufacturing employees and managers, or Fehr's game players. Silicon Valley employees are often said to be particularly self-ish (e.g., Borsook 2000).

Still, the only survey of Silicon Valley employees' attitudes toward fair-ness that I have found did not discover any interesting differences with other employee groups surveyed. Charness and Levine (2000) surveyed employ-ees in Vancouver, B.C., Toronto, and Silicon Valley, to determine which lay-offs were regarded as fair. Unsurprisingly, layoffs resulting from reduced product demand, from new technology, or when CEOs shared the pain were all more fair than layoffs without reciprocity by management, or when the firm could afford to retain employees. However, perhaps surprisingly, re-spondents in Silicon Valley were not more accepting of layoffs, on average, than the Canadians. Even Silicon Valley employees appear to regard some layoffs as unfair, and—since such layoffs are endemic—they risk affecting employee morale and resulting in loss of performance, just as in Bewley.

While this hypothesis about permatemps and employee morale is specu-lative, it is about the only hypothesis that occurs to me to explain permatemping. If permatemping performs no function except to fool em-ployees somehow, it could hardly be justified, and presumably there could then be no objection to decisions like *Vizcaino v. Microsoft,* making such permatemps statutory "employees" where they work. If, however, permatemping arrangements have some unknown psychological effect on other employees, the policy argument, to which we now turn, becomes much more interesting.

Legal and Policy Aspects of Permatemping

Companies that use permatemps, like CompTech and FlexTech, normally claim that the temporary help agency is the legal employer of those individu-als, and that they are merely the client of that agency. This claim may well be legally incorrect. Advocates for permatemps often insist that the client is the employer, which may be true, and that this is important to establish, which is normally not true.

Under U.S. employment law, a firm that hires employees from a normal temporary help agency (like Manpower) has all the advantages, and none of the obligations, of being their employer. The temporary help agency is nor-mally the legal employer. The agency is liable to pay promised wages and benefits (though there are normally few benefits), refer employees without discrimination, and obtain workers' compensation and unemployment insurance (though few of its employees will ever qualify for unemployment insurance [Pandya 1999]). Although the client has none of these liabilities of an employer, it nevertheless gets the only advantage of employer status. If the temp is injured on the job, the temp will not be able to sue the client in a personal injury suit. The temp will be relegated to the less-generous workers' compensation system, and in that system alone, the client will be considered a "special" employer. California is like other states in treating clients of temporary help agencies as "employers" of those temps for purposes of the workers' compensation statute, and for no other purpose (*Santa Cruz Poultry v. Superior Court*).

This legal framework resulted from political activity by the temporary help industry (Gonos 1997). It normally contemplates a genuine temporary help agency, such as Manpower.

Permatemps who work every day at the same employer, such as those at CompTech or FlexTech, are, by contrast, probably legal employees of those employers, under one of two theories. The first, already mentioned, is the theory applied by the Internal Revenue Service in Microsoft: that Microsoft controlled the means and manner of the temps' work and was therefore their common-law employer. This oversimplifies the unloved twenty factors that the IRS allegedly considers in determining "employee" status; however control of the means and manner of work is normally regarded as the most important of these factors. The second is a specific provision of the Internal Revenue Code [IRC §414(n)]. It applies to temporary and leased employees who have provided their services for a particular client, who primarily controls their work, "on a substantially full-time basis for at least a year." They must be treated as regular employees for purposes of retirement plans, employer-provided life insurance, and similar fringe benefits (but not health insurance). There is little case law applying this section. The federal Court of Appeals covering California, which decided the *Microsoft* permatemp case, has held that workers should first be evaluated, as the Microsoft employees were, as employees of the client firm. Only if they are not employees should §414(n) be applied (*Burrey v. Pacific Gas and Electric Co.*).

So no legal change is necessary in order to make CompTech or FlexTech the legal employer of its permatemps. This is probably already the law, at least for the temps who have worked full time for a year and, perhaps, under the IRS ruling regarding Microsoft, for some of the others. Of course, the law does not prevent either employer from excluding those permatemps from health insurance plans. After a year it must treat them like regular employees. This does not necessarily mean that it must include them in retirement and insurance plans. If it excludes in-house temps, it presumably may exclude the permatemps, too.

Except for the psychological factors discussed in the previous section, there is hardly any argument against making CompTech and FlexTech the legal employer of its permatemps. Either company could, as a legal matter, still structure highly contingent relations of employment. However, it would clearly be the responsible party for wage payments, application of discrimination and safety laws, and similar minimum legal obligations. We simply do not know, however, whether employers would face new pressure to include temporary employees in health insurance or retirement plans if they were forced to issue their paychecks and deduct their taxes. This might be a good thing, but it would not be costless and might result in creation of fewer temporary jobs. Would union organizing have more success if Silicon Valley workforces were not "artificially" divided into temps and permanent employees? If the "morale" of the permanent employees would be affected by poor treatment of their "fellow" employees, would they respond with union "voice" effects, exit, or what? The next generation of models of temporary employment should include measures of the psychological function it performs for regular employees.

6

HOW FLEXIBLE LABOR IS HIRED II:
INDEPENDENT CONTRACTORS

A *New York Times* article on October 11, 2000 (Ellin 2000) again told its
readers most of what they already knew about independent contractors in
high-technology employment. A manufacturer of medical devices in Fre-
mont, California (a manufacturing town on the East Bay usually included in
Silicon Valley) hired mostly independent contractors when it started up in
1993. Four years later, California state authorities determined that some of
the workers were legally its employees. The story ended with the
manufacturer's hiring of a company to manage its contingent workforce. Legal
specialists interviewed in the article called this a "smart move" since
misclassifying workers may have "grave unforeseen financial consequences."
The question of classification "has become more pressing as the hiring of
independent contractors has become more common." The story noted that
Microsoft had been ordered "to pay benefits to hundreds of workers that the
company said were independent contractors but that the courts found otherwise." The law is very complicated and companies need professional help.

This is a perfectly typical article about independent contracting in high
technology and strings together the usual misstatements and half-truths. People
who follow these issues in ordinary news media rarely learn:

- The percentage of independent contractors in the American workforce
  (6.4 percent) is at its historic *low*.
- Rates of independent contracting in Silicon Valley (6.2 percent of the
  workforce) are *even lower* than the national rate.
- Firms that misclassify their workforces rarely face significant liability.
- The plaintiffs in the famous Microsoft litigation (*Vizcaino v. Microsoft*)
  lost on every claim to be included in Microsoft benefits programs except for one, involving a very unusual stock purchase plan.

The lawyers and consultants interviewed in articles like this invariably reach
the self-serving conclusion that more firms should hire lawyers and consultants (cf. Edelman et al. 1992). This is unnecessary in most cases. Nevertheless, the law of independent contractors is a little tricky and one can imagine

some congressional fiddling with the definition of "employee" that would better serve both individuals and employers (Hyde 2000: 104).

The basic story of independent contracting in high technology, however, is that it is a useful legal mode of rendering services. Most independent contractors are economically successful. Less-well-paid independent contractors would not be better off if the opportunity to contract were denied them. There is no real evidence of widespread abuse of independent contracting (to remove individuals from the protection of labor statutes, for example), and certainly no need for regulation to add costs to the creation of independent contracting. Individuals who lose in a high-velocity workforce may need some legal and policy reforms. (I shall discuss retirement benefits and discrimination in chapters 11 and 12.) Status as an independent contractor, however, is not a good index of a need for any different legal protection. In short, independent contractor relations do not present any unusual problems in the economic or legal analysis of high-velocity labor markets. They are "flexible" relations, but not interestingly more flexible than relations of employment. They probably do not present any distinct issues of information.

Independent Contractors in Silicon Valley

The image of the "high-tech nomad" roaming "from company to company, attacking computer problems as a solo consultant," burst into media attention in the mid-1990s (Kanter 1995; Wysocki 1996). Two contrasting images appeared in the journalism. The successful consultants loved this way of working: they were in demand, made a fortune, constantly faced new challenges. They identified their work with their skills, craft, and technology and were happy to reject any loyalty to particular employers. A contrasting image then usually identified a stressful underside, in which the consultant yearned for a stable, steadier job with health insurance.

Part of the fascination of these images is the general fascination with short job tenures, the subject of this entire book. The contrast between the confident consultant and the stressed-out seeker of health insurance implicitly raises several questions addressed throughout this book. What drives the growth of a high-velocity labor market? Will those nomad jobs continue or eventually turn into more traditional jobs? Have the nomads chosen this existence or had it thrust upon them? Do these new nomad jobs reflect individuals' choices, or the incentives of the legal system? This chapter will try to focus only on the subset of issues raised by use of the legal form of self-employment or independent contracting.

It is important not to confuse this narrower inquiry with the larger inquiry into short-term jobs. As mentioned, most short-term jobs in Silicon

Valley are held by statutory "employees," enjoying all the legal privileges of employees.

The only statistical source for self-employment at the county level is the decennial census. The 2000 census revealed 52,302 self-employed individuals in Santa Clara County, around 6.2 percent of the workforce (U.S. Census 2000b: Table DP-3). This is the same number as in 1990, and thus a smaller percentage of the workforce (6.5 percent at that time) (Benner 1999: 12). This is almost identical to the national figure of 6.4 percent of the workforce who identified themselves as independent contractors, independent consultants, or freelance workers in the 2001 Supplement on Contingent and Alternative Work to the Current Population Survey (down from 6.7 percent in 1997 and 1995). California rates are higher: 9 percent of California's nonagricultural labor force was self-employed in 1999 (Austin, Mahoney, and Waskiewicz 2000). (It is a good idea to look only at the nonagricultural labor force, because the census category of self-employed includes farmers and ranchers along with "independent contractors" who render services for money. An "independent contractor" has jocularly been defined as a self-employed individual whom someone might consider an employee.)

Nationally, 83 percent of the self-employed prefer that arrangement to employee status. As a group, the self-employed are likelier than employees to be over thirty-five, white, male, and college graduates (BLS 2001).

The best, in-depth interviews with high-tech consultants, normally another term for the self-employed or independent contractors, suggest that they do indeed prefer working this way and would suffer from public policies that made independent contracting more difficult to arrange. Consider Kevin and Max, the 30-year-old freelance programmers in Po Bronson's *The Nudist on the Late Shift* (1999: 98–138). They are so much in demand that people starting companies use their names to reassure venture capitalists. They are frequently offered stock options and ownership shares that they routinely turn down, preferring to work at their hourly rate and spend the rest of their time flying or building airplanes. They always turn down employee positions, referring to offices as "cube farms" and themselves as "geeks" or "Contractor Boy." In the start-up observed by Bronson, launch date is jeopardized because Max refuses to reschedule a squirrel hunting trip in Tennessee with his cousin. We don't have to assume that Kevin and Max are typical; indeed the point of their story is that they are exceptionally well regarded. We should see though that they are very happy working as freelancers and could hardly be happier or more productive as employees, and we should think carefully about any proposals that would make it harder for them to work consistently as self-employed consultants.

A more systematic look at high-tech contractors is Kunda et al. (2002), interviewing fifty-two, of whom 58 percent worked in Silicon Valley. Their "underlying narrative of transformation" "begins with the lament of an expert for whom the tension between the ideal of technical rationality and the political reality of organizational life has become a source of simmering discontent" (p. 240). For them, discovering contingent work let them pursue the technical challenges they crave free of the organizational irrationality they detest. As contractors, they try to stay clear of organizational "politics" of companies, such as reorganizations and mergers, and managerial incompetence. Their values placed technical rationalism at the highest rung, so they were unsympathetic to financial or organizational obstacles to optimum technical performance. As independent contractors, they avoided involvement in company organizational "politics" and could largely define jobs in which they could pursue optimum technical performance. Only four subjects expressed a desire to return to employment as an employee; many, like Kevin and Max, had turned down such offers.

They also made a great deal more money than they would have as employees. When asked to work a twelve-hour day, they are paid at their hourly rate, working alongside salaried employees from whom such effort may be expected and who are not compensated extra for it [computer programmers are exempt from the provisions of the Fair Labor Standards Act requiring premium pay for overtime work, FLSA§13(17)]. Again, the sample is only of those who have chosen to work as contractors and so is not representative of all engineers or programmers. The point is that working as a contractor serves the needs of some firms and individuals; it is not necessary to decide that everyone should work this way.

Kunda's subjects are, by the way, entirely typical in seeing contracting as in their financial advantage. A salary survey conducted by Dice.com, a high-tech job board of EarthWeb, reported in the *Standard* for October 23, 2000, found that average salaries of information technology "consultants" are more than 40 percent higher than those of employees. The average salary for contract project managers was $123,521, while the highest-paid categories for employees and chief information or technology officers averaged $89,778. Kunda's subjects did point out three financial disadvantages in working as an independent contractor. You have to provide your own health insurance or forgo it; you are responsible for paying your own taxes and, while this provides opportunities to disguise income or inflate deductions (of which more later), it makes audits potentially costly; and you miss out on stock option compensation (discussed in chapter 10).

Kunda's subjects felt they had *more* job security than comparable employees. Most agreed with the technical writer who said:

Job security is the ability to get a job. Staff people don't have job security; you can be fired whenever the company likes. And they don't have the networks. They can't call someone and get a job tomorrow morning. They think they have job security but it's on paper. People don't realize that real job security is when you have a network of managers and recruiters where you simply call them and say, "OK my contract finished," and they say, "Great, I can place you somewhere tomorrow morning." The social reality is, the staff person has no connections to a next job. They don't have social relationships. They're isolated. A contractor has these relationships. That's real job security. That's the real game. (p. 251)

One may doubt that regular employees are really so isolated. In comparison with counterparts in Boston, they are quite networked (Saxenian 1994). Still, the contractors do probably have even better networks than the employees, though I know of no empirical literature making the comparison. The employees' "paper" job security, by the way, may be changed by employers at any time, so normally is not legally enforceable. During Silicon Valley's telecommunications boom, the old-line telephone company Pacific Bell had written policies securing stable careers. For example, managers had the right to reassignment and retraining, should their positions be eliminated. These were the years when PacBell managers who were any good were certainly approached about positions, potentially lucrative, in start-ups and newer firms developing wireless, digital, and other networks. Those who remained at PacBell undoubtedly valued its policies on job security and career stability, and must have felt betrayed when the California Supreme Court held that these might be revoked by the company at any time without legal liability (*Asmus v. Pacific Bell*).

Low-income workers in Silicon Valley, such as janitors and manufacturing workers, tend to be employees of temporary help agencies, often nominal (chapter 5), or labor contractors (chapter 8). Improving their lot might call for changed policies on joint employment, but does not raise issues of self-employment. They are rarely systematically classified as self-employed. The only potential advantages, to large Valley employers, in classifying janitors or manufacturing workers as self-employed, would be to defeat a union drive or avoid minimum labor standards. However, there are few union drives in the Valley. Most janitors at larger establishments are union members (chapter 9). It would not be surprising to encounter janitors or day laborers paid "off the books" in cash and reported to the Internal Revenue Service neither as employees nor independent contractors. These arrangements are largely limited to aliens not able to work legally.

When poor people in the Valley are self-employed, they normally really are self-employed, such as *paleteros* who sell popsicles (*paletas*) or sellers of jewelry or music tapes. Probably a majority of Mexican immigrant families have a member engaged in such informal economic activity (Zlolniski 1994: 2325–28). They are sometimes self-employed for the same reasons as are Kevin and Max (the computer programmers): they control their schedules, enjoy not being supervised, and make more money. Self-employment of this kind can provide income to an individual whose work as a manufacturing or janitorial employee is irregular.

Self-employment as an Economic and Social Institution

As mentioned, self-employment in the United States is close to its historic *low* as a percentage of the workforce, around 6.4 percent. Rates in Silicon Valley appear close to the national rate. This fact rarely appears in media treatment of "free agents," which usually state, incorrectly, that self-employment is "booming" or "exploding" or the like. At the beginning of the twentieth century, perhaps 25 percent of the workforce was self-employed. This figure dropped rapidly until around 1970, when it fell below 7 percent. It has been fairly stable, dropping slowly, ever since (Aronson 1991; Blau 1987). Some of the hoopla about free agents might more accurately be understood as referring to *employment* relations, which have indeed become shorter and less stable. However, *self-employment* is not a good proxy for this phenomenon. Since self-employment has been shrinking, it has obviously contributed nothing to recent job growth in the United States. (By contrast, in Canada, where payroll taxes are high, *all* net job creation in the 1990s was in relations of independent contracting; Manser and Picot [1996].)

Some "self-employment" does involve a relatively powerless individual and a more powerful customer, and suggests that the relationship might as easily have been structured as an employment relationship. For example, consider Arturo, the Mexican immigrant janitor turned *paletero* (Zlolniski 1994: 2326–28). Arturo pays the *paleta* factory 42 cents for each *paleta* sold. While in theory he might charge any price for them, *paletas* sell for a standard 75 cents, so Arturo keeps 33 cents. He also pays the factory $2 for cart rental and $2 for ice for each day he works. There are no formal agreements between the *paleteros* and the company. *Paleteros* work when they please and are paid in cash. No taxes are withheld by the factory or paid by the *paleteros*. Self-employed people have been included in Social Security since the 1950s, but Arturo is responsible for his own payments into it.

One can imagine labor market reforms that might help Arturo, but most of them would do so by benefiting all low-paid workers, rather than the self-employed as such. For example, he would benefit from health insurance, so long as it was not financed by a payroll tax that eliminated his job. His self-employed status is responsible for his exclusion from collective bargaining law. A union of self-employed *paleteros,* bargaining about the division of earnings, might well violate the antitrust laws. This makes good sense lest doctors, lawyers, or plumbers conspired to fix remuneration above-market rates. There would seem, however, to be little danger to the economy, and some benefit, in letting *paleteros* form an organization to negotiate with the factory. This might be accomplished by calling individuals in the bottom half or third of income distribution, or without capital invested in their work, "employees" for purposes of labor statutes irrespective of their status for purposes of tax laws. Given how few independent contractors in Silicon Valley are as poorly paid as Arturo, this book is not the place for development of such proposals.

What would happen if the law required that Arturo be treated as an employee for purposes of labor standards and tax laws? If the factory considered (or were required to consider) Arturo its employee, it might still hire him by the day or hour. It would have to keep records on his work hours, however, and would be liable if his earnings did not reach the minimum hourly wage. It would also have to withhold income tax from his pay. By contrast, since Arturo is self-employed, there are no limits on the hours he might work and no applicable minimum wage.

It is certainly possible that the factory calls Arturo self-employed in order to avoid labor standards or tax liability. In other cases, avoiding a labor union might also motivate the creation of self-employment. However, even in this simple case, there are advantages *to Arturo* in calling this self-employment. He pays no income tax or Social Security tax, though if he becomes retired or disabled in the United States, he will wish that he had paid the Social Security tax. And, of course he has a job, a flexible and adaptable one, that well might not be his if it had to observe wage and hours laws. In that case the *paleta* factory might demand a different kind of *paletero.*

Critics of self-employment (e.g., Linder 1989, 1992; Goldstein et al. 1999) have given prominence to such cases of "self-employment" of relatively low-paid and powerless individuals. It is therefore crucial to understanding the U.S. labor market generally, and Silicon Valley in particular, to understand that they are rare, not typical of low-wage labor (most of which is structured as relations of employment, perhaps temporary employment), and not typical of self-employment. The self-employed as a group are, as mentioned, disproportionately white, male, older, and college graduates. They earn more than traditional employees, overwhelmingly prefer working as self-employed, and do not, as a group, experience less job stability than regular full-time employees (BLS 2001, 1999; Houseman 1999; Houseman and Polivka 2000).

In other words, although the self-employed are excluded from most employment laws, they are rarely the sort of individuals who would present issues concerning minimum wage.

Legal and Policy Issues Concerning Self-employment

I do not wish to overemphasize the legal issues attached to self-employment. The basic story, as indicated, is that many people in Silicon Valley are self-employed; it is not difficult to create such relations; and most people in them are satisfied. The chief issues about self-employment involve some uncertainty as to how particular individuals should be classified, and the chief consequence of that uncertainty affects tax payment and recording, not labor standards. Nevertheless, legal tests for self-employment are famously vague. It is possible to imagine circumstances that might throw a spotlight on this underlying uncertainty, for example if the Internal Revenue Service once again went on a campaign against the self-employed, or unions seeking to represent programmers sought certification.

Defining "Employee" and "Independent Contractor"

Like "trade secrets," the concepts of "employee" and "independent contractor" were formulated in the old economy. In their case, however, the old economy was that of the late eighteenth century. The distinction arose in the law of accidents (what lawyers call "tort" law) to answer the question of when the person who hired a cart driver would be liable if the driver drove negligently and caused harm ("vicarious liability"). The answer was to examine a series of factors to determine who, the master or the driver, controlled the "means and manner" of the driver's work. If, for example, the master owned and maintained the cart and horse, determined what stops it would make, in what order, and under what time constraints, it is both fair and efficient under any theory of torts to hold the master liable if something goes wrong. If, by contrast, the driver made all these decisions himself, and the hiring party merely paid a set fee to deliver a particular item, it is fair and efficient to hold only the driver liable for his torts. Thus, determining the means and manner by which work is controlled, and doing so by examining multiple factors (ownership of equipment, other capital investment, ability to take other work), makes excellent sense in order to answer the question it was originally supposed to answer (Linder 1989: 133–146; Carlson 2001). (Deakin [1998, 2001] has instead emphasized the evolution of this control test in the context of interpretation of employment statutes.)

Congress is free to legislate concerning both employees and independent contractors and could include both groups in any legislation it passes. For example, both groups pay income tax, though the procedures and liability differ, and both are included in Social Security. However, most labor and employment legislation is written so as to apply only to "employees." The Supreme Court has held that this term, if used without further definition, means "common law" employees: that is, those who, on examination of multiple factors, do not, on balance, control the means and manner of their employment. This approach originated in the interpretation of the National Labor Relations (Wagner) Act of 1935, governing employee organization. There it reflects fairly clear congressional intent, expressed in the Taft-Hartley amendments of 1947, and also some antitrust policy, since difficult questions of restraint of trade would be raised if the federal government were free to certify unions of self-employed businessmen or professionals, setting uniform rates for their services.

However, the approach has been carried forward into more recent employment legislation, where it makes no sense at all. No reason has ever been given why a contracting party must be legally privileged to hire independent contractors on the basis of their race, religion, or sex; or to sexually harass independent contractors; or to withhold pension payments to an independent contractor in order to coerce some other conduct. None of these actions would be legal as to an employee. They would violate the Civil Rights Act of 1964 and the Employee Retirement Income Security Act of 1974, respectively. Nevertheless, until Congress provides otherwise, they are lawful as to independent contractors.

The use of the preindustrial "common-law" standards to define the reach of contemporary employment (and tax, as we shall see) statutes has three nonobvious consequences. First, an employer is not entirely free to create whichever relation it chooses. An employer (such as Microsoft) may tell technical writers (for example) that they are independent contractors; they may agree to this status; their income may be reported to the IRS on form 1099; and yet they may be statutory "employees." Second, should litigation arise over these issues, courts give no particular deference to the rulings of administrative agencies such as the Internal Revenue Service, National Labor Relations Board, or Department of Labor. The determination of employee status is a "common-law" decision as to which judges are competent and on which agencies are said to have no particular expertise. Third, "employees" are defined as people who do not control their work, following the orders of others. While, as we have seen, this definition originated long before Taylorist work organization separating conception from execution, it fit well with such jobs. By contrast, professionals and other individuals with substantial work control, such as university professors, may not be statutory "employees" but rather managers whom employers may keep out of unions (*NLRB v. Yeshiva University*; Klare 1983).

As we have seen, there are many workers in the new economy, as in the old, who present difficult cases of classification under the "common law" "means and manner" test. Almost all knowledge workers exercise sufficient control over their work so that they might be hired as independent contractors. It is also possible in particular cases (such as Microsoft's) that they were sufficiently under the employer's control as to be "employees." Their classification issues so far rarely arise under labor and employment statutes, because few are paid minimum wage, few form unions or experience discrimination that they care to remedy, and few have retirement income that can be appropriated by employers. If any of these things changed, there would be problems applying these employment and labor statutes to programmers and technical writers, as there already are with the truck drivers whose status is more frequently litigated. However, the distinction has arisen in the context of tax legislation, and this has recently (in the famous *Vizcaino v. Microsoft* litigation) begun to affect, in ways still uncertain, the law of work.

The Distinction Applied to Tax Collection

The principal economic impact of the institution of self-employment is probably reduced tax revenues. Computer programmers are an excellent example. Self-employed people are supposed to assess their own income tax and Social Security payments and mail them in. They thus have many more opportunities than employees to disguise or conceal income and thus pay no tax on it.

This is not simply a cynical observation by a critic of U.S. tax administration. It is an accepted and articulated part of the congressional budget process. For example, a provision of the tax laws makes it marginally more difficult to class computer programmers as self-employed, by denying them and their clients/employers use of some very simplified rules that others could normally use to establish self-employed status. [Revenue Act of 1978, §530 sets out the rules; §530(d), added in 1986, excludes engineers, designers, drafters, computer programmers, systems analysts, and similarly skilled workers.] This statute by itself is not particularly effective. As we have seen, thousands of such individuals in Silicon Valley are self-employed under conventional tests. However, the IRS has occasionally aggressively audited self-employed individuals, for example in the early 1990s. The combination of such audits, with the deprivation to programmers of the simplified rules, acted at that time to discourage them from self-employment.

Their exclusion from the simplified method of establishing self-employed status was a 1986 congressional deal. IBM sought a tax break for its overseas operations. While Congress was happy to grant the tax relief, congressional budgeting procedures required that the revenue loss be offset by a revenue increase. Since it is universally accepted that employees cheat less on their taxes than the self-employed, Congress estimated that, by classifying some programmers as employees, an additional $60 million would be raised over five years, enough to offset the break that IBM received (Johnston 1998). The reader might naively suppose that classifying programmers as employees would be inconvenient for businesses that would then have to pay time-and-a-half for workweeks exceeding forty hours, as programmers' often do. This potential problem was eliminated by simultaneously removing computer programmers from this aspect of the Fair Labor Standards Act [FLSA §13(17)].

The Department of the Treasury estimates that approximately $2.6 billion is lost each year in unpaid Social Security, Medicare, and federal unemployment insurance taxes because employees are misclassified as independent contractors. The same misclassification is responsible for an annual loss of $1.6 billion in income tax underpayment.

By contrast, consequences for an employer of such misclassification, contrary to the *New York Times* article cited at the beginning of this chapter, are normally minimal. Under §530, the statute mentioned before that simplifies claims to independent contractor status, the IRS may not collect back taxes, or even require reclassification of the workers, if the employer had ever been audited and not cited for misclassification, or if its misclassification is practiced by at least a quarter of employers in its industry (Revenue Act of 1978, §530, as amended in 1996).

"Employees" and "Independent Contractors" in the Law of New Economy Work Relations

The famous litigation involving Microsoft's permatemps (*Vizcaino v. Microsoft*) began as an IRS audit that determined that many individuals whom Microsoft had been treating as either independent contractors, or employees of temporary agencies, really worked under Microsoft's direction and were thus its employees for tax purposes. Microsoft agreed that its "independent contractors" were really employees, consented to their reclassification, and agreed to pay both back taxes and any overtime for which these employees should have been compensated. These were no small concessions by Microsoft. Had it asserted its rights under §530, the IRS could probably not have required any of this, since Microsoft would have been able to show such misclassification to be industry practice, hence in good faith for purposes of the tax laws. Most of the affected individuals were not programmers or systems analysts, so Microsoft might have been able to use §530. Indeed, some observers attribute Microsoft's distinction between permanent and temporary workers to its programmer culture in which "hackers and other hardcore software employees were at the heart of the company—and everyone else was, in one sense or another, temporary" (Lieber 2000).

In the subsequent lawsuit under employment laws, as a consequence, Microsoft conceded that the plaintiffs were common-law employees, and the courts never decided whether such a finding by the IRS would necessarily apply to labor and employment statutes. As mentioned in chapter 5, the only employment law consequence of this finding was that Microsoft had to include them in one very unusual stock purchase plan that few employers have ever adopted or will in the future. Even employees may lawfully be excluded from health insurance, pension, or 401(k) plans. So it is not likely that there will be many more suits by individuals classed as independent contractors who claim they are employees. In most cases, they will not have the benefit of either an IRS audit or an employer concession that they are employees; most employers will assert rights under §530; and few employers have the only kind of benefit plan into which all employees must be included.

One of the few lasting results of the *Vizcaino* litigation is the boost it gave to the business of "consultant brokerage firms," the labor market intermediaries who help recruit and place independent contractors. Many employers who previously hired consultants directly have become convinced by vague coverage of the Microsoft litigation, and articles like the *New York Times* article quoted at the beginning of this chapter, that they should use intermediaries instead (Benner 2000).

Intellectual Property Applications

It is possible that some relations of independent contracting are driven by the issues of ownership of intellectual property discussed in chapters 2 through 4. Merges (1999) asserts that the inventions and other information developed by independent contractors are normally their own property, as opposed to the information developed by employees, normally patentable or copyrightable by the employer. I was unable to find any examples of intellectual property concerns driving the creation of particular relations as those either of employment or consulting. Instead, as I tried to point out in those chapters, there is probably little practical difference in the intellectual property consequences of hiring a consultant rather than an employee, at least in information technology in California. In any state, the employer has the right to use the innovations of a consultant, either by contract, or through the application of the "shop rights" doctrine giving the employer a license to such innovations made using its facilities and equipment. The Federal Telegraph Company, as we saw in chapter 1, retained such shop rights in the inventions of its departed employees Cyril Elwell and Lee de Forest. The "shop rights" doctrine applies to the innovations of independent contractors (*Crowe*; *Franklyn*).

A distinction will arise if the employer tries to patent the invention of the consultant (the issue that concerns Merges). This is more important in some industries than in information technology. In information technology, speedy access to the innovation is more important than patent. At the same time, as I showed in chapter 2, in Silicon Valley, due to favorable law on noncompetes and trade secrets, employees are normally as free as independent contractors to depart their employer and trade on the information they learned or developed. It is possible that further empirical work will discover interesting differences between employees as a group, and consultants as a group, in diffusing or even creating valuable information. However, if any such differences exist, I would expect to find them outside of California information technology, in industries in which patentability is more important, and in jurisdictions that enforce employees' covenants not to compete.

We may thus leave further discussion of self-employment to discussions of tax policy, or advocates for the few employees who are disadvantaged by abusive exclusion from collective bargaining or minimum wage laws. While much has been written (some by this author, Hyde 2000) about the line between employees and independent contractors, such a discussion would not help in understanding Silicon Valley's high-velocity labor market. In Silicon Valley, although there are thousands of independent contractors who enjoy that status, their numbers are not remarkable by national standards. They are still a relatively small segment of the much broader high-velocity labor market. They present no distinct or difficult issues of law or policy, for which courts or policymakers need new economic analysis. Employers are largely free to hire genuine independent contractors like Kevin and Max, who work for many firms and control their own schedules. If employers guess wrong and misclassify an employee as an independent contractor, the consequences are rarely severe, if the employer is in good faith or, as will usually be true in the Valley, observing industry practice.

7

H-1B VISAS

The H-1B visa program, heavily employed in Silicon Valley, issues three-year visas, renewable once, to skilled foreign workers who take jobs with particular U.S. employers. The modal H-1B is a computer programmer from India (which provides almost half of all H-1Bs), twenty-eight years old and earning around $45,000 a year (USGAO 2000), perhaps sharing a house in Sunnyvale or Fremont with seven or eight other H-1Bs. The program is controversial, and there has been much speculation as to what would happen if the number of such visas were cut back from the current 195,000 per year to 65,000 (the minimum to which the United States is committed by treaty) or even lower. Employers would presumably react through some combination of the following three responses: they would outsource more programming to overseas locations; they would hire programmers already able to work in the United States as citizens or permanent residents; or they might forgo certain activities. Nobody has a very good idea which response would prevail.

I want to suggest in this chapter that this uncertainty reflects dominant paradigms in labor economics, in which something like an H-1B visa is normally understood, criticized, or defended as a particular instance of flexible employment contracting. That is, employers hire "labor," and if it is cheaper, they hire more of it. Certainly the H-1B visa permits employers to hire lots of cheap programming. However, our economic analysis should include from the outset the perspectives of the economics of information.

Thinking about labor migration is a good way to see how the economics of endogenous growth through information creation and diffusion can explain things that cannot be explained either by (1) flexibility paradigms; (2) human capital theories, or (3) other models of employment that emphasize longevity (such as life-cycle theories). Why does the Silicon Valley employer choose to employ an engineer in Silicon Valley whom it might just as well have employed in Bangalore? Explanations in terms of "flexible" labor contracting, or "human capital," or "efficiency wages" do not explain this.

Paying a programmer $45,000 a year, and acquiring no enforceable obligations to him or her, is as flexible as it gets for employers, even as compared with other Silicon Valley labor contracts, such as hiring an independent contractor or an employee of a temp agency. But it is not more flexible than outsourcing the work to an Indian contractor. The H-1B program is often criticized as a device for lowering the price of labor. But programmers on an H-1B visa, however poorly paid by Silicon Valley standards, are making more than they would have in India, or they would never have migrated in the first place (and indeed interviews with the programmers confirm this). So, as with permatemps and independent contractors, "flexibility" does not explain much about H-1B visas, at least in comparison with other "flexible" forms of hiring programming services.

Similarly, a graduate of one of the Indian institutes of technology has acquired a particular store of human capital, for those who like that particular concept-metaphor. But while the contents of his head are the same in Silicon Valley as in Bangalore, his "human capital" is not worth the same amount. The concept-metaphor "human capital" misleads. In classical economics, assets are normally worth more in markets in which they are scarce. Human capital is just the opposite. It is normally worth more in a market in which there are lots of other sellers of quality human capital, which is why human capital migrates from regions of low human capital to regions of high human capital (Lucas 1988). People who have more use for the "human capital" concept-metaphor than I do can fiddle (and have fiddled) with their models to reflect this "anomalous" feature of human (as opposed to other) capital. (We might say that labor markets display "supply side network effects.") But at some point "human" capital will become so "anomalous" that one might as well abandon what was only an analogy to conventional capital as an input in production.

Finally, this entire book is a critique or supplement of models of employment that emphasize the lifetime stability of employment contracts. While such models do not explain much about a high-velocity labor market, they have particular difficulty with immigration. At least, permatemp relations might be explained as a kind of probation period leading to more stable employment, and this does occur, although not in the majority of cases. But from the perspective of lifetime employment, bringing an engineer from India to Silicon Valley on a temporary visa forgoes all of the supposed advantages that an employer realizes from the employment relationship.

Obviously the starting point for a new law and economics of immigration must include the perspectives discussed in chapter 3—that is, the economics of endogenous growth through information creation and diffusion, and the economics of agglomeration in geographic districts. This supplements, not replaces, conventional labor economics accounts, and is the only way of explaining why the same programmer is worth more in Silicon Valley than in Bangalore.

Foreign-Born Labor in Information Technology

Heavy use of foreign-born scientists and engineers distinguishes the United States from other countries' high-tech sectors, and Silicon Valley from other U.S. high-tech regions.

Nationally, foreign-born scientists and engineers make up about 17 percent of the workforce in information technology (National Research Council 2001: 156), despite comprising around 11 percent of the U.S. population. (The studies cited in this chapter employ different definitions of "high technology" or "information technology" and different data sources. The differences do not matter for my purposes.) Most of these scientists and engineers are either naturalized U.S. citizens or hold permanent resident status (Ellis and Lowell 1999: III-2). No other country in the world absorbs such high numbers or percentages of foreign-born, though anti-immigrant sentiment is a potent political force in many countries with smaller numbers. At the other extreme lies Japan, where a vital high-tech sector employs only a negligible number of employees not born in Japan. Within the United States, Silicon Valley historically employs twice the percentage of foreign-born scientists and engineers as the high-tech district around Boston's Route 128 (Alarcón 1999: 1385). Unfortunately these figures have not been released from the 2000 Census. In 1990, one-third of the Valley's scientists and engineers were foreign-born (Saxenian 1999a: 11). Many observers expect that figure to have risen to about one-half by 2000 (e.g., Matloff n.d.: 83).

Critics of the practice characterize foreign-born labor as inexpensive, which it is, but this is obviously inadequate as an explanation either of U.S. practice generally or Silicon Valley's in particular. The U.S. story also involves some combination of high demand for labor of all kinds, including scientists and engineers; receptive laws and culture; and inadequate numbers and preparation of U.S.-born scientists and engineers. Katherine Stone (personal communication) has pointed out an additional reason, rarely discussed: the small U.S. welfare state (by European standards) can be extended to newcomers without raising such difficult issues of inclusion or diffusion. Efforts have been made to untangle these explanations, but for my purposes it is enough to note their coexistence.

The heavy foreign-born presence in Silicon Valley reflects two additional factors. First, the San Francisco Bay Area has a tradition of immigration, particularly from Asia and Latin America, certainly as distinguished from the high-tech districts around Austin, northern Virginia, or North Carolina. (Texas, the second largest state, is not even in the top twelve for employment of foreign-born workers in information technology; Ellis and Lowell [1999: III-3].) Migration to Silicon Valley in the first place, like most immigration, normally reflects social networks rather than classical economic factors, and the Valley's networks to Asia and Latin America are already quite dense (Alarcón 1999: 1394).

Second is the theme of this book. The Valley's high-velocity labor market not only creates demand for all kinds of labor, it enables a kind of career across firm boundaries that is particularly appealing to immigrants, who heavily start businesses of their own (as we will examine more closely in chapter 12; see Saxenian [1999a]). Start-ups are further enabled by the Valley's location in global production networks that make Silicon Valley contacts valuable to people who return home (or intend to) to start businesses in India, Taiwan, or China. While some aspects of formal immigration law appear incompatible with Silicon Valley's high-velocity labor market, the interesting story is how that market has been able to route around them.

Legal Modes of Employing the Foreign-Born

The procedures created by U.S. immigration laws to permit foreign nationals to work in the United States as permanent residents are incompatible with high tech's high-velocity labor markets and have been substantially supplemented by such other visas as student, intracompany transfers, and the controversial H-1B visa for "specialty occupation" skilled workers.

Award of permanent resident status ("green card") is slow, limited by country, and arbitrary and unpredictable from the point of view of employers and immigrants. Awards of permanent residence to individuals sponsored by employers might by law reach 140,000 a year, but in recent years the Immigration and Naturalization Service (INS) issues fewer than half that number annually. (Compare the slow pace of awarding permanent residence status to skilled employees sponsored by employers, with the sheer numbers of recent immigration. The 2000 Census counted 11 million foreign-born persons in the United States who had not been there in 1990; the real number is undoubtedly higher.) Permanent residents must have a skilled job, which the Department of Labor has certified to be without interest for U.S. workers, and for which employment of an alien will not adversely affect wages and working conditions of similarly employed U.S. workers. Armed with this certification (fairly routine in information technology and high tech), the employer and employee may then file a petition for permanent resident status. The petition may cover immediate family members, but they count against the 140,000 (so that figure results in considerably fewer workers). Award of permanent resident status is limited by country of origin. No more than 7 percent of green cards may go to applicants from any one country, even if that country is China or India. Earlier applications get priority for those countries, and the wait list is long. A green card is not automatic or fully predictable. At best the process takes two or three years, but for Indians or Chinese will take at least five or six; eight- or ten-year periods are not unusual (National Research Council 2001: 159). In information technology, this is a process that can reward employees of demonstrated ability, but cannot be used for recruiting, given rapid employee turnover and hiring on the basis of short-term needs, as employers have testified (National Research Council 2001: 171).

Instead, Silicon Valley employers make heavy use of other visas ("nonimmigrant" visas in the arcane and inaccurate parlance of the Immigration and Naturalization Service) that may be processed more quickly, such as intracompany transfers and special "NAFTA" visas for Canadians and Mexicans. Indians, Chinese, Israelis, Filipinos, and others often hold H-1B visas. I have never spoken to anyone in the Valley whose firm does not make heavy use of these. The H-1B visa is for "nonimmigrants" (who may, and often do, intend to pursue permanent immigration in the future) with needed job skills. (Intent to migrate both temporarily and permanently is known as "dual intent" in INS parlance and is not allowed under any temporary visa other than the H-1B.) Immigration law since 1952 has had an "H-1 nonimmigrant category" to assist U.S. employers who need temporary workers. The H-1B category for specialty occupations was created in 1990 and limited at the time to 65,000 visas annually. Congress has repeatedly reauthorized the program, most recently in 2000, authorizing 195,000 H-1B visas annually, effective for six years. (The United States is now committed by treaty, the General Agreement on Trade in Services, to admit at least 65,000 a year under this program.)

To obtain an H-1B visa, the employer (who may be a temporary help agency) must obtain certification from the Department of Labor for employment at particular jobs and salaries. The employer must attest, as with certification for permanent immigration, that prevailing wages will be paid and wages and working conditions of similar employees will not be adversely affected. However, unlike the application for permanent immigration, the employer need not show that U.S. workers are unavailable for the job. The employer must give a copy of the application to the H-1B worker, its employees' union (if any), and post it at the workplace. However, the application is not a contract enforceable by any of these individuals. By law, the Department of Labor has only seven days to decide whether to certify the employer's application, and may review it "only for completeness and obvious inaccuracies." As a result, 93 percent of applications are approved (and the remainder mostly approved on resubmission; U.S. GAO 2000: 19; Barnow, Trutko, and Lerman 1998: 75).

Department officials told the General Accounting Office (GAO) that they must approve prevailing wages that they know to be incorrect unless the employer's source for determining the prevailing wage is obviously inaccurate on its face. After the Department of Labor approves the Labor Condition Application, the employer files it and a petition with the INS containing information about the employer and worker. It also pays $610 in fees, which are used for grants and scholarships to train U.S. workers (discussed in chapter 12). Approval usually takes six to eight weeks. Around 91 percent of petitions are approved by the initial INS staff "adjudicator," and most of the rest are eventually approved by supervisors (GAO 2000: 26). Approval is so routine that in 1999 the INS discovered it had approved more than the allowable number of visas (GAO 2000: 28).

Statistical information on H-1B visa holders as a group is limited essentially to a single random survey conducted by the INS of 4,200 people admitted between May 1998 and July 1999 (GAO 2000; National Research Council 2001). Of that group, 56.7 percent worked in computer-related occupations, mostly systems analysts and programmers. (As recently as 1992, only around 6,000 H-1B visas were approved for information technology–related occupations [GAO 2000: 14].) Nearly one-half of the total H-1B group (47.5 percent) and almost three-quarters of the workers approved for information technology jobs were from India. China was the second largest sender of H-1Bs, making up 9.3 percent of the total group. Median salary for all H-1Bs was $47,000 a year. Student visas had previously been held by 22.9 percent of the computer-related group. The National Research Council study estimates that around 255,000 H-1B holders work in the core information technology workforce.

There is unfortunately no good data on the precise jobs that these programmers and systems analysts perform, and therefore no way to be certain how those jobs would be performed if the H-1B program were cut back or eliminated. The literature reflects two, somewhat contradictory, images.

One is that H-1Bs are used because of their specific recent training in new, hot programming languages such as Java and C++. (In the above-cited INS survey, the median age of an H-1B visa holder approved to work in information technology was 27.4 years [GAO 2000: 15].) Professor Norman Matloff of the Computer Science Department at the University of California at Davis, the most prominent academic critic of the H-1B program, makes just this charge (Matloff n.d.: 62–68). He frequently circulates to his e-mail list advertisements for programmers, requiring extraordinarily specific experience in particular applications of particular programs, and essentially requiring that the position be filled by an H-1B. This fits well with what the Stanford Project on Emerging Companies (chapter 1) calls an "engineering" model of personnel practices—the most common model among Silicon Valley start-ups and possibly Valley employers generally—in which employees are hired for specific skills at hiring, motivated by the challenge of work and peer control, and leave after eighteen months. Matloff thinks this is an inefficient way to obtain programming services, and that employers would be better off selecting clever programmers, hiring them for the long haul, and retraining them as new languages or applications emerge. While this book cannot show that this is wrong, few Valley employers see the advantages in such employment arrangements. Matloff is swimming against a tide that is far broader than just the H-1B program. One may therefore doubt that, even if the H-1B visa program were completely abolished, many employers would obtain Java programming by retraining their late career senior programmers (if any). They might hire recent graduates of less prestigious institutions. (I will show in chapter 12 that the demand for specific skills at hiring is simultaneously efficient for employers, meritocratic, and generates disparate labor market outcomes by race and age.)

A second image starts from the observation that programming covers a range of tasks. There is a big difference among high-level design of software; lower-level coding that may be broken into pieces and farmed out to inexpensive job shops in Bangalore; and the lowest end, at which the distinction between programmer and user becomes blurred as users use packaged software to write simple programs on personal computers (Ellis and Lowell 1999: I-3–4). While no one has a good picture of where H-1Bs fall on this spectrum, an engineer named John Ryskamp has claimed that H-1Bs increasingly perform routine application of "canned" software products. Such products may be applied by "software engineers" who "never even see, much less write, an algorithm" (Ryskamp n.d.: 2). Ryskamp claims that the Department of Labor will approve a Labor Certification Application, and the INS will approve an H-1B petition, for positions involving as little as a year of coursework in computer applications (much less theoretically intensive than computer science) (Ryskamp n.d.: 2). If this is correct, employers deprived of these H-1Bs would presumably replace them with other young people who had undertaken such brief training in computer applications. Ryskamp's analysis is not quantitative and is somewhat inconsistent with the educational attainment of existing H-1Bs, nearly all (98 percent) of whom have a bachelor's degree or higher, 41 percent of whom overall hold advanced degrees (35 percent of those working in information technology) (GAO 2000: 15). (By contrast, less than half of total U.S. computer scientists, computer engineers, systems analysts, and programmers have bachelor's or higher degrees with major or minor concentrations in information technology [Ellis and Lowell 1999: II-1].) However, Ryskamp has undoubtedly observed something true about programming and deserving of further research.

Critiques of the H-1B Program: Employers, Visa Holders, Abolitionists

Employer groups dominate the legislative process around H-1B visas, and this has resulted in visas that permit them to hire skilled labor on short order for salaries well below the prevailing rate for programmers, certainly in Silicon Valley. Employers still complain that the process is slow and somewhat unpredictable (National Research Council 2001: 171).

Visa holders have different complaints, some expressed through an organization called the Immigrants' Support Network (discussed in chapter 9) and others expressed individually to journalists and researchers. The program effectively creates indentured servitude with specific employers, particularly in connection with the process of acquiring permanent resident status; it makes it difficult for visa holders to change jobs and impossible for them to be self-employed; and subjects them to a real possibility that work will not be there for them (and they will be unable to obtain other work).

H-1B visas bind workers to employers, often for six years, while imposing no reciprocal obligations on the employer. The visa requires employer action and labor certification. It is not issued simply to an individual and may not be issued to a self-employed individual. Many if not most H-1Bs hope that their employers will sponsor them for permanent residence. Since that process normally takes around five years for an Indian, the employer must effectively initiate that process in the first year of H-1B employment, lest the H-1B be subject to deportation at the end of six years. The result is that the H-1B is effectively stuck with that employer for six years. Taking a different job, or being fired, may upset the permanent resident process or even be grounds for terminating the H-1B visa itself. (INS officials have been understanding during the recent round of layoffs in high technology and have not moved quickly to deport H-1B visa holders.)

The visa holder will certainly be docile and uncomplaining during the process, even if the employer is paying less than the promised wage, or has reneged on other promises. Such abuses are not rare. Despite these incentives for visa holders not to complain, some 135 to 140 complained about labor conditions to the Department of Labor in each of fiscal years 1999 and 2000. The department conducts investigations in twenty-five to thirty-five such cases each year. Violations were found in 83 percent of these—twice the rate under other employment standards investigations—and over $2 million in back pay was awarded to visa holders (GAO 2000: 21–22). These numbers are not large in comparison with the number of visas approved, varying in recent years between 65,000 and 195,000. Still, it took considerable courage for those victimized by employment law violations to complain at all.

Of course, California bans covenants in which employees agree not to compete with employers. A California court has recently applied this statute to an employee on an H-1B visa. His employment contract with a temp agency prohibited departing employees from joining clients, and required that any departing worker reimburse the agency for administrative, travel, and legal costs. The court voided these provisions as inconsistent with California's statutory ban on covenants not to compete (*Joshi v. Compubahn, Inc.*). While this decision will presumably dispose of such formal, contractual restrictions on employee mobility, the informal and practical restrictions, namely, the need not to upset the employer who is sponsoring one's green card, continue.

Visa holders also complain about "benching," the practice of not employing or paying the visa holder until work is available. In one case, far from unique, software engineer Biswajit De, a twenty-eight-year-old engineering graduate with four years of experience in India, came to Silicon Valley in February 2001, sponsored by JBAS Systems, Inc., a Santa Clara temp agency (often called a "body shop"). By May he had interviewed for only one job and been paid a total of $6,000 by JBAS. After he told his story to *India-West,* he was paid back salary and given a one-way ticket back to India (Sundaram 2001). De was wise to go the media (on advice of the Immigrants' Support Network), because such "benching" is expressly authorized by immigration law. (Labor standards laws require only that De be paid minimum wage on jobs to which he should be referred—overtime laws, as we have seen, do not apply to programmers—not that he actually be referred.) "Benching" is thought to be more common among such temporary help agencies ("body shops"), who may be "employers" of H-1B visa holders, though it is not limited to them.

Finally, a more radical critique seeks to abolish or radically trim the entire H-1B program, on the grounds that, if companies could not hire H-1Bs, they would be forced to hire U.S. citizens and permanent residents. (In press summaries of their position, this is often abbreviated as a demand to hire "Americans." These critics of the H-1B program justly complain that this attributes to them a xenophobia that they lack. They would be happy to see jobs filled by permanent residents, naturalized citizens of foreign birth, or anyone, of any nationality, who was both free to challenge his employer and was not depressing salaries for other workers.) Critics suggest that employers, deprived of H-1B visas, would be able to find plenty of programmers, including older programmers and graduates of less prestigious U.S. institutions, though they would have to pay these individuals more than $45,000 a year. The most prominent academic critic of the H-1B program is Norman Matloff; his constantly updated Web page is an invaluable source of information. This group is not well organized and has not historically received much if any support from professional associations or organized labor. Indeed, organized labor has not opposed the H-1B program as such, although the Communication Workers of America called for its repeal in June 2002 (Vaas 2002). I will suggest in chapter 9, when we take up employee organization, that organized labor may have a brighter future among the H-1Bs, who already have an organization (the Immigrants' Support Network), than among older programmers and systems analysts who never joined unions in the first place.

I will evaluate the entire program after setting out an economic analysis drawing on our models of endogenous growth. However, before doing so, I can state briefly that the numbers simply do not add up to support the claim that U.S. citizens and permanent residents are available to fill the quarter of a million jobs in information technology currently held by holders of H-1B visas. Despite numerous anecdotes of age discrimination in information technology (considered in more depth in chapter 12 on discrimination), such anecdotes are rarely followed by successful litigation challenging age discrimination (never, in Silicon Valley, where there appear to be no successful reported or unreported age-discrimination suits in high technology).

There are few systematic differences in the labor market experience of displaced older and younger information technology workers, according to an analysis prepared by Professor Henry Farber of Princeton for the National Research Council. Over 80 percent of either displaced group typically finds a new, full-time job in information technology within three years (National Research Council 2001: 143). Unemployment rates among programmers are simply too small to suggest that a quarter million, or anything like it, have been replaced by H-1Bs. For the argument to be plausible, Ryskamp would have to be on to something big—that is, it would have to be the case that H-1Bs were largely performing canned applications or other tasks that could be performed by individuals after a year or so of training.

Economic Analysis of Nonimmigrant Visas

Throughout this book, we have seen courts struggle to make sense of legal concepts that last made sense in an older labor market of stable careers, and fit poorly today's high-velocity labor markets. I have shown that this is true of "trade secrets," "employee," and "employer," and we will soon see the same of "employee organization" and "discrimination." Immigration law is mordantly interesting because of its reliance on concepts that make no sense under any known system of economics.

This is true of the crucial concept of "labor shortage," which in different ways is supposed to underlie awarding both permanent resident status and nonimmigrant H-1B visas. Economists do not normally assume that there could possibly be shortages in a well-functioning market. Of course, labor markets do not adjust as quickly as neoclassical markets for widgets. If exogenous technological developments have created sudden demand for programmers, new programmers will not appear suddenly from warehouses. (Again, this book tries to apply to legal problems models of *endogenous* technological change in which legal and economic systems themselves can be used to encourage those very technological developments and demands for programmers. This paragraph is trying to capture a classical analysis that the book normally tries to supplement.) Still, many of the jobs that are actually performed by H-1B holders do not require years of training. So, unless regulation prevents this, labor markets should be able to adjust to meet at least some demand for programmers.

Of course, this simple classical model cannot tell us whether our baseline labor market must include unlimited immigration, no immigration, or something in between. Is the classical labor market one of unlimited migration across borders, in which immigration law of any kind is "rent seeking" by incumbents that prohibits speedy adjustment of labor markets? Or is the classical labor market normally defined by national boundaries, so it is the admission of 195,000 H-1Bs a year that represents "rent seeking" by (or a "subsidy" to) employers? Both sides in this debate can (and do) tell a story of a self-regulating, efficient labor market undone by political interference! Employer defenses of the H-1B program that rest on a supposed "labor shortage" may work in Congress, but no objective assessment has ever found such a general "shortage" of information technology workers, though there are occasional "tight" markets for particularly hot skills (Computing Research Association 1999: Ch. 4; Ellis and Lowell 1999; U.S Department of Commerce Office of Technology Policy 1999; Barnow, Trutko, and Lerman 1998).

Like other critics of Silicon Valley's "flexible" labor markets, critics of H-1B visas have internalized many assumptions of traditional internal labor markets. In their case, the assumptions are unusually explicit, for example in the suggestion of Matloff and others that employers retain and retrain older programmers. If the case against H-1B visas is just another iteration of the debate about flexible labor relations, there is no basis for second-guessing employers. Those that will benefit from long-term careers and internal labor markets (for example, Intel, particularly at its facilities outside the Valley) will create those jobs, and those that will not, will not. Immigration is not an interesting problem in the "flexibility" debate, and that debate does not provide strong grounds for selecting any number of H-1B visas between 65,000 and 195,000, or indeed higher or lower than that range.

Finally, if we understand the H-1B visa and accompanying temp agencies as devices for hiring $45,000 programming, the issue immediately arises why employers would not just outsource the work to contractors or subsidiaries in India. The H-1B program, though well tailored for employer needs (and not by accident), still imposes costs (of applications) and uncertainty that could be avoided by assigning the same programming jobs to programmers physically in India. The value of software exported from India in fact grew 52 percent annually in the 1990s, amounting to billions annually, much of it from software technology parks fostered under the government's Software Technology Parks of India (STPI) initiative (the largest of which is in Bangalore), much by subsidiaries of U.S. and European companies (including IBM, Oracle, Digital Equipment, Novell, Texas Instruments, Unisys, HP, Apple, Honeywell, Citibank, Alcatel, and Motorola) (Arora, Arunachalam, Asundi, and Fernandes 2001; Sharpe 2001: 226). On the one hand, why do Silicon Valley employers ever import an H-1B rather than outsourcing his work to India? If we knew why employers used H-1B visas in the first place, we might have a better sense of how they would react if those visas became more expensive to them—for example, if they had to pay the genuinely prevailing wage for programmers.

Let us turn instead to the perspectives of endogenous growth theory. On this view, an H-1B visa is a device for increasing the value, short- and long-term, of an Asian software engineer. That increased value is not necessarily at the expense of another employee (though it might be). In endogenous growth models, information contributes to growth, so a particular organization of work might actually create growth, instead of merely redistributing it.

In a labor-information market, individuals are worth more because they work together with other individuals. We have already seen a number of ways in which this is true. Individuals are worth more in one place (Silicon Valley) than another (Bangalore) because they share information, or have particular incentives stemming from the temporary nature of their employment, or because of efficiencies resulting from convergence on particular protocols or diagnoses.

Which of these explains bringing in a programmer? I would suggest that this is an important research question. Intuitively, team production and supervision problems, and incentive effects, seem more important than information spillover effects. In Silicon Valley, the programmer will work in teams that will bring out better effort, or smarter effort, or simply induce extraordinary hours.

There must also be agency or supervision problems that are easier in the Valley than over the Web. I have not located any ethnographies of Indian software developers, nor did the budget for this book permit such research, but suggestive is the interesting brief participant's account of life in an Irish firm performing work under contract to a Silicon Valley startup in Ó Riain (2001). Small battles over how much they should disclose to their "supervisors" in the States, and how to keep "Silicon Valley" "informed" in a way that ensures more and better assignments in the future, are constant. Geography matters, and makes the programmer more productive in Silicon Valley than in Bangalore.

By contrast with my models in chapter 3, I do not think that Valley employers learn a lot from each H-1B with their median age of 27.4 years. Hiring an H-1B is not like Broadcom's hiring a team of Intel engineers (chapter 2). Still, every hiring, even of a temp, has an information-diffusion component. Employers do learn some things by employing H-1Bs that they would not necessarily learn from different programmers—including knowledge about what is being taught in Indian engineering programs and about problems that engineers have seen at other firms in India or the United States. Silicon Valley's emphasis on hiring youth is often equated with the sheer appetite for work hours or the discriminatory stereotyping of the aged. But there are information spillover effects here, too. The older programmer is not necessarily the one who has the most valuable information for a firm, if the firm has already seen most of the problems he has, while younger programmers know a different set of problems.

In a classical market, if scarcity raises the price of a production input from $45,000 to $65,000, the firm will demand less, or seek substitutes, or eventually produce less. Even ordinary labor markets, such as the market for fast-food employees, don't work like that. Firms have control over hiring policies and may derive benefits from above-market wages; they will not necessarily reduce hiring if the minimum wage goes up (Card and Krueger 1995). In information-labor markets, it is even more complicated to predict what firms will do if the price of engineers goes up. An information-labor market is not a true market for information, because the marginal cost of labor, unlike information, never equals zero (Shapiro and Varian 1999). Nevertheless, as we have seen, an information-labor market can display network effects, as here, where the value of an engineer depends on the network in which he functions. Some of these network externalities are available for redistribution, though it is hard to say in advance which, and I know of no helpful economic models on this point.

Suppose the Department of Labor heightened its scrutiny of employers' Labor Condition Applications (LCAs), rejecting any that did not include a realistic prevailing salary for programmers (say $75,000), and followed up with compliance efforts to ensure that employers actually paid that amount. What would happen to H-1Bs? Some employers would outsource their work to developers overseas; some would continue to employ H-1Bs, now paying them $75,000; some would hire locally. We have no way of estimating these proportions. Partly this is true of any labor market (Card and Krueger 1995); partly this is true of any labor market paying "efficiency" (above market) wages and realizing diverse benefits (reduced monitoring, reduced search costs, etc.) from doing so. But this case is harder yet, because of our knowledge that the geographic location of the worker changes his value, without good estimates of the magnitude of this externality.

My instinct is that this externality is quite large, reflecting all the reasons why Silicon Valley is so much more productive than even Route 128 (Saxenian 1994). This suggests that modest redistribution of this externality would not kill the Valley's international character or its firms' economic success.

If I am correct, several obvious reforms to the H-1B law follow. Employers should be required to be certified for salaries actually prevailing in the Valley. The LCA and visa petition should be binding contracts, enforceable in court by an H-1B not being paid as promised. The employer should actually be obligated to pay wages at the announced rate. It makes no sense whatever to permit employers to bring in foreign workers for supposed labor shortages and then keep them "on the bench," unpaid, because there are no such shortages. These reforms could then be evaluated. I would be surprised if they diminished use of the H-1B program, but nobody knows. The green-card process for highly skilled and needed labor should be speeded up, to diminish the long period of practical indentured servitude. (Matloff [2000: 21–22] claims that employers in the past have opposed speeding up green-card procedures, preferring to employ foreign workers as H-1Bs.) Such an increased suite of rights for visa holders should create market opportunities for their advocates and organizations (see also Hahm 2000). By contrast, it does not seem realistic to me to make changes in the H-1B program in the hope of benefiting older or younger workers already in the United States. As we will see more closely in chapter 12 on discrimination, older programmers are already well protected against discrimination, particularly in California; their problems do not appear widespread; and can best be dealt with in a discrimination framework.

Employee-Controlled Temp Agencies for H-1Bs?

A high-velocity labor market creates demand for particular kinds of labor market intermediaries (chapter 8), demand that in theory might be exploited by new kinds of employee organization (chapter 9). This is a good thing, for those who remember why employee organization was supposed to give the U.S. labor market a truer kind of flexibility than regulation (Barenberg 1993).

One such organization will round out our discussion of H-1Bs and lead us into the larger discussion of labor market intermediaries.

Samir Kosla graduated from Stanford Graduate School of Business in 1999 and founded TechLancer, a support community and employer for H-1B visa holders who are ready to enjoy the freedom of independent contracting, like Kevin and Max (chapter 6). Since their visas do not permit them to be true independent contractors, they become employees of TechLancer and virtual independent contractors. The appeal is principally to those who are leaving their first job. Employees normally come to TechLancer when they have lined up at least their first consulting job. Employees keep 90 percent of the billing rate. TechLancer is their employer for visa purposes, meaning that it certifies their employment to the INS, and handles all the paperwork for permanent residence, through its own immigration attorney. It also provides a full suite of benefits: health insurance, a 401(k) plan, and stock options in TechLancer. Kosla told me in February 2000 that while health insurance was particularly important to the employees, the 401(k) plan and stock options were less important to employees than he had supposed. TechLancer is proactive in finding consulting jobs for its employees (particularly as that first job comes to an end) and provides support and counseling for the freelance lifestyle, modeled on Web sites like guru.com and freeagent.com. Unlike "body shops," it won't send programmers "to Boise to do mainframe work." When I talked to Kosla, all the employees were Indian.

Only time will tell if this kind of hybrid temp agency/employee organization/freelance community will succeed, and it would not be surprising if some early versions do not. We will look at Working Partnerships, a union-sponsored temp agency/employee organization, in chapter 9. Such groups face stiff competition from proprietary temporary help agencies, which have increasingly taken on functions of employee training and advocacy, as we will see in the next chapter.

Part III

Labor Market Intermediaries:
Information and Flexibility

8

LABOR MARKET INTERMEDIARIES:
MATCHING WORKERS TO JOBS

It is common even in conventional labor economics to observe that labor markets are full of information asymmetries and other information that can be produced only by incurring high search costs. This book is not the first to "bring information into labor markets." Still, this insight is normally applied to a stock, limited set of information asymmetries. Typically, the worker knows whether he or she will shirk or not, but the employer does not know this. Or, in the models we reviewed in chapters 3 and 4, the worker may develop valuable ideas, but neither the employer nor worker knows this in advance.

In a high-velocity labor market like Silicon Valley's, the information problems are considerably more complex and serious, as a moment's reflection reveals. The employer may effectively know nothing about potential workers. The workers may know nothing about potential employers. And these very low levels of knowledge are then divided by the thousands annually, as firms with rapid employee turnover must repeatedly choose among employees who repeatedly move among firms.

Consider first the hiring employer. It needs employees with particular technical skills to be applied first to known, but thereafter to unknown, technical problems. Past work experience will be an imperfect source of information and educational attainment no help at all. Potential employees may describe the programs they created or products they designed on past jobs, but little objective evidence will be available to evaluate their claims. The best programmers may be high school graduates, not Ph.D.s in computer science from Stanford. Most relevant information about employee ability can be learned only on the job, and the short job tenures that are the subject of this book are in part explained as informational devices.

If conventional labor economics has simplified the employer's informational needs, it has positively neglected the employee's. However, the employer's "reputation"—the usual cure-all in conventional labor economics—conveys little information to an employee selecting among competing start-ups and perhaps evaluating them against an offer from a more established company. "You can't really know whether an e-commerce company is going to fly," said a twenty-five-year-old tech-support worker handing in a resume at a job fair. "It's a roll of the dice—just like investing in the Nasdaq." A job fair in San Jose in early 2000 had an "IPO Row" with more than fifty booths, each staffed by a start-up planning to go public within the year (Ethan Smith 2000).

It is a common but somewhat misleading abbreviation to refer to these as problems of "inadequate" or "low" information, as if the solution were merely more information. But in the words of Herbert Simon: "A wealth of information creates a poverty of attention" (quoted in Shapiro and Varian 1999: 6). The labor market intermediaries that we study in this chapter do more than increase the quantity of information about employers and employees; they put it into useful form.

So it is not surprising that Silicon Valley is marked by all kinds of new labor market intermediaries to facilitate information flow in the labor market. This chapter looks at new ways of matching people with jobs: online job boards, and new kinds of placement agencies. As with permatemp relations, independent contracting, and H-1B visas, these intermediaries are usually understood as institutions that facilitate "flexible" labor contracting, permitting quick matching of employees with short-term jobs. They do facilitate such "flexible" labor contracting, but, as with the institutions discussed before, their informational functions are more important. Understanding how people actually get jobs in Silicon Valley will later help us answer such questions as whether there is discrimination in this labor market (chapter 12). Silicon Valley's heavy use of new labor market intermediaries has suggested to many people a role for employee organizations. Chapter 9 takes up groups organized by or for employees that at least provide information about employers, and may also seek to defend employee interests. These include Web sites, chatgroups, in-house computer networks, ethnic- and gender-based groups (both employer-sponsored and employee-created), and special organizations created to serve mobile high-tech workers.

Electronic Recruiting

Literally thousands of Web sites devoted to job placement have sprung up since the mid-1990s. These include formal job boards, Web sites offering searchable databases of job listings and resumes, employer-initiated searches that target promising ("passive") candidates through their online credentials ("talent mining"), usenet bulletin boards and listservs, and systems internal to companies. It is probably impossible to get an accurate count of the number of Web sites, which is certainly in the thousands, let alone an overall picture of how they are used. Autor (2001b) cites estimates of 29 million jobs posted online (not necessarily unique) and over 7 million resumes. Benner (2000) lists the following sites as popular among information technology specialists in Silicon Valley (I have listed only those operating when I visited them in November 2000):

ants.com	fatjob.com	jobs.com
BayAreaCareers.com	headhunter.net	MetroVox.com
Bridgepath.com	hotjobs.com	net-temps.com
Bridgesonline.com	interbiznet.com	SanJoseJobs.com
careerbuilder.com	it.careershop.com	sdforum.org
careercity.com	javajobs.com	siliconvalleyjobs.com
careermagic.com	jobtrak.com	stc.org
dice.com	jobengine.com	techies.com

The list includes general national job boards like hotjobs, and specialized boards. For example, Bridgesonline is for women, stc for technical writers, and ants for contract work. Benner (2000) calls dice.com the "most prominent site in the Silicon Valley high-tech recruiting industry. . . . While the name actually stands for Data-processing Independent Consultants' Exchange, the gambling metaphor that accompanies the dice imagery actually captures fairly well the type of high-rolling lifestyle that high-end contractors aspire to." Each month, 20,000 distinct job seekers make over 3 million visits to the site (see Teuke 1999).

These online resources, like rapid turnover and short tenures, make labor markets more like classical markets than ever before. Individuals can advertise their skills to employers as well as the reverse, and each has access to unprecedented levels of information. Particularly telling is the heavy use by *employed* workers, some 11 percent of whom told the Computer and Internet Use Supplement to the Current Population Survey in August 2000 that they had used the Web to search for new jobs that month (Kuhn and Skuterud 2002: 5). This is believed to be many times the quantity of job searches by employed workers that took place before the Internet (Autor 2001b). More efficient matches to jobs should raise productivity.

New labor market intermediaries offer some potential for eliminating inefficiencies connected with information asymmetry, poor matches, and preferences falsified by employers or employee organizations. Crucially, they permit jobs to be defined, and filled, with highly specific requirements. Employers may demand, and receive, employees with actual experience writing particular narrow applications in particular programming languages on particular platforms. This is another nail in the coffin of the internal labor market, often defended as a way of ensuring companies access to employees with particular training, namely theirs. The Internet exacerbates earlier trends toward short-term hiring of individuals with highly particular skills, as opposed to long-term commitment to individuals who would be trained and retrained for changing roles. As we shall examine more closely in chapter 12, traditional analyses of employment discrimination often emphasize the unconscious discrimination that comes from subjective application of vague criteria. Tight, specific job descriptions, and Internet job boards that produce hundreds of qualified applicants, without regard to personal contacts or characteristics such as race, are an important force in helping to end the particular kind of discrimination that results from subjective job criteria and insider referral networks. However, as we shall see, they may enforce a different kind of "discrimination," if that is the word, against older employees and others who lack the hottest skills, even though they might come to be trained in them.

Internet job boards might even help address the collective action problems that show up as adverse selection problems, by raising the quality and quantity of information available about worker preferences. For example, recall Samir Kosla, whom we met in chapter 7 as the founder of TechLancer, the employer of record for mobile workers on H-1B visas. Samir had originally thought that the workers using his service would be very interested in 401(k) plans and options, but this turned out not to be true. They were, however, interested in health insurance. In conventional labor markets, such a demand for health insurance might be widespread but misperceived by employers, due to adverse selection. Employees particularly interested in health insurance will disproportionately take jobs in the public or old-economy sectors, even if they might otherwise prefer a high-velocity labor market and in fact be more productive there. Using Internet job boards, firms will be able to see that this demand is really widespread, and may worry less that the high-tech firm that institutes health insurance will become a magnet for time-servers.

Internet job boards convey unintended information to employers. All of Cisco's job openings, for example, are posted on its Web site. Whenever a job seeker logs on to examine the job posting, Cisco learns his or her Internet Protocol (IP) address. Cisco definitely watches these patterns as early warnings of trouble at particular companies; for example, if its job board gets over a thousand hits one month from a particular company. Cisco has also used its online job board to head off potential litigation, in which Lucent threatened to complain about Cisco's stealing its employees and trade secrets. Cisco was able to show that the Lucent employees had originally contacted Cisco by logging onto its job board.

Autor (2001b) raises some cautionary notes about the efficiency advantages of Web-based job sites. When applying for jobs becomes cost-free, employees will apply to jobs for which they would have considered themselves unqualified (if they had to pay to apply). The cost of distinguishing among these candidates is borne partly by employers, who must pay for additional information, and partly by other employees who must implicitly pay more to establish their qualifications. "A standard result of signaling models is that high quality workers pay to acquire a signal that distinguishes them from others. If the price of the signal falls, lower quality workers also acquire it and employers face more difficulty separating wheat from chaff." (2001b: 31 n. 4) Autor suggests possible responses. Employers might make greater use of, at the least, screening services (to find out whether individuals really have the credentials advertised). They might rely more on intermediaries like employment agencies to certify employees. They should do more of their own talent mining, or place greater reliance on personal contacts. Finally, employees may post richer online resumes that will include "project portfolios, dockets of customer evaluations, and even standardized personality assessments" (2001b: 36).

Temporary Agencies, Old and New

Temporary agencies of all types, which grew rapidly nationally in the 1990s, are, as mentioned in chapter 5, probably twice as important to Silicon Valley's labor market, where they make up 3.53 percent of jobs and are still growing. As just mentioned, the growth of Internet job placements may, if anything, increase the importance of temporary agencies. In the words of the owner of an agency that places independent contractors (Benner 2000: Ch. 4):

> The Internet has made it much easier for us to search for people, but it has also made it easier for everyone else to search too, which increases the competition. It allows our clients to go directly to our people, but that is very labor intensive and they don't have the relationships that we do. Half of the people we place every month we know well. They're reliable and we can vouch for them. If our clients put out an ad, they may get three hundred resumes but they still don't know who the people are. It is still a high-touch industry. That's what the clients are paying for, and the Internet has emphasized the importance of these relationships even more.

We saw in chapter 5 that close to 4 percent of Silicon Valley's workforce at any given moment is directly employed by temporary help agencies, and, while this number is not large, it has continued to grow rapidly even as the equivalent national figure has leveled off. All large private-sector employers in Silicon Valley told a telephone survey by Working Partnerships that they regularly use temporary agencies (Benner 2000: Ch. 4). Moreover, the number of people who work for a temporary help agency at some point during the year is larger than the number doing so on the date of any particular survey. Chris Benner estimates, based on studies conducted elsewhere, that between 7 and 10 percent of the Silicon Valley workforce is employed by a temp agency at some point during a year (2000: Ch. 4).

Silicon Valley employers do not need temporary help agencies to be able to hire and fire quickly, given Internet job boards and the general ability of U.S. employers to create short-term jobs without benefits. The chief, if unquantifiable, contribution of temporary help agencies to "flexible" employment, as discussed in chapter 5, may be their psychological impact on the more permanent workforce, permitting them to distance themselves from their coworkers' uncertainties. This explains why temporary help employment particularly grew after the economic downturn of 1985, when Valley employers like AMD learned that they could promise security only to some, not all, of their employees. The number of temporary help agencies in the Valley more than doubled from 1987 to 1997, and these firms became larger, not smaller. They also began providing professionals, technicians, managers, and manufacturing and warehouse workers, in addition to office staff (Benner 2000: Ch. 4).

Ethnographies of actual temporary help agencies make clear that their informational functions are more important than their "flexibility" functions. The best is by Esther Neuwirth (2002), who worked for the agency that she calls "Silicon Valley Temps" (SVT) from June to November 2000. She describes its testing, training, and employee advocacy functions, some of which sound more like a union than a temp agency. About 25 percent of its business was with a particular components manufacturer to which it supplied engineers, human resources staff, clerical and administrative staff, technicians, and assemblers. The largest group was production workers who soldered and assembled circuit boards. SVT set up a mirror of the client's job line at its own office, where it tested candidates on their knowledge of soldering, electrostatic discharge, general math, and English competency. Neuwirth "observed many instances where the staffing agency provided job-readiness assistance for workers in the form of job counseling, resume writing, and advice and tips on job interviewing. In these circumstances, the agency was providing a much-needed resource that people were not receiving elsewhere from either nonprofit organizations, government agencies, or other private institutions" (Neuwirth 2002: 10–11).

Perhaps most surprising was SVT's role as an advocate for employees. Neuwirth describes telephone calls to particular managers at their clients, in order to place particular individuals. SVT's branch manager had worked closely with managers at the component manufacturer on general strategies of recruitment, and was invited to meetings to discuss how to handle a manager whose treatment of staff was negatively affecting retention. She was now able to play an advocate's role for candidates. One candidate was offered a job at the manufacturer only after the SVT manager made a special call to a manager whom she knew personally. Another individual, a Filipina-American woman in her late thirties, sought placement in manufacturing, hoping eventually to become a manager. SVT's branch manager told her candidly that its manufacturing clients "use people up and spit them out." SVT placed her in a temp-to-perm position as a customer service representative in a company looking for a bilingual English-Tagalog speaker. "The job paid much more than assembly line work and even had the potential for upward mobility" (Neuwirth 2002: 13).

At other clients, SVT has a Vendor On Premises (VOP) agreement in which it sets up on the company premises, managing its temp-to-perm workers (some recruited by other agencies) and serving as their legal employer. Here, too, it served as an employee advocate. Neuwirth describes meeting a particular individual at a job fair and submitting his resume to this client as a Web developer. She learned that he was their second choice, because he was seen as too much of a "techie" for a job also requiring marketing and communication skills. She prepped the individual on how to prepare for his second interview, and he got the job.

SVT advocates for more than job placement. It has advised corporate clients to raise salaries that are out of touch with Valley standards, and to deal with particular managers whose harsh attitudes were affecting recruiting. Neuwirth also discusses negative aspects of working for SVT. These include confusion over who is the employer and mixups over paychecks. SVT employees also receive no health insurance or sick days, and paid holidays only after three consecutive months of work without interruption, which of course SVT does not guarantee.

We are not going to get very far in understanding why all large Silicon Valley employers use temp agencies like Silicon Valley Temps if we think only about "flexibility." "Flexibility" would be better served in some ways if SVT's clients did their own hiring. Personnel decisions would thus be made by one's own human resource managers employed at will, rather than managers who work for SVT and thus cannot be individually terminated by the client. Short-term workers, directly employed by clients, would not come trailing a built-in advocate committed to their retention by the organization. Either the psychological impact on the clients' regular employees of seeing coworkers terminated must be very great, as discussed in chapter 5, or the information provided by Silicon Valley Temps must be very valuable.

While there is much truth to both the flexibility and morale stories, this book is dedicated to demonstrating the information story, too. It is no mystery how Silicon Valley employers benefit from using labor market intermediaries. It is just another aspect of AnnaLee Saxenian's (1994) account of Silicon Valley's triumph over Route 128, as each was constituted in the 1980s. There are productivity gains when information circulates across the boundaries of many interlocked firms that outweigh any gains from more vertically integrated organizations. In models of endogenous economic growth like Paul Romer's (1906b), such information is the central element in economic growth. While this is true of technological information like how best to produce information technology products, it is also true of information about workers, jobs, and careers. The temp agency knows what other firms pay, do, and how they use workers. This is information that would be difficult for its clients to obtain. By contrast, the information that the temp agency has about individual workers could often be obtained for the same cost by the client itself (how well they solder or speak Tagalog). However, even as to the characteristics of individual workers, the temp agency may have different information than the client could obtain on its own. For example, each could learn, for more senior workers, how they have performed in different situations. But the client's knowledge would be limited to its own organization, while the temp agency's might, in particular cases, be greater. This would be more important when the temp agency is referring a chief financial or executive officer (cf. Bradach 1997) than when it refers a warehouse worker.

In theory, Silicon Valley's heavy use of labor market intermediaries opens opportunities for employee organizations that are now poorly established there. Labor unions, or something like them, could, like SVT, run hiring halls, train and certify employees, and advocate for them on the job. Yet there are very few union members working in the Valley. It is time to consider the comparative efficiency advantages of employee-controlled, and for-profit, labor market intermediaries.

9

EMPLOYEE ORGANIZATION: NETWORKS, ETHNIC ORGANIZATION, NEW UNIONS

Was the software and marketing company that I shall call Individuate one of America's one hundred best places to work in early 2000? Its human resources director, whom I shall call Farah, certainly thought it could be, and so did many of its employees. Its analytic software, analyzing customer behavior for online and offline shopping, was very successful. Individuate had successfully merged two very different companies to come up with the product. Originally a marketing company in San Francisco, selling to retailers, it was, Farah told me later, full of "hip, stylish people from marketing and advertising, dressed in black." In 1999 they realized they needed to merge with a database company, and chose an East Bay firm named after a character from Egyptian mythology and "full of kids wearing t-shirts and jeans" and snobbish about their degrees from M.I.T., Cal Tech, and Stanford. But the merger had worked out great—only two of the East Bay kids had quit, because they didn't want to commute into the City—and after the get-acquainted parties, Bay cruise, and community building, everybody now "loved the new company." Business was great, benefits and salaries were high—generous stock options, full medical and dental coverage, a 401(k) plan, free snacks and drinks, a recreation room, reduced rates on gym membership.

But like every information technology (IT) company in the Bay Area that year, it was hiring all the time. Executive management thought that it might help hiring and retention to have the company recognized widely as a great employer—for example, by having it named a "top company to work for" by business media. Farah looked into it and learned that to make these lists, Individuate would have to show that it was really meeting employee demands. So Farah called open meetings to find out what the staff wanted. The chief demand was for further professional development and training. "The engineers wanted classes in software skills. The salespeople and customer support staff wanted to know more about engineering." A small volunteer group formed to work up a plan, and Farah met with them weekly. Consultants had warned that it would be dangerous to raise expectations, but Farah was "green" (with but two years of experience as human resources director of the East Bay database company). The volunteer group also realized that they wanted more information about the company's finances, less hype. This demand became known around Individuate as "respect." After all, the employees, at least at the time of the merger, had just worked for a company in which they saw the CEO daily and asked whatever they wanted. A new Individuate CEO in early 2000 was exploring taking the company public and growing, and the employee meetings wanted more information about what this meant.

Although management had thought it would be "cool" to be one of the hundred best places to work in America, it never met these employee concerns. The company's stock fell, and management time was devoted to the basic objective of steering the company through a rough market. Employee initiatives, like training or sharing financial information, seemed like a diversion. Management even opposed a suggestion box for anonymous suggestions. More important, people felt demoralized and began to take jobs elsewhere, easily done in mid-2000. By then demand had peaked for Individuate's software. The company stopped hiring in late 2000 and downsized in early 2001. Its plans to go public have been shelved.

The Individuate story comes from an interview with its former personnel director on August 1, 2001. (I have changed the name of the interviewee, the company, and many details about the company.) Its lesson seems ambiguous to me. The company seems perfectly typical. Its only unusual feature was the project to be listed as one of the hundred best companies to work for; not many companies did that. But probably plenty of Bay Area companies in 2000 thought they belonged on that list. I think that most of them, had they pursued that listing, would have discovered—as the consultants warned Farah—that introducing employee consultation into an organization that lacks it can create false expectations. But what is the solution to this problem? Does the Individuate story show the need for new forms of employee organization in Silicon Valley? the need instead for old-fashioned employee organization like labor unions? the inevitability of informal modes of representation such as meetings, volunteer committees, and Intranet communication? or the harm that comes from consulting employees at all?

Ambiguity about formal employee organization pervades much of the literature on high-tech work. The Silicon Valley engineer or manager has symbolized both social isolation and high networking. Images of Bill Hewlett, David Packard, Steve Jobs, and Steve Wozniak, tinkering in garages, update a kind of Charles Lindbergh individualism. The first character introduced in the influential book *Habits of the Heart: Individualism and Commitment in American Life* (Bellah et al. 1985: 3–8), a Silicon Valley executive named Brian Palmer, stands in for devotion to work and family, commitment to individualism, and isolation from any kind of political or social organization.

By contrast, as we have seen, the managers and engineers in Saxenian (1994) pushed Silicon Valley ahead of Boston's Route 128 precisely because of their dense network of personal ties with counterparts at former employers, subcontractors, suppliers, and rivals. But, as Saxenian makes clear, these are instrumental ties. They are not what Robert Putnam (2000) calls "social capital." His attempt (2000: 324–35) to claim Silicon Valley as a kind of extension of the Homebrew Computer Club is not very convincing. Stephen S. Cohen and Gary Fields (1999) are closer to the mark (though, as we shall see, somewhat ethnocentric). Silicon Valley is not a community "of dense civic engagement. Silicon Valley is notoriously a world of strangers; nobody knows anybody else's mother there. There is no deep history, little in the way of complex familial ties, and little structured community. It is a world of independent—even isolated—newcomers." Most important, neither the isolate nor the networked seems to have much time for formal group membership.

Information-labor markets, as we saw in the previous chapter, create roles for new labor market intermediaries, like Internet job boards, that match employees to jobs and provide information. Does this create opportunities for employee organization, either old-fashioned unions, or some new kind of employee organization? A lot of people have speculated along these lines or worked to create such new organizations, but so far results are thin on the ground. This chapter will discuss, in addition to unions, four new kinds of employee organization and how they might relate to information-labor markets. They include:

- network-based employee groups that communicate on computer networks;
- ethnic- and gender-based groups that transcend firm boundaries;
- others organized as caucuses by firms; and
- new employee groups designed for mobile workers, such as Working Partnerships in San Jose, and Working Today, a New York-based group not yet active in Silicon Valley but a potential model.

These new forms of employee organization are full of vitality, play interesting roles, raise policy dilemmas that are best resolved by examining the full picture of a high-velocity labor market. They let employees raise demands characteristic of employees in high-velocity labor markets who expect to be back on the job market soon. Like the Individuate employees, workers use new organizations to demand more training and skills, and more transparency in their often opaque compensation. In other cases, they seek more stable benefits, lobbying (for example on immigration issues), or networking across firm lines with employees with whom one may work—or hire for one's start-up—in the future.

Like other work practices discussed in this book, they also raise questions at the cutting edge of economic analysis. Specifically, all are institutions of employee voice, that is, of information transmission. They have little bargaining or other labor market power. The economics of institutions of employee voice are, as we shall see, not well understood. In many ways, an information-labor market like Silicon Valley's creates demand for organizations of employee voice, as it does for temporary help agencies.

Yet whether any of them will endure in the new economy is somewhat doubtful, certainly as compared with Internet job boards and sites and temporary help agencies, the labor market intermediaries discussed in chapter 8. The dominant "employee organization" in Silicon Valley is the temporary help agency. Some of the new employee organizations seek to sell services already marketed by for-profit organizations, such as job placement services and insurance companies. The question that hangs over this entire chapter is whether an employee-directed organization, which seeks to provide assistance, support, and information to employees, offers any advantage over these proprietary organizations that seek to do the same thing.

For employees at the low end of the labor market such as circuit board stuffers, office temps, and perhaps even for programmers, I will argue that none of these new groups is a good substitute for a traditional union. If unionism ever comes to Silicon Valley's high-velocity labor market, it will, in my opinion, more closely resemble the old-fashioned American construction union. The construction union is the best organization ever devised for a mobile or contingent workforce—so good that we rarely think of unionized construction workers as "contingent." Today's temps, product testers, and low-level programmers would be much better off with an organization that administered, jointly with employer groups, funds that paid retirement, health, and vacation benefits, into which employers paid per hour worked, and that also trained and certified employees. Since, as we shall see, current labor law makes it unnecessarily difficult for temporary and mobile workers to form unions, that law should be changed. If unions among such groups were successful, they could in turn be the model for higher-end technical labor like customer service representatives or even programmers. I will sketch out such an organization after surveying the forms of employee organization that actually exist in the Valley. Let us start with actually existing unions.

Unions

Rates of union membership are not available by county, but most people think that Santa Clara County is very lightly unionized. In high technology, unions are hardly present at all. If you visit a high-technology company, the only employee you will see who is represented by a union is the janitor, who is likely to be represented by Local 1877 of the Service Employees International Union.

This is a remarkable organizing feat. Almost all the usual excuses for failed union organizing might have applied to that janitor. He or she is probably an immigrant from Mexico, with little English-language facility. The janitor has few job skills and can easily be replaced. Finally, the janitor is not an employee of Sun or Apple, but typically works for a cleaning contractor.

The Service Employees became their representative union after a brilliant organizing campaign built around appeals to Mexican cultural pride. It involved religious and political leaders, demonstrations, fiestas. The final decisive blow was a consumer boycott, of Apple computers and other products, sold by the companies that hire the cleaning contractors (Martínez Saldaña 1993: 115–25; Zlolniski 1994: 2313–16; Bacon 1997). (The consumer boycotts did not violate federal prohibitions on secondary boycotts, which do not reach consumer boycotts carried out by means other than picketing. *Edward J. DeBartolo Corp. v. Florida Gulf Coast Building and Construction Trades Council.*) Local 1877 now represents a majority of the Valley's janitors (Rivlin 2000b).

But that is about it for membership in labor unions in Silicon Valley. It was not always thus. In 1953 most Valley electronics firms were unionized by the United Electrical, Machine, and Radio Workers (UE), but became nonunion during the 1950s after the Cold War repression of that union (Eisenscher 1993). Valley employers placed importance on remaining nonunion, and were prepared to fight organizing vigorously. In the words of Bob Noyce, co-founder of Intel:

> Remaining non-union is an essential for survival for most of our companies. If we had the work rules that unionized companies have, we'd all go out of business. This is a very high priority for management here. We have to retain flexibility in operating our companies. The great hope for our nation is to avoid those deep, deep divisions between workers and management that can paralyze action. (quoted in Rogers and Larsen 1984: 191)

In the 1970s, when there was more manufacturing in the Valley, there were unsuccessful union attempts to organize production workers (Bacon 1997; Eisenscher 1993; Green 1983: 298). The UE eventually shut down its Electronics Organizing Committee in 1984 (Eisenscher 1993). The Communication Workers made some headlines in late 2000 with organizational efforts toward customer service representatives at the online retailers etown (in San Francisco) and Amazon (in Seattle), but these ended when etown went out of business and Amazon eliminated the unit of greatest union strength (Ewalt 2001; Kotkin 1999).

The only known unionized Web business is a special case. Online Television Network Services, Inc. (OTVnet.com) is a San Diego firm that develops online communication tools for labor union clients administering multiemployer benefits plans. Its management was happy to recognize Local 569 of the International Brotherhood of Electrical Workers as the representative of its five production and development technicians. Their collective bargaining agreement prohibits discharge without cause and offers unusual benefits (Roemer 2001).

Almost all the work practices discussed in this book are often said to be obstacles to union organizing, particularly short job tenures, heavy use of temporary labor, and heavy use of immigrant labor. But, as the example of the janitors' union suggests, they might as easily be seen as opportunities for union organizing. Other opportunities for employee organizing are suggested by the preceding chapter, on the heavy use of intermediaries in a high-velocity labor market.

Union image is, in my opinion, the biggest obstacle to union organizing. When unions come up in my interviews, people in the Valley (like Bob Noyce two decades ago) associate them with their traditional roles in traditional labor markets. It is instructive that, when the manufacturing employees at the contract manufacturer that Chun (2001: 140) calls FlexTech learned that their production line would be shut for two-and-a-half days because a strike at United Parcel Service (UPS) prevented delivery of parts, most felt the UPS workers "were ruining it for the rest of [them]." "Workers did not seem to identify with the strikers' demands as temporary workers" despite the fact, discussed in chapter 5, that FlexTech workers are all initially hired as temporary employees and most retain that status.

Like the economics and law of employment relationships, union practices have developed against an assumption of internal labor markets, typically in manufacturing. In this view, unions help members by negotiating detailed collective agreements, lasting several years, that link compensation and benefits to detailed job descriptions, with each job holding a place in a defined hierarchy. The benefits will be back-loaded, creating returns to seniority. This is why management agreed to them, to discourage turnover (Freeman and Medoff 1984). Companies that do not gain any such benefit from rewarding seniority will probably resist unions so thoroughly as to discourage employee interest (Freeman and Rogers 1999). In such a case, the union's only real weapon is to strike the employer, which exposes employees to risks of job loss and the stress of conflict, and will only succeed against some employers anyway.

This image of unions is at best a very partial picture of how unions work. It functions as what the cognitive scientists call a prototype. If we are asked to picture a bird, most people in our culture will picture a robin or bluebird. Few will imagine an ostrich or flamingo. Similarly, the prototype for unions for years has been the United Automobile Workers. When asked to picture a factory, or a worker, or a union, people automatically think cars. They also think detailed contracts, job descriptions, formal grievance systems, fixed compensation.

This model of unionism offers little to most employees in high-velocity labor markets and even less to their employers. There is much less manufacturing in Silicon Valley than there was before the 1990s. No new forms of employee organization emerged at that time. The work was largely conducted by immigrant women without unions (Bacon 1997; Friaz 1996; Hossfeld 1990). By now, as we have seen, much manufacturing has moved overseas. The surviving manufacturing is performed by a much more diverse workforce (Jayadev 2002), employed as temporary employees.But industrial unionism is not the only kind of unionism. Employees in Silicon Valley have developed some of their own forms of organization. This chapter discusses employee groups on electronic networks, ethnic- and gender-based networks and formal caucuses, and some new associations designed specifically to appeal to mobile, educated workers. Unions may adopt these organizational forms, possibly in combination with some traditional union forms. Or unions may never become established in Silicon Valley, but the new organizations themselves may flourish. I do not regard either of these outcomes as especially likely. I do not think the Valley (or any other portion of the U.S. economy) will ever become heavily unionized, and I do not think the organizations in this chapter—networks, caucuses, and new employee groups—will ever constitute more than small pockets of the labor force. However, the unconventional nature of these groups has already thrown up challenges to traditional labor and employment law. It is therefore important for this study to examine how the legal system responds to these challenges brought by new forms of employee organization, even though they are far less important, numerically or economically, than the challenges brought by (for example) employee mobility to the concept of trade secrets.

Employees and employers in Silicon Valley often associate labor unions with old labor markets, like they have back East, and therefore something that is antithetical to their high-velocity labor market. One of the most robust generalizations in industrial relations, however, is that unions take their structure from the employers they face; they certainly take the problems they work on from employers (Heckscher 1988). Unions that face small craft-oriented firms will organize on craft lines. Some European unions that face large corporatist national enterprises, largely directed from the national capital under government guidance, will focus their attentions on political parties and centralized bargaining. The economic story of the twentieth century was, until recently, the rise of the large corporation that realized economies of scope and scale. Of course unions that deal with such corporations are associated with detailed contracts, job descriptions, and seniority rights.

None of them, however, is inherent to labor unions, or would have much relevance in a high-velocity labor market, to invoke the contrast that structures this book. If that contrast is sometimes overdrawn here, my justification is the need to examine new high-velocity labor markets, as against a scholarly tradition in economics, law, and industrial relations that so often assumes the stable career ladders in large corporations.

Employee Action on Computer Networks

Employees with access to in-house computer networks can take collective action with a speed and efficacy that many a traditional union might envy. Let's consider in some detail the action at Apple Computer in 1990 described by Bishop and Levine (1999). Apple had encouraged employee use of an internal computer bulletin board. Its training materials noted that its recycling program "got started when someone suggested it in a [network] discussion" (p. 218). Other discussions had concerned policies on hiring minorities, smoking in buildings, and naming conventions for shared computers. Fifty top executives received periodic two-page summaries of the main issues discussed on the network, under the title "What employees want."

In January 1990, Apple management announced revisions in the profit-sharing plan that would have eliminated any payments to employees in quarters with slow sales growth. Bishop and Levine note: "Hundreds of postings were entered on [the electronic bulletin board] in the days immediately following the announcement. Over several weeks, about 1,000 messages were received, more than for any other event in the company's history" (p. 220). Most responses attacked the reductions, often bitterly, while a minority defended them. A common early theme was that employees wanted "a complete explanation of why the change in profit sharing was necessary, and how it would encourage growth, as management claimed." CEO John Sculley did write such explanations to the bulletin board, but many employees remained unconvinced. Ultimately, management caved in. Everyone interviewed for a Harvard Business School case attributed this to the effect of the electronic bulletin board (Gibbs 1991).

Meanwhile, one employee looked through bulletin board transcripts and recorded all the contributors to the profit-sharing debate who had used their actual names. He wrote to them, suggesting a meeting. A small group formed and met quietly several times that winter. Independently, a second employee posted a bulletin board message calling for formation of a concerned employees' league. The groups later merged under the name Employees for One Apple. Fifty employees attended the first meeting of the merged group, announced on the bulletin board, in May 1990. The group sought the restoration of the "corporate culture they recalled (perhaps in a somewhat idealized form) from a few years previous." They sought greater communication with top management, fewer management "perks" and other divisions among staff, and an institutionalized voice for employees. "Members of One [Apple] repeatedly pointed out that they loved [Apple]. . . . Moreover, most members we interviewed went out of their way to note that they were opposed to any form of more traditional employee protest such as a union. . . . They did not want outsiders involved, and they did not want a union bureaucracy to intervene between employees and managers" (p. 221).

Management, however, resisted formal employee representation. As of the date of Bishop and Levine's study, the only effect of the agitation over organization was the formation of an Employee-Executive Forum in which fifteen employees, randomly selected from among volunteers, discuss their concerns with top managers. The forum has no rights to information or consultation and no decision-making authority. It was supposed to meet quarterly but in fact met less frequently (p. 223).

Other companies that have announced changes in compensation, in and out of Silicon Valley, have similarly faced what the *New York Times* calls "The Electronic Rank and File" (Kahn 2000). IBM in 1999 reversed itself and more than doubled the number of employees permitted to keep a traditional, defined-benefit pension plan. The following year, Bell Atlantic similarly announced, then retracted, plans to switch employees to a "cash balance" plan with variable benefits. In each case employees set up Web sites that compared the two plans and were linked to government agencies, congressional offices, and other organizations on pension rights. The IBM site, www.cashpensions.com, was visited more than 97,000 times that year and became a model for employees at other firms. "I just don't see how we could have done it without the Web," said Lynda French, creator of the cashpensions Web site. Both companies denied that they had been influenced by the online pressure from employees, while offering no alternative explanation for their changes of mind.

Former employees of the defunct wireless data network firm Metricon, nearly all of whom still believe in its technology, maintain a Web-based bulletin board posting jobs and other opportunities (Corcoran 2002).

Economic Analysis of Employee Voice Groups

Let us analyze incidents like these from an economic point of view, before turning to the legal and policy issues that they raise. Economic analysis of unions often starts (since Freeman and Medoff [1984]) by distinguishing the effects of a cartel of labor, from the effects of a "voice" for labor. The economic analysis of unions as labor cartels is well developed, while few generalizations can yet be made about union "voice" effects.

In the case of a standard, old economy union, it may be very difficult to untangle the economic effects of its different functions. A unionized company, compared with a nonunion counterpart, will pay higher wages and benefits, have less turnover, will be more likely to terminate employees than adjust compensation. Do these effects, commonly associated with unions, reflect "cartels" or "voice"? The cartel effect shows up because of the union's ability to threaten, or organize, a strike. The voice effect occurs when the employer in a unionized workplace focuses on the median, as opposed to the marginal, employee. It might seem that this voice effect would never arise unless the union had its cartel power. Perhaps only the rare employer would really learn much about employee preferences from a union, given the more sophisticated tools available to learn about employee sentiments, including quality of work-life groups and teams. If you thought that employers were so well informed, you would think that collective bargaining could change their behavior only through its threat of economic harm. I think this view mistaken, for reasons I will now explain.

Groups like the networked groups at Apple or IBM offer a novel problem for the economic analysis of institutions of employee "voice." They have no cartel effects, nor are cartel effects feasible in a high-velocity labor market. They do not strike. Their effect on turnover and quits is unknown. It may be significant that neither Apple nor IBM is a stereotypical start-up with rapid turnover (like Individuate). I have not been able to find any published accounts of similar employee networked action at a high-turnover start-up, nor have any of my interviews turned up such an action. Surely there must have been such actions, at least over unhappiness about relatively minor job dissatisfactions. In a start-up, though, such actions could not be based on the rhetoric of restoration of the former regime. Perhaps such rhetoric might be more important to electronic action than it seems. Electronic action might be hard to organize except in defense of existing benefits.

My guess though is that employee action on electronic networks has a very bright future, far beyond the reported instances when it was mobilized in defense of existing benefits. Network mobilization is a spectacular institution for employee voice, which it can mobilize cheaply, quickly, and effectively. Management concedes the point, even though it cannot be said to face a threat of a strike. The Apple employees did not understand their own power. It is ironic that so much employee follow-up went into creating silly and ineffective new institutions of employee voice. These employees had already demonstrated their command over as effective an institution of employee voice as has ever been observed, one that mobilizes not only employee complaints, but even managerial responses. A deeper irony is that employees were effective without formal organization. When they were simply complaining on the network, they got management both to respond to them and to change its course. After forming an organization and seeking permanent channels of communication, they accomplished little. While these Apple employees were in no sense poor people, they would seem to represent another illustration of the thesis of Piven and Cloward (1977) that popular protest or insurgency often becomes ineffectual once organizers transform it into mass permanent organization.

Of course, employee action on computer networks faces some severe limitations. So far, it has been limited to the reactive. It is hard to see how network groups could ever plan, or link up with other groups, or employ professional assistance. Network groups are also limited to whatever communications networks employers set up for their own purposes. This does not seem to be a serious limitation yet, because the communications network will meet the employer's needs only if it is rapid, interactive, and perceived as such. An unidentified Silicon Valley executive told Dean Hal Varian that "downsizing was now much easier than it used to be, because companies could use intranets to communicate with employees more effectively. This allowed them to squelch rumors quickly and to minimize, to some extent, the productivity hit that inevitably accompanies layoffs" (Varian 2002).

Nevertheless, as a way of mobilizing employee voice for management response, it has a bright future, and will generate more legal cases in addition to those discussed below. So what do we know about the economics of employee voice organizations like network groups? Why does management give in to employee groups that will not strike and cannot threaten economic harm?

Employee Voice and "Morale"

What do we know about the economics of organizations of pure employee "voice"? It is not surprising that there is no developed economic analysis of (pure) employee voice groups, since the concept appears for the first time here. Such economic analysis might start however with the importance of employee morale, the striking and unexpected finding of Bewley (1999).

Bewley conducted over three hundred interviews during the first Bush recession of the early 1990s in order to learn why employers are so much more likely to shed labor than they are to adjust wages downward. Most subjects named employee morale, a factor difficult to model economically and often dismissed by economists. Bewley's informants use "morale" to cover all the factors that motivate high employee performance without immediate reward and often without direct monitoring by managers. "Employers want workers to operate autonomously, show initiative, use their imagination, and take on extra tasks not required by management; workers who are scared or dejected do not do these things" (p. 431). Good morale includes employee satisfaction, a sense that effort will be reciprocated, that employees will cooperate spontaneously and share information among themselves and with supervisors—the last two being particularly difficult to motivate either with threats or financial incentives. Pay cuts cause bad morale in several different ways. The best employees will leave. Others will shirk or retaliate. Reducing compensation just for new hires is not a good idea either. "Managers regarded anything that upsets internal equity as potentially disruptive. Lack of equity spawns jealousies, resentments, and perceptions of unfair treatment" (p. 433).

Bewley does not specifically discuss collective bargaining. There was a union presence in 35 of the 248 companies in his sample (pp. 32–33), but those companies rarely appear to behave in any special way.

Nevertheless, I think his book represents the most interesting vantage point from which to rethink collective bargaining. It certainly captures the dynamic of the Apple, IBM, and Bell Atlantic stories better than conventional models of collective bargaining. Why did these employers give in to the disgruntled employees on the internal network, when those employees did not threaten a strike or boycott? When we understand the importance of what management calls "morale," we can understand how "voice" institutions might work even without a strike threat. Management will go to great lengths to avoid bad morale. Perceived injustice or inequity leads to bad morale. Institutions of employee voice that publicize potential injustice or inequity transmit this information to employees and managers, and lead to swift management response, lest the best employees leave, and all of them slacken their voluntary cooperation.

Once again, a problem in the economics of labor and employment turns out to be, to a significant degree, a problem in the economics of information. Employee organizations that have *only* information effects may, under some circumstances, be as effective or more effective than organizations that can threaten or inflict economic harm through a strike. Future models, of even the prototype version of collective bargaining, will have to account more fully for this potent informational effect.

Networks would be appealing mainly if they involve less than a majority of employees, or if the employer would oppose union organization. Obviously, either or both of these situations obtains in most U.S. workplaces, certainly including Silicon Valley. By contrast, if the employer does not oppose employee unionization, and a union represents a majority, it is hard to think of any advantage to the *employees* in maintaining a network as opposed to a union. If a union represents a majority of the employees in an appropriate bargaining unit, it would have privileges that a network would lack. It could use the law to require employer bargaining, or have dues deducted off from employee paychecks, or impose certain limited discipline on its members. A network with these privileges, added to its rapid mobilization of employee voice and employer response, would (in theory) be more effective than a network without them. As Al Capone is alleged to have said, in a kind of ultimate comment on the economics of information: you can go further in life with a kind word and a gun than with a kind word alone. However, in practice, these legal privileges of a union might cut against the power of employee networks, by triggering the kind of employer opposition that so far networks have not. Employers do have legal ways of not cooperating with unions, such as refusing to recognize them until the government conducts an election, then campaigning against them. Many employees, like those surveyed in Freeman and Rogers (1999), fear such employer opposition. They might be drawn to network organization, since employers don't seem to fight network organization, particularly if the employees were more interested in employer responsiveness than in formal bargaining.

Legal Issues Raised by Networked Employee Voice Groups

No new legal framework is necessary to accommodate the new network organizations of employee voice. They are already protected by existing labor law, which gives them two major privileges: protection against employer retaliation, and some rights to equal treatment by the employer, if the employer has a preferred employee organization. These legal rights of such groups, and employees who participate in them, come from the federal National Labor Relations (Wagner) Act. This is another irony, since the employees involved are always careful to point out, as they did at Apple, that they do not like unions and aren't trying to organize one.

Nevertheless, the Wagner Act protects the right of employees to engage in "concerted activities for the purpose," not merely of collective bargaining, but of "other mutual aid or protection." Suppose an employee were fired, or otherwise punished, for complaining on internal networks about bonus changes, or for trying to get other employees to do something about it. I have not encountered any stories of such retaliation in Silicon Valley. But if it happened, it would violate the National Labor Relations Act and would be corrected by the National Labor Relations Board on complaint by the employee (*Timekeeping Systems Inc.*). The latter case specifically protects employee internal e-mails, cast in the sarcastic tone so often found in e-mail (Wallace 1999: 110–32; Kiesler and Sproull 1992).

If the employer has its own preferred forms of employee organization, it may have to extend its privileges to the employee-organized group (Hyde et al. 1993a). For example, at the time of the action on Apple's internal network, Apple promoted black or Asian employee caucuses. Apple let those groups have e-mail boxes, meeting spaces, and bulletin boards, and therefore probably has to extend the same privileges to an employee network group (*Black Grievance Committee*), even if neither group is a statutory "labor organization" (*National Labor Relations Board v. Northeastern University*).

There is really no dispute with the abstract proposition that employee action on computer networks, or other informal group action without a union, is nevertheless protected by federal labor law. There are, however, two significant areas of legal uncertainty surrounding this protection. First, the law on protected activity under the Wagner Act has often been applied so as to deny protection to common action by unorganized employees, as I have shown in more detail elsewhere (Hyde 1993b). This is particularly true when orders of the National Labor Relations Board come before federal appeals courts. Judges simply insist (incorrectly) that a union is necessary to obtain the act's protection, or deny protection because of the Rabelaisian language often favored by unorganized employees (particularly on e-mail), or invoke vague rules about protest going "too far." I think this comes about largely because of judicial hostility to the act itself. However, the decisions also reflect, in part, the power of that prototype of union organizing (the robin, not the flamingo), and a refusal to understand that protecting the actual activity of unrepresented employees is equally a priority of the act. This protection requires protecting the ways that employees without unions actually present their grievances, not merely those channels that seem appropriate to federal judges.

The more difficult legal question concerns access to company e-mail systems. Intel has been involved in litigation here, too. Ken Hamidi is a former Intel engineer, bitter about his termination, who is the most prominent figure in Former And Current Intel Employees (FACE). They maintain a Web site (http://www.faceintel.com) with information on lawsuits against Intel by former employees alleging wrongful termination, and other information critical of Intel. (A lightly fictionalized account of his activities is Lessard and Baldwin [2000: 182–97].) FACE is a kind of network group, as we have been

using the term. An Intel employee could not be fired or disciplined for joining or participating in it.

Hamidi has raised the legal stakes by sending e-mail messages to current
Intel employees over Intel's internal network, activity that a California court
has enjoined as a trespass (*Intel Corp. v. Hamidi*). "Trespass" may seem like
a ridiculously old-fashioned way of thinking about an e-mail network, or any
system of communications. Intel probably could not enjoin Hamidi from
mailing letters to each of its employees. But "trespass" is a surprisingly important concept in labor law, and is turning out to be equally important in the
law of electronic data. It is a good example of a concept defined in traditional
labor markets, like "trade secret," that yields strange results when applied to
today's high-velocity labor market.

Labor law has, for nearly fifty years, solved the tension between employees' federal organizational rights, and employers' managerial and property rights,
by making a sharp distinction between current employees and nonemployees.
In labor law, the concept of trespass permits an employer to bar anyone who is
not an employee from its physical property. That includes union organizers
who are not employees. While employees have a federally protected right to
talk about organization among themselves, or hand out literature, the employer
does not have to assist this process by letting union organizers—or any other
nonemployees—onto its property. This is conceptualized as a matter of property rights. The employer does not need to have any reason, and it does not
matter if its property is normally open to the world, like a shopping center
(*Lechmere, Inc. v. NLRB*). (There is a dispute between the NLRB and some
lower courts, that the Supreme Court will eventually resolve, whether an employer that permits charitable solicitation of employees using company property must extend similar privileges to union organizers.) Finally, state courts
may enjoin trespasses even if the NLRB might have held them protected, at
least where the alleged trespasser did not make any effort to get the case before
the NLRB (*Sears, Roebuck & Co. v. San Diego Carpenters*).

Hamidi is not a current Intel employee. In fact, his position is that he was
wrongfully terminated. Nevertheless, under this way of thinking, if the internal network is Intel "property" under California law, the California court
was not wrong to enjoin Hamidi, a nonemployee, from using it. States are
largely free in the constitutional system to define "property," and California
has in fact decided that owners of shopping centers and other property open
to the world do not have a "property" right to keep out union organizers
(*PruneYard Shopping Center v. Robbins*). People who do not have a state
property right to exclude trespassers do not have any federal labor law right
to do so, either (*Bristol Farms, Inc.*). However, Intel's internal e-mail system
is not routinely open to people other than Intel employees.

Hamidi represented himself in the California courts, and did not raise issues of the National Labor Relations Act, or its preemptive effect on California law. That figures. As I have said, people in Silicon Valley typically mistakenly believe that federal labor law has nothing to offer them. It is possible that, had Hamidi raised the issue of labor law preemption, he might have convinced a California court that his activity was "arguably protected" by federal law (the legal standard: *San Diego Building Trades Council v. Garmon*). That is, he was and is attempting to organize employee group action, through FACE at Intel. If the state courts found that Hamidi's organizational efforts were "arguably protected" by federal law, it might have had to dismiss Intel's suit. But it is more likely that the state court would not have dismissed, even if Hamidi had argued preemption. The state court would probably have found either that Hamidi, as a former Intel employee, was not even "arguably" protected by federal labor law, or that even if his conduct was "arguably protected," California courts retain jurisdiction over his "trespass" (*Sears, Roebuck*). These are two different ways of making his case turn on a sharp distinction between employees and nonemployees.

While labor law has traditionally yielded to state property law when dealing with nonemployees (like union organizers), it provides different rules for employees. A traditional labor lawyer, advising Ken Hamidi, would tell him that all these problems could be avoided in the future if FACE messages were sent by Intel employees lawfully authorized to send messages over the network. Sending such messages would be presumptively protected by the National Labor Relations Act. Employees could not be disciplined for sending them, unless Intel could show some unusual disruption or harm, or the system (like some hospitals', e.g., *Washington Adventist Hospital*) was not open to employee messages of any kind. Certainly an employer with an e-mail or bulletin board open to all employees for their own use couldn't have a rule forbidding union or organizational messages.

E-mail systems and databases of addresses are held to be property in cases involving either spam (unsolicited bulk e-mail) or what is now called hacking (unauthorized breach of system security). If an outsider gets into a data system and obtains information, or causes harm, the owner may sue under the Computer Fraud and Abuse Act. It has become normal in such suits to include a separate claim under state trespass law (see, e.g., *Register.com v. Verio, Inc.; Ebay, Inc. v. Bidder's Edge, Inc.; America Online Inc. v. National Health Care Discount, Inc.*). Hamidi probably did not violate the statute, since he did not damage Intel's data, or acquire any for himself. But his messages were a kind of unsolicited bulk e-mail or spam, and spam is so unpopular that courts are unlikely to be criticized when they hold that owners of networks are empowered to keep it off. It has been argued that courts should allow people like

Hamidi to send messages to employee e-mail (Malin and Perritt 2000; Harvard Law Review 1999). I would be surprised to see it happen on behalf of former employees or union organizers. Recall that *employees* with access to internal networks may send such messages, and are protected by federal law if they do. So even if Hamidi loses his case, it will not have a practical impact so long as employees can be found who will post messages from FACE.

The biggest problem with this traditional labor law analysis seems to me to be not its practical effect, but the rigid distinction between "employee" and "nonemployee." The distinction originated in a United States Supreme Court opinion in 1956 (*NLRB v. Babcock & Wilcox Co.*). Before then, it had not been thought important. But this is obviously a very "old economy" way of thinking about employee organization. It calls up a world in which employees form communities; the communities take place at work; employees are people who will stay at work for a long time. This, of course is not the world of Silicon Valley, in which employee mobility is high, loyalty is to teams or technology, normally spanning many firms, often heightened by ethnic ties, and such mobility is highly positive for economic growth. The new employee organizations, forming in the Valley and discussed in this chapter, do not make rigid distinctions between employees and former employees, and could not function if they did. Conceptualizing employee organizational rights as limited to incumbent employees at one employer never fit the statute very well. It is on a collision course with labor market trends toward shorter tenures, high mobility, and strong formal and informal ties among employees across firm lines—ties that benefit society by transmitting information crucial to endogenous economic growth.

Cases like *Intel v. Hamidi* rest on the traditional distinction between Hamidi's rights to communicate with Intel employees (none that an employer need assist) and the extensive rights of those employees. That is why a traditional labor lawyer might see Hamidi's conduct as unnecessary to protect, because his messages could "just as well" have been sent by an Intel employee. It would be better, however, if cases like this began to redefine the meaning of employee communication in high-velocity labor markets. A court might start by noting that the relevant community is broader than merely employees at Intel at a particular time. The community of people who have worked at Intel, or who might work at Intel, and therefore are interested in Hamidi's litigation against Intel, is much larger. Recall that, as recounted in chapter 2, when Intel sued employees departing to start-ups in the late 1980s, "chat groups lit up all over the Valley," and the issue was raised frequently in its recruiting interviews. The court might also note that the communication itself, e-mail, is cheap and not disruptive. This might suggest greater rights for "nonemployee" Hamidi than those recognized in the 1950s.

The most interesting legal issues raised by network groups and other "employee voice institutions" may arise in the long term. It is conventional to assert that labor law recognizes some of the harm to the public from unrestrained cartel effects, and on many issues takes the form that it does in order to trim some of those cartel effects. This might be true of limitations on union secondary boycotts, application of antitrust laws to certain labor activities, and obligations that labor unions observe internal democracy and offer fair representation to individuals. If one really were faced with employee action that involved strictly "voice" effects without risk of cartel, one might expect greater scope for its action.

Ethnic Organizations and Networks

The popular picture of the isolated Silicon Valley engineer (e.g., Bellah et al. 1985; Cohen and Fields 1999), while not totally inaccurate, turns out to be somewhat ethnocentric. Silicon Valley's large immigrant population makes extensive use, not only of informal ethnic ties, but of formal, ethnic-based network organizations. (Here I use "network" in the older sociological sense, and not to imply use of computer-mediated communication.)

About 30 percent of the Valley's high-tech workforce was foreign-born in 1990, about one-third of all scientists and engineers. Of these, almost two-thirds were Asian, the majority Chinese or Indian. By contrast, Massachusetts and Texas have half this proportion of foreign-born scientists and engineers. Chinese and Indian engineers run one-quarter of the region's technology businesses started since 1980, companies that collectively account for more than $12.5 billion in annual sales and 46,290 jobs (Saxenian 1999a).

Saxenian shows the importance of formal organization in this economic success story (although most immigrant engineers do not participate in formal ethnic associations [Dossani 2002: 6]). She lists thirteen formal professional associations of Chinese or Indian engineers that foster networking and support along fairly narrow ethnic lines. For example, there are distinct associations of engineers with origins in Taiwan (who speak Mandarin at meetings), Hong Kong (Cantonese), mainland China, and English-speaking Chinese. Another association was named The Indus Entrepreneur to include Pakistanis, Bangladeshi, and Nepalese; however, its members are in fact almost all Indian. These associations put professionals in touch with role models and sources of venture capital, serve as important sources of information about market or job opportunities, and offer formal and informal lessons in the basic facts of entrepreneurship, management, and (for Chinese) English communication. Almost 80 percent of participants in these ethnic associations are male (Dossani 2002: 7).

Now if unions may seem a little old-fashioned to fit with high-technology culture, what about ethnic-based network groups? They link the Valley with the immigrant cultures of the last century. They also link the Valley's richest and poorest immigrants. The Mexican janitor and gardener is also likely to be part of a network of relatives and friends, often from the same city in Mexico, who share living and economic arrangements and provide information on job opportunities (Zlolniski 1994). These ethnic networks were central in the successful organization of their union (Martínez Saldaña 1993). (The Mexican networks, however, are rarely formal organizations with names and meetings and are not linked electronically.) As I have mentioned, my interest in Silicon Valley work relations originally stemmed from my concerns about low-wage contingent labor. I believed that successful contingent workers would be employing new forms of organization, savings, and benefits, which might be adapted to low-wage contingent labor. The only employee organization that can truly be said to be employed by both high- and low-end contingent workers in the Valley is the ethnic-based network.

For Chinese and Indian engineers, the chief economic aspect of the ethnic network is a path toward entrepreneurship. A survey of several thousand Chinese- and Indian-born engineers showed that participation in formal ethnic associations was strongly linked to desire to start one's own business. Sixty percent of the Indians participating in formal Indian associations were involved in start-ups, and 75 percent of the group that wasn't, planned to start one. Fewer of those born in the People's Republic of China were involved in start-ups (only 30 percent), but 77.2 percent of that group planned a start-up (Dossani 2002: 15).

Entrepreneurship opportunities are also provided by the Mexican networks, though these also assist union organizing. (Both networks also perform some aspects of the labor market intermediaries discussed in the previous chapter that provide information to match employees to opportunities.) The engineer meets role models and sources of venture capital. The janitor advances by becoming a contractor himself or herself, or uses the network for an informal sales business, or even an informal dentistry practice (Zlolniski 1994: 2328–30). The entrepreneurship path is crucial in understanding the groups as employee organizations, and in understanding immigration. It also raises again the role of business ownership in a high-velocity labor market, in which employers do not offer lifetime careers, and individual advancement normally requires exit from the firm and entry into new employment, self-employment, or business ownership.

We saw in chapter 2 that employees in such a high-velocity labor market can outperform employees in a traditional internal job tournament. The promise of advancement outside the firm can be a powerful motivator of performance. For this to be true, the promise must be bound—as it is in the Valley—in a new implicit contract. The employee will leave this firm with skill and experience that he or she lacked coming in, and will be able to exploit that knowledge at the next employer, or at the employee's own business. We now see how the promise of entrepreneurship shapes employee organization, and I will suggest momentarily that other new employee organizations will take account of this. In chapter 12, I will discuss the role of entrepreneurship in civil rights or antidiscrimination strategies for high-velocity labor markets.

By contrast with their entrepreneurship functions, ethnic-based networks of employees, transcending particular employers, have not yet taken on any functions of advancing employee interests *as employees.* (One group that does is the Immigrants Support Network that lobbies and organizes for changes in the treatment of immigrants on temporary visas. I will take them up separately later in this chapter; although dominated by Indians, they aspire to speak for immigrants more generally, so I will treat them as a "new organization" rather than a "formal ethnic-based organization.") Ethnic-based networks do not appear to have provided the basis for such informal protests as the Apple profit-sharing or IBM pension protests discussed earlier in this chapter. They do not go to bat for individual employees with grievances against particular employers or labor contractors. Sometimes this must happen informally, but I could find no specific example of it.

So we might ask the following questions about ethnic-based networks of employees. Are they creatures simply of the recent immigrant experience, in which case we might expect them to fade away as immigrant groups become more acculturated? Or are they prototypes for new forms of employee organization that can be used by other groups of employees—not merely new immigrant groups, but other groups of employees? Will such networks take on any more of the functions of new labor market intermediaries: information, job matching, possibly benefits? Will they remain best suited to advancing job exit through entrepreneurship? Or ever take on representational functions for employees? While it is obviously too soon to answer any of these questions definitively, tentative answers may emerge from examining two other kinds of employee group: formal ethnic caucuses organized by, or with the cooperation of, large firms; and women's networks.

Formal Ethnic Caucuses for Large Employers

While no Silicon Valley employer has a union of technical personnel, several encourage formal caucuses. For example, Apple Computer has had a formal Multicultural Alliance including Asian, black, Hispanic, lesbian and gay, professional women, and Viet caucuses. These caucuses are defined almost exclusively as vehicles for the advancement, within firm hierarchies, of individual group members. They play little or no role in linking women or Latino or Asian or African-American employees across firm boundaries. Their inability to perform the latter function impedes their utility in the emerging high-velocity labor market.

The basic model of an employee identity caucus is familiar from the work of Friedman (1996) and Friedman and Carter (1993). "The issue that African American network groups deal with is, broadly speaking, the acceptance, comfort, and career achievement of Black employees" (Friedman and Carter 1993: 3). Just the same might be said (as they note) of other network groups. Their main activities include mutual support, networking, exchange of information (particularly about managerial vacancies), and advice. Within a sample of Fortune Service 500 companies responding to a survey, 29 percent had network groups, typically African-American, women's, or both. Groups often arise on initiative of managers not part of the group, who seek assistance in recruiting, or who bring the group together for some other purpose, such as reviewing an affirmative action plan or planning Black History month, the group then staying together to pursue its own purposes.

Groups tend to be dominated by professional or managerial employees even when nominally open to others (Friedman and Carter 1993: 16). They almost never make formal demands or requests of management. When managers express concerns about the formation of such groups, it is a fear that they will be confrontational and union-like. Groups are sensitive to this fear and avoid confrontation or demands. This is certainly true of the Silicon Valley groups I could research. The sole categorical exception that I was able to find in database news searches and personal discussions was gay and lesbian caucuses, which typically at some point request that corporate benefits programs be opened to nonmarried domestic partners. When this request is granted, such groups generally make no further demands and revert to a more typical social-and-support group (Scully 1997). Sometimes African-American or women's caucuses, particularly when asked to review an affirmative action plan, may suggest numerical goals. They have also requested changes in formal job posting, evaluation, or mentoring programs or sensitivity training or cultural awareness programs. Still, the human resources managers surveyed by Friedman and Carter ranked "influence policies" the second-lowest among potential functions actually accomplished by network groups. Thus, while almost no problems or downside can be identified in the existence of identity caucuses, their positive role seems largely limited to career and psychic support for their particular members.

Silicon Valley firms often have active caucus systems that largely replicate this pattern of corporate loyalty and devotion to career advancement. For example, Apple Computer, at the time of my interviews in March 1996, had a formal Multicultural Alliance consisting of six employee groups (Asian, black, Hispanic, lesbian and gay, professional women, and Viet). A "senior specialist, multicultural programs" publicized their efforts and acted as liaison with management. Christian fellowship and Jewish cultural groups were at that time functioning outside the alliance. All groups are "identity caucuses." The specialist in 1996, Toni Tomacci, told me laughingly: "There are no Employees for a Democratic Apple or for Higher Bonuses." Groups, funded mostly by individual contribution, got e-mail boxes, meeting places, and permission to plan public events. All their activities consisted either of "social, networking" functions or of helping the company use diversity for business success, such as tapping Asian or Latin American markets. Groups have persuaded Apple to fund conferences of professional women, or mentoring programs at historically black colleges. Particularly when planning conferences, groups may link up informally with counterpart caucuses at Hewlett-Packard or Xerox, but nobody knows of any links with larger community or political organizations.

At least one group formally links identity caucuses, though it still excludes larger community or political organizations. A National Hispanic Employee Association (NHEA) is active in the Bay Area and perhaps elsewhere. I attended their Second Annual Breaking Barriers Awards Conference in San Jose, California, on March 15, 1996. The group is not, however, even the beginning of an "associational union" (Heckscher 1988). Rather, it describes its "mission and vision . . . to promote the upward mobility of Hispanics in the corporate and public sectors." Indeed, the conference, sponsored by Silicon Graphics, Sun Microsystems, Apple Computers, AT&T, and similar employers, was largely aimed at high school and college students and advised them on self-presentation and career planning. The mission was clearly to facilitate inclusion of Hispanics in existing corporate culture, and transforming that culture only in the sense of including more Hispanics.

I do not wish to denigrate the importance of these goals or the efficacy of the National Hispanic Employee Association's efforts. I wish simply to raise as a question the disjunction between the corporate world uniformly invoked in the literature and communications of employee network groups (like NHEA or the Apple caucuses), and Silicon Valley. The literature and speeches at the conference invoked a world of loyalty to the corporation, advancement through internal promotion ladders ("upward mobility"), and fitting in to an existing corporate culture. There was no reference to a high-velocity labor market involving frequent job changes, start-ups, informal exchange of information among networked employees, and know-how sharing among firms. There was certainly no sense that the Hispanic Employee Association could facilitate start-ups or job changes by Hispanic employees, as Asian organizations do (Dossani 2002). The intense devotion of NHEA and the Apple identity caucuses to the world of corporate loyalty, careers, and promotions may show that world to be in better shape than this book has too quickly assumed. On the other hand, it may be that there is a kind of deeper affinity between network groups and the hierarchical corporation with internal labor markets. This affinity may impede the network groups' recognition of newer and more vital ways of operating labor markets.

Employee network groups, if they link with groups at other firms and then community groups, could play a more important role in future labor markets than they currently play. They could take on some of the intermediary functions we have discussed (job matching and information, benefits delivery) as well as additional functions of political and community advocacy. Such linked organizations could play a larger role in remedying problems of discrimination; I will take that up in chapter 12. It will be necessary, however, for them to transcend a model of loyalty to hierarchical corporations with career ladders, and imagine functioning in high-velocity labor markets. Unless something like this happens, it is hard to imagine anything interesting coming out of corporate-oriented ethnic caucuses.

Women's Groups

Women's networks will surely provide an interesting test over the next few years of the potential of identity-based groups to cross the boundaries of the firm and perform informational or other economic functions in a high-velocity labor market. The record to date is rather sparse.

In chapter 12, I will take up the ways in which women's experience working in high tech differs from men's, in connection with issues of equal opportunity and discrimination. For now, we can proceed on the unremarkable premise that there are such differences, and that Silicon Valley simultaneously offers unusual opportunities and obstacles to the careers of women as a group. A few formal network organizations of women transcend firm boundaries. Like the Chinese and Indian organizations studied by Saxenian and Dossani, they are particularly oriented toward facilitating entrepreneurship through access to capital and other technical support. The best known is the Forum for Women Entrepreneurs, which claims through programs and networks to have assisted women in raising over $600 million in starting businesses in 2000 (Women of Silicon Valley 2001: 14). They run formal programs in which women entrepreneurs teach small groups of potential entrepreneurs. Other formal groups include Silicon Valley Webgirls, San Francisco Women on the Web, and Women in Multimedia (Solomon 2000). These groups are known entirely by self-description and journalism. There are no ethnographies of these formal or informal organizations, and they never came up in my interviews with women in the Valley, despite my questions.

For women who plan to remain employees (or self-employed, but not entrepreneurs), but who seek support in career planning, there seem to be fewer formal organizations. A typical informal network would consist simply of people one knew from former jobs, neighbors, and other social acquaintances. Naturally people hear about jobs, new products, and so on through whatever informal networks they employ, but I did not hear any stories (despite asking for them) to suggest that informal networks of women play any special role.

I think it is too soon to conclude that women's networks will function just like any other kind of network, such as engineers who were classmates together at an Indian institute of technology, or Web site designers who all once worked together. There are some intriguing hints in the literature that they may play unique roles. For example, the Stanford Project on Emerging Companies (SPEC) has reported the unexpected fact that start-ups with high initial representation of women in core technical and scientific roles will have significantly fewer administrators in subsequent years. Their typical firm was about 25 percent female in these roles in its founding year. Such a firm would have only 80 percent as many full-time administrators in subsequent years, as compared to an all-male firm (Baron, Hannan, and Burton 1999). The numbers were large and held across different variables. Why should this be? They suggest a number of possible explanations, such as that men like having titles. But in more recent work, they explore precisely the role of network ties. Women are common in start-ups typically when they enter through network ties to the founders, and a firm with such network ties has richer informal control and needs fewer formal administrators (Baron, Hannan, Hsu, and Kocak 2002: 263–65). Surveys reveal that women in high-tech attribute unusual importance to networks and mentors in advancing careers (Women of Silicon Valley 2001: 22). In short, there is much to learn about informal networks in high-velocity labor markets and any gender differences in their use.

New Organizations for the Mobile Workforce: Working Partnerships, Immigrants Support Network, Communication Workers Projects, Working Today

New organizations have been created for mobile, high-tech workers, partly for their own sake but partly because existing unions and some foundations regard them as potential prototypes for other contingent workers. They have attracted some of the most thoughtful, imaginative, and energetic people interested in labor issues, though successes are limited to date. Particularly active in Silicon Valley are Working Partnerships, affiliated with the South Bay Labor Council AFL-CIO, and the Immigrants Support Network. Two other particularly interesting organizations are not yet active in the Valley. I include them here because the Valley would be an obvious next location for them if they achieve success. They are the specialized projects of the Communication Workers aimed at employees of Microsoft in Seattle and IBM in upstate New York, and Working Today in New York City.

Working Partnerships/South Bay Labor Council AFL-CIO

The union movement in the Valley itself has chosen some unusual forms through which to organize low-wage workers, particularly temporary and contingent workers. Working Partnerships USA, founded in 1995, is affiliated directly with the South Bay Labor Council (rather than any particular affiliated union). "Partnerships" is supposed to convey a desire to build bridges between organized labor and nonunion workers. The group has issued a series of research reports on the Silicon Valley economy, work organization, and housing (e.g., Benner, Brownstein, and Dean 1999). It has organized political campaigns around "living wage" ordinances enacted to raise labor standards in the contracts of local governments, and on behalf of favored candidates. It runs leadership training courses for members of neighborhood associations in San Jose and other community leaders.

Most intriguingly, it has opened its own temporary help agency, hoping to compete with existing temp agencies despite maintaining high labor standards. When I interviewed its president, Amy Dean, in October 2001, it was placing forty or fifty individuals a week, for 1,200 hours on average. Its members work both in entry-level positions like office temps, receptionists, and administrators, and as systems administrators, network administrators, and cablers sourced to Pacific Gas & Electric.

The staffing agency incorporates training and upward career mobility. It offers training in software skills and programming languages like Java and Juniper; A+, a standard training in hardware literacy; and Cisco and other certifications for network administrators and support staff. The unique advantage of a union-affiliated staffing agency is this combination of job placement, training, and employee mobility. Junior colleges offer some training, but not linked to specific jobs. Employers offer some training, but rarely for mobile employees. Many staffing agencies offer little or no training. The theoretical and practical advantage of an employee-run organization is the combination. Its employees currently are enrolled in a Kaiser health plan for mobile employees during the time they are working. The next project will be the creation of a trust fund, on the model of construction unions, into which employers will pay pennies per hour worked. The point will be to permit some coverage of employees during brief periods they are between placements.

All these initiatives reflect a strategy of positioning worker organizations in larger political and geographic communities, not merely inside traditional firms, reflecting the decline in internal labor markets and one-firm careers. Thus, the political and community activity is not merely a device to organize a traditional union; it is a new model of union organizing that, if successful, will result in a very different type of union. For example, its training courses and self-directed tutorials are administered jointly with the Black Chamber of Commerce. It has warm, though less formal, ties with the Hispanic and Vietnamese Chambers of Commerce. Dean pointed out how unusual these business ties are for a union. Every Labor Day, Working Partnerships, like other unions, send representatives to speak at over eighty churches and synagogues, where congregants are asked to sign cards supporting its issues. While this publicity technique is not unique to Working Partnerships, it takes on a different meaning in an organization devoted to community advocacy as much as worker representation. American unions have been organized around specific industries, or specific crafts, but we have little experience with unions organized around regions and communities. Nor can we point to successful unions organized around a way of working (temporary, contingent), as opposed to a craft or job description (such as carpentry or waitressing). Working Partnerships draws on imaginative recent thinking on new ways to organize unions (Stone 2001). It combines elements of an associational union (Heckscher 1988), a regional craft union (Cobble 1991); a union of low-income service workers, organized around their work organization, as opposed to craft or industry (Wial 1993), a union-run job referral system (Silverstein and Goselin 1996); and an institution providing training to workers in dead-end jobs so as to create career paths that lead out of those dead-end jobs (Herzenberg, Alic, and Wial 1998). A project this ambitious cannot be expected to achieve instant success. It will take time to sort out what works.

Immigrants Support Network

More successful numerically is a group focused (so far) entirely on political representation, the Immigrants Support Network, representing mainly individuals working under "H1-B visas," the program discussed in chapter 7 in which temporary visas are issued to skilled individuals to fill supposed labor shortages.

H-1B visa holders' most frequent complaints are that they would like smoother transitions to permanent resident status and greater ability to move to jobs with employers other than their original visa sponsor. The Immigrants Support Network (ISN) was formed after the 1998 congressional process by visa holders who felt they required representation for these concerns, independent of the employer groups that dominate the legislative process (as discussed in chapter 7). It appears to be funded largely by successful entrepreneurs of Indian origin, such as Kanwal Rekhi (Chhabra 2001). These businessmen have no direct financial interest in reforming the H1-B program to meet visa holders' complaints, but rather seem to fund the organization out of pride in Indian contributions to high technology and desire to assist their nationals in immigration. Still, it seems only a matter of time before the interests of H1-B visa holders conflict with some interests of the businessmen who fund their organization. Matloff (2001) claims that ISN spent heavily to employ expensive lobbyists in the 2000 legislative process, despite receiving contributions from only about 700 of the 15,000 individuals it claims as "members." It achieved some success in that 2000 congressional process, obtaining extensions of H1-B visas for those whose permanent resident applications are in process, and permitting employers to expedite the H1-B process for a fee. ISN's next goal is abolition of the country quota on permanent resident cards (Jayadev 2001).

Does the ISN belong in a chapter on employee organization? It is limited to immigrants, receives funds from employers, and largely lobbies around particular political interests. Does that mean that it is not an employee organization? Or rather, is this the kind of employee organization of the future: linking employees across employers, moving from political to workplace advocacy, drawing strength from identity ties? Its future will tell us a great deal about the future of employee organization.

Will it form links with other employee groups: for example, the South Bay Labor Council, or its Working Partnerships project? Could ISN and organized labor (say, Working Partnerships) make common cause around their joint interest in mobility of workers among employers, ease of immigration, and high employment standards? The AFL-CIO's position on immigration has changed sharply recently. It no longer opposes immigration as a threat to current U.S. jobholders; it now welcomes immigration and seeks to organize immigrants. Consistent with that position, it did not oppose extension of the H1-B program, but has not made efforts to organize H1-Bs.

In such a hypothetical "mobile workers' alliance," labor would be turning its back to older programmers allegedly displaced by immigrants. However, that might not be an obstacle. There are questions about how large that group is anyway. Labor might well conclude that its future lay with the newer immigrants, rather than older IT professionals who never affiliated with labor in the first place. Could ISN, alone or with assistance from organized labor, become an advocate for immigrants in disputes with their employers or sponsors, not merely with Congress? Could the ethnic pride and energy of Silicon Valley's immigrant communities fuel successful organizing for programmers, as it has for janitors?

Communication Workers Projects Aimed at IT Workers

The Communication Workers of America (CWA) union, which represents many workers at older telephone companies, has set up two innovative projects to advance the interests of information professionals, Washington Alliance of Technology Workers (WashTech) in Seattle, and Alliance@IBM in Endicott, New York. Both projects advance workers' interests without any legal status as bargaining representative, and thus have been described as "virtual unions" (Diamond and Freeman 2001: 15–16).

WashTech is actually Local 37083 of the Communication Workers (duRivage 2000), but does not yet function as a bargaining representative for any of its members or for the much larger group that visits its Web site. Its particular focus is the individuals working at Microsoft but nominally employees of temporary help agencies. Some of these individuals were found to be legally employees of Microsoft in litigation in the mid-1990s—*Vizcaino v. Microsoft,* discussed in chapter 5. Microsoft has changed its practices since then, and presumably most individuals whom it classes today as agency employees would also be found to be agency employees in law. WashTech provides lobbying, training, and informational services to these temporary employees. While WashTech did not initiate the *Vizcaino* litigation, it keeps members informed about it. It has lobbied in Washington State for access to personnel records and favorable employment standards treatment for agency employees, and offers training classes in software and other skills. It has requested bargaining recognition from at least four temporary agencies but without success so far. However, like Working Partnerships, WashTech aspires to anchor organization in an industry and geographic area, not just in a collective bargaining relationship. In the words of Larry Cohen, executive vice president of the CWA, at WashTech "what sustains people is not collective bargaining, but creating a community of people" (Greenhouse 2000). Like the Immigrants Support Network or any Web-based organization, it has many more individuals visiting its Web page, and joining for specific actions, than it has dues-paying members: only 225 as of June 2001 (Littman 2001).

Alliance@IBM, another CWA affiliate, was formed in summer 1999, growing out of the electronic protests of IBM's proposed reductions in pensions, discussed earlier in this chapter. Its main constituency appears to be long-time IBM employees concerned about outsourcing and downsizing (Littman 2001). Alliance@IBM doesn't appear to have reached out yet to the kind of temporary employee served by WashTech, whose interests may conflict with the career IBM employees. Perhaps at some point the CWA will have to confront this conflict between older career employees and younger temps (served by WashTech) or immigrants (served by ISN). At the moment it is free to organize opportunistically: what *RedHerring* magazine calls "the venture capital approach to unionizing" (Littman 2001). The CWA is not yet active in Silicon Valley, but this would be an obvious next arena if it feels that either WashTech or Alliance@IBM has been succesful.

Working Today

Working Today was founded to represent mobile individuals, mostly self-employed, but in any case lacking ties to a single employer. So far it is funded more by foundations than by members. Some of its founders (such as the Columbia sociologist Herbert Gans) contemplated a group that would seek to convert such contingent work into more traditional, stable work, but the group eventually followed the path of other organizations reviewed in this section. It accepts the appeal of self-employment and a mobile workforce, and now hopes to learn what kinds of benefits appeal to such a group, how to market benefits to them, and what other kinds of economic and political representation they need (Horowitz 2000). Its first pilot project, launched in 2001, is aimed at Web site designers in New York City and seeks to market health insurance to them. The group has designed what it believes will be an attractive package of portable benefits, though still fairly expensive. It remains to be seen whether a participatory or democratic employee organization will have any advantage over the private sector in the marketing of benefits such as health insurance. I cannot think of any practical or theoretical reason why it should.

Summing Up: The Future of Employee Organization in High Technology

The brutal truth is that Silicon Valley attained its present technological and economic preeminence essentially without formal employee organization. It is difficult to see why this will change any time soon. The nascent organizations discussed in this chapter may be interesting straws in the wind, and may present intriguing legal or economic issues. But none has really achieved much importance. Put another way: employee organizations come up in my interviews only when I specifically ask about them. If the conversation concerns "tell me about the last company where you worked/were HR director/counseled," employee organization will never come up.

Certainly many managers still believe, as Robert Noyce did, that employee organization is fundamentally incompatible with high-technology employment, particularly the flexibility and energy demanded of (and received from) employees. When I asked whether Cisco had formal women's or black caucuses like Apple's, Michael LaBianca, the lawyer who handles employment matters, laughed: "People are too busy to think about anything else." The managers to whom I have talked would nearly all interpret a story like the Individuate story (with which I opened this chapter) as one in which naive attempts at formal organization actually took discontent that was minor and manageable and converted it into a serious problem. Nor can I be optimistic about the new groups that hope to get employees into formal organizations by meeting employee desires for training (WashTech), benefits (Working Today), or job placement (Working Partnerships). Private organizations already exist to meet these needs, and there seems no practical or theoretical reason why an employee organization should be able to provide better courses, or insurance plans, than private companies.

It is easier to imagine a role for employee organization at the low end of the Silicon Valley labor market: the office temps, product testers, and perhaps low-level programmers. The model that would work best for them, however, is not any of the fancy new organizations designed for mobile workers. What they need is a good, old-fashioned construction union. The employer on a unionized construction job pays contractual amounts, per hour worked, into trusts, jointly administered by the union and employers, that pay health, vacation, and retirement benefits. This is the best institution ever designed, in my opinion, for providing income stability, insurance, and retirement to what is really a very contingent workforce. It is puzzling that so much energy has been put into designing new organizations for a mobile workforce, when U.S. law and practice already provide an excellent blueprint.

Part of the problem in adapting the construction union model is simply the cognitive one of recognizing that construction work is a kind of contingent work, but one in which unions make earnings less contingent. Many construction workers work, over the course of a year, for many different contractors, on many jobs. Despite this uncertainty, construction workers are not usually included in discussions of "contingent" work. The difference is the union. Construction workers who are represented by a labor union typically have health insurance (87.1 percent), paid vacations, and a pension (67 percent). Construction employees who are not represented by a union normally have no health insurance (only 41.4 percent get it through work) or pension (only 22 percent have one) (Center to Protect Workers' Rights 1998: charts 3, 26, 27). While the oldest construction unions involve highly skilled employees, the form has also been employed by laborers and others who have less formal training. Construction unions also often operate hiring halls that provide labor to contractors on request. While this can facilitate administration of the benefit plans, it is not necessary to them. So there is no obvious reason why office temps and other mobile, less-skilled employees could not be organized into unions that would administer benefits and might, or might not, take on training and job placement functions.

The legal impediments to such unions are so serious—and so artificial—that I have no confidence that temps would not join unions, if they could. Of course, many people feel that this is true of U.S. unions as a general matter: that the legal obstacles to their organization are so serious as to depress levels of organization below existing demand (the best introduction is still Weiler [1990], and Freeman and Rogers [1999]). Unions for mobile temps face problems apart from these general impediments to unionization. The chief specific legal impediment, to the organizations proposed for mobile employees, is the lack of authority in the National Labor Relations Board to certify a bargaining unit with multiple employers. Such bargaining takes place, but is voluntary with the employer, who is free to withdraw from multiemployer bargaining at any time except when new contract negotiations are actually under way.

The Board has retreated from some extensions of this doctrine that have really impeded union organization among temporary help workers. For years, the Board took the position that including temporary help employees in a bargaining unit with regular employees was a kind of multiemployer bargaining that required the mutual consent of the temporary help agency and the client firm. The Board will now certify a unit of all employees working at one client, including regular employees and those jointly employed by the temp agency, to bargain with the client. For the temps discussed in chapter 5 who have little contact with the temp agency and work every day at the same employer, this is really all the bargaining they need. The Board will also certify a unit of all the temporary employees working at various locations but referred by the same temp agency, in order to bargain with that temp agency. It is possible that these changes will spark new union organizing among temporary help employees. However, they represent the outer limits of the Board's power. A unit of all the temps working at many different clients, to bargain with those clients, is a multiemployer unit, voluntary with each client, (see *M.B. Sturgis, Inc.*). Nor does the Board have authority to force any client, and the temp agency, to bargain jointly with the employees whom they employ jointly. Congressional amendment to the National Labor

Relations Act to facilitate multiemployer units is not imminent, and the *Sturgis* decision is likely to be reversed once appointees of George W. Bush gain an effective majority on the Board; its reconsideration was announced in October 2002.

However, such multiemployer bargaining for temps might also come about through employer voluntary actions, which are not totally far-fetched in Silicon Valley. After all, Valley employers preferred that their cleaning contractors bargain with the Service Employees, rather than face potential product boycotts. So while the most realistic assessment of the future is that rates of union organization in Silicon Valley will continue to be very low, I now feel that, if organization increases, it will not be the newfangled caucuses, associations, and networks that I have written about before. Rather, the construction union form will turn out to be adaptable to other individuals who work for many different employers.

Part IV

Flexible (and Informational) Compensation

10

STOCK OPTIONS:
THEIR LAW AND ECONOMICS

Compensating managers, and in some cases employees, through stock options has become the practice at perhaps one-third of American employers, according to a survey by the Federal Reserve (Lebow et al. 1999: 11 [Table 2]). In particular, stock option compensation has become a symbol of America's high-growth sectors, nowhere more so than in Silicon Valley's high-velocity labor market, where stock options are often more important than salary, not only for CEOs, but for ordinary employees. In the words of Mark Edwards, president of iQuantic, a compensation consulting firm: "If you don't do stock options, you won't get off the ground" (Southwick 1999: 176). Hotmail convinced all fifteen of its earliest employees to work only for stock options until its product was launched in 1996 (Bronson 1999: 86–87). By the fall of 2000, newly hired executives in the Valley were given options averaging $685,234, while hourly workers received options with an average value of $12,567 (Muto 2000).

As this book was being completed in 2002, several high-profile bankruptcies (none in Silicon Valley) focused national attention on executive pay generally and stock options in particular. Reform proposals have been raised concerning how companies account for stock options. A comprehensive legal discussion of stock options is not feasible here and would be out of date almost immediately. Instead, I will stick to my usual method. I will point out certain recurring legal problems, resulting in litigation, concerning stock options: specifically, promises to provide them, fraudulent representations concerning them, and valuing them if the recipient is wrongfully terminated. These problems recur frequently, potentially daily, when stock options are used. They are not limited to massive bankruptcies. Since, as I mentioned in chapter 1, most hiring of professionals or managers in Silicon Valley still involves stock options, these problems will continue, whether or not changes are made in accounting for stock options.

They are also essentially impossible to resolve under existing law. This difficulty again reflects the fact that both law and economics (to the extent that there is an economics of stock options) approach stock options through such traditional analogies as compensation, investment securities, or retirement benefits. Stock options in practice do something different than any of these three analogies, and, not surprisingly, the function they perform is one of transmitting information. I will identify a legitimate use of stock options as an informational device, analogous to use of a labor market intermediary or short-term employment, and suggest the illumination that this informational perspective casts on recurring legal problems. From this informational perspective, stock options perform a useful and important role in a high-velocity labor market. Understanding this informational role leads one to favor more helpful accounting and disclosure of such options, although I will not discuss specific proposals here. However, understanding the informational role that stock options play in high-velocity labor markets also leads to the conclusion that there is no good reason to discourage them through taxation or other regulation.

Stock options are something of a legal anomaly in the world of employee compensation, and current litigation over stock options often displays a search for the best analogy. They are normally conceptualized solely as creatures of state contract law, and can be structured to lie outside of both federal securities law and federal benefits law. They may thus be uncovered by any fiduciary, antifraud, or antidiscrimination rules. Courts, particularly courts now facing suits over stock options brought by ordinary employees and managers, sometimes rebel against this fact and attempt to assimilate stock options to other employee benefits, such as pensions or actual stock bonus plans, that are covered by federal fiduciary and antidiscrimination rules. At least one court has treated stock options as wages for purposes of a state wage payment statute (*Scully v. US Wats, Inc.*, contra, *IBM v. Bajorek*).

This chapter argues that courts should resist this temptation. The actual use of stock options, though not fully understood, suggests that they serve different functions than other forms of employee compensation and should not lightly be assimilated to existing statutory schemes. In particular, stock options are primarily used to send information to outside investors about management's (and sometimes employees') belief in the value of the company. Their secondary use is to recruit employees who are not averse to risk. (Congress also intended them to function to link the incentives of top executives to those of shareholders, though they do not fill this function particularly well.) They are understood by employees as speculative. Reported abuses in stock option compensation could and should be remedied by new federal or accounting industry rules on disclosing information. However, there are good reasons for keeping stock options out of ERISA's fiduciary and nondiscrimination rules, state wage payment statutes, or other regulation that would destroy their chief function of transmitting accurate information to investors.

Stock Options in the Economy

Just as stock options often elude legal categories, they also elude the categories in which official statistics on compensation are collected. This omission probably considerably understates recent inflation in compensation.

The wage data released by the Current Population Survey, on which most labor economists focus, excludes fringe benefits entirely. Another measure published by the Bureau of Labor Statistics (BLS), the employment cost index (ECI), includes many fringe benefits, but expressly omits stock options (Lebow et al. 1999: 2–3). A third BLS figure, the compensation per hour (CPH), divides national income and product accounts (according to Department of Commerce surveys) by hours worked (according to BLS surveys). In theory it captures all methods of pay, but agglomerated into other data; moreover, stock options are not included until the option is exercised. If, as appears to be the case, there has been a national trend toward putting compensation into forms not measured, or measured well, by BLS measures, wage inflation may be understated.

Economists for the Federal Reserve Board have recently attempted to study the growth in variable pay generally (including profit sharing and performance bonuses) and in stock options in particular. Nearly 90 percent of firms surveyed use some kind of variable pay. Just over 33 percent have stock option plans that are not limited to top executives, though the plans typically are limited to managers. Fewer than 10 percent had stock option plans available to employees below the managerial and professional level (Lebow et al. 1999: 12). An appendix to this report calculates the value of stock options (in Black-Scholes terms) in the annual reports of the largest 125 nonfinancial corporations in the S&P 500; had these been included in the ECI, which grew annually 3.1 percent per year from 1994 to 1998, the true figure would have been closer to 3.4 percent (pp. 22–24).

If stock options have been growing generally in the economy, they have been exploding in information technology. Technology firms grant options (in proportion to shares outstanding) three times as aggressively as nontechnology firms, and to a much broader range of employees. One hundred percent of executives in high-tech firms surveyed received stock options in 1997, as did 85 percent of managers and 42 percent of individuals. For high-tech CEOs and CFOs, stock options made up 58 percent and 55 percent of total compensation; for quality assurance engineers, 16 percent of compensation came as stock options, 12 percent as incentives, and only 72 percent as base pay (Southwick 1999: 176, 241). A different survey, using data on the top five executives in 1,724 firms, showed options accounting for more than 40 percent of the compensation of executives in the information technology area and less than 25 percent of the compensation of non-IT executives. By relating information on executive compensation to data on firm compensation, it also confirmed that stock options are used much more generously to compensate employees throughout IT firms and particularly generously in Silicon Valley firms (Anderson, Banker, and Ravindran 2000; see also Ittner, Lambert, and Larcker 2002).

Moreover, the relative importance of compensation through stock options is increasing. That 16 percent of engineers' compensation as stock options represented an increase of one-third between 1992 and 1997. This is important, because it is often asserted that technology start-ups are becoming more like conventional companies in the sense that, in a tight labor market, they must pay high base salaries and cannot expect people to work just for options. These assertions were media staples even in Silicon Valley's boom years, and are even more frequent now. I have not found one based on an actual survey.

On the contrary, as of the summer of 2002, more Western technology firms are increasing stock option awards than are decreasing them (William M. Mercer, Inc. 2002). Two different trade associations found the same thing in national surveys in summer 2002. Among semiconductor manufacturing and materials suppliers, 74 percent of employees received stock options, and over 86 percent of options went to rank-and-file employees rather than executive management (PR Newswire 2002). The trade association AeA reported that 84 percent of high-tech employees were receiving stock options. Sixty percent of firms surveyed give stock options to all their employees ("AeA Survey Finds 84% of High-Tech Workers Receive Stock Options" 2002). My informal interviews have not encountered any drop in the importance of stock options in Silicon Valley, and indeed some firms, like Cisco, have increased their use.

A Typical Stock Option

Stock options give the employee or manager the right but not the obligation to buy a share of the company's stock at a prespecified price, called the "exercise" or "strike" price. As we shall see, stock options are legally creatures of contract and may be set up in almost any way one likes. However, at least when Kevin Murphy (1999) collected data in 1992, there was remarkably little variation. I will describe a typical plan, with the caveat that it is derived from surveys covering CEOs. The plans that reach more ordinary employees may look different, though nobody knows.

In a typical plan, the options cannot be exercised immediately. They "vest" over time—that is, become capable of exercise by the recipient. (This use of the word "vest" is different from its use under ERISA, where it means nonforfeitability. By contrast, as we shall see, stock options that have "vested" in the stock option sense—that is, were capable of exercise by the recipient but not yet exercised—normally are forfeitable if the recipient leaves the firm, and hence were not "vested" in an ERISA sense.) Common vesting periods are around three or four years, and vesting is linear, such as 25 percent at the end of each of four years. The employee or manager, as mentioned, typically loses any "unvested" or "unexercised" options on departure from the firm. Although options may be exercised as soon as they vest, they do not have to be exercised at that time. Eventually, though, they will expire: after ten years, for 85 percent of options. About 95 percent of options are granted "at the money" or at "fair market value," which means that the exercise price is set equal to the stock price at grant date. On that date, the value of the option is the chance that the stock will increase in value. The remaining 5 percent of options are either "discount" options or "in the money," meaning that the exercise price is below the stock price at grant date, or "premium" or "out of the money" options, where the exercise price is above the stock price at grant date (Murphy 1999: 16; Hall and Liebman 2000: 8).

Why Stock Options?

Stock options are conventionally explained as part of a larger trend toward flexible, performance-based pay, and as a potent way of motivating managers and employees, or, more precisely—since managers and employees are well motivated under many compensation arrangements—of aligning their motivation with that of shareholders. Both these explanations are surely correct as far as they go. Certainly, there is an overall trend away from fixed compensation and toward compensation that responds more to firm performance (e.g., Bertrand 1999; Lebow et al. 1999; Cannon et al. 2000). Congress in 1993 made all forms of compensation that are linked to firm performance more attractive, with the adoption of Internal Revenue Code §162(m), placing a cap of $1 million on the deductibility of an individual's compensation, unless it is "performance based." However, there are many ways besides stock options of delivering pay that is flexible and based on firm performance. These include stock bonus plans, or any performance-based bonus plan, or bonuses linked to the price of company stock (called "stock appreciation rights" or SARs). So understanding the popularity of stock options requires that additional factors be considered.

Edward Lazear (1999) argues by contrast that stock options are valuable more for their "sorting" and "signaling" functions. That is, they help recruit managers or even employees who are willing to assume risk ("sorting"), and provide this information to potential investors ("signaling"). He first debunks two alternative explanations.

The claim that stock options ally management interests with shareholder interests, while containing some truth, can only be a part of the story. In a multiagent firm, the incentives on any agent, even the CEO, will be so diluted as to be trivial. To truly align the CEO's interests with the shareholders', he would have to be the residual claimant, and then there would be no way of aligning any other employee's interests with shareholders' (see also Stabile 1999). Calvin Johnson (1999) makes a different, and, frankly, more telling argument to the effect that stock options do not really align managers' interests with shareholders'. Someone holding stock options may have incentives to pursue risky investments. If share prices go up, the manager exercises the options; if share prices decline, he or she simply does not buy any stock. The interests of actual shareholders include a stronger interest in avoiding large downsides. The most recent studies suggest that firms that pay less in equity grants than their peers will indeed suffer poorer performance, while firms that pay more in equity grants than the median will not enjoy unusually better performance (Ittner, Lambert, and Larcker 2002). This, too, seems more consistent with a sorting story than an incentives story.

Lazear debunks the claim (e.g., Oyer and Schaefer 2002; Stephen C. Smith 1988) that granting nonvested options assists in employee retention. He notes that "nothing requires that non-vested pay take the form of equity" (p. 8). Lazear observes that "To the extent that the typical worker is more risk averse than the outside suppliers of capital, non-vested pay should take the form of bonds rather than equity" (p. 8). U.S. corporations in the 1950s and 1960s that really did try to bind employees to the firm for the long haul, employed a complex of well-known devices, including internal labor markets, promotion ladders, and back-loading compensation in the form of pensions and health insurance (typically more valuable to older employees). These are all considerably more effective than stock options in binding employees to the firm, where the firm believes this is in its interest.

Studies have failed to show any relation between grants of stock options and retention of employees (Ittner, Lambert, and Larcker 2002). Stock options at most bind employees for a few years. My observation, and that of others, of Silicon Valley suggests that many employees cash in stock options as soon as they vest and then move on, although data on cashing in do not seem to be available. "Many corporate employees behave less like old-fashioned workers than they do like investors. Rather than think, I need to stay here and do my best because I have an investment in this company, they think, I am going to keep a close eye on this ship, in case it starts to sink and my options become worthless" (Lewis 2000: 46–47). That is what this book is about. Stock options, in short, are a pretty lame device for creating employees or managers who are loyal for any but the short haul. Stock options may, in fact, lead to increased turnover, either from employees jumping ship or employers reevaluating the costs of keeping them. A perverse illustration of the latter is *Scully v. US Wats, Inc.,* where the court found that the company had promised so many stock options, that would soon have to be disclosed to the Securities and Exchange Commission (SEC), that it fired its president before his options vested—a firing that the court held was a breach of contract.

Lazear's explanation for stock option compensation, by contrast, contains elements of sorting and information. His example—drawn from real life—involves a manufacturer of pajamas who is considering moving into lingerie. The owner of the pajama firm (Gladys) has no expertise in lingerie and does not know the prospects in the lingerie market. Jim, with managerial expertise in lingerie, claims that Gladys can enter lingerie profitably, with his assistance. "Jim may be correct, but his statement may be wrong for two reasons: Jim's assessment of the lingerie market may be wrong or Jim may know the truth, but may gain personally by drawing Gladys into the venture, even if it is unprofitable" (p. 9). Gladys could sell a factory to Jim, or auction it among other lingerie managers, but this is not feasible:

> the manager must be in a position to buy the entire firm outright at the present value of its future profit stream. In most situations, this is infeasible and is part of the reason why managers are managers and not owners. Managers neither have the capital nor can they borrow enough to buy the firm outright. Borrowing introduces severe moral hazard problems. (p. 16)

Gladys can solve both the moral hazard and adverse selection problems by making Jim's pay contingent on profit. "It is sensible for a capitalist to be more willing to commit to an organization where all the knowledgeable people accept contingent pay than to an organization where those people demand a guaranteed wage." She will attract the managers who both believe that the new division will be profitable and estimate that they will make more running that new division than doing whatever they are currently doing. This recruiting (or "sorting") story seems right as far as it goes, but is subject to the same criticism that Lazear makes of other explanations: it does not distinguish stock option compensation from bonuses or other ways of linking pay to performance.

Lazear's second story—the "signaling" or "information" story—does.

> The idea is that insiders have more information about the profitability of an enterprise than outsiders. Outsiders, who might be inclined to invest in an enterprise, would like some assurance that the firm is likely to make a

positive profit. By taking compensation in a contingent form, insiders put their money where their mouths are. (p. 4)

This story, finally, distinguishes stock options from other performance-based pay, because stock options must be disclosed, and are therefore transparent enough to represent clear signals to outside investors.

Hall and Liebman's (2000: 18 and Table 3) data offer confirmation of this story: firms with a higher fraction of their shares owned by institutional investors use more stock options, while firms with large shares of inside directors are less likely to use stock options. While Lazear does not extend his analysis to the Silicon Valley start-up, the signaling story seems intuitively powerful there. Every potential entrepreneur, pitching an idea to venture capitalists, will suggest its enormous potential. Venture capitalists would be unlikely to finance a venture in which key personnel nevertheless assumed no risk. Stock options, despite all the recent revelations about accounting for them, nevertheless must be disclosed, and are therefore easier for outsiders to monitor than other bonus plans in which compensation is linked to performance. This is particularly true where "performance" itself is measured in something murkier than stock price. It is essentially impossible for outsiders to monitor pay that is linked to "productivity" or "sales," for example.

Lazear's sorting-and-information story has important legal implications. It suggests that the most important function served by stock options is the transmission of information to potential investors about managerial, and sometimes employee, assessment of the firm's prospects. To perform this function, stock options must retain their flexibility of structure. The informational function would be destroyed if stock options were forced into particular legal molds, as would be the case if particular employees had to be included or excluded, particular vesting schedules were required, and so on. Stock options are thus not analogous either to pension or benefit trusts, or to shares sold to investors on the market. As we shall see, legal regulation of stock options generally complies with this understanding.

Legal Treatment of Stock Option Compensation

A stock option is an unusually flexible form of employee compensation. There are no necessary formalities. Any enforceable contract giving someone the right to purchase shares of stock by tendering specified amounts of money can be a stock option. The contracts are governed by state law; a stock option is not covered by the federal ERISA legislation, so state law is not only not preempted, it is the only game in town.

If an option has a readily ascertainable fair market value—for example, an option to purchase stock publicly trading at $30 for $25 (an option that is "discounted" or "in the money")—its grant to an employee is income to that employee and a deductible expense to the employer. The typical high-technology start-up, though, may be handing out options to purchase stock that is not even tradable yet. In such a case, the option is a kind of gift until exercised by the employee: the firm does not take a deduction for giving it and the employee realizes no income in receiving it. While accountants do not require companies to take a charge to earnings when stock options are issued, because of the difficulty of valuing them at that time, since 1998 they require the company to disclose their dilutive effect. Financial Accounting Standards Board, Financial Accounting Standards No. 123, at 49 (1998), is discussed in Yablon (1999: 284). (The pre-1983 history of tax treatment of stock options is lucidly explained in Melton [1983]). If the start-up later goes public, existing options will have to be disclosed and valued fairly. A detailed and amusing journalistic account of this process can be found in Bronson (1999: 67–71).

The tax treatment of a stock option agreement turns on its classification as an incentive stock option (ISO) or nonstatutory stock option (NSO). The ISO is a nonmandatory, tax-favored form that entered the Internal Revenue Code in 1981. Any stock option that does not meet the form of an ISO is an NSO. An ISO must be given to an employee, and requires shareholder approval. Its advantages are: (1) income is deferred until the employee sells the *underlying stock;* the employee realizes no income on either the receipt or the exercise of the option itself; and (2) the appreciation in the underlying stock is taxed, on sale of that stock, as a capital gain. There are no tax consequences either to the grant or the exercise of an ISO, so long as the recipient remains an employee and holds the stock for a year. The disadvantages of the ISO are its restrictions (options are nontransferable; plans may not last more than ten years, options may not exceed $100,000 per executive per year, etc.), and the fact that it does not permit a deduction to the employer. (In the typical start-up without tax appetite, the absence of a deduction should not matter, and ISOs may be more common there, though data seem unavailable.) For this reason, ISOs are less popular than NSOs, constituting only 5 percent of options (Hall and Liebman 2000: 5). Presumably, however, if capital gains taxes became substantially lower (while personal income taxes remained the same or declined less), ISOs might become more popular.

Whether an ISO or NSO, however, the stock option permits a great deal of flexibility in its construction, particularly if compared to other devices for transferring stock to employees, such as qualified stock bonus plans or employee stock ownership plans. Both of these must be open to a broad range of employees under ERISA nondiscrimination rules (as Microsoft learned with respect to its employee stock purchase plan). By contrast, even an ISO, and of course an NSO, may be limited to a few employees. Top executives will be ERISA fiduciaries if stock is put into an Employee Stock Ownership Plan (ESOP), but not when stock options have been given. Stock in a qualified stock bonus plan may not exceed $30,000 per year, while stock options may be granted up to $100,000 per year in an ISO and without limit under an NSO. If shares involved fraud, the employee-shareholders may not sue under the securities laws (*McLaughlin v. Cendant;* Bodie 2003).

Stock options may also be made impermanent. As mentioned, they do not "vest" in an ERISA sense. Their exercise may be conditioned on various good behavior by employees long after their pensions would be nonforfeitable under ERISA. Normally employees leaving the company must sell back their options. (This makes sense. If employees leave the company, stock options no longer either align their interests with shareholders', bind them to the company, or provide information to investors.) The options may also be subject to revision or revaluation by the company.

Many start-up employees are naive about legal and financial matters and insufficiently aggressive in protecting their interests. In my experience, engineers, women, and people just out of school are particularly vulnerable. As a result they are often fleeced by management. At one point, for example, our lawyers explained to me that companies often retained the right to repurchase employee stock options at their original strike price. That sounded unfair to me, so we didn't do it, but I later learned that it does occur. It is one of many tricks used against the innocent and unwary.

Most people have heard of Pixar, the company that did the animation for the movie *Toy Story* and that made its principal owner, Steve Jobs, a billion dollars when it went public in 1995. Pixar was founded by Alvy Ray Smith and Ed Catmull, who are legends in the world of digital animation. Smith is a veteran of Xerox PARC from the 1970s where, far ahead of his time, he created some of the earliest technologies for manipulating images. In 1979, Smith and Catmull were recruited by George Lucas's Industrial Light and Magic—Smith was its first director of computer animation.

At Lucasfilm, Smith created a stir with a spectacular 3-D sixty-second sequence in Paramount's *Star Trek II: The Wrath of Khan*, which would have been impossible with conventional technology. But Lucas got into financial trouble, and in 1986 Smith and his team were spun off as Pixar and sold to Jobs, who'd been kicked out of Apple and was looking for something to do. Jobs made himself CEO and kept about 60 percent of the stock for himself, while the rest was widely distributed among employees. Jobs was his usual impossible self, and Smith finally left in despair in 1992.

He's a good man, and I'm pleased to say has done well since. He founded a software company that was eventually purchased by Microsoft, where he seems to have found a home as their top graphics guru.

Jobs put a lot of money into Pixar—Smith guesses $50 million over ten years. But the company's future, including the *Toy Story* contract and a long-term relationship with Disney, had been constructed before Smith left, the result of fifteen years' work. At this point, however, Jobs reorganized the company, selling off a money-losing hardware business to focus on software. Then Jobs pulled a neat trick. "Old" Pixar was shut down and all of its shares sold to "New" Pixar, which Jobs created solely for this purpose. The paperwork was easy. The controlling shareholder of Old Pixar and the controlling shareholder of New Pixar, both of whom happened to be Steve Jobs, simply voted the deal through.

As part of the reorganization, Jobs exercised a clause in the employee stock option agreements that allowed him to buy back their options at the original strike price, which was a pittance. Peter Arnstein had worked at Pixar, and all he knew was that one day he had stock options, and the next day he didn't. During the public offering, the underwriters forced Jobs to distribute about 15 percent of the stock among key employees, because nobody would have invested otherwise. Smith was allowed to buy a small allocation of stock at Catmull's insistence, but many employees were shut out entirely, including some who had spent many years creating the technology. (Ferguson 1999: 98–99)

Employee-Employer Suits About Stock Options

Nobody likes to see employees swindled, or the powerful pushing around the less powerful. The current exceedingly light regulation of stock options gives employers a lot of flexibility, and no doubt there are abuses. For example, stock options, the features of which are unknown to employees, neither provide valuable information to outside investors nor motivate or bind employees. Honest employers could hardly object to regulatory changes that required accurate annual disclosure to employees of the terms of stock option compensation (unless the disclosure were very expensive or redundant).

Employees recruited with promises of stock options, that are then never set up, get next to no protection under current law. In a typical scenario, the employee is reluctant to leave PacBell or 3Com and is assured that she will be given stock options "as good as what you have there." Life in the start-up turns out to be chaotic, and for one reason or another no such plan is ever created. As mentioned, such a promise is analyzed as a matter of each state's common law of contracts, and, in the reported cases, is normally found too "vague" or "indefinite" to enforce (*Ekedahl v. Corestaff, Inc., Catex Vitol*

Gas Inc. v. Wolfe). (Lawyers have suggested to me that the reported cases may be an unrepresentative sample. If the plaintiff really can convincingly prove such an oral promise, the employer is likely to settle.)

But if courts may give too little protection to the employee who never receives any promised stock options, they may give too much where the stock option plan has actually been set up. A trend seems to be emerging under which courts analogize stock options to the wrong thing—wages, pensions, benefits, shares purchased in the market—and miss the unique role that options play, namely the attraction of employees willing to assume risk, and the provision of information to investors.

Vizcaino v. Microsoft: *Exclusion from the Stock Purchase Plan*

We have now referred several times to the famous lawsuit by "permatemps" working at Microsoft, wrongfully classified by Microsoft as independent contractors or employees of a temporary help agency. We mentioned that the lawsuit was successful in including the permatemps in exactly one Microsoft benefit program, its employee stock purchase plan (ESPP). It is time now to look at that plan. Although it is not, technically, a stock option plan, the judicial treatment may be similar.

Microsoft maintains a stock purchase plan under which any employee may purchase Microsoft stock, through payroll deductions up to 10 percent of gross compensation, at 85 percent of fair market value. Such a stock purchase plan is a little different from the stock option plans we have been discussing so far. Like them, it is not covered by ERISA but governed by state law.

Unlike other stock option compensation, however, it must be open to all employees in order to receive favorable tax treatment. Internal Revenue Code Section 423(b)(4), covering employee stock purchase plans, requires that they be open to all employees, with exceptions for, inter alia, part-time employees or employees with less than two years of service. This is an unusually strict antidiscrimination provision. Benefits actually covered by ERISA vesting and fiduciary rules, like pensions and insurance, are normally covered by one of a variety of antidiscrimination rules, designed to prevent the creation of tax-favored plans that provide benefits only to highly compensated employees. However, these normal ERISA nondiscrimination rules normally permit exclusions of various kinds. (ERISA nondiscrimination rules are inordinately complex. An excellent introduction and critique is Bankman [1988: 795–800; 1994a: 599–601]).

By contrast, employee stock purchase plans must be open to all full-time employees who have worked longer than two years. This strict antidiscrimination provision, applying only to employee stock purchase plans, made them a relatively unattractive way for employers to give stock to employees, even before the *Vizcaino v. Microsoft* litigation presumably delivered its lethal blow. Alvin D. Lurie, the IRS's first deputy commissioner for employee benefits, and a veteran practitioner and consultant in the employee benefit field, told my seminar at New York University School of Law in March 2000 that he had never seen a plan like Microsoft's. It is not easy to explain why the tax laws impose such uniquely strict antidiscrimination rules, requiring the plan to be open to all employees, for a plan unregulated by ERISA; I have been unable to locate a convincing account. Probably because of this unattractive feature, employee stock purchase plans are normally not included when people make generalizations about "stock options" (e.g., "stock options are either ISOs or NSOs"). However, there is no technical reason why they could not be considered "stock option compensation," a term that (as we have seen) lacks technical legal meaning.

The *Microsoft* litigation was a state-law contract action under the contract law of the state of Washington, in federal court as supplementary to plaintiffs' unsuccessful ERISA claims about other benefits programs. The court of appeals ordered the permatemps included in the employee stock purchase plan. The plan had been drafted to qualify as an employee stock purchase plan under Section 423 of the Internal Revenue Code. It contained the language: "It is the intention of the Company to have the Plan qualify as an 'employee stock purchase plan' under Section 423 of the Internal Revenue Code of 1954. The provisions of the Plan shall, accordingly, be construed so as to extend and limit participation in a manner consistent with the requirements of that section of the Code." As noted, such plans must be open to all employees. The court reasoned that, rather than construe the plan to discriminate against some employees (and therefore risk its §423 qualification), it would effectuate Microsoft's supposed intent by maintaining that qualification, and opening the plan to all common-law employees. It then remanded the case to the district court to determine appropriate relief for each employee.

Microsoft eventually settled the case by agreeing to pay $97 million. This will be distributed among the 8,000 to 12,000 individuals who worked at Microsoft for at least nine months between 1986 and 2000 while classed either as independent contractors or employees of temporary help agencies. The settlement formula presumes that each worker would have bought stock in any six-month period at the average rate of those eligible to purchase stock, that the stock would have been held for one year, then sold (Virgin 2000). Had the case not settled, it is far from clear what relief a court might have ordered.

The *Vizcaino v. Microsoft* litigation has captured much public imagination and has been extensively discussed, though normally misunderstood. It seems rarely appreciated that the decision applies only to the subset of so-called freelancers who were actually full-time Microsoft employees, and thus offers little to most independent contractors, let alone temporary employees— issues discussed earlier in this book. It also is rarely observed that even these individuals, found to have been Microsoft employees, lost on every claim to be included in Microsoft benefits, with the sole exception of the ESPP, a claim they won only because of this specific, quirky antidiscrimination rule. The case then offers little to most temps or freelancers, so we now turn to its implications for the law of compensation through stock options.

The main interest of the case for present purposes is as a prominent example of a court misunderstanding stock option compensation, through analogy to legal abstraction, rather than attempting to understand what functions it served for the company that created it. The court made no effort to understand the ESPP as a unique legal entity: why it is given special tax treatment; or the meaning of its unusually strict antidiscrimination rules. Nor did it attempt to understand the plan from Microsoft's perspective: why the plan was created; or what Microsoft hoped to achieve. Rather, the court treated the plan as an attempt to realize the benefits of §423—without, as noted, discussing the precise tax benefits that Microsoft received from having the plan qualify under §423. While Microsoft's intent was indeed to achieve such qualification, one doubts that this was—as the court seemed to believe— at any cost. The court should have compared the costs to Microsoft of a plan that included just the individuals that Microsoft selected (and therefore lost the tax benefits of §423), with the cost of a plan that qualified for those tax benefits by enrolling many more individuals than Microsoft had intended. Absent such comparison, it is hard to decide if the court is correctly construing the document. Surely Microsoft's resistance to the court's reading is some evidence that the court got it wrong. However, this aspect of the case is unlikely to affect anyone but Microsoft. As mentioned, §423 is an unusually comprehensive requirement of nondiscrimination. Future employers that want to set up stock option plans open only to some employees will avoid §423 and instead create other types of stock option compensation, as most already did, and to which we now turn.

Knox v. Microsoft: *If the Manager Is Fired, What Happens to the Stock Options?*

When Knox was terminated from Microsoft, his unvested stock options were cancelled, as is typical. When a jury later determined that the termination was a breach of contract, the issue arose whether Knox's damages should include the loss of those stock options. Before trial, Microsoft had been awarded summary judgment on Knox's claim for damages for loss of stock options. Knox appealed this dismissal. Microsoft did not appeal the jury finding that the termination breached its contract with Knox. (Knox's lawyer, Jerry McNaul, told me that the breach of contract claim was based on the Microsoft handbook, and oral promises to Knox contained in his performance improvement plan, that the jury found were enforceable promises to let him improve his performance.) The Washington Court of Appeals, in a straightforward application of contract law's principles of expectation damages, held that Knox should be compensated for the loss of stock options, in order to put him into the same financial position he would have occupied absent Microsoft's breach of contract. The case then settled before any trial on damages. While the amount of the settlement is confidential, McNaul told me that it permitted Knox, among other things, to fly his lawyers and sixty close friends to Paris in order to celebrate.

The decision is probably right, but it does treat stock options purely as a matter of employee compensation, and ignores their sorting and signaling functions. As we have seen, the economic analysis of stock options suggests they perform three functions. In descending order of importance, they signal commitment to outside investors; they attract employees willing to assume risk; and they align managers' and employees' interests with shareholders'. (While they do not perform that function particularly well, Congress thought that performance-based pay, including stock options, did.) After an employee has been terminated, all these functions cease. Information about the employee is of no value to investors; he need not be recruited; he cannot effectuate shareholder interests. In such a case, the correct analogy is Knox's base salary, which he can also recover as damages for wrongful termination, even though the employer no longer receives the value it anticipated from paying that salary.

It is easy, however, to imagine apparent extensions of *Knox* that would be wrong. While it is appropriate to analogize Knox's stock options to his salary, the analogy succeeds in the Microsoft context because of the entirely contingent fact that both the Microsoft stock option program and Knox's behavior were stable and orderly. For example, Knox's lawyers would have been able to establish his consistent pattern of holding his stock options and exercising them at the last minute. In other cases, defendants should surely be permitted to argue that the stock options would have been revalued, revised, or repurchased, in ways that might be less likely for salary (cf. Bewley 1999) but are the very reason for flexible, performance-based pay. The decision would certainly be wrong if it treated stock options like a pension.

Microsoft was not obligated to pay stock options at all, or extend them to all employees, or maintain its current plans forever, or refrain from repricing or otherwise altering existing options. All these would be important to consider in determining the likelihood that others in Knox's position missed out on much due to wrongful termination.

An intermediate appeals court in New York has extended the approach of Knox in a decision that is almost surely wrong (*Williamson v. Moltech*). Williamson, like Knox, was an executive in a high-tech company who was terminated before he could exercise certain promised stock options. Williamson, like Knox, argues that his termination was wrongful, a claim yet to be tried. In pretrial motions for summary judgment (appealable in New York), the court ruled, as in *Knox*, that if Williamson can show that his termination was a breach of contract, he should be compensated for his inability to exercise stock options.

The step beyond *Knox* is that Williamson sought, not damages for the loss of the options (the remedy in *Knox*), but the actual issuance of the options themselves. Moltech was not yet publicly traded at the time of the decision. Williamson claimed that his estimate of the value of options to purchase their stock exceeds the likely estimates the experts would produce. (Apparently he does not argue that his firing as CEO will do anything to harm the prospects of the company; by contrast, he maintains that the company will really take off now that he is no longer CEO.) Counsel for defendant informed me that it agreed to compensate him for the economic value of lost options, should it lose on the underlying wrongful termination claim, but Williamson wanted the options themselves, and that is what the appellate court found he should have.

This seems an award of equitable relief without a showing that legal relief was inadequate. It also misunderstands the functions of stock options. Because stock options are designed to signal investors, attract risk-takers, and realign managerial incentives, they are typically limited to employees. Indeed, the stock option plan in the case was an incentive stock option plan in which options may be granted only to employees and are not transferable. The court did not discuss the tax regulatory aspects of the plan.

The *Williamson* decision creates dangers for high-tech start-ups, because it misunderstands that flexible compensation is designed to be, well, flexible. The chief contribution of American employment law to the high-tech sector, as we have emphasized repeatedly, is its hands-off attitude toward extensive use of short-term employment, even at the managerial level. The new firm has to be able to replace employees, without thereby saddling itself with extensive obligations to nonemployees, perhaps competitors if they stay in the industry and move to a competitor or rival. Although Williamson himself was the CEO, his lawyer told me that Moltech used exactly the same stock options for employees throughout the organization. Apparently other individuals were terminated along with Williamson. The prospect of a start-up with substantial shares claimable by former employees is troubling, although perhaps the biggest complaint might come from a competitor who hired Williamson, unaware that he stands to benefit from a rival's success.

Here again, the court gropes for an analogy to stock options and settles on employee compensation—not wrong, but not identical either, for it ignores the aleatory quality of stock option compensation that can be revalued, re-purchased, or diluted. These individuals knew they were working for a high-tech start-up that might or might not ever go public or make it big. They were compensated under a plan designed to attract risk-takers. Absent allegations of fraud or deceit (discussed in the next section), they should not be permitted to turn uncertain compensation—far less certain than the Microsoft bonuses involved in the *Knox* case—into something that vests like a pension.

Finally, ordering the company actually to issue stock options is totally unnecessary even to protect Williamson's idiosyncratic subjective valuation of them. Instead, Williamson could have been issued stock appreciation rights, which would guarantee him the financial equivalent of increases in the price of the stock. While this would still seem like a kind of equitable relief, it would fully protect his supposed interest in his idiosyncratically high sub-jective valuation of the stock, while avoiding the dangers of having options in a start-up's shares dispersed among former employees.

Silicon Valley employers, and other high-tech employers on the West Coast, have started to respond to cases like *Knox* and *Williamson* with negotiated written contracts that specify what happens to stock options even if an employee or executive is dismissed without cause. The judicial response so far has been mixed. Oracle's contract, and its interpretation by Oracle's com-pensation committee, received deference in *Oracle Corp. v. Falotti*. Falotti's contract provided that, if he were terminated without cause, a portion of his unvested options would vest, and the others would be lost. The court de-ferred to the administration of this provision by Oracle's compensation com-mittee, noting that the options were incentives, not salary.

By contrast, the decision of Worldcom's committee was reversed. Scribner's contract provided that his options could be executed immediately if he were terminated "without cause." Scribner was terminated as his division was sold to another company, which then hired him. Scribner attempted to exercise his options. Worldcom's compensation committee ruled that he had been terminated with cause. The federal court of appeals reversed this ruling, re-fusing to defer to the committee and insisting that "without cause" had to be read in their "ordinary meaning," that is, "without deficient performance"

(*Scribner v. Worldcom*). I have no particular sympathy for Worldcom, since revealed to have committed much greater frauds. I am skeptical, however, that "without cause," when used in individual employment contracts, has any such plain meaning that would permit a court to substitute its judgment for the compensation committee's. The coexistence of these two cases suggests considerable uncertainty as to when decisions of compensation committees will receive judicial deference or scrutiny, and, if the latter, what standards will be applied.

Cendant Litigation: Are Managers Paid in Options Investors?

Employees so far have been unsuccessful in using federal securities law to redress fraudulent promises made to induce acceptance of stock options as compensation. In the massive litigation involving securities fraud at Cendant Corporation, employees holding options were excluded from the plaintiff class because they did not "give anything of value for stock other than the continuation of employment." Stock options are securities for purposes of federal securities legislation. For example, they have to be registered. Stock options sold to employees are thus also securities that have to be registered (*Securities and Exchange Commission v. Ralston Purina Co.*). However, the portions of the securities laws dealing with fraud, including the SEC's famous Rule 10b5, are limited to those who directly purchase or sell securities (*Blue Chip Stamps v. Manor Drug Stores*). When options are distributed to large groups of employees, some courts, including the court in the *Cendant* litigation, have found that the employees do not "purchase" the options. Thus, though other investors could sue alleging securities fraud, employees could not. "To 'purchase or sell' stock options [under Rule 10b5], employee purchasers must 'give up a specific consideration in return for a separable financial interest with the characteristics of a security.' Conversely, '[w]hen an employee does not give anything of value for stock other than the continuation of employment nor independently bargains for such stock,' there is no 'purchase or sale' of securities" (*In re Cendant Corp. Securities Litigation*; see also *McLaughlin v. Cendant Corp.*).

There are several things wrong with this. First, it is in such tension with cases like *Knox*, *Williamson*, and *Scully* as to threaten the coherence of the law of stock options. I criticized those cases for treating stock options as if they were fixed compensation, and not recognizing that options carry the riskiness of an investment. *Cendant* goes to the opposite extreme. Other investors may sue if they were induced to invest because of fraudulent representations, but employees were not investors, so are treated worse than those who were. Employees who go to work for a company that extensively uses stock option are, as Lazear says, accepting risk and signaling this fact to others. But they do not accept the risk that the company is falsifying income or assets or committing other kinds of stock fraud.

Second, as Matthew Bodie (2003) shows in a careful review of the cases, the rule, that giving labor is not purchasing for value, creates numerous anomalies and inconsistencies. For example, the very same stock option plan that is not "purchased" by employees who work under it, can become a "sale" of securities when used—as any stock option plan might be—to recruit an engineer from a rival company (e.g., *Collins v. Rukin*). This permits top executives and others who individually negotiate recruitment terms to be protected by securities laws, while ordinary employees holding the same fraudulent options may not. Moreover, under Lazear's sorting model, the option always is used, at least in part, to recruit non-risk-averse employees. So employees "purchase" stock options when they go to work for a company in which options make up some of their pay. They trade security for risk in a very real sense. Recall the Hotmail employees, and others, who worked exclusively for options. Did they not "purchase" those options? And if they did, where should the line be drawn between them and employees who didn't? Bodie argues that employees should be held to purchase stock options when they exchange their labor for them, pointing out that the statutory term "sale" is neither narrow nor technical, and that other nonmonetary exchanges have been held to be "sales" of stock.

Third, decisions like *Cendant* violate Congress's basic principle governing stock options, the alignment of managerial and employee incentives with shareholders'. *Cendant,* by contrast, literally splits managers and employees from the shareholder class, thus splitting managerial incentives from shareholder incentives, contrary to Congress's understanding in treating stock option compensation as performance-based pay. As we have seen, stock options are used to align managers' interests with shareholders', in two ways: to signal commitment to investors and perhaps realign managers' incentives. One should therefore be suspicious of anything that splits the manager- or employee-option holders from other investors with whom they were supposed to be aligned. Specifically, the decision weakens the incentives for managers and employees, not themselves guilty of securities fraud, to root it out. Do their incentives to uncover and resist such fraud, in the interests of outside investors, weaken if the discovery of such fraud will eliminate all market value in their own shares, as well as any value they might have had, even as choses in action?

On balance, then, employees holding options that they were induced to accept by fraudulent representation should be permitted to sue for securities fraud like any other investor. This would help reinforce the idea that stock options are risky and are not just like other compensation. Particular problems in including managers and employees in the shareholder class can be solved without depriving them entirely of the securities laws. For example, if shareholders allege that specific individuals wrecked the company, obviously those individuals should not be included in the shareholder class. Other employees who are insiders with respect to stock fraud, or employee groups that opportunistically bring securities litigation for other purposes, might also be separately represented. But the blanket exclusion of all employees paid in stock options on the ground that they did not "purchase" them is unwarranted. It misses the role that stock options play and harkens back to an earlier era when "fringe" benefits in employment were seen as "gratuities."

The *Cendant* court also held that top managers were not ERISA trustees for the employees' stock options. Stock options are not pensions or substitutes for them. They do not defer income until retirement. Nor are they welfare plans under ERISA. They do not create a special trust of assets, and thus a conflict between that trust's use for employee benefit and its use for other corporate functions. Rather, the entire idea of stock option compensation is that those who get it should have just the same incentives as shareholders to increase the value of those shares. Thus, normally managers' duties to shareholders should also take care of increasing the value of employee stock options. It is hard to think of an important example where managers' duties to employee-shareholders, qua shareholders, could conflict with their duties to other shareholders. However, if such a conflict arose, it would be undesirable to have duties as ERISA trustee overruling duties to shareholders. This would defeat the entire point of using stock options as compensation, as Congress saw it. On the other hand, the fact that employees who are victims of real fraud in stock options may not use ERISA's fiduciary provisions, may be another reason to let them use the securities laws, like other investors. It seems odd to hold, as the *Cendant* court did, that managers and employees holding stock options are too investor-like to sue under ERISA and simultaneously too employee-like to sue under the securities laws.

Conclusion

Ultimately none of our existing analogies works for all aspects of stock options compensation. They partake of elements of wages, benefits, contractual entitlements, and securities, without comfortably equating to any. Meanwhile, the relevant law concerning them is being fashioned piecemeal, in state courts hearing common law contract actions, with little attention to the function of stock options to the employer or in the economy at large, and no effective means of coordinating diverse state decisions.

A simple and uniform set of conventions for the disclosure of stock options is probably desirable. I have no opinion whether or not this should be done as a matter of accounting conventions, or by the SEC or IRS. Employees and investors certainly have a right to know the terms of stock option compensation. Perhaps limits on revaluation will be desirable.

However, in developing special rules for stock option compensation, its unique features must be kept in mind. It is not a pension or benefit plan, in which funds are set aside for employee benefit and must be kept from the self-dealing of corporate officials. It is still part of the compensation package mainly of well-paid and sophisticated professional and managerial employees. Its primary functions—sending information to investors, attracting employees with a taste for risk, and aligning managers with shareholders—should not be impeded. Nor should the flexibility that has been such an important contributor to the growth of American high-technology industry.

11

MARKET FAILURE IN RETIREMENT SAVINGS AND HEALTH INSURANCE

When I first began studying Silicon Valley's high-velocity labor market in the early 1990s, there was enormous concern about the emerging national "contingent" labor force, without stable attachment to any employer, changing jobs frequently, perhaps a temporary employee or self-employed, but in any case without retirement or health benefits. One of my several goals in studying a high-end, well-paid, but quite contingent labor force was to learn things that might be adaptable to lower-end contingent workers. Had mobile programmers and engineers, or businesses marketing to them, developed interesting ways of marketing retirement benefits, health insurance, or training? Did these functions support employee organizations or for-profit companies that might be adapted to meet the needs of temporary manufacturing or office workers? This aspect of the study has been a complete failure. Such institutions have not emerged for Silicon Valley's well-paid workers, and we may therefore be confident they will never emerge for other contingent workers, absent some expensive public policy initiatives. This critique is the subject of this chapter.

The three most serious criticisms that one could make of Silicon Valley's high-velocity labor market might well give pause to the hypothetical country or region considering adopting its laws and institutions. This book can assure that country that the Valley's laws and institutions do not lead to reduced investment in information or psychotic employees. It cannot assure that country that ready solutions are at hand for the following three problems.

First, Silicon Valley's is a highly unequal labor market, even by American standards.

Second, Silicon Valley has failed to develop market (or governmental) institutions permitting mobile employees to provide for their retirement or current health insurance needs. This is most significant, for if such institutions failed to arise for America's wealthiest and most sophisticated workers, in the metropolitan area with the greatest concentration of college degrees, in the most booming years of the U.S. economy, we may be fairly confident they will never arise anywhere else. Similarly, the Valley has failed to produce child care institutions or employer family policies compatible with careers for women with family responsibilities (Carnoy 2000).

Third, Silicon Valley's labor market almost completely excludes African-Americans and Latinos and may, although this point is controversial, be hard on older workers. The mechanisms producing these disparate outcomes do not, for the most part, constitute illegal discrimination, so redressing them would require substantial changes in our national understandings of discrimination or equality.

This chapter will take up the general problem of inequality, and the failure of the private market to develop health insurance or retirement savings. This will include an analysis and critique of the 401(k) plan, the usual vehicle for retirement savings in Silicon Valley. The next chapter will address disparate labor market outcomes by race, national origin, sex, and age.

An Unequal Labor Market

Silicon Valley's is an extraordinarily unequal labor market, even by American standards. The rosiest way of summing up the 1990s in America is that all groups made gains in real earnings, but those at the top made much more (e.g., U.S. Economic Report of the President 2001). A more critical generalization is that incomes in the lower half of the population were largely stagnant (e.g., Ellwood et al. 2000). Silicon Valley breaks both generalizations. It is one of the few regions in the country in which income of the lowest 20 percent of the population actually declined in real terms (Census 2000b). This reflects heavy immigration into the region, and not a decline in the income of many individual households. In the middle, median pay is more than twice the national median ($76,500 and $35,300, respectively, Joint Venture 2002). Median salary in the computer industry in 2000 was $166,100, and in software, $165,200. At the top, the accumulations of income are legendary (Lewis 2000; Kaplan 1999). The ratio of annual income of the Valley's top hundred executives to that of the average production worker rose from 42:1 in 1991 to 220:1 in 1996 (Benner 1999: 20).

Of course, this is just an extreme example of a national trend toward inequality, a trend that has provoked a great deal of academic analysis that cannot be summarized here. It has not yet converged on a simple theory. Studying Silicon Valley does not move that particular debate forward, as most of the theories that have arisen to explain increasing U.S. income inequality would seem to apply very well to Silicon Valley. The most popular explanations combine an account of rising return to education and skills, with the unraveling of institutions that promoted modest redistribution toward the poor, such as labor unions, and public education and welfare schemes. Both elements present problems, however.

No one disputes the increasing returns to education. In 1979 a male college graduate in the United States earned on average 30 percent more than a high school graduate. By 1995, this figure had jumped to 70 percent (Gottschalk 1997). But the micromechanisms of this process are not understood. Is it job skills that are being rewarded (Juhn, Murphy, and Pierce 1993)? Examination of compensation data for over 50,000 managers at large industrial corporations, whose jobs were evaluated for skill by the same compensation consultant, revealed that, while skill differentials powerfully predicted inequalities of income within each firm, they had little value in predicting the increasing, and increasingly important, inequalities among firms. (During the six years studied, 1986–92, inequality increased 20 percent among firms but only 8 percent within firms [O'Shaughnessy, Levine, and Cappelli 2000].) Why should job skills or education command higher rewards now than formerly? Is increasing spending on information technology responsible (the so-called "skill-based technological change" hypothesis; see Autor, Katz, and Krueger [1998])? The old view that computers substituted for some kind of labor has given way. It seems that firm spending on information technology is positively correlated with level of employee skill and adoption of such work reorganization practices as delegation to teams or line workers (Bresnahan, Brynjolfsson, and Hitt 1999). (Once again, as in Paul Romer's (1990b) model of endogenous economic growth, intellectual labor exhibits increasing returns; capital investment cannot substitute for it.) Card and DiNardo (2002) point out other problems with the skill-based technological change hypothesis: the sharpest rise in inequality was in the early 1980s, not a period of increased spending on information technology; scientists and engineers have earned smaller wage premiums than other groups; gender gaps have been closing, although women do not use information technology more than men. I would also add, what seems to me obvious but does not figure much in the studies in this paragraph, that the really big earnings gains have been with top corporate executives and consultants. Their jobs have not in the last decade really called for any new skills at all, let alone rocket (or computer) science. They just make a lot more money.

Technology can result in jobs that are upskilled and earn more, downskilled, or eliminated when technology substitutes for human labor. In the banking industry, information technology has facilitated deskilling of jobs and their relocation to off-site call centers where wages are low, work fast and closely monitored, and career ladders weak (Hunter et al. 2001).

This book has urged a new economic perspective on labor markets, focusing on the creation and diffusion of nonrivalrous information. What is the relationship between investing in information and inequality? Does investing in information require increasing returns to intellectually productive workers? Possibly, but the link is not obvious and there may be offsetting trends. For example, as we have seen, the best incentive structure for inducing intellectual creativity among employees may well be one in which they change jobs rapidly and take much of their compensation linked to performance. Once information is produced, it does not mandate any particular distribution of the returns. Creating or holding information can increase returns to the most creative workers, but cannot create "superstars" (cf. Rosen 1981). Like other creators of information, scientists and engineers cannot monopolize it and must live with its spillover. (We noted in chapter 4 the particular asymmetry here: individuals with valuable information must disclose it to venture capitalists or employers in order to make money from it.) Such spillover may increase the output of all other workers in the network over which information spills. In the model of Saint-Paul (1999: 27), poorest workers cannot lose from an improvement in information technology; inequality might rise as the size of the network of the spillover grows, but inequality later falls. "[W]hen networks get larger, the ideas of a given, highly creative worker, are less valuable because it is more likely that somebody else in the network would have had an idea almost as good." Of course, we do not in fact see this wage compression in Silicon Valley, but we do not see it in the U.S. economy generally, and it is hard to specify anything specific about information technology that should make things more unequal in that industry. One possibility, soon to be tested, is that extraordinarily high returns to professionals in that labor market reflected a bubble in technology stocks rather than a permanent feature of the labor market.

Similarly, there is not much argument that nationally, some institutions that raised incomes for workers at the bottom end have had a rough time in the 1990s. I refer to labor unions, whose density continued to decline; oligopolies sheltered from foreign competition; and internal labor markets in which individuals with few skills at hiring could nevertheless look forward to stable careers and orderly income increases. (These three things often went together, though not necessarily.) Participation in foreign trade is correlated with a wage structure that responds more to market forces and less to the orderly progression from a starting point that was so typical of old-style internal labor markets (Bertrand 1999). Silicon Valley lacks any of these institutions that once redistributed income downward, relative to the rest of the U.S. labor market. Silicon Valley participates heavily in international trade, has weak internal labor markets, and is very lightly unionized (and its informal employee organizations, as we saw in chapter 9, do little to affect wage distribution). On the other hand, Silicon Valley has always participated in foreign trade, had comparatively weak internal labor markets, and (since the early 1950s) been lightly unionized. These factors did not change in the 1990s.

Blame for inequality has also been placed on such features of Silicon Valley's high-velocity labor market, discussed earlier in this book, as temporary help agencies (said to depress earnings at the bottom) and stock options (said to raise it at the top). I have argued that this mistakes the legal form for the economic substance. If employers could not easily hire through temporary help agencies, they would hire temporary help directly, paying them minimum wage and no benefits, or outsource more production. The existence of the temporary help agency may exert some uncalculated effect on the morale of the regular workforce, but is not essential to create low-wage jobs. Moreover, temporary jobs can be extremely important to working people with few skills, particularly if they have a temporary job and would not have any other kind (Vicki Smith 2001; Chun 2001). This is true when temporary jobs serve as transitional jobs, created in the early months of recovery from recession, or through which workers pass after, or on the way to, permanent employment (Farber 1999). Recall that few individuals really spend lifetimes trapped in temporary employment (Finegold et al., in progress; Farber 1999). Still, the uncertainty created by all forms of contingent and temporary employment probably encourages wage restraint by workers, even as it encourages job creation and low unemployment (Katz and Krueger 1999).

Similarly, stock options are indeed the vehicle for top executives to realize extraordinary sums, but if stock options were capped, or subjected to strict nondiscrimination rules, they would pay themselves other bonuses. Most important, it is unrealistic to expect employers in industries of such constant technological and economic change to make implicit contracts for lifetime employment, commitments to retrain and never lay off, or job ladders from unskilled to engineering positions. Silicon Valley companies that had similar institutions have regretted this and eliminated them.

But while I see no reason to reproach Silicon Valley for adopting institutions adapted to technological change that also encourage inequality, it may certainly be reproached for failing to adopt any response to the resulting inequality. Many people outside the Valley, who have come to regard some kinds of contingent employment as either desirable or inevitable, have worked on policy initiatives to create ladders for careers that span firm boundaries and permit individuals to lift themselves (see generally Herzenberg, Alic, and Wial 1998; Osterman 1999; Bernhardt et al. 2001: 191–99). For example, there are formal programs of training, or transition from temporary to permanent employment, or links between temporary help firms and firms that offer more permanent careers. Silicon Valley is not a hotbed of such initiatives. The most interesting I have found is the Working Partnerships program of the South Bay Labor Council, discussed in chapter 9, a union-operated temporary help agency that combines placement with training, but so far it is very small.

Virtually all the institutions of a high-velocity labor market, discussed in this book, could be adapted for the benefit of the comparatively unskilled janitor or production worker. This book's emphasis on the Valley's networked economy hopes to do just that. In fact, such adaptations are occurring, but rarely as a result of policy initiatives that could help them to become more widespread. The following four adaptations could be considered helpful starting points:

- Building self-employment and other entrepreneurial options into the incentive structure is perhaps the most important. Formal programs to assist gardeners to develop their own landscaping companies are more relevant to low-income workers in today's economy than programs that think only inside the boundaries of particular firms. Such networked service firms will grow like some of the start-ups discussed in chapters 9 and 12. They will use formal and informal ethnic networks, here Mexican, Filipino, or Vietnamese, that offer advice, English training, training in business ownership, and some capital.
- Labor laws that permitted bargaining by organizations enrolling current employees, former employees, and others in a larger community would help unions play this role facilitating cross-firm careers.
- New kinds of temporary help agencies could build on the attractive features of the agencies studied by Esther Neuwirth (2002). They could provide more training, assist clients in thinking about careers, not merely the current job placement, and develop a reputation for quality workers.
- The H-1B visa program could be reoriented toward introducing skilled workers into a regional network, freeing them from indentured servitude at a single employer.

None of these is any kind of magic cure for an unequal society, but each would help particular individuals with entry-level or even low skills to build a more productive career relevant to a high-technology sector. It is long since past time for large employers in the Valley to begin to fund small initiatives along these lines. Instead, they have permitted the Valley to evolve so as to make clear that its large African-American and Latino/Latina populations, as we will see in more depth in the next chapter, have essentially no stake in its success.

So far, Valley employers have done very well in Congress. They have successfully fought congressional initiatives to trim stock option compensation, H-1B visas, or temporary help agencies. Future political battles may, however, require different coalitions. Some attention to inequalities in the Valley may be a price worth paying for companies, if it broadens the number of people who consider themselves stakeholders in Silicon Valley's economy.

Market Failure in Retirement Planning: The 401(k) Plan

I have tried throughout this book to understand the function performed by various aspects of Silicon Valley's labor market institutions, including those that have been heavily criticized. It is difficult, however, to find anything good to say about the 401(k) plan, the primary vehicle for retirement savings in the United States.

The United States in recent years has seen a stampede away from the traditional, defined-benefit pension, toward plans defined only by set contributions that do not guarantee particular results. Employers have made this change for their own benefit. Defined-benefit plans place heavy administrative and fiduciary duties on employers, who bear the risk of the investments' loss of value. By contrast, in defined-contribution plans, the employer's obligation is largely complete when the contribution is made. Risks thereafter are borne by employees.

The most popular defined-contribution plan, in turn, has been the highly flexible 401(k) plan, funded by some mix of employer and employee contributions and invested in shares of stock after varying mixes of employer advice and default rules, and employee direction. Employees are permitted to choose among several different investment options, such as different stock portfolios or a fixed-income fund. It is not possible to obtain figures on this trend by region. However, I have never found a Silicon Valley employer that has defined-benefit pensions, despite my searching for a firm that might represent an attempt to apply old practices to the new economy. Virtually all employees above the very bottom of the labor market have a 401(k) plan.

The mythology of the 401(k) plan is that it is perfectly suited for mobile workers whose careers span several firms. The reality is considerably different. The truth is that for two-thirds of U.S. households, all pensions, including both defined-benefit and defined-contribution plans, essentially missed the bull market of 1982–98. In these two-thirds of U.S. households, retirement wealth from pensions was just the same or less in 1998 as it had been in households headed by people of comparable age in 1983. For the median U.S. household, retirement wealth *dropped* 13 percent from 1983 to 1998 (Wolff 2002). Overall, retirement accounts increased in value, but *all* of this increase went to the very rich. Those in the 95th percentile saw their pension wealth increase 176 percent in those fifteen years. How could this happen? There are five reasons: (1) too many workers have no pension coverage; (2)

the plans in existence are not really portable, while the workforce has become more mobile; (3) workers are rarely in a position to fund their own retirement; (4) those who are do not invest enough or wisely; (5) employers, as we have seen, have been terminating plans.

First, more than half the population is not covered by any kind of retirement plan. Coverage peaked in 1979 when 49 percent of the workforce was covered by some kind of retirement plan and has dropped since. About 44 percent of civilian workers now participate in a company pension plan. The drop in pension coverage is dramatic for some groups. Coverage of male workers with no education past high school dropped 22 percentage points from 1979 to 1993, reflecting the elimination of mandatory defined-benefit pensions for which unions once bargained, and their replacement with voluntary defined-contribution plans in nonunion jobs (Even and Macpherson 2000). (Coverage in health insurance has similarly dropped. The proportion of full-time workers in firms with more than 100 employees who participate in a company health plan declined from 92 percent in 1989 to 76 percent in 1997. The comparable figures for small firms are 69 and 64 percent [1990–96] [statistics available at the Bureau of Labor Statistics' Web page].)

Workers in the new short jobs are particularly unlikely to participate in these benefits. Only 4.3 percent of agency temporaries participate in a pension plan through their employer; the figure for on-call workers and temps directly hired by employers is around 20 percent. The figures are similar for health insurance. Only 7.3 percent of agency temporaries obtain health insurance through their employer, and only about 20 percent of on-call workers. The disparity, between workers in flexible and regular relations, remains large even when controlled for age, education, union status, and occupation, suggesting that employers simply don't offer these benefits to workers in flexible arrangements (Houseman 1999: 24).

Second, those mobile workers in 401(k) plans normally cash in those plans every time they change jobs. About two-thirds of workers under age fifty-nine take cash distributions when they change jobs; only one-third "roll over" their account balances, despite a federal tax on such cash distributions, designed to discourage them (Bassett et al. 1998; Hewett Associates 2000). Thus, about 14 percent of the total investment in 401(k) plans between 1988 and 1992 was paid out to workers changing jobs. Why?

Defined-contribution plans, such as 401(k) plans, are normally not portable from employer to employer. There is no legal impediment to making such plans portable. Most professors at large U.S. colleges and universities are enrolled in the TIAA-CREF plan, a defined-contribution plan that is fully vested from the first day, and fully portable if the professor moves to another university that participates in TIAA-CREF. When federal legislation on pensions was first enacted in 1974, the pension experts around Ralph Nader, major proponents of some legislation, favored encouraging such portable plans for all workers, but this proposal was not adopted.

Rather, when a worker leaves an employer with a 401(k) plan, the worker must choose between receiving a cash distribution of the account, or instructing the corporate trustee to "roll over" the balance into an Individual Retirement Account or a plan at the new employer. If the employee elects the cash balance and is under the age of fifty-nine and a half, a 10 percent penalty tax will be placed on the withdrawal. It is thus remarkable that a large study by the leading U.S. benefits consulting firm showed that 68 percent of participants in 401(k) plans, who switch jobs between the ages of twenty and fifty-nine, take a cash distribution of their retirement savings (Hewitt Associates 2000). Workers between jobs may need cash to live on, or take this opportunity to remodel their home. Such uses of 401(k) plans support the conclusion that workers do not really think of them as their retirement savings (Bassett et al. 1998). Of course, workers are not the only ones confused by 401(k) plans. Jeremy Siegel of the Wharton School favors some privatization of Social Security, noting: "Our 401(k) plans generate winners and losers; we've certainly accepted that." (Brock 2002). Why should plans for retirement savings generate losers?

Third, workers do a very poor job of investing. As a general matter, employees do not contribute to their plans at the level to which they aspire, or which would be appropriate given their aspirations for retirement (Laibson 1998). Few people really manage their 401(k) accounts. Most people are highly responsive to default policies and suggestions by the sponsoring employer, even when those suggestions are made entirely for its own purposes (Madrian and Shea 2001). Many employees invest too much in the stock of their own employer and are not diversified if that stock falls. Other employees do pay close attention to their holdings and make frequent trades. Unfortunately, as a group they are not particularly successful (Choi, Laibson, and Metrick 2002).

Fourth, if wages are stagnant, as they have been for most Americans not at the very top, neither retirement plan contributions nor employer matches can grow. Finally, during the years in question many pension plans were terminated, and employees lost the value of those assets.

As I said, it is not possible to obtain similar data for Santa Clara County, or for 401(k) plans separately. All I can report is a negative: all employees and consultants to whom I spoke had 401(k) plans, but none had anything unusual; all had ordinary plans. If they are like other Americans, a few have done well, most have not.

Similarly, my search for innovative ways of marketing health insurance came up empty in the Valley. (In chapter 9 I reported on the New York-based organization Working Today, with its pilot benefits plans for freelance Web designers. There does not appear to be a Silicon Valley equivalent.) Consultants and freelancers to whom I spoke had health insurance when their spouses were working, and if not, not.

I regard this as a telling experiment that failed. Silicon Valley in the 1990s has been described as "the greatest legal creation of wealth at one place and time in the history of the planet" (Lewis 2000: 14). (The quotation is usually attributed to the venture capitalist John Doerr.) Unlike some other areas of the U.S. economy, that wealth was shared with employees down around and below the median, though not with the manufacturing, service, and clerical employees in the bottom quartile. Yet this wealthy, intelligent, sophisticated workforce largely acquired no retirement wealth and often worked without health insurance. If private markets did not serve them, why does anyone think that Social Security could be privatized? Once again, we see that flexible labor markets are not necessarily deregulated markets. While my study of Silicon Valley has helped me see some virtues in employment at will, job turnover, and temporary and self-employment, it has also, most unexpectedly, given me new arguments in favor of national health insurance and a robust, publicly funded retirement benefits system.

Part V

Inequality

12

EMPLOYMENT DISCRIMINATION? HOW A MERITOCRACY CREATES DISPARATE LABOR MARKET OUTCOMES THROUGH DEMANDS FOR SKILLS AT HIRING, NETWORKS OF EMPLOYEES, ENTREPRENEURIAL TENDENCIES

Silicon Valley is the true land of opportunity, "the MOST meritocratic labor market I've seen anywhere in the world," according to one of its leading observers (Saxenian, personal communication). Programmers, engineers, and designers have poured in from around the world, knowing no one, but willing to work hard, and have achieved remarkable economic success. "I make integrated circuits," says T.J. Rogers, the blunt president and CEO of Cypress Semiconductors, "and electrons obey the laws of nature, and they don't care if the engineer pushing them is male or female, black or white or brown" (Molineaux and Frazier 2001).

Silicon Valley is rife with discrimination, one of the most unequal labor markets in a country with generally skewed earnings distributions. African-American and Latino/Latina representation in the workforce of all the large employers is so low, below 4 percent, as to invite litigation, were the employer a Home Depot (Angwin and Castaneda 1998). Engineers older than forty often feel they are essentially unemployable. Many high-tech firms have a fraternity-house atmosphere, full of men with undeveloped social skills and demanding long hours of employees. Sexual relations with coworkers are common and many are harassing (Orenstein 2000). Menial manufacturing and maintenance jobs are performed by poorly paid members of immigrant groups without possibilities for advancement (Siegel 1998; Hossfeld 1990).

It is not necessary to choose between these accounts. Both are true. Understanding how both are true can illuminate much about the nature of discrimination in American labor markets generally. I will argue that Silicon Valley's high-velocity labor market offers a particularly vivid example of several trends in the larger labor market, trends that existing discrimination law (and literature) do not deal with well, or at all. The Valley can be proud of the success of its immigrants, particularly Asians. This success shows the declining significance of overt—perhaps, even covert—racial and ethnic discrimination. The Valley's practice of hiring for very specific skills, without additional requirements that applicants "fit" into firm culture, is a bulwark against certain kinds of discrimination. So are the Internet job sites and agencies that reinforce this culture of immediate skills. Finally, its entrepreneurial culture of start-ups and careers across firms helps ameliorate any residual discrimination against Asians, and could conceivably be made to ameliorate other discrimination.

Yet Silicon Valley also shows that African-Americans and Latinos/Latinas, as groups, may still do poorly even in a labor market that is rapidly expanding and hires from many nonwhite groups. At least three reasons for this failure seem particularly important in explaining Silicon Valley. While all three have been discussed in the academic literature, putting them together provides a distinct model of discrimination (or disparate labor market outcomes) that is different from the pictures assumed in conventional law or economics.

First, employers put increased emphasis on present skills and relevant experience. They do not train employees or maintain ladders from assembly lines to white-collar jobs, as was true in the older industrial economy. While from one perspective this is highly meritocratic, it may well have highly disparate outcomes across ethnic lines.

Second, career ladders in high-velocity labor markets reward, as we have seen repeatedly, entrepreneurs who at some point leave the employer, armed with information and contacts, and start a new firm. Yet for reasons not well understood, racial and ethnic groups differ sharply in their ability to make effective use of entrepreneurial options.

Third, people who hire, particularly founders of start-ups, employ networks that may favor people like themselves and not experience this as prejudice against others. This may be particularly true in industries of interlocked firms dominated by a particular ethnic group, such as computer distribution is for Taiwan-born Chinese. This bears some resemblance to what some academics call, provocatively, "aversive racism." I prefer, however, to view hiring through networks of contacts as an efficient reduction of information costs.

All of these phenomena exist outside of Silicon Valley and high-velocity labor markets, but become even more acute within them, when turnover is heavy, hiring constant, information low, and informal networks of contacts crucial.

There are no reported legal cases of employment discrimination (other than sexual harassment) against prominent Silicon Valley employers, and few unreported cases that really address discrimination. I am employing a somewhat subjective definition of "real employment discrimination" suits here, but not, I think, a controversial one. When the mercurial Larry Ellison at Oracle fires another executive who sues for his or her stock options, that individual may throw in a count alleging race or sex discrimination, and the case will eventually settle (e.g., Farmer 2000; see also Delevett 2002 [age discrimination suit by cousin of Hewlett-Packard director]). This, however, is not a "real discrimination" suit by my lights, and neither is a suit alleging sexual harassment by a boss against a single employee (e.g., Rai 2002). The unreported discrimination cases that I have found all raise highly individual claims of this type. I do not believe there has ever been a suit challenging a firm's practice applying to more than a single individual. Yet, if I am correct in identifying demand for skills at hiring, contacts in networks, and unequal entrepreneurism as the three most likely explanations for the Valley's low employment rates for African-Americans and Latinos/Latinas, it is entirely possible that employers might be vulnerable to successful suits alleging discrimination. The social pressures against bringing such suits are great and are analogous to, though different from, the social pressures against employers' suing to protect their trade secrets, discussed in chapter 2.

Yet it seems only a matter of time before Silicon Valley hiring goes under the litigation microscope. When that happens, the legal system will be faced with an extraordinarily difficult choice. It could redefine concepts of discrimination so that most Valley employers would end up in violation of the statute. Arguably, this might not even require "redefinition." As we shall see, statistics on African-American hiring in particular are so poor that employers might already be guilty of what lawyers call "disparate treatment, statistically proven." But would this be a good idea? How would such discrimination be remedied? Are the personnel practices associated with civil rights remedies compatible with a high-velocity labor market? Could Silicon Valley's distinctive personnel practices—entrepreneurism and cross-firm careers, information intermediaries, high turnover—be harnessed instead to serve employment equity?

This chapter reviews data on discrimination in Silicon Valley; explains these patterns as the result of demand for skills at hiring, hiring through networks, and unequal resort to entrepreneurism, and shows how these three phenomena assume crucial importance with the decline of internal labor markets and the rise of high-velocity labor markets. These practices are then analyzed under the law of employment discrimination and determines that some large Valley employers might be discriminatory, in a legal sense. If this is the case, why are there no employment discrimination suits, for practical purposes, in the Valley? Looking to the future, the chapter discusses whether the high-velocity personnel practices that have generated such wealth for so many can be made to work better for those who have yet to benefit from them—or whether, by contrast, expanding legal remedies to include Silicon Valley's disparate racial outcomes would do more harm than good.

Protected Groups in the Silicon Valley Labor Market

Asians: The Success Story

Almost one-third of the high-technology workforce of Silicon Valley was foreign-born in 1990, one-third of scientists and engineers. (Data from the 2000 Census are not yet available, but many observers predict that one-half of scientists and engineers in the Valley are now foreign-born [e.g., Matloff 2001].) Of that one-third in 1990, two-thirds were born in Asia, half of them Chinese, about one-quarter Indian, and the rest mostly divided among Vietnam, the Philippines, Japan, and Korea (Saxenian 1999a: 11–12). Close to one-quarter of technology firms started in the Valley between 1980 and 1998 had CEOs with Chinese or Indian surnames (Saxenian 1999a: 23). Po Bronson describes one of these, KillerApp.com, founded by Ben Chiu, Taiwan-born, who arrived in the Valley knowing no one, was turned down for money all along Sand Hill Road, and eventually sold the company for almost $50 million (Bronson 1999: 15–17, 26–27, 31–33, 38–39). Michael Lewis set out to tell the story of Silicon Valley by following Jim Clark, but soon realized this missed a big part of the start-up story. In his words: "The definitive smell inside a Silicon Valley start-up was of curry" (Lewis 2000: 116).

People who describe Silicon Valley as a meritocracy are thinking of stories like these. It is not my purpose to debunk them. Silicon Valley's strength is its openness to hard workers from whatever origin. As mentioned in chapter 7, openness to immigrants is a significant part of the Valley's advantage over Boston and Austin, and something all these high-technology districts share in comparison with foreign equivalents. Silicon Valley participates in global production networks, and for those in the Valley who experience that globalism every day, meritocracy and nondiscrimination are daily experiences, and have been for many years. For example, when Intel in 1983 opened new assembly plants in Chandler, Arizona, and Ireland, they were set up by engineers from Intel's Malaysian facility (Ernst 2000: 15). Two particular aspects of Asian success in the Valley, however, complicate the pure model of careers open to talent: ethnic networks and entrepreneurial options. Each is important. Each reinforces the other.

Asian engineers' success reflects not only their individual effort, but the working of formal and informal organization, as stressed in chapter 9 (Saxenian 1999a; Dossani 2002). Informal ties are more important than formal organization. Ben Chiu's story, from Bronson (1999), is an example. As mentioned, his company, a comparison shopping engine, was not funded by Sand Hill Road venture capital. His investors were Taiwanese. Like the nightclub business in Taiwan that Chiu had left, Silicon Valley was "guanxi all over again: connections" (Bronson 1999: 31). His attorneys recommended a personal financial adviser who had been an accountant for Jerry Yang (of Yahoo!) and Mark Andriessen (of Netscape), and that man introduced Chiu to investment bankers and facilitated the sale of the company. The several thousand Chinese- and Indian-born engineers who responded to a survey ranked their most important network to be family and friends, followed by current and former colleagues, school alumni, members of formal ethnic associations, and, in last place, other professional organizations (Dossani 2002: 22).

The start-ups founded by immigrant engineers also reflect, not simply the larger start-up culture of Silicon Valley, but also the glass ceiling. While Asians are statistically overrepresented in professional positions in the Valley, they are less common in managerial positions. "A 1991 survey of Asian professionals in the region found that two-thirds of those working in the private sector believed that advancement to managerial positions was limited by race" (Saxenian 1999a: 19, quoting Asian Americans for Community Involvement 1993). For those surveyed, this did not mean "racial prejudice and stereotypes" so much as a perceived "old boys' network that excludes Asians" and "lack of role models." When these Asian professionals felt blocked in the companies for which they worked, they were particularly likely to start their own.

The New Economy, then, includes some very Old Business forms: networks of ethnically linked businesses that provide goods or services to the larger community. These networks do not just involve Chinese laundries or Korean greengrocers, but the design, manufacture, and distribution of computers and components, linking California with Taiwan or Singapore (Saxenian 1999a: 53–71). Asian networks also dominate aspects of high technology that do not require particular scientific or technical expertise, and might otherwise represent opportunities for other groups, such as distributing computers to retailers. (For another example, in the 1980s Asians were preferred for unskilled assembly jobs [Park 1999]; recent ethnographies have reported more diverse workforces [e.g., Chun 2001; Lüthje 1997].)

Retailing and distribution are not particularly high-tech jobs and do not figure much in this book, but I include them here for two reasons. First, just because they do not require computer or engineering skills, they might be a way for less-skilled workers to share in the wealth created by a high-tech economy. Compare, for example, how African-American truck drivers were able to benefit from deregulation (Agesa 1998). Second, we have a splendid ethnography of Chinese immigrant computer distributors in Los Angeles that shows precisely why this business is not open to anyone who might want to enter it (Zhou 1996).

Chinese-owned companies constitute 25 percent of the companies that distribute computers in Los Angeles County, despite making up only 9 percent of retailers, and less than 3 percent of the county population. Virtually all the owners were born outside the United States, three-quarters in Taiwan, and came to the United States as adults. Most became computer distributors because of family members in the computer business, gained experience in Chinese-owned firms, and now employ relatives in their own firm. Even as the companies grow larger, propensity to employ family members does not decline. Capital usually comes from the manufacturers in Taiwan, and otherwise disproportionately from personal savings, friends, and Chinese-owned financial institutions. Unlike some ethnic enclaves, the workforce is not all Chinese. Only 30 percent of firms have an all-Chinese workforce, and 29 percent have non-Chinese managers. However, jobs reflect ethnicity. Whites typically work "in the front" in sales or as secretaries; the technicians and accountants "in the back" are Chinese. The Mexicans work in shipping or assembly (Zhou 1996). I have not found a similarly detailed study of hardware distribution in northern California, but this picture certainly seems to apply there as well.

Women: A Pressing Research Agenda

There is an amazing absence of research on women as a group in the Silicon Valley economy. My impressions are just that: impressions. In every interview I conducted with a woman, for example in her capacity as human resources director or information manager, I always asked about distinct experiences of women as a group. These were nearly always denied to exist, in keeping with the general meritocratic ethos of the Valley; but, in truth, as I probed respondents for more specific examples, these rarely fell into clear patterns.

On balance, Silicon Valley appears to be an excellent place for women, as for anyone who welcomes challenge and opportunity. Women's economic gains largely reflect incorporation into high-skilled and high-paid jobs within sectors (Carnoy and Gong 1996). One often encounters women who are vice presidents or general counsels at an age where one would not expect to find this "back East," as Californians say. One of the few surveys of Silicon Valley women was conducted in November 2000 of 826 women. It reported that some 51 percent of women think that advancement opportunities for women are better in Silicon Valley than outside; 41 percent think they are about the same; and only 8 percent think they are better outside (Women of Silicon Valley 2001: 15). Women nevertheless feel that opportunities for men are still better than for women (60 percent agreed with that statement). Women in technology are more than twice as likely as the general sample to agree that gender has been a significant barrier to their career advancement (28 versus 15 percent). Some 41 percent of women in technology believe that they have to "fit into a masculine workplace" in order to advance (p. 22).

As mentioned in chapter 9, while formal and informal networks restricted to women exist, they are much less influential than the Chinese or Indian networks. Rather, the crucial network for women appears to be the relationship with the company founder (usually male). Companies with lots of women usually started with lots of women brought in by the founder, and thereafter have lower levels of supervision (Baron, Burton, and Hannan 1999: 14; Baron, Hannan, Hsu, and Kocak 2002).

If women without family responsibility could be broken out for separate analysis, it seems possible that their work experience would not differ from that of similarly situated men, something that is increasingly true across the U.S. economy. However, such similarity is elusive for women with children. The Women of Silicon Valley survey reported: "The number one source of stress for women in Silicon Valley is in balancing work with personal or family responsibilities. Some 67% say that this balancing act always or sometimes causes them stress" (Women of Silicon Valley 2001: 16). Working hours are long, and child care is not available to meet the demand (see generally Carnoy 2000).

As mentioned, I have been unable to find a single lawsuit alleging structural discrimination against women (or any other group). There are, however, some unreported suits alleging sexual harassment (e.g., Rai 2002). This is not surprising, for reasons explored in journalism on high-technology companies elsewhere (e.g., Orenstein 2000). Companies filled with young people working extremely long hours are likely to see relationships between co-workers. Men in Silicon Valley are often arrogant, and often there are suggestions that career advancement will be assisted by the relationship. When it ends, particularly if employment ends too, there may be a lawsuit.

African-Americans, Latinos, Latinas: Missing

You can spend a whole day at any large Silicon Valley employer and never see a black face. In 1998 the *San Francisco Chronicle* requested the forms that government contractors file with the U.S. Department of Labor, and confirmed what everyone knew. Staff at thirty-three of the most prominent firms in the Valley are, on average, about 4 percent African-American and 7 percent Latino, even though African-Americans and Latinos make up 8 percent and 14 percent, respectively, of the Bay Area labor force (Angwin and Castaneda 1998).

Silicon Valley's high-tech labor force was also about 4 percent African-American in 1980. Those blacks were disproportionately in production work, lost jobs along with others in the industry recession in the mid-1980s, and were one-third less likely to be rehired than whites, Hispanics, or Asians (Mar and Ong 1997). Managers hiring for unskilled assembly jobs interviewed from 1989 to 1993 were quite open in their preference for Asians over Latinos, Latinas, and African-Americans (Park 1999). Four government contractors were fined by the Department of Labor in the 1990s for denying a job to a qualified applicant rejected on racial grounds: Apple, Oracle, Solectron, and Everex Systems. Low numbers of these groups in technical and scientific positions are normally attributed today to low numbers of African-Americans and Latinos/Latinas studying math or science and poor networks of recruiting, since so few people from those groups work in the industry now (Angwin and Castaneda 1998).

The story sparked some interest in the federal Equal Employment Opportunity Commission (EEOC), specifically in Vice Chair Paul Igasaki, who encouraged its office in San Jose to focus on the technology industry (Rivlin 2000a; Lubman 2002). The only reported result of this effort was a relatively small ($50,000) settlement at Acropolis Systems, Inc., of Milpitas, to a fired African-American human resources manager and two others. She claimed she was fired for refusing to "do something" about "too many blacks in the office." The company denied wrongdoing and disputed the incident but claimed to want to avoid the expense of further litigation (Johnson 2001). Of course, that is what companies always say, but if the case settled for $50,000, the EEOC must have doubted that it could prove the allegation.

Age Discrimination

There are many anecdotes of middle-aged technical workers who had difficulty finding jobs in information technology, even in the tight labor markets of the last few years of the 1990s (e.g. Matloff n.d.: Ch. 5). To quote a U.S. Department of Commerce Technology Administration study (1999: 17) (not limited to Silicon Valley):

> The IT industry is populated by many younger workers. Approximately 75 percent of computer systems analysts and scientists, and nearly 80 percent of computer programmers are under the age of 45. Many managers in the

IT industry are in their 20s and 30s, and may be uncomfortable hiring or managing older and more experienced workers. A Network World survey [Weinberg 1998] of 200 readers with some hiring responsibility showed that younger network managers are less likely to hire older workers than younger workers. Almost half of respondents 20 to 30 years of age had never hired a person over the age of 40.

It is hard to know what to make of surveys like this (see also Cowley 2001; Alster 1998), or of the many letters to computer magazines by older IT professionals claiming discrimination (e.g., Thorne 2002, who invented a resume of himself, fifteen years younger, in order to get interviews: it didn't make much difference). The National Research Council (2001: 139–51) was skeptical of any claims of systematic age discrimination. Its report relied on unpublished research by Professor Henry Farber. Farber analyzed national data on information technology workers from the Bureau of Labor Statistics. It showed little systematic difference between workers over forty and younger workers. The entire IT workforce is younger than workforces of similar educational attainment. Information technology workers over forty are more likely to lose jobs than younger workers. (The reverse is normally true.) However, they are just as likely to find new jobs as younger workers, in similar amounts of time. Within three years of job loss, 82 percent of the above-forty group, and 84 percent of the under-forty group, find new jobs. The new jobs are comparable. In particular, the older workers are not more likely to work part-time or outside information technology than the younger workers. The older workers may take a larger pay cut, even accounting for the fact that they were paid more than younger workers at the time of job loss. Farber was unable to determine why older IT workers are more likely to lose their jobs. The reasons conventionally given are employer preference for newer programming languages, other hot job skills, and cost factors. Even if there is some illegal discrimination occurring against IT workers over forty, ending it "would not have a significant impact on tightness in the IT workforce in the long term" (NRC, p. 148).

A related interpretive problem, in my view, is that we lack any longitudinal studies of the careers of computer programmers or other computer professionals. Computer programming, in particular, is in many ways not a particularly good job, and it is perhaps not surprising that few people do it all their lives. As Peter Cappelli observes (2001: 94): "In brief, aside from pay, many IT jobs—but especially computer programming jobs—would qualify as lousy work. Most of the understanding about how to design work to meet the psychological needs of workers seems to have bypassed the IT professions." Programming tasks are divided into small jobs; programmers work in isolation from each other and from the organization; work under considerable time pressure; and receive little recognition (Barr and Tessler 1997: 4–5). So it may not be surprising that one sees so few programmers (in particular) over forty. A National Science Foundation analysis of census data shows that, "six years after finishing college, 57 percent of computer science graduates are working as programmers; at 15 years the figure drops to 34 percent, and at 20 years—when most are still in their early 40's—it is down to 19 percent. In contrast, the figures for civil engineering are 61 percent, 52 percent and 52 percent" (Matloff 1998).

The question is, what happens to them? It is at this point that very well informed observers of the Silicon Valley labor market (e.g., professors at Stanford Graduate School of Business) typically tell me a story about somebody whose kid played soccer on their kid's team. Some proportion of those who wrote code in the 1980s are now working elsewhere in IT firms, working for venture capital firms, teaching at community colleges, practicing law, or selling real estate in Oregon. Some founded their own companies, so are no longer in the employment statistics as employees at all, but are self-employed. Some are happy with how life turned out, some are not, but nobody has any systematic picture. Few were unemployed, at least not in 2000 when unemployment rates in the Valley were below 2 percent. But, as Norman Matloff (1998), who argues strongly that there is age discrimination, observes: "A programmer who becomes, say, an insurance agent after failing to find programming work counts in the statistics as an employed insurance seller, not an unemployed software worker."

The case that systematic age discrimination is taking place may be another of those assertions that presupposes the old world of internal labor markets that Silicon Valley has largely left behind. In an internal labor market, thin representation of workers in their forties often suggests age discrimination, breach of implicit promises, or both. In a high-velocity labor market, no such inference follows. What appears as age discrimination may be a different phenomenon: demand for very specific skill sets at hiring, as a way of reducing information costs as firms constantly search for the best workers in a situation in which information of any kind is thin and unreliable. Firms will hire only programmers who can program in Java already. They will not train or retrain programmers they have worked with before, and do not value experience in older programming languages. Most published complaints about "age discrimination" go on to include just this charge (e.g., Cappelli 2001; Matloff 2000; Weinberg 1998). I will look more closely at this demand in the section that follows, and later in this chapter I will consider whether it might represent discrimination in a legal sense.

Still, even if systematic age discrimination is difficult to prove, there are undoubtedly individual cases of age discrimination in high technology. There are even journalistic anecdotes in which employers actually display prejudicial stereotypes about older workers, what lawyers call "direct evidence" of discrimination (Cowley 2001; Alster 1998). It is all the more surprising, then, that there appear to be no reported or unreported cases of age discrimination against high-tech firms in the Valley, apart from the occasional individual executive's suit for stock options. I will discuss why later in this chapter.

Why Divergent Labor Market Outcomes by Race and Ethnicity?

In the classical economic account of discrimination (Becker 1971), individual employers may indulge a taste for discrimination. Such discrimination is economically subrational, but has little economic effect. It merely creates a labor market opportunity for another employer. More recent scholarship on disparate labor market outcomes has criticized the classical account and substituted a highly nuanced understanding of modern discrimination (Charny and Gulati 1998; Krieger 1995, 1998; Wilkins and Gulati 1996). In these accounts, the natural habitat of discrimination is the large firm with internal job tournaments, and discrimination reflects a combination of unconscious racism, subjective hiring criteria, failures to mentor, high information costs of learning about employees, and inefficient signaling.

The disparate labor market outcomes by race in Silicon Valley do not reflect either the classical account ("taste for discrimination") or the tournament account. I do not believe there is much taste for discrimination, and certainly no taste for association with whites as such (given the success of Asians). Disparate labor market outcomes do not reflect internal tournaments or promotion ladders, which are weak. Failures to mentor are a factor, certainly for women, yet mentoring is haphazard at best and also not extended proportionately to Asians. Nor are hiring criteria excessively subjective. The usual charge is that they are excessively specific.

Rather, disparate labor market outcomes in Silicon Valley are the very result of the distinctive features of employment in the Valley, identified throughout this book: short tenures, rapid turnover, cooperation among networked firms, start-ups and self-employment as career options built into the reward structure, and flexible compensation. I have argued that these aspects of working in Silicon Valley are responsible for a good portion of its remarkable technological and economic growth. This chapter shows that these features can result in labor markets with strong racial disparities.

Rapid turnover creates a constant need to hire, despite generally low levels of information about individual applicants. Three employer responses, each individually rational, create racially disparate outcomes. First, employers require very specific skill sets at hiring and are not willing to train or retrain employees who lack those skills. This has a particularly negative impact on older, African-American, and Latino/Latina employees. Second, employers rely heavily on contacts, connections, and hiring entire teams. Social and business contacts continue to be segregated and thus reinforce disparate labor market outcomes. Third, low rates of entrepreneurial activity among African-Americans have direct labor market consequences.

In a high-velocity labor market or similar network, racial discrimination by an individual employer is not irrational and does not create labor market opportunities for another employer, as predicted by classical economic theory. Instead, as Kenneth Arrow (1998: 98) observes, in a network, there are rewards to discrimination, and no costs.

Introduction: Job Searches, for Top Employees, Without Tournaments

I have pointed out repeatedly that in a high-velocity labor market, employers hire all the time, often with little information. Constant hiring spreads information among firms as discussed in chapters 2–4, and creates a need for the kind of labor market intermediaries discussed in chapters 8 and 9. Let us look more closely at how this works in the market for programmers, who have been frequently discussed in the popular and academic literature. Programmers are the most common example in discussions of age discrimination and probably illustrate racial disparities as well as any other occupational group.

Discussions of computer programmers often observe that the best are vastly superior to the mean, more productive by a factor of twenty or so (e.g., Cappelli 2001; Matloff 1998: Ch. 7.2). Whether this is true or not, employers act as if it is true. They devote enormous time and energy to identifying superior workers.

Some years ago, my brother and I invented the concept of a "tequila distribution" to describe a distribution in which a handful are excellent while the mass are mediocre. Tequila distributions thus look quite different from "normal" bell curves; they contain a mass near the left axis and a long, thin, tail extending to the right. They take their name from my (highly subjective) observation that really good tequilas are excellent, as good as the best whiskeys, while the masses are undrinkable. My brother, a radiologist, believes that ability among orthopedic surgeons is also distributed according to a tequila curve. I have no independent opinion on that question. In any case, employers behave as if programmers were distributed along a tequila curve.

Older companies used to find good employees through what economists call job tournaments (Carmichael 1983; Lazear and Rosen 1981; Nalebuff and Stiglitz 1983). In these models, employers do not worry much about the job skills that they cannot observe at hiring anyway. They hire a bunch of people who look pretty good and then offer them incentives if they perform really well. Some will not make it and will get washed out as probationary employees; some look better and may get trained by the employer; some will ascend to the top of the heap. The partnership or fat salary is the price the employer pays in order to induce the entering employee to work as hard as possible. In the interesting variant by Charny and Gulati (1998), the employer will be able to distinguish a small group of superstars (and hire them), but will be relatively indifferent to which subset of a mass of fairly standard applicants are hired. Charny and Gulati show how such tournaments may result in racially disparate outcomes.

The tournament device is not available to a typical Silicon Valley start-up, which obviously cannot promise a long career ladder, back-load benefits, or even maintain long probationary periods. Instead, employers try to find excellent employees at the hiring stage. Matloff (n.d.: Ch. 4.1) interviewed a number of prominent information technology employers in 1997 and 1999—that is, during the years they complained of "desperate shortages." They were nevertheless extremely picky. All employers admitted being flooded with resumes, and nevertheless hiring no more than a maximum of 5 percent of applicants (Cisco). Many companies hired fewer than 1 percent. The devices employed to do so also contribute to racially disparate outcomes.

Demand for Specific Skills at Hiring

Employers in high-velocity labor markets are less likely than older employers to search for generalists with multiple aptitudes—the kind of engineer or lawyer who would be the best contributor to a firm over a forty-year career. Instead, jobs are defined to include highly particular skill sets, and actual experience in using them (Angel 1991: 130–34). During the period of my research, programmers had to be able to program in Java. Matloff (n.d.: Ch. 4.2) cites job advertisements like "Must have experience writing C++ code for TCP/IP applications on SPARC platforms." In 2002, despite the elimination of half a million jobs in information technology nationally, employers continued to search for database administrators, Web architects, and others with very specific skills (Dubie 2002).

To employers, these specific skill requirements refute any implication of bias or discrimination, the kind of discrimination that would, by contrast, creep in if employers were looking for someone to "fit into firm culture" or "make partner" someday. "If we find someone who programs fast in Java, we will hire them today," I was told dozens of times, "whatever they look like or whatever planet they come from." The success of programmers from Asia is supposed to demonstrate the lack of discrimination resulting when jobs are tightly defined by objective, job-related performance criteria.

Such jobs do look like the Holy Grail to human resources professionals and lawyers, accustomed to identifying discrimination either with intentional hostility, or subjective job requirements unrelated to performance yet with disparate racial impact. If African-Americans are not hired as programmers and engineers—and they are not—this simply reflects, in this way of thinking, their lack of skills, or human capital, and not discrimination. (I warned you in chapter 4 that contemporary invocations of "human capital" typically serve to justify inequality.) There is much truth to this story.

Matters are not so simple, however, for specific required skill sets may be an instrument generating discriminatory outcomes, even if not necessarily illegal discrimination. First, obviously, they take the education system and labor market as they find them. If African-Americans do not learn Java somewhere else, that is not the companies' problem. What if companies are the most efficient trainers in Java, and no other institution even offers such training in the Valley? A democratic society cannot conscript employers to train employees. It could offer incentives to encourage conversion of a high-velocity labor market into one of more stable employment: by taxing separations, limiting flexibility, enforcing covenants not to compete—but these risk harming the very scientific and economic vitality of the district. Possibly, as mentioned in chapter 9, the unwillingness of companies to train employees creates a market opportunity for a labor market intermediary to train, certify, and place employees, whether a proprietary school, community college, or employee organization like Working Partnerships. Second, a job requirement such as "ability to program in Java" (or some other hot language) will clearly favor younger programmers over older. I will return to these points later, when I analyze whether either of these disparate outcomes violates civil rights laws.

Connection Networks

One of the most attractively meritocratic aspects of Silicon Valley's labor market are the stories of young people arriving from distant places, knowing nobody, and succeeding in establishing reputations based entirely on their competence (Bronson 1999; see also Jon Katz 2000, although his eponymous "geeks" ended up in Chicago, not California). This is no myth. On the other hand, there is no reason to think that employer openness to unknown job candidates is the whole story, or functions in a racially neutral manner. As managers of temporary help firms say, personal contacts become more, not less, important in the age of Internet job boards and employer access to thousands of resumes. Hiring may often reflect contacts from past work assignments, though in today's Silicon Valley rarely social contacts. Hiring often involves entire teams. Phil Schneidermeyer, managing director of Advanced Technology Practice at the search firm Korn/Ferry International: "You go out to look for one, but your expectation is that whomever you hire will bring in five to eight other members of his or her previous team" (Millard 2000).

We know essentially nothing systematic about how different groups protected by discrimination laws make use of networks of contacts. Some assumptions are plausible. Older workers should be advantaged over younger workers in markets in which personal contacts are important. Ethnic ties to workers already in the industry probably reinforce the likelihood of being hired. As mentioned, firms with the highest percentage of women employees are those that rely most heavily on recruiting those personally known to founders (Baron, Burton, and Hannan 1999: 14; Baron, Hannan, Hsu, and Kocak 2002). Once inside the firm, a large California high-technology engineering firm, networks were closely associated with mobility but did not function differently for nonwhites and women, though both groups were lightly represented in the sample (Podolny and Baron 1997).

Entrepreneurial Preference

In the entrepreneurial version of the American success story, the successful founder often prefers members of his own ethnic group. It is not possible to break down Silicon Valley workforce statistics by the ethnicity of the firm founder. The difference may not be great. All Valley employers employ lots of Asians, and none employs many African-Americans.

Still, if Valley employers are just like America here, it adds up to another strike against African-Americans. African-Americans are less than one-third as likely as white Americans to be self-employed, a ratio that has been constant for many years (Fairlie 1999; Fairlie and Meyer 1996). Rates of entrepreneurship by ethnic group are almost perfectly negatively correlated with unemployment rates for that group, suggesting a strong tendency for entrepreneurs to prefer their own kind (Bloch 1994: 39–40). By contrast, a survey of several thousand Chinese and Indian engineers active in formal associations found that they were most likely to be employed in a firm that has at least two founders from their country of birth. Almost 60 percent of Indian engineers, and 54.5 percent of engineers born in the People's Republic of

China, work for firms in which more than 10 percent of the workforce shares this characteristic (Dossani 2002: 20).

Like every other empirical and theoretical picture in this book, its explanation of racial disparities will be clarified with future research, or even journalism. For the rest of the chapter, though, let us assume the following stylized portrait of discrimination in high-velocity labor markets. Firms hire constantly for the relatively short term. They demand experience in narrowly defined skill sets, and rely on intermediaries that can credibly confirm individuals' skills. They derive no particular benefit from workplace diversity as such, given short tenures and high turnover. Hiring personnel have no particular objection to employees of different ethnicity, but no incentive whatever to go find them.

Under these conditions, getting a job depends mainly on ability to acquire hot skills, connections to individuals at other firms, and rates of entrepreneurial activity among one's own ethnic group. Recent graduates of technical institutes, even foreign, will do well. Older workers should have good network connections, but if they lack entrepreneurial aptitude—that is, if they have not already started their own firm—they will face constant pressure to update skills. African-Americans will do particularly poorly: their schools will disproportionately prepare them poorly in mathematics and science; they will find few African-Americans inside companies; and even fewer owning them.

Are Silicon Valley Employers Violating Civil Rights Laws?

If a Home Depot store has very few women in high-paying sales or managerial jobs, as used to be common, it can expect to be sued under the discrimination laws, as also used to be extremely common. In 1997 Home Depot settled multiple discrimination suits for $104.5 million, eventually making major changes in its personnel processes (Sturm 2001: 509–19). Are large Silicon Valley employers with poor records of employing African-Americans, Latinos/Latinas, or people older than forty similarly vulnerable? The difficulties in analysis show some of the problems involved in mapping our existing law of employment discrimination onto high-velocity labor markets.

Stable Career Jobs as the Natural Habitat of Employment Discrimination Law

We have seen how the law of trade secrets and employee organization reflects an assumption of stable long-term careers inside individual firms. It may surprise readers that the law of employment discrimination makes the same assumption. If asked to name an employment practice forbidden by the civil rights laws, I suppose most people would name the refusal to hire some-one because of that individual's race, color, sex, or religion. While such a refusal does indeed violate the Civil Rights Act, in practice there are very few lawsuits growing out of refusals to hire. Rather, the natural habitat of the law of employment discrimination is the discharge, or failure to promote (Donahue and Siegelman 1991). In these two situations, the law normally assumes stable employment, which would have continued had it not been disrupted by an act of discrimination.

Refusal-to-hire cases are almost impossible to prove. There is rarely a presumption that any individual will be hired for any particular job, and indi-viduals rarely are told, or find out independently, why they did not get any particular job. Employers are not normally required to keep records of job applications, and few do. Finally, such suits are rarely worth an attorney's time. Until the statute was amended in 1991, remedies were limited to com-pensatory damages. If someone does not get a job because of discrimination, but gets a different job instead that pays about what the old one did, there may have been discrimination but there is no legal damage. Since 1991, pu-nitive damages are theoretically possible, but again almost impossible to es-tablish in hiring cases.

By contrast, loss of a stable job, well into the employment life cycle, is worth fighting over. The same is true if the employer signals that the em-ployee will not proceed further up a promotion ladder. Damages may well be substantial, as the employee's earnings may exceed significantly his or her opportunity wage. Something will have been said about the discharge or failure to promote, and that statement may turn out to be evidence of dis-crimination, if either direct evidence of prejudice or pretextual. Comparison will be possible between the potential plaintiff and other employees. Particu-lar hiring practices, such as subjective criteria, might turn out statistically to have disparate impacts across protected groups.

Applying Discrimination Law to a High-Velocity Labor Market

General Problems

There is thus little case law, and little academic literature, on applying dis-crimination law to labor markets in which hiring is constant, job tenures are short, internal labor markets weak, and racial disparities appear at the hiring stage. (By contrast, the literature on discrimination in internal labor markets, identified with tournaments, patterns of mentoring, subjective criteria, and inefficient signaling, is quite sophisticated.) The problems in proving dis-crimination are severe. Some have already been suggested.

First, discrimination that occurs at the hiring stage is difficult to document.

Second, many plaintiffs who are in fact victims of discrimination will not bother to sue if other jobs are available. It is obviously a good thing if jobs are available and unemployment is low. I am not suggesting these things should be changed for the sake of developing antidiscrimination law. Rather, I am just reinforcing the point that the natural habitat of antidiscrimination law is the lucrative late-career job up the career ladder.

Third, the highly flexible forms of acquiring labor bedevil statistical analysis. For example, programmers (like just about any other business service in the Valley) may be obtained, as we have seen, by hiring an employee; subcontracting to a self-employed individual, unincorporated business, or incorporated business, inside or outside the United States; or hiring a temporary employee referred by an agency, or an immigrant on a temporary visa. (In chapter 2, I mentioned Cisco's acquiring a company to obtain its chief technology officer.) Collecting and presenting the relevant statistical evidence, on all these modes of acquiring programming services, is obviously far more complex than comparing the resumes of all the accountants or legal associates to see which made partner and which did not. Civil rights laws forbid discrimination in "employment," but not, as a general matter, discrimination in contracting for business services (Suggs 1991).

Fourth, and, I believe, most important, disparate outcomes are, as shown above, generated largely through the practices of demand for skills and experience at hiring, skewed sources of information in networks, and skewed distribution of business ownership. The demand for skills and experience at the time of hiring is just the sort of thing often proposed as an antidote to the discrimination generated by subjective hiring criteria, yet it, too, may generate disparate outcomes, particularly by age and ethnicity. Yet it is difficult to imagine a successful challenge under the discrimination laws to a hiring criterion for being too specific. This will require some legal discussion.

The Problem of Demands for Specific Skills and Experience at Hiring

In some circumstances, disparate treatment, violating the Civil Rights Act, can be proved simply statistically, where a protected group is underrepresented in a workforce at a rate that is two standard deviations away from a predicted normal representation (*Hazelwood School District*; see generally Bloch 1994: 53–70). The very low percentages of African-Americans in Silicon Valley firms may suggest exploration of these theories. Such statistical proof is relevant under two slightly different legal approaches that are often confused with each other: "statistical proof of disparate treatment" and "disparate impact." In the *Hazelwood School District* case, involving a suburban school district with very few nonwhite teachers, the Supreme Court held that a distribution two standard deviations away from normal distribution might alone constitute proof of disparate treatment. However, on the facts of that case, the low numbers of African-American teachers hired triggered instead an obligation in the employer to explain what was going on. For example, the Court held, the school district might show recent improvement in its hiring, or dispute the definition of the relevant labor market.

Proving disparate treatment (called, since 1991, "intentional discrimination") solely through statistical evidence might appear an attractive option to plaintiffs' lawyers. In fact, however, lawyers prefer not to make much use of this theory. An unsuccessful suit against Sears by the federal Equal Employment Opportunity Commission in the 1970s relied almost exclusively on statistical proof of gendered patterns in job assignments, women rarely being assigned to the more remunerative commission sales. The courts were unimpressed with the statistics, imagining that women might not have been interested in the better jobs (Schultz 1990). The plaintiffs' bar learned the lesson that no statistics are good enough by themselves. One must present vivid anecdotes of individual discrimination.

The procedure is similar but not identical where plaintiffs allege that a particular hiring practice has a "disparate impact," a judicially created interpretation of the Civil Rights Act, added in terms to the statute in 1991 [Civil Rights Act of 1964, §703(k)]. Plaintiff identifies a particular employment practice with a disparate impact, and then the employer explains what is going on. The difference is that the employer has an additional defense to a "disparate impact" case. In such a case, the employer is permitted to show that the facially neutral employment practice, producing the disparate impact, is "job related for the position in question and consistent with business necessity." By contrast, "business necessity" is not a defense where the plaintiff has demonstrated "intentional discrimination," that is, disparate treatment.

A hypothetical suit alleging race or age discrimination by a Silicon Valley employer might scrutinize the practice of highly specific job qualifications under both lenses. It is not clear that the difference would be important. Plaintiffs could easily show the low representation of programmers or engineers, and the role of specific qualifications (e.g., experience in programming in C++ of TCI/IP applications on SPARC platforms) in generating disparate outcomes. Employers, however, could probably defend the practice. To the charge that such skill requirements have a "disparate impact," employers would argue that they are justified by "business necessity." As mentioned, there is room for debate here. Advocates insist that good programmers trained in older languages can adapt to newer problems (Matloff n.d.). However, it is difficult to imagine a court substituting its judgment for the employer's on an issue like that. (I should mention that in California, unlike the nation as a whole, it is quite clear that an age discrimination suit may be based on a theory that a particular employment practice or hiring criterion has a "disparate impact" on older workers. Calif.Gov.Code §12941.1, added to California's fair employment law in 1999, declares a legislative "intent that the disparate impact theory of proof may be used in claims of age discrimination," an issue still unresolved as to the federal Age Discrimination in Employment Act.)

The employer could also probably defend its skills requirement against a "disparate treatment" charge, to which "business necessity" is not a defense. The issue here would involve the definition of the labor market. Defining the relevant labor market was one of the issues that the Supreme Court refused to decide in the *Hazelwood* case. Since few cases have used the theory, there remains much uncertainty about how to define labor markets. Surely a high-tech employer will successfully argue that the standard is not the total number of African-Americans (for example) in the Bay Area labor market. But is the standard the market for programmers, or Java programmers, or Java programmers with experience on highly specific applications?

The answer doesn't much matter for African-Americans. Nobody believes there are enough African-American programmers in any of these labor markets to establish deviation from an ideal distribution. (Advancing African-Americans would require attention to exclusion from other, less technical positions; from networks of information; and from educational opportunity. I will take these up later.)

However, the definition of labor market would be critical to a suit by older programmers alleging intentional age discrimination and relying on statistical proof. While the employer will be unable to argue that Java experience is a "business necessity" in terms, it will surely argue that its distribution of older programmers must be measured against the ideal distribution in the market for programmers with relevant experience. The "business necessity" defense, that the statute excludes in cases of intentional discrimination, will come back as part of defining the labor market. There must be some limit to this argument, but it will take much litigation to learn what it is.

So it is difficult to imagine a successful case demonstrating discrimination in hiring programmers based on statistical proof. Ironic confirmation of this statement comes in a recent publication suggesting the widespread presence of intentional discrimination, statistically proven, in the U.S. workforce, and advocating greater use by plaintiffs' lawyers of the theory (Blumrosen and Blumrosen 2002). In this study, discrimination is established by comparing a particular employer's employment statistics with other employers in its industry. If a given industry employs a workforce that is 15 or 20 percent African-American, a particular employer that employs only 2 or 3 percent may well have some explaining to do. Using this test, it is impossible to establish discrimination in the computer or software industry. So few African-Americans or Latinos/Latinas work in the industry that no individual employer deviates much from its normal distribution (pp. 209–10). (Under this method of proving discrimination, the most discriminatory employers in the United States turn out to be large hospitals (p. 202). Conclusions like this suggest why the law has made little use of the theory of statistical proof of disparate treatment.)

Statistical proof might be more useful in demonstrating intentional discrimination for positions without such rigorous entry requirements. It is indeed difficult to explain why Intel's office clericals are only 4 percent African-American (Angwin and Castaneda 1998).

The Problem of Exclusion from Information Networks

It is not surprising that employers who hire all the time, and cannot observe job performance, will rely heavily on networks: hiring an individual in the expectation that he or she will bring along a team; hiring individuals known to current employees from past work. Networks are efficient solutions to high information costs, even though they will magnify racial and ethnic disparities existing at the time of labor market entry (and thus reduce incentives in excluded groups ever to enter that labor market).

Still, this kind of racially disparate outcome would seem to be a much easier legal case than disparate outcomes resulting from requiring specific skill sets at hiring. Recruiting through particular contacts may be efficient, but if it has a disparate impact, it is unlikely to be justified by business necessity—not in a world in which Internet job boards and job sites make thousands of resumes available (Autor 2001b; see chapter 8). If exclusion from networks reflected only the fact that it is quicker and easier to hire your friends and your friends' friends, the law could correct this problem, particularly as to those Valley employers who are government contractors subject to affirmative action requirements.

Silicon Valley employers therefore balance, delicately, the convenience of hiring through referral networks with their genuine commitment to nondiscrimination, as they understand it. Even the lowest ranks of the industry, the manufacturing jobs, are considerably more diverse by ethnicity and gender today (Chun 2001; Lüthje 1997) than ten or twenty years ago, when one more frequently observed white men supervising "short, brown, foreign" women (Hossfeld 1990; Park 1999). They too now share an express ethos of nondiscrimination. Chun (2001) worked at a contract manufacturer in the summer of 1997. She observed her supervisor, a man of Vietnamese origin, simultaneously encourage workers to let him know if they had a friend or cousin who needed a job, and then tell a story about having to fire a Vietnamese speaker.

> On the line, you hear me speak Vietnamese to other workers. Some people think I favor them if you speak my language. They think I give better treatment. But, he speaks my language. I still let him go. . . . It doesn't matter if you speak my language or if you don't. I treat everyone equally. (Chun 2001: 148)

If a workforce is already unbalanced ethnically yet recruits largely or entirely by word of mouth, it will not hire workers from groups not already represented. Is this illegal discrimination? The answer is somewhat unclear. Judge Richard Posner once decided a case of a janitorial firm owned by a Korean immigrant with an overwhelmingly Korean workforce. It hired employees strictly on referral from current employees and received few if any serious applications from non-Koreans. Posner held that this was not intentional discrimination. Rather, it was the cheapest method of recruitment, resulted in the best information about job applicants and some screening of them (*EEOC v. Consolidated Service Systems*). However, in that case, there was no claim that employee referral constituted discrimination because of its "disparate impact."

Since that decision, the law of "disparate impact" has been made somewhat more proplaintiff by the Civil Rights Act of 1991. Today, an employer that relied exclusively on employee referral would be challenged because of its disparate impact. It could defend such reliance only on a showing that it was a business necessity. It is not clear how this "business necessity" defense would apply to low-tech jobs like Posner's Korean janitorial firm, or the 30 percent of Taiwanese Chinese-owned computer distributors in Los Angeles County that lack any non-Chinese employees. (Does "business necessity" simply mean the cheapest and most efficient way of proceeding, or something without which the business would fail?) However, high-tech employers could hardly show any kind of business necessity for relying solely on employee referral to fill high-tech positions, since Internet job boards make thousands of resumes available for high-tech positions. Moreover, Posner's opinion was not applied in a later case, when an employer actually received applications from African-Americans, and still did not hire any. This turned reliance on employee referrals into illegal intentional discrimination (*EEOC v. O&G Wire Spring and Forms Specialty Co.*) However, few Silicon Valley employers receive many applications from African-Americans.

So, in theory, the kind of heavy reliance that some Silicon Valley employers place on referrals by current employees—a practice that helps to generate racially disparate outcomes—might constitute unlawful discrimination because of its disparate impact. This conclusion seems somewhat pedantic, however. My reading of the cases—and conversations with lawyers—suggest that such a claim would not be brought without additional strong anecdotal evidence of qualified African-American applicants who actually applied but were turned down.

The Weak Claim of "Diversity"

Workforces like Silicon Valley's, with low representation of African-Americans and Latinos/Latinas, raise the question of how strong is the legal system's commitment to "diversity" as such. Suppose I am correct that the low representation of these groups primarily reflects employers' demand for high skills on hiring, and unequal access to information and entrepreneurial networks. A strong advocate of workplace "diversity" might claim this misses the point. Such firms would benefit, it might be said, from a more diverse workforce, and thus should be required to recruit one.

The evidence on the advantages of "diversity" as such is not that strong, even as to large and general workplaces. Perhaps there is a case for requiring ethnic and racial diversity in newsrooms or elementary schools. However, I do not know of any literature looking specifically at diversity in highly technical or scientific work teams. It is hard to imagine that diversity as such would contribute anything at all to a technical project. It is difficult to describe any advantage, to the employer putting together a project on wireless data networks (for example), employing a few dozen engineers, programmers, and managers for a defined period and then likely to be spun off or sold, in diversity as such. At least if most of the staff is from India or Taiwan, an additional source of venture capital opens up.

For a generation or more, our discourse of workplace equity, fairness, or justice has given way to a discourse of diversity. It may be doubted that diversity as such could ever have borne the weight placed on it. For this book, however, we need only note that the case for opening more jobs in Silicon Valley to excluded groups must rest on arguments of equity or justice, not on diversity as such.

Existing Discrimination Law Targets Employers, Not Networks

Our existing law of discrimination, like our law of employee organization, locates the relevant employee community within the boundaries of a single employer. The discriminating unit is the single employer. (As mentioned, statistical proofs of discrimination single out individual employers who are deviant in their industries, not entire networks of discrimination.) Remedies for discrimination, if found, will similarly fall on particular employers, who might be ordered to promote particular individuals or modify particular practices with discriminatory impact.

Much of this apparatus assumes the internal labor markets and promotion ladders of an earlier era. The EEOC, or counsel to the private plaintiff, asks the employer: "Are there any female vice presidents? Do any African-Americans serve in this agency above GS-14?" We do not know what questions to ask of an employer with flat managerial hierarchies, 25 or 30 percent turnover a year; where one-quarter or so of the people working on any day are either self-employed consultants or employees of a temporary help agency; where no one expects to make a lifetime career, where successful careers inevitably involve changes among employers, stints as a self-employed consultant, and ultimately founding one's own company. Obviously there will be no cases alleging discriminatory failure to promote or discharge. Even discriminatory failure-to-hire cases may have difficulties in defining what it means to "hire." These ambiguities would be tolerable if Silicon Valley's high-velocity labor market were delivering employment equity, in some rough-and-ready fashion. But it is not, and so our intellectual failure to define equal employment in terms of today's jobs becomes a serious one.

I had thought that in talking to plaintiffs' lawyers, I would learn of potential discrimination suits against Silicon Valley employers that foundered on definitional and statistical questions of this kind. This turned out to be untrue. Instead, there has never been a systematic discrimination suit against a Silicon Valley employer. The problems in this section remain, however. They may lie a few years in the future. I think, however, a time will come when we will want our law of discrimination to come to grips with careers that do not take place entirely within the boundaries of a single firm.

Conclusions on Discrimination

The low representation of older workers, African-Americans, and Latinos/Latinas in Silicon Valley most probably represents a combination of legal and illegal discrimination. The numbers are so low as to trigger some burden on employers to justify them. Employers could, however, probably justify the highly specific skill sets required, despite their exclusory effects. Only against a background assumption of old-style internal labor markets, in which firms employ for entire careers and expect to train, do these skill requirements appear suspicious. I have argued throughout this book that courts should not impose the picture of internal labor markets on high-velocity labor markets, and I must maintain that position despite my sympathy for those excluded. So I think that a general preference for specific skill sets, and refusal to train, do not violate the civil rights laws, even where the effect is to exclude older, African-American, and Latino/Latina employees and result in workforces that are almost entirely white and Asian.

Illegal discrimination, however, probably occurs when employers act on prejudicial stereotypes, or recruit solely through networks known to them. The stereotyping particularly harms older workers, while the networks particularly exclude African-American and Latino/Latina workers, especially from less-skilled jobs. Both kinds of cases are difficult to win in practice. A stereotyping case normally requires direct evidence of the prejudice. Such prejudice against old people is sometimes expressed. A case of "hiring through referral" normally requires showing actual application by, and rejection of, qualified members of excluded minority groups. Journalism suggests that both scenarios are found in Silicon Valley.

Why Are There No Reported Legal Cases Finding, or Even Alleging, Discrimination in Silicon Valley?

So the question is raised of why there are no reported or unreported cases challenging systemic exclusion of older workers, or African-Americans, or Latinos/Latinas, from the Silicon Valley job market.

Reported cases are of course useless for social science purposes; they are not a representative sample of any social practice, including litigation, and not accurate accounts even of the facts in the reported case (Shuchman 1979). Reported employment discrimination cases are even less representative of employment discrimination cases than other reported cases are of their class. Lawyers who practice in the area confirm that the "best" cases from plaintiffs' points of view nearly always settle, and the price of the settlement is a confidentiality order—for which defendant was willing to pay quite a bit—that forbids counsel or the parties from discussing the case. So I was not surprised to discover no officially reported cases finding a high-tech employer in Silicon Valley guilty of discrimination. I fully expected to interview lawyers, and to that end interviewed numerous lawyers who represent either plaintiffs or defendants (occasionally some of each) in employment litigation.

As nearly as I can determine, there has never been a case attacking any Silicon Valley employment practice as a systemic exclusion of, or discrimination against, older, or African-American, or Latino/Latina, or female employees. The absence of age discrimination is particularly striking. There is a handful of unreported cases, all involving highly individual claims, such as an individual woman sexually harassed by a particular supervisor, or a discharged Oracle executive suing for stock options who adds a discrimination count to a breach of contract claim. Yet nearly everyone believes that there are employers that do systematically discriminate against older workers, and the statistics on African-Americans and Latinos/Latinas would prompt litigation in other industries. Why not here?

At least three explanations have been suggested to me, but I think we can reject two of them. (1) There is no shortage of capable lawyers who represent plaintiffs in discrimination suits. (2) California law is not unfavorable to discrimination plaintiffs (as it is to trade secrets plaintiffs); if anything, it is more favorable to plaintiffs. In my judgment, the absence of successful discrimination suits in Silicon Valley, even against stereotyping and exclusion from referral networks, reflects: (3) the availability until recently of alternative, even preferable, employment for victims of discrimination and the costs of suing.

The Plaintiffs' Lawyers

There is no shortage of lawyers in the Bay Area, and no shortage of lawyers willing to take a discrimination case on behalf of a plaintiff. The lawyers are not in bed with, or in any way dependent on, the large Valley employers.

I found plaintiffs' lawyers by tracing lawyers involved in cases mentioned in news articles, and by referral from other lawyers in the area. Most resemble the lawyers drawn into employment discrimination practice after the 1991 amendments to the Civil Rights Act created jury trials and increased damages. My generalizations about these lawyers are commonplace in the field, though lack comprehensive academic treatment. They approach discrimination litigation like personal injury litigation. They conceptualize discrimination as a bad event that happens to an individual, like a car accident or defective product. They are compensated from contingent fees, so have incentives to put their energies into cases that offer the possibility of really large jury verdicts. In the employment discrimination field, such a case involves a sympathetic plaintiff, subject to an affront that is easy to explain and comprehend, that caused her to leave or be fired from a well-paid job, leaving her with substantial documentable losses (such as medical bills), and out of well-paid work for a substantial period. An incident, or course of incidents, of sexual harassment, fills the bill well. By contrast, there will be little incentive to take cases for people who did not get hired in the first place (discrimination hard to prove); people who did not get one job but got another (no damage); poorly paid employees (low damage); or victims of discrimination that is subtle or difficult to grasp.

Nationally, such lawyers take few cases of race or national origin discrimination, and their California counterparts are no different. However, nationally, such lawyers gravitate toward age discrimination cases, with their sympathetic plaintiffs, unlikely to work again, suffering the losses of high-income positions appropriate to their late stage in the life cycle (Rutherglen 1995). This makes the absence of such cases in the Valley more surprising.

The Bay Area, however, also contains an unusual number of lawyers who conceptualize discrimination as something that happens to classes of people, particularly ordinary working people, not just to affluent individuals. I spoke to three of the ablest.

Patricia Shiu and Joan Graff are veteran plaintiffs' advocates at the Employment Law Center, a project of the Legal Aid Society of San Francisco. Originally founded to assist immigrants, the center now specializes in all aspects of discrimination litigation on behalf of poor and working people. (It does not concern itself with "glass ceiling" issues of promotion to or within managerial ranks.) It employs around twenty lawyers and does not receive funds from the federal Legal Services Corporation.

Its last case in Silicon Valley concerned Atari (which dates it fairly effectively), a class action concerning its obligation before layoffs to inform workers under a California statute that predated the federal Worker Adjustment and Retraining Notification (WARN) Act. Some of its other cases involve worker classification issues and thus might help low-income workers in the Valley. One involved a class of janitors misclassified as independent contractors, settled (without published opinion) when their employer reclassified them as employees. In another, they cooperated with the Equal Employment Opportunity Commission in a suit against a temporary help agency that was the vehicle for its clients' race discrimination (*EEOC v. Recruit USA;* Pender 1992).

They confirmed the difficulty in applying the kinds of discrimination litigation they usually do to Silicon Valley, largely because of the high job mobility, lack of loyalty, and low aspirations for workplace community. People who feel discriminated against either leave, or stay because they are making money, but do not fight. But Joan Graff thought that the absence of discrimination complaints in the Valley was a sign of a weak sense of community (which she termed "narcissism"). Valley employees do not have any sense of a larger community, she said, citing the recent bankruptcy of the United Way of Santa Clara County. All they care about is work, like the employees in Juliet Schor (1991) who would rather stay at work than go home. That makes work the only place left to be a community, the only place to overcome narcissism. But it is not a community either, given the end of loyalty and short tenures. In this environment, a focus on nondiscrimination or workplace diversity or community will not succeed.

Barry Goldstein is a partner at the Oakland firm of Saperstein, Goldstein, Demchak & Baller. They do not bring individual discrimination suits, only class actions or other attacks on systemic practices, and are famous for their suits reforming job assignments at Home Depot, based largely on statistical disparities in men's and women's assignments (Sturm 2001: 509–19). Goldstein agreed that many Valley employers had statistics that resembled Home Depot's and said that his firm has considered suits in the Valley but never brought one. He pointed out some of the problems. Companies do not really have entry-level positions. Where compensation is flexible, as it normally is for white-collar employees of all types, it is difficult to frame a class of plaintiffs since courts often hold that individual issues will predominate over the group's. He suggested that sales might be an area of discrimination, based on his representation of sales employees at a technology company in a different part of the country, where none of the sales force had degrees in computer science and whites seemed to be making more money than African-Americans. In that case, the clients preferred that he send a confidential letter to the employer and then work together with the employer on fairer sales assignments. By contrast, he has never even sent such a letter, or heard of one, in the Valley. If there is any discrimination in sales assignments, he thought it would reflect relations with purchasing vice presidents and other cultures in which women or African-Americans might not "fit in." He also told me that Asians of all types in the Bay Area labor market simply do not sue. In the entire history of his firm, during which they have always had Asian lawyers in the office, they have brought only one case on behalf of Asian plaintiffs, against the San Francisco Fire Department.

I will return to some of these points later. I have given a fuller account of these interviews to dispel any notion that the absence of discrimination suits in the Valley reflects a lack of imagination or courage by lawyers. I do not believe any area of the country has more thoughtful or courageous lawyers practicing employment law, either on behalf of employees or employers.

Legal Obstacles

In chapter 2 I discussed some of the difficulties in deciding whether one state's law is really different from another's. It is necessary to examine both formal law "on the books," and informal aspects of the sociology of litigation. In that chapter, both turned out to be essential to understanding why employees are normally free to depart Silicon Valley firms and start competing firms. That is, formal California law prohibits enforcement of covenants not to compete. Understanding the trade secrets story required understanding social factors. Formal trade secrets law in California is little different from other states' (it has the same Uniform Statute but does not give independent weight to negotiated trade secret agreements), and interpretations of that statute have been adopted by courts inside and outside California that would make it the functional equivalent of enforcing noncompetes. Nevertheless, employers rarely sue, because such suits cause them reputational harm, rarely succeed, and threaten them as hirers as well as losers of labor.

Does California law provide any formal or informal obstacles to civil rights plaintiffs? We can be definitive that there are no formal obstacles. Federal civil rights laws against race, sex, and age discrimination apply as minima in all states. States may extend additional protection to plaintiffs (and, as mentioned, California has, to age discrimination plaintiffs). They are allowed to proceed under state law by showing that a putatively neutral employment practice, such as targeting highly paid employees for layoff, has a "disparate impact" on older workers. There has been little reported litigation under this statute, enacted in 1999. It is hard to believe that it means what it says. A job that requires Java programming certainly has a "disparate impact" against older employers. California courts will eventually have to define what kinds of business justifications will support such practices with "disparate impact" against older workers.

My interviews disclosed only one informal aspect of California law that might discourage discrimination suits, and even this is impressionistic and mostly understood as a change from past practice. Bay Area juries used to have a reputation for being generous to victims of all kinds of legal harm, including accident as well as discrimination plaintiffs. Many observers believe that this is less the case as San Francisco in particular becomes less working class, more professional class. However, high-velocity labor markets are also blamed. Karen Jo Koonan of the National Jury Project/West in Oakland observes the influence of New Economy workers in employment cases. "Dot-commers jump from job to job" and "have no sense that the employers owe anything to the employees" (Opatrny 2000) (or vice-versa: they also think that employees owe no duties of loyalty or confidentiality to employers, at least where this would inhibit their own employability and the employer undertakes no reciprocal duties to employ them). However, it does not appear that even these dot-commers are less generous than juries elsewhere, as opposed to San Francisco juries in former times.

Social Obstacles to Discrimination Suits

In general, people will not sue to protect their rights against discrimination if there are other jobs to be had, or if they can leave and start their own company. They sue when they are about to lose late-career jobs paying above opportunity wage. So much employment discrimination litigation is endogenous to internal labor markets, which create the job that is the subject of the typical discrimination suit.

In a dynamic and expanding economy, employees who lose or fail to get a job due to prejudice normally get a different, better job. As Henry Farber has shown, this is true for job losses in general, comparing older information technology professionals with younger (National Research Council 2001: 135–51). Farber's data include job losses for many reasons, including incompetence or poor performance. Perhaps he has hold of two offsetting trends. There is some stereotyping against older professionals in information technology, which results in some job losses, and longer job searches, which younger workers would not experience. But by the same token, those older workers have a persuasive explanation of some of those job losses that younger workers would not—they were forced out because of discrimination. (This matters if the job lost was at an information technology employer that normally offers somewhat stable employment but chose not to do so for this individual. Nobody has to explain being laid off from most Silicon Valley employers.) So most information technology workers who lose jobs, even for illegal reasons, are able to find other jobs and are not stigmatized by the illegal discrimination.

By contrast, suing that former employer in a discrimination suit could have a powerful negative impact on future employability, powerful in a high-velocity labor market in which employees are back on the job market every eighteen months or two years. Lawsuits and lawyers are not well regarded in the Valley, which also believes itself, with considerable justification, to be meritocratic. Network hiring, with its heavy emphasis on colleagues' and intermediaries' vouching for specific individuals, makes it easy to retaliate against people with reputations as troublemakers. So long as victims of discrimination can get other jobs, they have every incentive to do so, and little incentive to pursue legal remedies. If the U.S. economy generally were really able to keep unemployment rates low through adopting more high-velocity work practices (Katz and Krueger 1999), one might see similar decreases in discrimination suits across the economy.

It is harder to explain why employees at the very end of their careers do not sue. I think there are not many such employees who are really victims of discrimination. As we discussed in chapter 7 on H-1B visas, the woods do not seem to be full of unemployed or underemployed older programmers who would really prefer today's programming jobs to their current occupation, whatever it is.

In the United States in the 1990s, essentially no new Net jobs were created in traditional internal labor markets. Manufacturing employment declined and public employment held steady. All new Net jobs were in the services. Some of these jobs were extremely remunerative (the expanding information technology, financial, and legal sectors) and some were not, but few were in traditional internal labor markets with implicit contracts for lifetime employment. As fewer such jobs are created and existing jobs disappear, discrimination law will either change or die.

Silicon Valley's labor market challenges many ways in which lawyers and economists have understood labor markets, but no challenge is greater, or more intellectually difficult, than its challenge to our legal and conceptual apparatus for understanding discrimination and equal opportunity. If the law does not change, Silicon Valley will continue to be essentially all white and Asian, and disproportionately young. I have argued throughout this book that there is a national interest in growth and innovation that supports such legal institutions as bans on covenants not to compete, narrow enforcement of trade secrets, self-employment, temporary help agencies, and H-1B visas. It is more difficult to defend high-velocity labor markets if they will forever exclude African-Americans and Latinos/Latinas in significant numbers. It is tempting to suggest that law should be less focused on discrimination and more on job creation and growth, but it is simply hypocritical to say this if one knows that such growth policies will not help African-Americans or Latinos/Latinas.

If existing legal tools were more widely used, they would still not bring these discriminated groups into the Valley's labor market. Statistical proofs of discrimination do not work in industries in which no employer hires many members of minority groups (Blumrosen and Blumrosen 2002). Other statistical proofs would at best trigger employer obligations to explain disparate outcomes. Since narrow skill requirements are probably easier to defend than network hiring, more legal scrutiny of employment might result in even stricter skill requirements at hiring, and the loss of the valuable informational functions of the Valley's labor market intermediaries. None of these strategies would accomplish anything if, as is true today, potential victims of discrimination do not sue.

In order for law to bring discriminated minorities into high technology, it would have to become more intrusive in ways that might lose public support and might stifle some of the Valley's flexibility and information-based institutions. Law could, for example, mandate more rigid quotas, particularly for government contractors; or make statistical proof of discrimination easier (by rejecting most explanations of it); or insist on duties to train employees and applicants in protected groups before hiring individuals on H-1B visas. Any of these policies would represent a major change in the Valley's distinctive labor market, moving it away from the flexibility represented by short-term hiring for specific existing skills, and by networks and other intermediaries, and toward traditional labor markets that are simply less productive of high-technology growth and innovation. Again, if a national consensus ever developed in favor of restoring older labor markets, it could be implemented by restricting temporary and self-employment and enforcing covenants not to compete and trade secrets agreements), at considerable cost to innovation and wealth creation.

Critics of high-velocity labor markets and advocates for more traditional labor markets typically minimize the costs imposed by such markets, which include excessive termination of employees and insufficient adjustment; legal and other battles over the rents accruing to such fixed jobs; and too much aggregate unemployment. I also doubt that there would be much public support for policies like quotas, discrimination suits based entirely on statistics, or conscripting employers to train. However since African-Americans as employees benefit little from such innovation (although they benefit along with all consumers of information technology) they might favor such labor market reforms.

Public Policy Initiatives to Open Up High-Tech Jobs to Excluded Groups: African-Americans, for Simplicity

I see no easy solution to this problem, and none that emerges entirely within the realm of what we have traditionally regarded as the law of discrimination. I have also considered and rejected two other policies sometimes advocated on antidiscrimination grounds. I do not favor either a national policy favoring traditional internal labor markets, or a major cut in the H-1B visa program, at least on an antidiscrimination rationale. Eliminating the H-1B program entirely would create the most opportunities for programmers in India and Ireland; a few opportunities for older programmers; and none at all for African-Americans and Latinos/Latinas. I therefore favor experimentation with a variety of other public policy initiatives. The goal would be to find levels of information technology at which African-Americans and Latinos/Latinas might feasibly be employed, and then preferably to create incentives for employers to find ways of doing so. The problem of disparate labor market outcomes will test Silicon Valley's high-velocity labor market. In theory, its distinctive labor market institutions, ideal for transmitting information, providing incentives to employees, and creating wealth, should be able to address problems of disparate labor market outcomes with an efficacy unknown to present approaches.

Create Incentives for Employers to Improve the Numbers

Large information technology employers that receive government contracts are subject to formal affirmative action requirements and informal pressure. Before subjecting all employers to more liability for statistical discrimination, we should try more targeted pressure on particular employers, which can afford to do so, to improve their hiring from excluded groups. They would be given relatively free reign to design recruitment and training programs. Those that were effective could become more widespread. In evaluating results, the law would have to be sensitive to the aspects of a high-velocity labor market that makes genuine contributions to growth. For example, regulators should be responsive to employer programs that create opportunities for African-American contractors or permatemps, if the employer is already making use of these contracts and the opportunities are genuine. Obviously if such requirements affect rates of economic and technological growth, they will not be developed further, but there is no reason to assume in advance that no progress is possible here.

Hi-tech Solutions to High-tech Problems

As with retirement plans and health insurance, there is a lamentable gap between the creativity that has gone into the design of some aspects of high-velocity work practices while ignoring others. Perhaps some existing institutions can be adapted to serve equal employment opportunity. Internet job boards and job sites (cf. chapter 8) for African-American, or older, employees could help demonstrate that such individuals are available. Of course, as we have seen, Internet job sites appear to reinforce meritocracy, but with so many resumes available, these sites make contacts and networks even more important. This creates opportunities for temporary help agencies and advocacy groups focused on older or African-American workers. As discussed in chapter 9, existing organizations advocating employment equity could focus much more on networks of employees spanning firms, facilitating mobility, and self-employment.

Some Silicon Valley employers have developed distinctive ways of organizing human resources (besides outsourcing to a temp agency). Sturm (2001: 499–509) describes human resources problem solvers at Intel, who were delegated unusual authority to treat human resources complaints as symptoms of deeper problems, then to work on the problems. These are probably unique to Intel and would not export easily. As we saw in chapters 1 and 2, Intel is an unusual Silicon Valley employer. Its core business is to dominate chips for personal computers, and in that aspect of its business, it is more interested in stability and maintaining its dominance than are most Valley employers. (Intel also was on a buying spree in the late 1990s to find some market to dominate other than the personal computer, but none of those acquisitions yet plays anything like the role of its core business.) Intel is a place at which people make careers, where departing employees may well face trade secrets suits (invariably unsuccessful), and product lines may well be moved to remote locations with few other high-tech opportunities to tempt departing Intel employees. Intel is also unusually "paranoid" about outside scrutiny (Grove 1996). While its human resource problem solvers may have many achievements to their credit, employment opportunities for members of minority groups are not among them. Intel's statistics are if anything worse than most Valley employers (Angwin and Castaneda 1998).

Equal Employment for Careers, Not Within Single Employers

If there ever are discrimination suits against employers in networks, like Silicon Valley's, counsel, in seeking relief, must be sensitive to the networked aspect of contemporary careers. Law needs a period of experimentation with remedies for discrimination that cross firm lines. These might include several firms agreeing to fund particular training efforts, or a new placement agency. Perhaps a victim of discrimination might receive funding from the discriminatory employer for his or her own start-up, rather than accept a promotion from that employer. I cannot report on successful efforts here. There are not any. It will take some time to learn what works.

A basic problem is that artificial cooperation among entities in a network is never as effective as the kind of natural cooperation that has been the subject of this book: the natural sharing of information, cooperation among firms in bringing products to market, technology licensing and second sourcing, and the like. For example, consider the failure of the Talent Alliance. AT&T, after announcing the elimination of 40,000 managerial positions in 1996, "proposed to a group of 'peer corporations' that they form a network to help laid-off employees find work more easily and conversely to help the companies find the right talent quickly. It seemed an exciting idea at the time: fourteen large companies jumped quickly on the bandwagon, including leaders such as DuPont, Johnson & Johnson, and UPS." However, the idea never got "off the ground." No employers joined after the initial group, at least one dropped out, and fewer than ten people were ever placed through this network (Heckscher 2000: 277–78).

Similarly, if the EEOC somehow found the resources to sue the ten or twenty largest firms in Silicon Valley alleging disparate treatment in hiring for some positions without rigid entry requirements, it (just) might be able to win a suit. I am suggesting, though, that if it did, it would still not know what to ask for in relief. Would a decree requiring hiring (perhaps by contractors, monitored by the large firms) of a certain number of African-American cablers accomplish anything? Would it result six months later in a lot of unemployed cablers? Or would this be a "foot in the door" that would alter lives and aspirations for many individuals not even the subject of the decree?

A "Talent Alliance" linking large Valley employers under EEOC decree might seem like a good remedy if all were found to have discriminated. It might work, or might be as unused as AT&T's. Throughout this book I have been urging further study of how people really match with jobs in a world of networked careers, Internet job boards, new labor market intermediaries, and the like. I stress that this is not some academic ritualized professing of humility; it is necessary if we are to think straight about problems of equity and discrimination.

Equity in Business Contracting

Increasing the distribution of African-American programmers, engineers, and scientists calls for thinking over the extremely long term—the opposite of "Internet time." There are few such individuals now and no trend toward their increase. Certainly the United States should target science and tech education for minorities.

It seems desirable to me to find nontechnical niches in the information technology industry that would be more feasible targets for shorter term integration. If one generation of African-Americans works somewhere in information technology, learning the players and some of the vocabulary, it seems more likely that their children will aspire to higher jobs in the industry, like cars in Detroit, though there is little relevant literature on the point. Finally, since companies do not maintain promotion ladders up from entry-level positions, targeted positions should be those that are often held by the self-employed. A strategy of using public policy and funds to encourage subcontracting to minority-owned contractors accomplishes several goals, since business ownership is especially low among African-Americans. However, existing African-American small business owners employ workforces that are overwhelmingly African-American (Bates 1997). Application by government of antidiscrimination and affirmative action principles to business contracting raises difficult constitutional issues that I cannot explore here, but that do not bind voluntary efforts by employers. There is much to be gained from modest experiments to create more African-American entrepreneurs running technician, service, and outsourced manufacturing businesses, particularly if these could be carried out by companies, with public participation limited to technical assistance grants and the like. The modal existing self-employed African-American male is a truck driver (Kalleberg et al. 1997: 14 [from CPS Supplement]), so channeling more distribution work to them is a very feasible first step.

H-1B Technical Skill Training Grant Program

Employers who apply for H1-B visas since the last congressional reauthorization of the program in 2000 now pay a $1,000 fee, much of which is used for targeted technical training of minority technicians and repair people. This has turned out to be a very good program. It creates some rewards to human capital investment by African-Americans and could yield the fabled "foot in the door" of the information technology industry that is currently lacking. Minority repair people and technicians may, over time, found their own small businesses. By watching them, we will learn things about how to open opportunities in a high-velocity labor market.

This program, however, was sold to Congress under the inaccurate claim that such training would alleviate the need for H-1B visas. This is inaccurate because H1-Bs are normally programmers and engineers, not repairers or technicians. In my view, there is no feasible short-term way of eliminating the need for H1-B visas; certainly there is no reason to think that idle minority and older U.S. programmers are available in anywhere near the numbers required. So I think a program to train minority repair persons and technicians is an excellent one; over the very long term it will help readjust minority attitudes toward education and their place in the information technology industry. However, the Bush administration is seeking to abolish the training program as this book is being completed (Bjorhus 2002).

CONCLUSION

The New Implicit Employment Contract

When I interviewed Will Poole in 1996, he had just joined eShop, one of the new companies developing use of the Internet for marketing. He had already worked for Sun Microsystems (in Massachusetts and Silicon Valley) and Pen Computer Solutions, and thought there was "something wrong" with a resume that showed five years at the same place. I told Will about the economists' concept of an "implicit contract" (chapter 4), and asked him whether he thought there was a similar implicit contract for Silicon Valley professionals like himself who changed jobs frequently. He understood that being hired by Sun or Pen or eShop involved absolutely no implicit or explicit promise to be retained. Nevertheless, he thought that there was an implicit contract, very different from the economists'. "I normally get a year to show what I can do; I get a month's notice before I'm let go; and I will be more marketable when I leave this job than I was when I got here."

The last comment struck me as the most crucial. Indeed, the others follow from it. In Silicon Valley, increasingly throughout the economy, workers willingly, happily, excitedly take jobs that they know will not last, and they do so even when more traditional possibilities exist. They expect that the employer who offers such a short time commitment will not interfere with their next job search. Will Poole expected to be, and was, more attractive to other employers because of what he had learned at Sun, Pen, and eShop. He was able to trade on that information and be free of threatened lawsuits by his old employers. That is why I believe that a promise not to sue departing employees, though rarely as explicit as Cisco's, is nevertheless implicit in Silicon Valley employment contracts.

Since that conversation, "employability" has become prominent in the discourse of European labor law. A distinguished study commission has counseled acceptance of more employee mobility, with the goal of labor law to be the guarantee, not of a particular job, but of each worker's "employability" (Supiot 1999). In the United States, in California, no analogous official document sketches our new implicit contract for employability. That is not how Americans make labor and employment law.

This book has tried to put that contract together and provide its economic rationale. Its rationale is to achieve the wealth creation, low unemployment, and rapid technological and economic growth that come from labor markets oriented around the twin poles of flexibility and information. The employer's legal privileges are sweeping, while the limitations on them, though crucial to their acceptance by employees, are implicit. The employer is privileged to create and destroy jobs; terminate individuals at will; hire temporary employees, employees of contractors, self-employed consultants, and programmers on H-1B visas; outsource personnel functions to temporary help agencies; set compensation and benefits at any level; employ such flexible compensation as stock options that may be terminated or reevaluated. Yet such arrangements can be popular with employees, induce extraordinary amounts of labor, and be rewarding and exciting. The limitations on them, though implicit, are crucial. The employee will be back on the labor (or venture capital) market and will not face interference. Employees have a right to learn about employers and other opportunities, so there will be no interference with the Web sites, chat rooms, and informal networks through which they exchange information about opportunities. Obviously there will be no discrimination. These are modest reciprocal obligations on employers, and perhaps someday law will impose others, but they are the most that one can tease out of the cases and corporate practices so far.

An information technology worker, in Silicon Valley on an H-1B visa, told researchers:

> You see the thing is, it's not like a relationship with a woman or your girl friend or your wife. It's just a company and you think like. . . ok, if I get emotional each and every time with a company then I won't be able to, you know, increase any level of knowledge. I'll be stuck to where I am and I know people who've been working for the same company for 20/30 years . . . that's it. So the only thing that they can say is ok, I'll be getting a pension after I retire. I don't want to be there. I want to be a jack of all trades. (Anand, Ashforth, and O'Leary-Kelly 2002)

This worker, like Will Poole, has traded certainty in order to learn new things, "increase level of knowledge." He also expects to be more employable when he leaves his current position than he was going in, and further expects not to be interfered with as he makes his way through the labor market. These commitments are implicit, not explicit, but underlie the entire Silicon Valley labor market.

Charles Heckscher (2000: 283–84) has suggested a similar implicit employment contract for today's professional relationships. The employee and organization are committed to the mission or project, with a typical time frame of three to five years, not permanent; there will normally be no layoffs while the mission continues; if layoffs are necessary employees will be supported; employees will not harm the mission by leaving before adequate back-up is in place; the employer will fully and honestly disclose business information and strategy; the employee will disclose his or her goals and commitments; and each will reasonably accommodate the other.

The old implicit contract for lifetime employment was developed in practice in the 1950s, though with earlier antecedents; modeled by economists beginning in the late 1970s; and became a legal concept only in the 1980s, as the underlying arrangements fell apart. Today's new implicit contract of employment in a high-velocity labor market will not enjoy an equally leisurely trajectory from practice to theory. Many people are employed under such arrangements; they have survived economic downturn; they raise legal and policy issues that cry out for economic analysis.

We can be confident however that some of the criticism they have received misses the mark. The rise of high-velocity labor markets has induced in many social critics on the left a nostalgia for lifetime careers inside the corporation, jobs for which they had little use when they were still expanding. Once, the Left promised to free workers from wage-slavery, not merely the misery of industrial production, but (at least in the New Left version), the drudgery of routine depicted in such works of fiction as Herman Melville's *Bartleby the Scrivener* and Fernando Pessoa's *Livro do desassossêgo* (Book of Trouble). Today, by contrast, a leftist critic like Richard Sennett (1998) writes with nostalgic yearning of the days when bakers knew how to make bread, and hopes for short jobs only that they will finally convince U.S. workers of the value of socialism.

Sennett argues that today's short jobs are leading to a "corrosion of character" as anxious Americans become unable to make commitments of any kind. (His research sample consists of one man whom he sat next to on an airplane.) His very metaphor shows the problem. Things do not corrode from excessive motion but from standing around. The closed internal labor markets for managers formerly common in U.S. corporations did not, as Heckscher (1995) shows brilliantly, foster mature psychological and emotional relationships. These jobs particularly impeded adjustment to change.

It is possible that high-velocity labor markets will reinterest workers in socialism. As I write, there is no sign of this happening. As this book has shown, short jobs are not the weapon of strong employers against weak workers. They offer much to workers with considerable bargaining power. Those workers respond to the excitement of short jobs with unparalleled creativity and output, shared among those workers and their employers. The task is now to make these job markets work for everybody.

Future Research

Let me close by pulling together the unanswered questions, scattered throughout the book, calling for more research.

Empirical and Sociological

1. The contrast between Silicon Valley and other high-technology districts continues to be stylized and derivative of Saxenian (1994). We need much more precise measures of output in geographic districts, not merely Silicon Valley and Route 128, but control districts such as New Jersey or in Germany, and more precise and comparable data on job tenure and turnover in local labor markets. High-technology districts in Singapore, India, Taiwan, and the Philippines would provide good test cases for the thesis that the "Silicon Valley" model of networked firms and mobile personnel will outperform firms with stable internal labor markets.

2. The contrast between old careers and new short jobs is also stylized. While we have good data on tenures and turnovers, it is not broken down by industry and geography for either the old or new economy. For example, we do not know the extent to which apparently short tenures among programmers reflect normal dissatisfaction with the job, stable if implicit career ladders, or age discrimination.

3. Contrasts among firms with similar technology are an obvious research project. They do not all offer the same implicit career paths.

4. Employees who change job frequently necessarily make use of networks of contacts: former coworkers, friends and social acquaintances, and so on. We know next to nothing systematic about how such networks are used; whether different kinds of employees make different use of them.

5. Women employees as a group have received little attention. Personnel administrators and advocates who seek to open opportunities for women throughout the economy can find many attractive features of the Valley's labor market: opportunities open to women; high subjective satisfaction. It is unclear whether women as a group are disadvantaged by high-velocity labor markets, whether they use networks differently, face unusual demands on time or in combining family with work.

6. Firms' choice among different modes of acquiring technological expertise (hiring an individual, hiring a team, acquiring a company, licensing technology, forming a joint venture) remain a black box.

7. Training in new economy firms is also known mainly through a stylized contrast with old economy firms in which people made careers. We know little specific about the kinds of training that are or are not offered to highly mobile employees. It seems foolish for educational systems to undertake training that will not be valued in the market. There might, however, be scope for better meshing between public and employer training.

8. There is surprisingly little psychological literature on temporary and contingent workers. What little there is often fails to discover meaningful differences with standard workers (e.g., Allan and Sienko 1997). There are undoubtedly stresses attached to new jobs, but the sweeping condemnation in Sennett (1998) is unsupported and premature.

Economic

1. The most important problem is also the least manageable. In economic theory, information is alternatively nonconvex (yields increasing returns) and convex. The world has both kinds of information, but there is no metatheory for linking them. One metaphor is to identify the nonconvex information with statements in code and the convex kind with practical know-how embodied in individuals, but this is only a metaphor and still does not much advance the project of linking the two.

2. We do not have good models of information that is a more valuable factor of production because it is "too valuable to be kept secret." Normal economic approaches make information valuable if it is a monopoly of one user, or property that is therefore contractible. This is often, but not always, true. We still do not understand when, and why, a firm rationally enters into arrangements under which its technology diffuses throughout a network, often carried by mobile employees.

3. Networks of firms have economic properties that are not reducible to those of individual members. In networks, transfer of personnel, transfer of information, and discrimination all may be efficient for the network.

4. The incentive and productivity effects of different methods of compensation remain poorly understood. The actual behavior of employees under different compensation schemes often deviates from expectations. Much needs to be learned about the tendency of mobile workers to cash in their stock options and 401(k) plans before better programs for today's workers can be developed.

5. Informational asymmetries between employers and employees go far deeper than questions over whether the employee will shirk or not.

6. We lack models of the choice among institutional forms for hiring services: subcontracting, hiring an employee, hiring a self-employed consultant, hiring an employee of a temporary help agency. The choices undoubtedly reflect problems in the economics of contracting and information. They may also have different psychological consequences for workers other than those hired.

7. The role of geographic location in productivity of the same worker is not understood. It presumably raises problems in costs of monitoring, incentives, and the effects of information-sharing.

8. The economics of labor organizations that have only voice, not cartel, effects are not well understood. They play important informational roles.

9. The information that compensation arrangements transmit to investors is conjectural.

Legal and Policy Recommendations

1. Organizations of mobile employees might play important roles in their training, delivery of health and retirement benefits, better matching of workers with employers, and advocacy with employers. Artificial legal restrictions on their development should be eliminated. These include definitions of protected concerted activity limited to employees communicating with other employees at the same employer (in industries in which careers span firm boundaries); restrictions on the certification of multiemployer bargaining units; secondary boycott laws that restrict union pressure to a single employer in industries in which employers have fused in network organization.

2. Current legal definitions of trade secrets can be enforced as written only by threatening both employee mobility and a culture of economic growth through start-up firms. Trade secret law should formalize the practices of California courts that permit employee mobility. Employers suing departing employees should be required to identify specific trade secrets, not merely allege "inevitable disclosure."

3. The market has failed to produce private health insurance even for well-compensated self-employed and other mobile workers and shows no sign of doing so. Health insurance should, therefore, be a public responsibility.

4. Only a comparatively few, very highly compensated managers increased their retirement savings in the boom market of the 1990s. Consequently, retirement savings must retain a public and compulsory component.

5. There should be much more experimentation with public policy initiatives to sponsor transition from temporary to permanent work and from contingent work to self-employment. Employee organizations should play a key role in these transitions.

6. While low participation of African-Americans and Latinos/Latinas in Silicon Valley probably reflects primarily poor job qualifications, there must be more public attention to ways of overcoming this problem. Representation is low even in secretarial or distribution jobs, suggesting that other mechanisms are generating disparate labor market outcomes apart from human capital. Firms should be encouraged to experiment with voluntary projects for more inclusive workforces.

The legal and contractual institutions of a high-velocity labor market are not fads, not adventitiously associated with a young industry, not statistical flukes. They are long-lived, have survived boom and bust, and appear strongly associated, not accidentally, with a high-growth culture of start-ups and rapid technological advance. We have much to learn about this relationship, and much more about how to spread its accomplishments to other industries and workers.

APPENDIX

Interview Subjects

Elizabeth Adler, writer and graphic designer
Richard Adler, SeniorNet
John Aguirre, attorney, Wilson Sonsini
Fred Alvarez, attorney, Wilson Sonsini
David Anderson, Sutter Hill Ventures
Kenneth Arrow, Stanford University
Joseph Bankman, Stanford University
Stephen R. Barley, Stanford University
James Baron, Stanford University
Chris Benner, Pennsylvania State University
David Berger, attorney
Carol Blitzer, writer
Roy Blitzer, independent consultant
Steven Bochman, attorney, Wilson Sonsini
Cynthia Cannady, Apple Computer
Mark Chandler, Cisco
Evan Chesler, attorney, Cravath, Swaine and Moore
Amy Christin, independent consultant
Timothy Clark, The FactPoint Group
Phil Constantinou, Driveway
Jeffrey C. Dannenberg, attorney, Kestenbaum, Dannenberg and Klein
Amy Dean, Working Partnerships
Denise DeRose, attorney, Crosby Heafey Roach and May
Paul R. De Stefano, attorney, Pennie and Edmonds
Peter Detkin, Intel
Jennifer Drobac, attorney
Garth Gantrell, attorney, Fenwick and West
Ronald Gilson, Stanford University
Barry Goldstein, attorney, Saperstein Goldstein Demchak & Baller
William J. Gould IV, Stanford University
Joan Graff, Employment Law Center
Paul Hall, attorney, Nixon Peabody
Cary Heckman, Stanford University
Charles Heckscher, Rutgers University

Sara Horowitz, Working Today
Carol Huebenthal, journalist
Robert Kaplan, Apple Computer
Dru Ann Keegan, attorney
Gerry Keeler, Andersen Consulting
Samir Kosla, TechLancer
Michael LaBianca, Cisco
Michael Ladun, attorney
Edward Lazear, Stanford University
Michael Leventhal, Mayfield Fund
David I. Levine, University of California at Berkeley
Deborah Levinger, eShop
Janet Levinger, independent consultant
Art Lim, graphics designer, Lumisys
Sarah Lubman, *San Jose Mercury News*
Alvin Lurie, attorney, former assistant secretary of the Treasury for
    Employee Benefits
Laura Macaulay, U.S. Infogrames
Jean McCown, attorney
Jerry McNaul, attorney
Ann Moncus, Andersen Business Consulting
Daniel Niehans, attorney, Gunderson Dettman Stough Villeneuve Franklin
    and Hachigian
Thomas J. Nolan, attorney, Nolan and Armstrong
Michael Papuc, attorney
Will Poole, eShop
James Pooley, attorney
Nils Reimers, Intellect Partners
Paul Romer, Stanford University
Bertram Rowland, attorney, Fleur, Hohbach, Test, Albritton and Herbert
Melinda Rykwert, attorney, Brobeck
Deborah Satten, Walmart.com
AnnaLee Saxenian, University of California at Berkeley
John Schoch, Asset Management
John Shea, attorney, Twomey, Latham, Shea and Kelley
Patricia Shiu, Employment Law Center
Darby Siempelkamp, Tibco Software
Claudia Slovinsky, attorney
Margaret Steen, *San Jose Mercury News*
Susan Sturm, Columbia University
Katherine Sure, attorney
Ravya Taghavi, human resources consultant
Toni Tomacci, Apple Computer
Charles Yablon, Yeshiva University
David Stewart Zirk, software engineer

Table of Cases and Statutes

Cases

Ebay, Inc. v. Bidder's Edge Inc., 100 F.Supp.2d 1058 (N.D. Cal. 2000).

Edward J. DeBartolo Corp. v. Florida Gulf Coast Building and Construction Trades Council, 485 U.S. 568 (1988).

Ekedahl v. Corestaff, Inc., 183 F.3d 855 (D.C. Cir. 1999).

Electro Optical Industries v. White, 2000 Cal.LEXIS 3536 (Cal., Apr. 12, 2000).

Equal Employment Opportunity Commission v. Consolidated Service Systems, 989 F.2d 233 (7th Cir. 1993).

Equal Employment Opportunity Commission v. O&G Spring and Wire Forms Specialty Co., 38 F.3d 872 (7th Cir. 1994), cert. denied 513 U.S. 1198 (1995).

Equal Employment Opportunity Commission v. Recruit USA Inc., 939 F.2d 746 (9th Cir. 1991).

Francklyn v. Guilford Packing Co., 695 F.2d 1158 (9th Cir. 1983).

Gordon v. Landau, 321 P.2d 456 (Cal. 1958).

Hazelwood School District v. United States, 433 U.S. 299 (1977).

Intel Corporation v. Broadcom Corporation, California Superior Court, County of Santa Clara (unpublished order, No. CV 788310, May 25, 2000).

Intel Corporation v. Hamidi, 94 Cal.App.4th 325, 114 Cal.Rptr.2d 244 (3d Dist. 2001).

International Business Machines v. Bajorek, 191 F.3d 1033 (9th Cir. 1999).

Joshi v. Compubahn, Inc., California Superior Court, County of San Mateo (Unpublished order, No. 411674, Feb. 28, 2001).

Knox v. Microsoft Corp., 962 P.2d 839 (Wash. App. 1998), review denied 980 P.2d 1280 (Wash. 1999).

Lechmere, Inc. v. National Labor Relations Board, 502 U.S. 527 (1992).

M.B. Sturgis, Inc., 331 NLRB No. 173 (2000).

McLaughlin v. Cendant Corp., 76 F.Supp.2d 539 (D. N.J. 1999).

Morton v. Rank America, Inc., 812 F.Supp. 1062, 1073–74 (C.D. Cal. 1993).

National Labor Relations Board v. Babcock & Wilcox Co., 351 U.S. 105 (1956).

National Labor Relations Board v. Northeastern University, 601 F.2d 1208 (1st Cir. 1979).

National Labor Relations Board v. Yeshiva University, 444 U.S. 672 (1980).

National Starch & Chemical Corp. v. Parker Chemical Corp., 530 A.2d 31 (N.J.App.Div. 1987).

Oracle Corp. v. Falotti, 187 F.Supp.2d 1184 (N.D. Cal. 2001).

Peggy Lawton Kitchens Inc. v. Hogan, 466 N.E.2d 138 (Mass.App. 1984).

People v. Eubanks, 927 P.2d 310 (Cal. 1996).

Pepsico, Inc. v. Redmond, 54 F.3d 1262 (7th Cir. 1995), on remand 1996 WL 3965 (N.D. Ill. 1996).

PruneYard Shopping Center v. Robbins, 447 U.S. 74 (1980).

Register.com Inc. v. Verio, Inc., 2000 US Dist LEXIS 18846 (S.D.N.Y. 2000).

Salsbury Laboratories, Inc. v. Merieux Laboratories, Inc., 735 F.Supp. 1555 (M.D. Ga. 1989), affirmed as modified 908 F.2d 706 (11th Cir. 1990).

San Diego Building Trades Council v. Garmon, 359 U.S. 236 (1959).

Santa Cruz Poultry v. Superior Court, 194 Cal.App.3d 575, 239 Cal.Rptr. 578 (6th Dist. 1987).

Schlage Lock Co. v. Whyte, 107 Cal.App. 4th 1443, 125 Cal.Rptr.2d 277 (4th Dist. 2002).

Scribner v. Worldcom, Inc., 249 F.3d 902 (9th Cir. 2001).

Scully v. US WATS, Inc., 238 F.3d 497 (3d Cir. 2001).

Sears, Roebuck & Co. v. San Diego County District Council of Carpenters, 436 U.S. 180 (1978).

Securities and Exchange Commission v. Ralston Purina Co., 346 U.S. 199 (1953).

State Farm Mut. Auto Ins. Co. v. Dempster, 174 Cal.App.2d 418, 344 P.2d 821 (1st Dist. 1959).

Timekeeping Systems, Inc., 323 NLRB 244 (1997).

Vizcaino v. Microsoft Corp., 120 F.3d 1006 (9th Cir. 1997), cert. denied 522 U.S. 1098 (1998) (ordering inclusion of reclassified employees in Employee Stock Purchase Plan).

Vizcaino v. Microsoft Corp., 2002 U.S. App LEXIS 9188 (9th Cir. 2002) (approving $97 million settlement).

Washington Adventist Hospital, Inc., 291 NLRB 95 (1988).

Williamson v. Moltech Corp., 690 N.Y.S.2d 628 (App. Div. 1999).

Statutes

Federal

Age Discrimination in Employment Act of 1967, 29 U.S.C. §621 *et seq.*

Civil Rights Act of 1964, Title VII (Equal Employment Opportunity), 42 U.S.C. §2000e *et seq.*

Computer Fraud and Abuse Act, 18 U.S.C. §1030.

Economic Espionage Act of 1996, 18 U.S.C. §1831 *et seq.*

Employee Retirement Income Security Act, 29 U.S.C. §§1001–1461.

Fair Labor Standards Act, 29 U.S.C. §§201–219.

Family and Medical Leave Act, 29 U.S.C. §2601 *et seq.*

Internal Revenue Code §414(n), 26 U.S.C. §414(n) (temporary and leased employees).

National Labor Relations (Wagner) Act, 29 U.S.C. §157 *et seq.*

Revenue Act of 1978, §530(d) (simplified method of establishing self-employment; exclusion for computer programmers). This statute has never been codified in the Internal Revenue Code but is reproduced in the notes following 26 U.S.C. §3401.

Worker Adjustment & Retraining Notification Act, 29 U.S.C. §§2102–2109.

Uniform

Uniform Trade Secrets Act, 14 *Uniform Laws Annotated* 438 (1990).

California

Business and Professional Code §16600 [covenants not to compete are unenforceable].

Civil Code §3426.1 [Calif. version of Uniform Trade Secrets Act].

Government Code §12941.1 [age discrimination may be shown by disparate impact].

REFERENCES

Acemoglu, Daron, and Jörn-Steffen Pischke. 1999. "The Structure of Wages and In-vestment in General Traning." *Journal of Political Economy* 107: 539–72.

"AeA Survey Finds 84% of High-Tech Workers Receive Stock Options." 2002. *Business Wire*, August 14.

Agesa, Jacqueline. 1998. "The Impact of Deregulation on Employment Discrimina-tion in the Trucking Industry." *Atlantic Economic Journal* 26: 288–303.

Aghion, Philippe, and Jean Tirole. 1994. "The Management of Innovation." *Quarterly Journal of Economics* 109: 1185–1209.

Aghion, Philippe, and Peter Howitt. 1998. *Endogenous Growth Theory.* Cambridge, MA: MIT Press.

Akerlof, George A., and Janet L. Yellen. 1986. *Efficiency Wage Models of the Labor Market.* New York: Cambridge University Press.

———. 1990. "The Fair Wage-Effort Hypothesis and Unemployment." *Quarterly Journal of Economics* 105: 255–83.

Alarcón, Rafael. 1999. "Recruitment Processes Among Foreign-born Engineers and Scientists in Silicon Valley." *American Behavioral Scientist* 42(9): 1381–97.

Allan, Peter, and Stephen Sienko. 1997. "A Comparison of Contingent and Core Workers' Perceptions of their Jobs' Characteristics and Motivational Properties." *SAM Advanced Management Journal* 62(3) (Summer): 4–9.

Almeida, Paul, and Bruce Kogut. 1999. "Localization of Knowledge and the Mobility of Engineers in Regional Networks." *Management Science* 45(7) (July): 905–17.

Alster, Norm. 1998. "Too Old for High Tech." *Upside*, December 8.

Anand, Bharat N., and Alexander Galetovic. 2000. "Weak Property Rights and Hold-up in R&D." *Journal of Economics & Management Strategy* 9(4): 615–42.

Anand, Vikas; Blake E. Ashforth; and Anne M. O'Leary-Kelly. 2002. "Being Contin-gent and International: The Experiences of H1-B Information Technology Work-ers in the U.S." Paper presented at the annual meeting of the Academy of Manage-ment, Denver, Colorado.

Anderson, Mark C.; Rajiv D. Banker; and Sury Ravindran. 2000. "Executive Com-pensation in the Information Technology Industry." *Management Science* 46(4) (April): 530–47.

Angel, David P. 1989. "The Labor Market for Engineers in the U.S. Semiconductor Industry." *Economic Geography* 65(2): 99–112.

———. 1991. "High-Technology Agglomeration and the Labor Market: The Case of Silicon Valley." *Environment and Planning* A23: 1501–16. Reprinted in Martin Kenney, ed. 2000. *Understanding Silicon Valley: The Anatomy of an Entrepre-neurial Region.* Stanford, CA: Stanford University Press, 124–40.

Angwin, Julia, and Laura Castaneda. 1998. "The Digital Divide: High-Tech Boom a Bust for Blacks, Latinos." *San Francisco Chronicle,* May 4, A1.

Anton, James J., and Dennis A. Yao. 1994. "Expropriation and Inventions: Appropriable Rents in the Absence of Property Rights." *American Economic Review* 84: 190–209.

———. 1995. "Start-ups, Spin-offs, and Internal Projects." *Journal of Law, Economics, and Organization* 11: 362–78.

Aronson, Robert L. 1991. *Self-Employment: A Labor Market Perspective.* Ithaca, NY: ILR Press.

Arora, Ashish; V.S. Arunachalam; Jai Asundi; and Ronald Fernandes. 2001. "The Indian Software Services Industry." *Research Policy* 30(8): 1267–87.

Arora, Ashish; Andrea Fosfuri; and Alfonso Gambardella. 2001. *Markets for Technology: The Economics of Innovation and Corporate Strategy.* Cambridge, MA: MIT Press.

Arora, Ashish, and Alfonso Gambardella. 1990. "Complementarity and External Linkages: The Strategies of the Large Firms in Biotechnology." *Journal of Industrial Economics* 38(4): 361–79.

Arrow, Kenneth. 1962a. "The Economic Implications of Learning by Doing." *Review of Economic Studies* 29: 5–73.

———. 1962b. "Economic Welfare and the Allocation of Resources for Invention." In *The Rate and Direction of Inventive Activity: Economic and Social Factors.* Princeton, NJ: Princeton University Press.

———. 1996a. "The Economics of Information: An Exposition." *Empirica* 23: 119–28.

———. 1996b. "Technical Information and Industrial Structure." *Industrial and Corporate Change* 5: 645–52. Reprinted in Glenn R. Carroll and David J. Teece, eds. 1999. *Firms, Markets, and Hierarchies: The Transaction Cost Economics Perspective.* New York: Oxford University Press, 156–63.

———. 1998. "What Has Economics to Say About Racial Discrimination?" *Journal of Economic Perspectives* 12: 91–100.

Arthur, Michael B., and Denise M. Rousseau. 1996. *The Boundaryless Career: A New Employment Principle for a New Organizational Era.* New York: Oxford University Press.

Arthur, W. Brian. 1994. *Increasing Returns and Path Dependence in the Economy.* Ann Arbor: University of Michigan Press.

Asian Americans for Community Involvement (AACI). 1993. *Qualified, But . . . A Report on Glass Ceiling Issues Facing Asian Americans in Silicon Valley.* San Jose, CA: Asian Americans for Community Involvement.

Audretsch, David B. 1996. "International Diffusion of Technological Knowledge." In *The Economics of High-Technology Competition and Cooperation in Global Markets,* ed. Georg Koopmann and Hans Eckart Scharrer, 107–26. Baden-Baden: Nomos Verlaggesellschaft.

———.1998. "Agglomeration and the Location of Inventive Activity." *Oxford Review of Economic Policy* 14: 18–29.

Audretsch, David B., and Maryann P. Feldman. 1996. "R&D Spillovers and the Geography of Innovation and Production." *American Economic Review* 86(3): 630–40.

Audretsch, David B., and Paula E. Stephan. 1996. "Company-Scientist Locational Links: The Case of Biotechnology." *American Economic Review* 86(3): 641–52.

Austin, Janet; Mary Mahoney; and Andrew Waskiewicz. 2000. "Self-Employment in Nonagricultural Industries in California." California Employment Development Department, Labor Market Information Division, *California Labor Market Trends* 00(1) (October). www.calmis.cahwnet.gov/specialreports/self-employmentreport.pdf.

Autor, David H. 2001a. "Why Do Temporary Help Firms Provide Free General Skills Training?" *Quarterly Journal of Economics* 116(4): 1409–48.

———. 2003. "Outsourcing at Will: The Contribution of Unjust Dismissal Doctrine to the Growth of Employment." *Journal of Labor Economics* 21(1): 1–42.

———. 2001b. "Wiring the Labor Market." *Journal of Economic Perspectives* 15: 25–40.

Autor, David H.; Lawrence F. Katz; and Alan B. Krueger. 1998. "Computing Inequality: Have Computers Changed the Labor Market?" *Quarterly Journal of Economics* 113: 1169–1213.

Ayres, Ian, and Robert Gertner. 1989. "Filling Gaps in Incomplete Contracts: An Economic Theory of Default Rules." *Yale Law Journal* 99: 87–130.

Baccara, Mariagiovanna, and Ronny Razin. 2002. "From Thought to Practice: Appropriation and Endogenous Market Structure with Imperfect Intellectual Property Rights." Mimeo, Princeton University.

Bacon, David. 1997. "Organizing Silicon Valley's High Tech Workers." www.igc.org/dbacon/Unions/04hitec0.htm.

Bahrami, Homa, and Stuart Evans. 1995. "Flexible Re-Cycling and High-Technology Entrepreneurship." *California Management Review* 37(3): 33–51. Reprinted in Martin Kenney, ed. 2000. *Silicon Valley: The Anatomy of an Entrepreneurial Region.* Stanford, CA: Stanford University Press, 165–89.

Bajaj, Vikas. 2000. "Alcatel Guards Its Trade Secrets." *Dallas Morning News,* September 3, 1H.

Baldoz, Rick; Charles Koeber; and Philip Kraft. 2001. *The Critical Study of Work: Labor, Technology, and Global Production.* Philadelphia: Temple University Press.

Balkin, David B., and Luis R. Gomez-Mejia. 1986. "Compensation Practices in High-Technology Industries." *Personnel Administrator* 30(6): 111–23.

Ballon, Ian C. 1998. "Keeping Secrets: Courts Are Becoming More Amenable to Suits Aimed at Stopping Job-Hopping Techies from Revealing Trade Secrets." *IP Magazine* (March).

Bankman, Joseph. 1988. "Tax Policy and Retirement Income: Are Pension Plan Anti-Discrimination Provisions Desirable?" *University of Chicago Law Review* 55: 790–835.

———. 1994a. "The Effect of Anti-Discrimination Provisions on Rank-and-File Compensation." *Washington University Law Quarterly* 72: 597–618.

———. 1994b. "The Structure of Silicon Valley Start-Ups." *UCLA Law Review* 41: 1737–68.

Bankman, Joseph, and, Ronald J. Gilson. 1999. "Why Start-ups?" *Stanford Law Review* 51: 289–308.

Baptista, Rui. 1998. "Clusters, Innovation, and Growth: A Survey of the Literature." In *The Dynamics of Industrial Clustering: International Comparisons in Computing and Biotechnology,* ed. G.M. Peter Swann, Martha Prevezer, and David Stout. Oxford: Oxford University Press.

Barenberg, Mark. 1993. "The Political Economy of the Wagner Act: Power, Symbol, and Workplace Cooperation." *Harvard Law Review* 106: 1379–1496.

Barker, Kathleen, and Kathleen Christensen. 1998. *Contingent Work: American Employment Relations in Transition.* Ithaca, NY: ILR Press.

Barnow, Burt S.; John Trutko; and Robert Lerman. 1998. "Skill Mismatches and Worker Shortages: The Problem and Appropriate Responses. Final Report Submitted to Office of the Assistant Secretary for Policy, U.S. Department of Labor." Washington, DC: Urban Institute.

Baron, James N. 2000. "Comment." In *The New Relationship: Human Capital in the American Corporation,* ed. Margaret M. Blair and Thomas A. Kochan, 90–101. Washington, DC: Brookings Institution.

Baron, James N.; M. Diane Burton; and Michael T. Hannan. 1996. "The Road Taken: The Origins and Evolution of Employment Systems in Emerging High-Technology Companies." *Industrial and Corporate Change* 5: 239–76. Reprinted in Glenn R. Carroll and David J. Teece, eds. 1999. *Firms, Markets, and Hierarchies: The Transaction Cost Economics Perspective.* New York: Oxford University Press, 428–64.

———. 1999. "Engineering Bureaucracy: The Genesis of Formal Policies, Positions, and Structures in High Technology Firms." *Journal of Law, Economics and Organization* 15: 1–41.

Baron, James N.; Michael T. Hannan; and M. Diane Burton. 1999. "Building the Iron Cage: Determinants of Managerial Intensity in the Early Years of Organizations." *American Sociological Review* 64: 527–47.

———. 2001. "Labor Pains: Organizational Change and Employee Turnover in Young, High-Tech Firms." *American Journal of Sociology* 106(4): 960–1012.

Baron, James N.; Michael T. Hannan; Greta Hsu; and Ozgecan Kocak. 2002. "Gender and the Organization-Building Process in Young, High-Tech Firms." In *The New Economic Sociology: Developments in an Emerging Field,* ed. Mauro F. Guillén, Randall Collins, Paula England, and Marshall Meyer, 245–73. New York: Russell Sage Foundation.

Barr, Avron, and Shirley Tessler. 1997. "Notes on Human Resource Issues in the Software Industry and Their Implications for Business and Government." Paper presented to the NSTC Presidential Advisory Committee on High-Performance Computing and Communications, Information Technology, and the Next Generation Internet, Washington, DC, October 30. www.stanford.edu/group/scip/avsgt/NSTC.pdf.

Baru, Sundari. 2001. *Working on the Margins: California's Growing Temporary Workforce.* San Diego: Center for Policy Initiatives. www.onlinecpi.org.

Bassett, William F.; Michael J. Fleming; and Anthony P. Rodrigues. 1998. "How Workers Use 401(k) Plans: The Participation, Contribution, and Withdrawal Decisions." *National Tax Journal* 51(2): 263–89.

Bates, Timothy. 1997. "Utilization of Minority Employees in Small Business: A Comparison of Nonminority and Black-owned Urban Enterprises." In *African Americans and Post-Industrial Labor Markets,* ed. James B. Stewart, 391–99. New Brunswick, NJ: Transaction.

Beard, Kathy M., and Jeffrey R. Edwards. 1995. "Employees at Risk: Contingent Work and the Psychological Experience of Contingent Workers." *Trends in Organizational Behavior* 2: 109–26.

Becker, Gary S. 1971. *The Economics of Discrimination.* 2d ed. Chicago: University of Chicago Press.

———. 1993. *Human Capital.* 3d ed. Chicago: University of Chicago Press.

Bellah, Robert N.; Richard Madsen; William M. Sullivan; Ann Swidler; and Steven M. Tipton. 1985. *Habits of the Heart: Individualism and Commitment in American Life.* Berkeley: University of California Press.

Benkler, Yochai. 1999. "Free as the Air to Common Use: First Amendment Constraints on Enclosure of the Public Domain." *New York University Law Review* 74: 354–446.

————. 2002. "Intellectual Property and the Organization of Information Production." *International Review of Law and Economics* 22: 81–105.

Benner, Chris. 1999. "Silicon Valley Labor Markets: Overview of Structure, Dynamics and Outcomes for Workers." Task Force on Reconstructing America's Labor Market Institutions Working Paper 07. http//mitsloan.mit.edu/iwer.

————. 2000. "Navigating Flexibility: Labor Markets and Intermediaries in Silicon Valley." Ph.D. dissertation, University of California, Berkeley.

Benner, Chris; Bob Brownstein; and Amy B. Dean. 1999. *Walking the Lifelong Tightrope: Negotiating Work in the New Economy. A Status Report on Social and Economic Well-Being in the State of California.* San Jose: Working Partnerships USA and Economic Policy Institute. www.wpusa.org/pubs.html.

Benner, Chris, and Amy Dean. 2000. "Labor in the New Economy: Lessons from Labor Organizing in Silicon Valley." In *Nonstandard Work: The Nature and Challenges of Changing Employment Arrangements,* ed. Françoise Carré, Marianne A. Ferber, Lonnie Golden, and Stephen A. Herzenberg, 361–75. Champaign, IL: Industrial Relations Research Association.

Bennet, James. 1994. "Who Owns Ideas, and Papers, Is Issue in Company Lawsuits." *New York Times,* May 1.

Bernhardt, Annette; Martina Morris; Mark S. Handcock; and Marc A. Scott. 2001. *Divergent Paths: Economic Mobility in the New American Labor Market.* New York: Russell Sage Foundation.

Bertrand, Marianne. 1999. "From the Invisible Handshake to the Invisible Hand? How Foreign Competition Changes the Employment Relationship." National Bureau of Economic Research Working Paper 6900.

Bewley, Truman F. 1999. *Why Wages Don't Fall During a Recession.* Cambridge, MA: Harvard University Press.

Bishop, Libby, and David I. Levine. 1999. "Computer-Mediated Communication as Employee Voice: A Case Study." *Industrial and Labor Relations Review* 52(2): 213–33.

Bjorhus, Jennifer. 2002. "Tech Job Training Risks Getting Sacked." *San Jose Mercury,* April 15.

Blau, David M. 1987 "A Time-Series Analysis of Self-Employment in the United States." *Journal of Political Economy* 95(3): 445–67.

Bloch, Farrell. 1994. *Antidiscrimination Law and Minority Employment: Recruitment Practices and Regulatory Constraints.* Chicago: University of Chicago Press.

Blonigen, Bruce A., and Christopher T. Taylor. 2000. "R&D Intensity and Acquisitions in High-Technology Industries: Evidence from the U.S. Electronic and Electrical Equipment Industries." *Journal of Industrial Economics* 48(1): 47–70.

Blumrosen, Alfred W., and Ruth G. Blumrosen. 2002. *The Reality of Intentional Job Discrimination in Metropolitan America—1999.* www.eeo1.com/1999_NR/1999_n1.htm.

Bodie, Matthew T. 2003. "Aligning Incentives with Equity: Employee Stock Options and Rule 10B-5." *Iowa Law Review* 88: 539–600.

Boldrin, Michele, and David Levine. 2002. "Perfectly Competitive Innovation." Centre for Economic Policy Research Discussion Paper No. 3274. www.cepr.org.

Borsook, Paulina. 2000. *Cyberselfish: A Critical Romp Through the Terribly Libertarian Culture of High Tech.* New York: Public Affairs.

Boyle, James. 1996. *Shamans, Software, and Spleens: Law and the Construction of the Information Society.* Cambridge, MA: Harvard University Press.

Bradach, Jeffrey L. 1997. "Flexibility: The New Social Contract Between Individuals and Firms?" Harvard Business School Working Paper 97–088, May.

Bresnahan, Timothy F.; Erik Brynjolfsson; and Lorin M. Hitt. 1999. "Information Technology, Workplace Organization, and the Demand for Skilled Labor: Firm-Level Evidence." NBER Working Paper 7136, May. Also in *The New Relationship: Human Capital in the American Corporation,* ed. Margaret M. Blair and Thomas A. Kochan, 145–93. Washington, DC: Brookings Institution Press.

Brock, Fred. 2002. "Social Security and the Ballot Box." *New York Times,* October 6, BU8.

Bronson, Po. 1999. *The Nudist on the Late Shift.* New York: Random House.

Brown, John Seely, and Paul Duguid. 2000. "Mysteries of the Region: Knowledge Dynamics in Silicon Valley." In *The Silicon Valley Edge: A Habitat for Innovation and Entrepreneurship,* ed. Chong-Moon Lee et al., 16–39. Stanford, CA: Stanford University Press.

Bui-Eve, Hanna. 1997. "To Hire or Not to Hire: What Silicon Valley Companies Should Know About Hiring Competitors' Employees." *Hastings Law Journal* 48: 981–1016.

Burrows, Peter. 1997. "A Nest of Software Spies?" *Business Week,* May 19.

Cannon, Sandra A.; Bruce C. Fallick; Michael Lettau; and Raven Saks. 2000. "Has Compensation Become More Flexible?" Board of Governors of the Federal Reserve Board Finance and Economics Discussion Paper 2000/27, April.

Cappelli, Peter. 1999. *The New Deal at Work: Managing the Market-Driven Workforce.* Boston: Harvard Business School Press.

———. 2001. "Why Is It So Hard to Find Information Technology Workers?" *Organizational Dynamics* 30(2): 87–99.

Cappelli, Peter; Laurie Bassi; Harry Katz; David Knoke; Paul Osterman; and Michael Useem. 1997. *Change at Work.* New York: Oxford University Press.

Card, David, and John E. DiNardo. 2002. "Skill-Based Technological Change and Rising Wage Inequality: Some Problems and Puzzles." *Journal of Labor Economics* 20(4): 733–83.

Card, David, and Alan B. Krueger. 1995. *Myth and Measurement: The New Economics of the Minimum Wage.* Princeton, NJ: Princeton University Press.

Carlson, Richard R. 2001. "Why the Law Still Can't Tell an Employee When It Sees One and How It Ought to Stop Trying." *Berkeley Journal of Employment and Labor Law* 22: 295–368.

Carmichael, Lorne. 1983. "Firm-Specific Human Capital and Promotion Ladders." *Bell Journal of Economics* 14: 251–58.

Carnoy, Martin. 2000. *Sustaining the New Economy: Work, Family, and Community in the Information Age.* New York: Russell Sage Foundation, and Cambridge: Harvard University Press.

Carnoy, Martin, and Weimin Gong. 1996. "Women and Minority Gains in a Rapidly Changing Local Labor Market: The San Francisco Bay Area in the 1980s." *Economics of Education Review* 15(3): 273–87.

Carnoy, Martin; Manuel Castells; and Chris Benner. 1997. "Labour Markets and Employment Practices in the Age of Flexibility: A Case Study of Silicon Valley." *International Labour Review* 136: 27–48.

Carr, Chris A., and Larry Gorman. 2001. "The Revictimization of Companies by the Stock Market Who Report Trade Secret Theft Under the Economic Espionage Act." *Business Lawyer* 57: 25–53.

Cassiman, Bruno, and Reinhilde Veugelers. 2002. "Complementarity in the Innovation Strategy: Internal R&D, External Technology Acquisition and Cooperation." Centre for Economic Policy Research Discussion Paper No. 3284. www.cepr.org.

Castaneda, Laura. 2001. "The Impact of Contingent Workers on Knowledge Flow Within the Firm." Ph.D. dissertation, Stanford University School of Engineering.

Center to Protect Workers' Rights. 1998. *The Construction Chart Book.* 2d ed. Washington, DC: Author.

Chan, William. 1996. "External Recruitment versus Internal Promotion." *Journal of Labor Economics* 14: 555–70.

Chandler, Alfred Dupont, Jr. 1990. *Scale and Scope: the Dynamics of Industrial Capitalism.* Cambridge, MA: Belknap Press of Harvard University Press.

———. 2001. *Inventing the Electronic Century: The Epic Story of the Consumer Electronics and Computer Industries.* New York: Free Press.

Chang, Chun, and Yijiang Wang. 1996. "Human Capital Investment Under Asymmetric Information: The Pigovian Conjecture Revisited." *Journal of Labor Economics* 14: 505–19.

Charness, Gary, and David I. Levine. 2000. "When Are Layoffs Acceptable?: Evidence from a Quasi-Experiment." *Industrial and Labor Relations Review* 53: 381–400.

Charny, David. 1996. "The Employee Welfare State in Transition." *Texas Law Review* 74: 1601–43.

Charny, David, and G. Mitu Gulati. 1998. "Efficiency Wages, Tournaments, and Discrimination: A Theory of Employment Discrimination Law for 'High-Level' Jobs." *Harvard Civil Rights-Civil Liberties Law Review* 33: 57–105.

Cherensky, Steven. 1993. "A Penny for Their Thoughts: Employee-Inventors, Preinvention Assignment Agreements, Property, and Personhood." *California Law Review* 81: 597–669.

Cheung, Steven N.S. 1982. "Property Rights in Trade Secrets." *Economic Inquiry* 20: 40–53.

Chhabra, Aseem. 2001. "Rekhi's Visa Stand Raises a Ruckus." www.rediff.com/news/2001/may/10usspec.htm.

Choi, James J.; David Laibson; and Andrew Metrick. 2002. "How Does the Internet Affect Trading? Evidence from Investor Behavior in 401(k) Plans." *Journal of Financial Economics* 64: 397–421.

Chun, Jennifer JiHye. 2001. "Flexible Despotism: The Intensification of Insecurity and Uncertainty in the Lives of Silicon Valley's High-Tech Assembly Workers." In *The Critical Study of Work: Labor, Technology, and Global Production,* ed. Rick Baldoz, Charles Koeber, and Philip Kraft, 127–54. Philadelphia: Temple University Press.

Clark, Don. 1993. "Intel Lawyer Commands Chip War—Rivals Say Dunlap Is a Darth Vader Guarding a Microchip Empire." *San Francisco Chronicle,* June, E1.

Clark, Elizabeth. 2000. "Gigabit Ethernet Over Copper: A Progress Report." *Network,* February 1. www.network magazine.com/article/NMG20000426S0013/3.

Coase, R.H. 1937. "The Nature of the Firm." *Economica* 4: 386–403.

Cobble, Dorothy Sue. 1991. *Dishing It Out: Waitresses and Their Unions in the Twentieth Century.* Urbana: University of Illinois Press.

Cohany, Sharon R. et al. 1998. "Counting the Workers: Results of a First Survey." In *Contingent Work: American Employment Relations in Transition,* ed. Kathleen Barker and Kathleen Christensen, 41–68. Ithaca, NY: ILR Press.

Cohen, Stephen S., and Gary Fields. 1999. "Social Capital and Capital Gains: An Examination of Social Capital in Silicon Valley." *California Management Review* 41(2): 108–30. Reprinted in Martin Kenney, ed. 2000. *Understanding Silicon Valley: The Anatomy of an Entrepreneurial Region.* Stanford, CA: Stanford University Press, 190–217.

Cohen, Wesley M., and Daniel A. Levinthal. 1989. "Innovation and Learning: The Two Faces of R&D." *Economics Journal* 99: 569–96.

Colclough, Glenna, and Charles M. Tolbert II. 1992. *Work in the Fast Lane: Flexibility, Divisions of Labor, and Inequality in High-Tech Industries.* Albany: State University of New York Press.

Collins, H.M. 1974. "The TEA Set: Tacit Knowledge in Scientific Networks." *Science Studies* 4: 165–86.

Computing Research Association. 1999. "The Supply of Information Technology Workers in the United States." www.cra.org/reports/wits/cra.wits.html.

Cooper, David Pepper. 1999. "Essays on Innovation and Intra-industry Information Flows." Ph.D. dissertation, University of California, Los Angeles.

———. 2000. "Innovation and Reciprocal Externalities: Information Transmission via Job Mobility." *Journal of Economic Behavior and Organization* 45: 403–25.

Corcoran, Elizabeth. 2002. "Digital Diaspora." *Forbes,* February 18.

Cortright, Joseph, and Heike Mayer. 2001. "High Tech Specialization: A Comparison of High Technology Centers." Center on Urban and Metropolitan Policy, Brookings Institution, Washington, DC. www.brookingsinstitution.org/urban/cortright/specialization.pdf.

Cowan, Robin; Paul A. David; and Dominique Foray. 2000. "The Explicit Economics of Knowledge Codification and Tacitness." *Industrial and Corporate Change* 9: 211–53.

Cowley, Stacey. 2001. "Survey: Age Bias Seen by Over-45 Techies." *Network WorldFusion News,* April 23. www.nwfusion.com/news/2001/0423agebias.html.

Darrah, C.N. 1999. "Temping at the Lower End: An Incomplete View from Silicon Valley." Task Force on Reconstructing America's Labor Market Institutions Working Paper 10. http://mitsloan.mit.edu/iwer.

Dataquest. 1990. *A Decade of Semiconductor Startups.* San Jose, CA: Dataquest.

David, Paul A. 1985. "Clio and the Economics of QWERTY." *American Economic Review Papers and Proceedings* 75: 332.

———. 1993. "Intellectual Property Institutions and the Panda's Thumb: Patents, Copyrights, and Trade Secrets in Economic Theory and History." In *Global Dimensions of Intellectual Property Rights in Science and Technology,* ed. Mitchel B. Wallerstein, Mary Ellen Mogee, and Roberta A. Schoen, 19–61. Washington, DC: National Academy Press.

Deakin, Simon. 1998. "The Evolution of the Contract of Employment 1900–1950: The Influence of the Welfare State." In *Governance, Industry, and Labour Markets in Britain and France: The Modernising State in the Mid-twentieth Century,* ed. Noel Whiteside and Robert Salais. London: Routledge.

———. 2001. "The Contract of Employment: A Study in Legal Evolution." *Historical Studies in Industrial Relations* 11: 1–36. www.cbr.cam.ac.uk/pdf/WP203.pdf.

Delevett, Peter. 2002. "HP Age-bias Lawsuit Is All Relative." *San Jose Mercury-News,* February 8.

Demski, Joel S.; Tracy R. Lewis; Dennis Yao; and Hüseyin Yildirim. 1999. "Practices for Managing Information Flows Within Organizations." *Journal of Law, Economics and Organization* 15: 107–31.

Diamond, Wayne J., and Richard B. Freeman. 2001. "Will Unionism Prosper in Cyber-Space?: The Promise of the Internet for Employee Organization." NBER Working Paper 8483, October.

Donahue, John J., and Peter Siegelman. 1991. "The Changing Nature of Employment Discrimination Litigation." *Stanford Law Review* 43: 983–1033.

Dossani, Rafiq. 2002. "Chinese and Indian Engineers and Their Networks in Silicon Valley." Asia/Pacific Research Center, Stanford University. http: //aparc.stanford. edu/docs/Dossani_Survey.pdf.

Douglass, Marcia Lynn. 1991. "The Myth of Meritocracy: Race, Gender, and Class in Silicon Valley." Ph.D. dissertation, University of California, San Diego.

Drennan, Matthew P. 2002. *The Information Economy and American Cities*. Baltimore, MD: Johns Hopkins University Press.

Dube, Arindrajit, and Ethan Kaplan. 2003. "Outsourcing, Wages, and Benefits: Empirical Evidence from the Service Sector." Paper presented at the American Economics Association Annual Meeting, Washington, DC, January 5.

Dubie, Denise. 2002. "Résumés Pile Up, Yet Key Jobs Open." *Network World,* August 5. www.nwfusion.com/news/2002/0805hiring.html.

DuRivage, Virginia L. 2000. "CWA's Organizing Strategies: Transforming Contract Jobs into Union Jobs." In *Nonstandard Work: The Nature and Challenges of Changing Employment Arrangements,* ed. Françoise Carré et al., 377–91. Champaign, IL: Industrial Relations Research Association.

Edelman, Lauren B.; Steven E. Abraham; and Howard S. Erlanger. 1992. "Professional Construction of Law: The Inflated Threat of Wrongful Discharge." *Law and Society Review* 26: 47–83.

Eisenscher, Michael. 1993. "Silicon Fist in a Velvet Glove." Unpublished manuscript.

Ellin, Abby. 2000. "A Start-Up's Hiring Attracts Unwanted Attention." *New York Times,* October 1, C5.

Ellis, Richard, and B. Lindsay Lowell. 1999. "The Information Technology Workforce Data Project." United Engineering and Alfred P. Sloan Foundations. www.uefoundation.org/itworkfp.html.

Ellwood, David T. 2000. "Winners and Losers in America: Taking the Measure of the New Economic Realities." In *A Working Nation: Workers, Work, and Government on the New Economy,* ed. David T. Ellwood, Rebecca M. Blank, Joseph Blasi, Douglas Kruse, William A. Niskanen, and Karen Lynn-Dyson. New York: Russell Sage Foundation.

Ellwood, David T.; Rebecca M. Blank; Joseph Blasi; Douglas Kruse; William A. Niskanen; and Karen Lynn-Dyson. 2000. *A Working Nation: Workers, Work, and Government in the New Economy*. New York: Russell Sage Foundation.

Ernst, Dieter. 1997. "From Partial to Systemic Globalization: International Production Networks in the Electronics Industry." Working Paper 98, Berkeley Roundtable on the International Economy, University of California. http: //brie.berkeley.edu/ pubs/pubs/wp/wp98.html.

———. 2000. "Carriers of Cross-Border Knowledge Diffusion: Information Technology and Global Production Networks." Schumpeter Society Conference, ESRC Centre for Research on Innovation and Competition, University of Manchester, June 28–July 1. http: //les1.man.ac.uk/cric/schumpeter/papers/18.pdf.

Ernst, Dieter, and David O'Connor. 1992. *Competing in the Electronics Industry: The Experience of Newly Industrialising Economies.* Paris: OECD.

Esping-Andersen, Gøsta, and Marino Regini, eds. 2000. *Why Deregulate Labour Markets?* Oxford: Oxford University Press.

Even, William E., and David A. MacPherson. 2000. "The Changing Distribution of Pension Coverage." *Industrial Relations* 39(2): 199–227.

Ewalt, David M. 2001. "IT Workers Look at the Union Label—Dissatisfied Dot-com Workers Look to Labor Organizers to Blunt Effects of Economic Slowdown." *Information Week,* March 19.

Fairlie, Robert W. 1999. "The Absence of the African-American Owned Business: An Analysis of the Dynamics of Self-Employment." *Journal of Labor Economics* 17: 80–108.

Fairlie, Robert W., and Bruce D. Meyer. 1996. "Ethnic and Racial Self-employment Differences and Possible Explanations." *Journal of Human Resources* 31: 757–93.

Farber, Henry S. 1997. "The Changing Face of Job Loss in the United States: 1981–1995." *Brookings Papers on Economic Activity: Microeconomics* 1997: 55–128.

———. 1998. "Has the Rate of Job Loss Increased in the Nineties?" Princeton University Industrial Relations Section Working Paper No. 394, January.

———. 1999. "Alternative and Part-Time Employment Arrangements as a Response to Job Loss." *Journal of Labor Economics* 17: S142–69. Reprinted in David Neumark, ed. 2000. *On the Job: Is Long-Term Employment a Thing of the Past?* New York: Russell Sage Foundation, 398–426.

———. 2000. "Trends in Long Term Employment in the United States, 1979–96." *Proceedings of New York University Annual Conference on Labor* 52: 63–98.

Farmer, Melanie Austria. 2000. "Ex-Oracle VP Wins Wrongful Termination Suit." News.cnet.com/news/0-1003-202-2554287.html (August 18).

Fehr, Ernst et al. 1998. "When Social Norms Overpower Competition: Gift Exchange in Experimental Labor Markets." *Journal of Labor Economics* 16(2): 324–51.

Fehr, Ernst, and Klaus M. Schmidt. 1999. "A Theory of Fairness, Competition, and Cooperation." *Quarterly Journal of Economics* 114(3): 817–68.

Feinberg, Ian N. 1998. "Inevitable Disclosure of Trade Secrets: A New Problem for Companies Hiring Experienced Technical Employees." www.gcwf.com [no longer available].

Feinstein, Jonathan S., and Jeremy Stein. 1988. "Employee Opportunism and Redundancy in Firms." *Journal of Economic Behavior and Organization* 10: 401–14.

Ferguson, Charles H. 1999. *High Stakes, No Prisoners: A Winner's Tale of Greed and Glory in the Internet Wars.* New York: Times Books.

Finegold, David; Alec Levenson; Ann Majchrzak; and Mark Van Buren. In press. "The Temporary Staffing Industry and the Career Prospects of Lower-Skilled Workers." Russell Sage/Rockefeller Foundations.

Finn, Christine. 2001. *Artifacts: An Archaeologist's Year in Silicon Valley.* Cambridge, MA: MIT Press.

Fisher, Lawrence M. 1992. "The Winery, Not the Winemaker, Owns the Secrets, a Court Rules." *New York Times,* July 2, A1.

Florida, Richard, and Martin Kenney. 1990. *The Breakthrough Illusion: Corporate America's Failure to Move from Innovation to Mass Production.* New York: Basic Books.

Fosfuri, Andrea; Massimo Motta; and Thomas Rønde. 2001. "Foreign Direct Investment and Spillovers through Workers' Mobility." *Journal of International Economics* 53: 205–22.

Franco, April Mitchell, and Darren Filson. 2000. "Knowledge Diffusion Through Employee Mobility." Federal Reserve Bank of Minneapolis, Research Department Staff Report 272, July.

Freeman, Richard B., ed. 1994. *Working Under Different Rules.* New York: Russell Sage Foundation.

Freeman, Richard B., and James L. Medoff. 1984. *What Do Unions Do?* New York: Basic Books.

Freeman, Richard B., and Joel Rogers. 1999. *What Workers Want.* Ithaca, NY: ILR Press.

Friaz, Guadalupe M. 1996. "Labor Stratification and Downsizing in Computer Manufacturing: Effects on White Women and Women of Color." Working Paper No. 23, Julian Samora Research Institute, Michigan State University.

Friedman, David D.; William M. Landes; and Richard A. Posner. 1991. "Some Economics of Trade Secret Law." *Journal of Economic Perspectives* 5: 61–72.

Friedman, Lawrence M.; Robert W. Gordon; Sophie Pirie; and Edwin Whatley. 1989. "Law, Lawyers, and Legal Practice in Silicon Valley: A Preliminary Report." *Indiana Law Journal* 64: 555–67.

Friedman, Raymond A. 1996. "Defining the Scope and Logic of Minority and Female Network Groups: Can Separation Enhance Integration?" *Research in Personnel and Human Resources Management* 14: 307–349.

Friedman, Raymond A., and Donna Carter. 1993. *African American Network Groups: Their Impact and Effectiveness.* Washington, DC: Executive Leadership Council.

Friel, Thomas J. 2000. "Shepherding the Faithful: The Influence of Executive Search Firms." In *The Silicon Valley Edge: A Habitat for Innovation and Entrepreneurship,* ed. Chong-Moon Lee et al., 342–54. Stanford, CA: Stanford University Press.

Fuller, Brian. 1993. "Cleared, ULSI's Hwang Picks Up Pieces." *Electronic Engineering Times,* September 20.

Gersbach, Hans, and Armin Schmutzler. 1999. "Endogenous Spillovers and Incentives to Innovate." Unpublished manuscript.

Gibbs, Michael J. 1991. "Apple Computer (B): Managing Morale and Corporate Culture." Harvard Business School Case 9-491-041.

Gilson, Ronald J. 1999. "The Legal Infrastructure of High Technology Industrial Districts: Silicon Valley, Route 128, and Covenants Not To Compete." *New York University Law Review* 74: 575–629.

Goldstein, Bruce; Marc Linder; Laurence E. Norton II; and Catherine Ruckelshaus. 1999. "Enforcing Fair Labor Standards in the Modern American Sweatshop: Rediscovering the Statutory Definition of Employment." *UCLA Law Review* 46: 983–1163.

Gonos, George. 1997. "The Contest over 'Employer' Status in the Postwar United States: The Case of Temporary Help Firms." *Law and Society Review* 31: 81–110.

Goodin, Dan. 1996. "AMD, Hyundai Resolve Litigation Over Trade Secrets." *The Recorder,* November 19, 1.

Gordon, Wendy J. 1993. "A Property Right in Self-Expression: Equality and Individualism in the Natural Law of Intellectual Property." *Yale Law Journal* 102: 1533–1609.

Gottschalk, Peter. 1997. "Inequality, Income Growth, and Mobility: The Basic Facts." *Journal of Economic Perspectives* 11(2) (Spring): 21–40.

Gould, Susan B.; Kerry J. Weiner; and Barbara R. Levin 1997. *Free Agents: People and Organizations Creating a New Working Community.* San Francisco: Jossey-Bass.

Green, Susan S. 1983. "Silicon Valley's Women Workers: A Theoretical Analysis of Sex Segregation in the Electronics Industry Labor Market." In *Women, Men, and the International Division of Labor,* ed. June Nash and María Patricia Fernández-Kelly, 273–331. Albany: State University of New York Press.

Greenhouse, Steven. 2000. "Five Questions for Larry Cohen: Renewing a Union in the New Economy." *New York Times,* December 24, BU 4.

Gregory, Kathleen L. 1984. "Signing-up: The Culture and Careers of Silicon Valley Computer People." Ph.D. dissertation, Northwestern University.

Griliches, Zvi. 1979. "Issues in Assessing the Contribution of Research and Development to Productivity Growth." *Bell Journal of Economics* 10: 92–116.

———. 1992. "The Search for R&D Spillovers." *Scandinavian Journal of Economics* 94: S29–S47.

Grossman, Sanford, and Oliver D. Hart. 1986. "The Costs and Benefits of Ownership: A Theory of Vertical and Lateral Integration." *Quarterly Journal of Economics* 94: 691–719.

Grove, Andrew S. 1996. *Only the Paranoid Survive.* New York: Currency/Doubleday.

Hahm, Jung S. 2000. "American Competitiveness and Workforce Improvement Act of 1998: Balancing Economic and Labor Interests Under the New H-1B Visa Program." *Cornell Law Review:* 85: 1673–1701.

Hall, Brian J., and Jeffrey B. Liebman 2000. "The Taxation of Executive Compensation." National Bureau of Economic Research Working Paper 7596.

Hannan, Michael T.; M. Diane Burton; and James N. Baron. 1996. "Inertia and Change in the Early Years: Employment Relations in Young, High Technology Firms." *Industrial and Corporate Change* 6: 503–36. Reprinted in Glenn R.Carroll and David J. Treece, eds. 1999. *Firms, Markets, and Hierarchies: The Transaction Cost Economics Perspective.* New York: Oxford University Press, 465–98.

Hardie, Christa. 1996. "AMD, Hyundai Settle Flash Squabble." *Electronic News* 42, November 25, 16.

Hart, Oliver. 1995. *Firms, Contracts, and Financial Structure.* Oxford: Clarendon Press.

Hart, Oliver, and John Moore. 1990. "Property Rights and the Nature of the Firm." *Journal of Political Economy* 98: 1119–58.

Harvard Law Review. 1999. "Development: The Law of Cyberspace." *Harvard Law Review* 112: 1610–1704.

Hayes, Dennis. 1989. *Behind the Silicon Curtain: The Seductions of Work in a Lonely Era.* Boston: South End Press.

Heckscher, Charles C. 1988. *The New Unionism: Employee Involvement in the Changing Corporation.* New York: Basic Books.

———. 1995. *White Collar Blues: Management Loyalties in an Age of Corporate Restructuring.* New York: Basic Books.

———. 2000. "HR Strategy and Nonstandard Work: Dualism Versus True Mobility." In *Nonstandard Work: The Nature and Challenges of Changing Employment,* ed. Françoise Carré et al., 267–90. Champaign, IL: Industrial Relations Research Association.

Hellmann, Thomas. 2002. "When Do Employees Become Entrepreneurs?" http: // faculty-gsb.stanford.edu/hellmann/index.htm.

Hellwig, Martin, and Andreas Irmen. 2001. "Endogenous Technical Change in a Competitive Economy." *Journal of Economic Theory* 101: 1–39.

Henton, Doug. 2000. "A Profile of the Valley's Evolving Structure." In *The Silicon Valley Edge: A Habitat for Innovation and Entrepreneurship,* ed. Chong-Moon Lee et al., 46–58. Stanford, CA: Stanford University Press.

Herzenberg, Stephen A.; John A. Alic; and Howard Wial. 1998. *New Rules for a New Economy: Employment and Opportunity in Postindustrial America.* Ithaca: ILR Press.

Hewitt Associates. 2000. "Hewitt Study Shows Majority of 401k Plan Participants in U.S. Opt for Cash When Changing Jobs." Hewitt Associates Press Release, May 30. http: //was.hewitt.com/hewitt/resource/newsroom/pressrel/2000/05–30–00.htm [no longer available].

Hiltzik, Michael. 1999. *Dealers of Lightning: Xerox PARC and the Dawn of the Computer Age.* New York: Harper Business.

Hirshleifer, Jack. 1971. "The Private and Social Value of Information and the Reward to Inventive Activity." *American Economic Review* 61: 561–74.

Hirshleifer, Jack, and John G. Riley. 1992. *The Analytics of Uncertainty and Information.* Cambridge, UK: Cambridge University Press.

Hoefler, Don C. 1971. "Silicon Valley, U.S.A." *Electronic News,* January 11.

Holmström, Bengt, and Paul Milgrom. 1991. "Multitask Principal-Agent Analysis: Incentive Contracts, Asset Ownership, and Job Design." *Journal of Law, Economics, and Organization* 7 (special issue): 24–52.

Horowitz, Sara. 2000. "New Thinking on Worker Groups' Role in a Flexible Economy." In *Nonstandard Work: The Nature and Changes of Changing Employment,* ed. Françoise Carré et al., 393–98. Champaign, IL: Industrial Relations Research Association.

Hossfeld, Karen J. 1990. " 'Their Logic Against Them': Contradictions in Sex, Race, and Class in Silicon Valley." In *Women Workers and Global Restructuring,* ed. Kathryn Ward, 149–78. Ithaca, NY: ILR Press.

Houseman, Susan N. 1997. "Temporary, Part-Time, and Contract Employment in the United States: A Report on the W.E. Upjohn Institute's Employer Survey on Flexible Staffing Policies." Final Report submitted to the U.S. Department of Labor. www.upjohninst.org/ptimerpt.pdf.

———. 1999. "Flexible Staffing Arrangements: A Report on Temporary Help, On-Call, Direct-Hire Temporary, Leased, Contract Company, and Independent Contractor Employment in the United States." www_.dol.gov/asp/programs/history/human/reports/staffing/staffing_/futurework/conference.htm.

Houseman, Susan N., and Anne E. Polivka. 2000. "The Implications of Flexible Staffing Arrangements for Job Stability." In *On the Job: Is Long Term Employment a Thing of the Past?* ed. David Neumark, 427–62. New York: Russell Sage Foundation.

Howeth, Linwood. 1963. *History of Communications-electronics in the United States Navy.* Washington, DC: U.S. Government Printing Office.

Howse, Robert, and Michael J. Trebilcock. 1993. "Protecting the Employment Bargain." *University of Toronto Law Journal* 43: 751–92.

Hunter, Larry W.; Annette Bernhardt; Katherine L. Hughes; and Eva Skuratowicz. 2001. "It's Not Just the ATMs: Technology, Firm Strategies, Jobs, and Earnings in Retail Banking." *Industrial and Labor Relations Review* 54(2): 402–24.

Hyde, Alan. 1991. "In Defense of Employee Ownership." *Chicago-Kent Law Review* 67: 159–211.

————. 1993a. "After Smyrna: Rights and Powers of Unions That Represent Less Than a Majority." *Rutgers Law Review* 45: 637–69.

————. 1993b. "Employee Caucus: A Key Institution in the Emerging System of Employment Law." *Chicago-Kent Law Review* 69: 149ff. Reprinted in Matthew Finkin, ed. 1994. *The Legal Future of Employee Representation.* Ithaca, NY: ILR Press.

————. 1998. "The Wealth of Shared Information: Silicon Valley's High-Velocity Labor Market, Endogenous Economic Growth, and the Law of Trade Secrets." http: //andromeda.rutgers.edu/~hyde/WEALTH.htm.

————. 2000. "Classification of U.S. Working People and Its Impact on Workers' Protection: A Report Submitted to the International Labour Office."

Irwin, Douglas A., and Peter J. Klenow. 1994. "Learning-by-Doing Spillovers in the Semiconductor Industry." *Journal of Political Economy* 102: 1200–27.

Issacharoff, Samuel, and Erica Worth Harris. 1997. "Is Age Discrimination Really Age Discrimination?: The ADEA's Unnatural Solution." *New York University Law Review* 72: 780–84.

Ittner, Christopher D.; Richard A. Lambert; and David F. Larcker. 2002. "The Structure and Performance Consequences of Equity Grants to Employees of New Economy Firms." http: //papers.ssrn.com/paper.taf?abstact_id=296275.

Jackson, Tim. 1997. *Inside Intel.* New York: Dutton.

Jayadev, Raj. 2001. "Look Who's Organizing—High-level Tech Workers Form New Labor Group." www.pacificnews.org/content/pns/2001/aug/0815techlabor.html.

————. 2002. "Silicon Valley's Underbelly: High-tech's Temp Troops: Overworked, Underpaid, Essential." *San Francisco Chronicle,* January 20.

Jefferson, Thomas. 1984 [1813]. "Letter to Isaac McPherson." In *Thomas Jefferson: Writings,* 1286–94. New York: Library of America.

Johnson, Calvin H. 1999. "Stock Compensation: The Most Expensive Way to Pay Future Cash." *Southern Methodist University Law Review* 52: 423–54.

Johnson, Carrie. 2001. "Settlement Shows How Hard Life Is for Minorities at Tech Firms, Critics Say." *Washington Post* (July 22).

Johnston, David Cay. 1998. "How a Tax Law Helps Insure a Scarcity of Programmers." *New York Times,* April 27, D1.

Joint Venture Silicon Valley Network. 1999. *Workforce Study: An Analysis of the Workforce Gap in Silicon Valley.* www.jointventure.org/initiatives/edt/work_gup/workforce99.pd8.

————. 2001. *Next Silicon Valley: Riding the Waves of Innovation.* www.jointventure.org/nsv/nsvpaper.pdf (December).

————. 2002. *Index of Silicon Valley.* www.jointventure.org/resources/2002Index/2002Index.pdf.

Juhn, Chinhui; Kevin M. Murphy; and Brooks Pierce. 1993. "Wage Inequality and the Rise in Returns to Skill." *Journal of Political Economy* 101(3): 410–42.

Juravich, Tom. 1985. *Chaos on the Shop Floor: A Worker's View of Quality, Productivity, and Management.* Philadelphia: Temple University Press.

Kahn, Virginia Munger. 2000. "The Electronic Rank and File." *New York Times,* March 8, G1.

Kalleberg, Arne L. et al. 1997. *Nonstandard Work, Substandard Jobs: Flexible Work Arrangements in the U.S.* Washington, DC: Economic Policy Institute and Women's Research & Education Institute.

Kanter, Rosabeth Moss. 1995. "Nice Work if You Can Get It: The Software Industry as a Model for Tomorrow's Jobs." *American Prospect* 23 (Fall): 52–59.

Kaplan, David A. 1999. *The Silicon Boys and Their Valley of Dreams.* New York: William Morrow.

Katz, Eliakim, and Abraham Ziderman. 1990. "Investment in General Training: The Role of Information and Labour Mobility." *Economics Journal* 100: 1147–58.

Katz, Jon. 2000. *Geeks: How Two Lost Boys Rode the Internet out of Idaho.* New York: Villard Books.

Katz, Lawrence F., and Alan B. Krueger. 1999. "The High-Pressure U.S. Labor Market of the 1990s." *Brookings Papers on Economic Activity* 1999(1): 1–65.

Katz, Naomi, and David S. Kemnitzer. 1983. "Fast Forward: The Internationalization of Silicon Valley." In *Women, Men, and the International Division of Labor,* ed. June Nash and María Patricia Fernández-Kelly, 332–45. Albany: State University of New York Press.

Kenney, Martin, ed. 2000. *Understanding Silicon Valley: The Anatomy of an Entrepreneurial Region.* Stanford, CA: Stanford University Press.

Kenney, Martin, and Urs von Burg. 1999. "Technology, Entrepreneurship and Path Dependence: Industrial Clustering in Silicon Valley and Route 128." *Industrial and Corporate Change* 8(1): 67–103.

Kiesler, Sara, and Lee Sproull. 1992. "Group Decision Making and Communication Technology." *Organizational Behavior and Human Decision Processes* 52: 96–123.

Klare, Karl. 1983. "The Bitter with the Sweet: Reflections on the Supreme Court's *Yeshiva* Decision." *Socialist Review* 13(71) (September–October): 99–129.

Kleingartner, Archie, and Carolyn S. Anderson, eds. 1987. *Human Resource Management in High Technology Firms.* Lexington, MA: Lexington Books.

Koch, James L.; Ross Miller; Kim Walesh; and Elizabeth Brown. 2001. *Building Community: Social Connections and Civic Involvement in Silicon Valley. Preliminary Findings Report.* Peninsula Community Foundation, Community Foundation Silicon Valley, and John F. Kennedy School of Government, Harvard University. www.cfsv.org/communitysurvey/docs/scsrfd.pdf.

Kotkin, Joel. 1999. "Unions See Fertile Fields at Lower End of High Tech." *New York Times,* September 26, BU 4.

Krieger, Linda Hamilton. 1995. "The Content of Our Categories: A Cognitive Bias Approach to Discrimination and Equal Employment Opportunity." *Stanford Law Review* 47: 1161–1248.

———. 1998. "Civil Rights Perestroika: Intergroup Relations After Affirmative Action." *California Law Review* 86: 1251–1333.

Kubes, Steven. 1999. "PHY IC Technology at the Crossroads." *Electronic Buyers' News,* March 8.

Kuhn, Peter, and Mikal Skuterud. 2002. "Internet and Traditional Job Search Methods and Unemployment Durations." Institute for the Study of Labor (IZA). Discussion Paper 613, October. http://ssrn.com/abstract_id-343887 or www.iza.org.

Kunda, Gideon; Stephen R. Barley; and James Evans. 2002. "Why Do Contractors Contract?: The Theory and Reality of High End Contingent Labor." *Industrial and Labor Relations Review* 55(2): 234–61.

Kusterer, Ken C. 1978. *Know-How on the Job: The Important Working Knowledge of "Unskilled" Workers.* Boulder, CO: Westview Press.

Kvamme, E. Floyd. 2000. "Life in Silicon Valley: A First-Hand View of the Region's Growth." In *The Silicon Valley Edge: A Habitat for Innovation and Entrepreneurship,* ed. Chong-Moon Lee et al., 59–80. Stanford, CA: Stanford University Press.

Laberis, Bill. 1999. "The $6 Billion Question: Has Your Vendor Gone Buyout Crazy?" *Computerworld* 33(36): 34.

Laibson, David. 1998. "Self-Control and Saving for Retirement." *Brookings Papers on Economic Activity* 1998: 91–196.

Lamoreaux, Naomi R., and Kenneth L. Sokoloff. 1999. "Investors, Firms, and the Market for Technology in the Late Nineteenth and Early Twentieth Centuries." In *Learning by Doing in Markets, Firms, and Countries,* ed. Naomi R. Lamoreaux, Daniel M.G. Raff, and Peter Temin, 19–57. Chicago: University of Chicago Press.

Langlois, Richard N. 1992. "External Economies and Economic Progress: The Case of the Microcomputer Industry." *Business History Review* 66: 1–50.

Langlois, Richard N., and Robertson, Paul L. 1996. "Stop Crying over Spilt Knowledge: A Critical Look at the Theory of Spillovers and Technical Change." MERIT Conference on Innovation, Evolution and Technology, Maastricht, the Netherlands, August 25–27.

La Pedus, Mark. 1999. "PHY-IC Delays Pester OEMs." *Electronic Buyers' News,* August 7.

Lashinsky, Adam. 2001. "The Incredible Shrinking Engineer." *Fortune,* December 10, 40–42.

Lazear, Edward. 1979. "Why Is There Mandatory Retirement?" *Journal of Political Economy* 87: 1261–84.

———. 1995. *Personnel Economics.* Cambridge, MA: MIT Press.

———. 1999. "Output-Based Pay: Incentives or Sorting?" National Bureau of Economic Research Working Paper 7419.

Lazear, Edward, and Sherwin Rosen. 1981. "Rank-Order Tournaments as Optimum Labor Contracts." *Journal of Political Economy* 89: 841–64.

Lebow, David; Louise Sheiner; Larry Slifman; and Martha Starr-McCluer. 1999. "Recent Trends in Compensation Practices." Board of Governors of the Federal Reserve System, Finance and Economics Discussion Series 99/32, July. http: //papers.ssrn.com/sol3/delivery.taf?7118&UserReference=26857C745BDE52563887BE8B.

Lécuyer, Christophe. 2000. "Fairchild Semiconductor and Its Influence." In *The Silicon Valley Edge: A Habitat for Innovation and Entrepreneurship,* ed. Chong-Moon Lee et al., 158–83. Stanford, CA: Stanford University Press.

———. 2001. "Making Silicon Valley: Engineering Culture, Innovation, and Industrial Growth 1930–1970." *Enterprise & Society* 2(2): 666–72.

Lee, Chong-Moon. 2000. "Four Styles of Valley Entrepreneurship." In *The Silicon Valley Edge: A Habitat for Innovation and Entrepreneurship,* ed. Chong-Moon Lee et al., 94–123. Stanford, CA: Stanford University Press.

Lee, Chong-Moon; William F. Miller; Marguerite Gong Hancock; and Henry S. Rowen, eds. 2000. *The Silicon Valley Edge: A Habitat for Innovation and Entrepreneurship.* Stanford, CA: Stanford University Press.

Lerner, Josh, and Robert P. Merges 1998. "The Control of Technology Alliances: An Empirical Analysis of the Biotechnology Industry." *Journal of Industrial Economics* 46: 125–56.

Leslie, Stuart W. 1993. "How the West Was Won: The Military and the Making of

Silicon Valley." In *Technological Competitiveness: Contemporary and Historical Perspectives on the Electrical, Electronics and Computer Industries,* ed. William Aspray. New York: Institute of Electrical and Electronics Engineers.

———. 2000. "The Biggest (Angel) of Them All: The Military and the Making of Silicon Valley." In *Understanding Silicon Valley: The Anatomy of an Entrepreneurial Region,* ed. Martin Kenney, 48–67. Stanford, CA: Stanford University Press.

Leslie, Stuart W., and Robert H. Kargon. 1996. "Selling Silicon Valley: Frederick Terman's Model for Regional Advantage." *Business History Review* 70: 435–72.

Lessard, Bill, and Steve Baldwin. 2000. *NetSlaves: True Tales of Working the Web.* New York: McGraw-Hill.

Lessig, Lawrence. 2001. *The Future of Ideas: The Fate of the Commons in a Connected World.* New York: Random House.

Lester, Gillian. 1998. "Careers and Contingency." *Stanford Law Review* 51: 73–145.

Lester, Gillian, and Eric L. Talley. 2000. "Trade Secrets and Mutual Investments." University of Southern California Law School Olin Research Paper No. 00–15.

Levine, David I. 1991. "Just-Cause Employment Policies in the Presence of Worker Adverse Selection." *Journal of Labor Economics* 9: 294–305.

Lewis, Michael. 2000. *The New New Thing: A Silicon Valley Story.* New York: Norton.

Lewis, Tracy R., and Dennis Yao. 2001. "Innovation, Knowledge Flow, and Worker Mobility." http: //rider.wharton.upenn.edu/~yao/research/lewyaowpjuly3101.pdf.

Lieber, Ron. 2000. "The Permatemps Contretemps." *Fast Company* no. 37 (August): 198–216.

Liebeskind, Julia Porter. 1997. "Keeping Organizational Secrets: Protective Institutional Mechanisms and their Costs." *Industrial and Corporate Change* 6: 623–63.

Linder, Marc. 1989. *The Employment Relationship in Anglo-American Law: A Historical Perspective.* New York: Greenwood Press.

———. 1992. *Farewell to the Self-Employed: Deconstructing a Socioeconomic and Legal Solipsism.* New York: Greenwood Press.

Littman, Jonathan. 2001. "Phone Union Attempts Dial-up Internet Connection." *RedHerring:* www.redherring.com/insider/2001/0619/420019642.html (June 19).

Lodge, David. 1984. *Small World: An Academic Romance.* New York: Macmillan.

Lubman, Sarah. 2002. "Race Bias Suits Are Few at Tech Firms." *San Jose Mercury News,* July 15. www.bayarea.com/mld/mercurynews/3664217.htm.

Lucas, Robert E. 1988. "On the Mechanics of Economic Development." *Journal of Monetary Economics* 22: 3–42.

———. 1993. "Making a Miracle." *Econometrica* 61: 251–72.

Lüthje, Boy. 1997. "Industrial Restructuring, Production Networks, and Labor Relations in the Silicon Valley Electronics Industry." www2.ucsc.edu/cgirs/publications/cpapers/leuthje.pdf.

———. 2001. "Electronics Contract Manufacturing: Transnational Production Networks, the Internet, and Knowledge Diffusion in Low-Cost Locations in Asia and Eastern Europe." East-West Center Working Paper, Economics Series No. 18. www.eastwestcenter.org.

Machlup, Fritz. 1952. *The Economics of Sellers' Competition: Model Analysis of Sellers' Conduct.* Baltimore, MD: Johns Hopkins University Press.

Madrian, Brigitte C., and Dennis F. Shea. 2001. "The Power of Suggestion: Inertia in 401(k) Participation and Savings Behavior." *Quarterly Journal of Economics* 116(4): 1149–87.

Malin, Martin H., and Henry H. Perritt, Jr. 2000. "The National Labor Relations Act in Cyberspace: Union Organizing in Electronic Workplaces." *University of Kansas Law Review* 49: 1–64.

Malsberger, Brian M., ed. 1996. *Covenants Not to Compete: A State-by-State Survey.* 2d ed. Washington, DC: BNA Books.

Manser, Marilyn E., and Garnett Picot. 1996. "The Role of Self-employment in U.S. and Canadian Job Growth." *Monthly Labor Review* 122(4) (April): 10–25.

Mar, Don, and Paul M. Ong. 1997. "Race and Rehiring in the High-Tech Industry." In *African-Americans and Post-Industrial Labor Markets,* ed. James B. Stewart, 337–48. New Brunswick, NJ: Transaction.

Markoff, John. 2001. "Ignore the Label: It's Flextronics Inside. Outsourcing's New Cachet in Silicon Valley." *New York Times,* February 15, C1.

Markoff, John, and Matt Richtel. 2002. "Down, but Not Out, in the Valley." *New York Times,* January 14, C1.

Marshall, Alfred. 1961 [1920]. *Principles of Economics.* 9th (Variorum) ed. London: Macmillan.

Martínez Saldaña, Jesús. 1993. "At the Periphery of Democracy: The Binational Politics of Mexican Immigrants in Silicon Valley." Ph.D. dissertation, University of California, Berkeley (Ethnic Studies).

Matloff, Norman. n.d. "Debunking the Myth of a Desperate Software Labor Shortage." http: //heather.cs.ucdavis.edu/itaa.real.html.

———. 1998. "Now Hiring! If You're Young." *New York Times,* January 26, A19.

———. 2001. "Why ISN Feels an 'Entitlement.'" E-mail communication (May 7).

McKendrick, David G.; Richard F. Doner; and Stephen Haggard. 2000. *From Silicon Valley to Singapore: Location and Competitive Advantage in the Hard Disk Drive Industry.* Stanford, CA: Stanford University Press.

Melton, Michael W. 1983. "The Alchemy of Inventive Stock Options: Turning Employee Income Into Gold." *Cornell Law Review* 68: 488–520.

Mendelson, Haim, and Ravindran R. Pillai. 1999. "Information Age Organizations, Dynamics and Performance." *Journal of Economic Behavior and Organization* 38: 253–81.

Merges, Robert P. 1999. "The Law and Economics of Employee Inventions." *Harvard Journal of Law and Technology* 13: 1–63.

Miles, Thomas J. 2000. "Common Law Exceptions to Employment-at-Will and U.S. Labor Markets." *Journal of Law, Economics, and Organization* 16: 74–101.

Milgrom, Paul, and John Roberts. 1990. "The Economics of Modern Manufacturing." *American Economic Review* 80: 511–28.

Millard, Elizabeth. 2000. "Luring Techies." *The Industry Standard* (January 31). thestandard.com/article/0,1902,9007-0, 00.html.

Milner, Joseph M., and Edieal J. Pinker. 1997. "Optimal Staffing Strategies: Use of Temporary Workers, Contact Workers, and Internal Pools of Contingent Labor." W.E. Simon School of Business Working Paper CIS 97–7, University of Rochester.

———. 2001. "Contingent Labor Contracting Under Demand and Supply Uncertainty." *Management Science* 47(8): 1046–62.

Mintz, Howard. 2001. "Jail Terms Handed Down in Avant! Software Theft." *San Jose Mercury News,* July 26.

Møen, Jarle. 2000. "Is Mobility of Technical Personnel a Source of R&D Spillovers?" NBER Working Paper 7834, August.

Molineaux, Charles, and Stephen Frazier. 2001. "Diversity in Silicon Valley." Broadcast on Cable News Network Financial, January 15, 2001. Transcript available on LEXIS.

Moss, Philip; Harold Salzman; and Chris Tilly. 2000. "Limits to Market-Mediated Employment: From Deconstruction to Reconstruction of Internal Labor Markets." In *Nonstandard Work: The Nature and Challenges of Changing Employment,* ed. Françoise Carré et al., 95–121. Champaign, IL: Industrial Relations Research Association.

Motta, Massimo, and Thomas Rønde. 2002. "Trade Secret Laws, Labor Mobility, and Innovations." Discussion Paper 3615. London: Centre for Economic Policy Research. www.cepr.org/pubs/dps/DP3615.asp.

Murphy, Kevin. 1999. "Executive Compensation." *Handbook of Labor Economics,* vol. 3, ed. Orley Ashenfelter and David Card. Amsterdam: North Holland. www-rcf.usc.edu/~kjmurphy/ceopay.pdf.

Muto, Sheila. 2000. "Stock Options Spur Lawsuits as Mergers Roil High Tech." *Wall Street Journal Interactive Edition,* September 27.

Nalbantian, Haig R., ed. 1987. *Incentives, Cooperation, and Risk Sharing: Economic and Psychological Perspectives on Employment Contracts.* Totowa, NJ: Rowman and Littlefield.

Nalebuff, Barry J., and Joseph E. Stiglitz. 1983. "Prizes and Incentives: Towards a General Theory of Compensation and Competition." *Bell Journal of Economics* 14: 21–43.

National Research Council, Computer Science and Telecommunications Board. 2001. *Building a Workforce for the Information Economy.* www.cstb.org or www.nap.edu/books/0309069939/html.

Neumark, David, ed. 2000. *On the Job: Is Long Term Employment a Thing of the Past?* New York: Russell Sage Foundation.

Neumark, David, and Deborah Reed. 2002. "Employment Relationships in the New Economy." NBER Working Paper 8910, April.

Neumeyer, Fredrik. 1971. *The Employed Inventor in the United States: R&D Policies, Law, and Practice.* Cambridge, MA: MIT Press.

Neuwirth, Esther B. 2002. "'Silicon Valley Temps': An Ethnographic Account of the Staffing Industry." www.ucop.edu/ile/conferences/grad_conf/pdf/neuwirth.pdf.

Newman, Nathan. 2002. *Net Loss: Internet Prophets, Private Profits, and the Costs to Community.* University Park: Pennsylvania State University Press.

O'Connor, Marleen A. 1991. "Restructuring the Corporation's Nexus of Contracts: Recognizing a Fiduciary Duty to Protect Displaced Workers." *North Carolina Law Review* 69: 1189–1260.

Opatrny, Dennis J. 2000. "S.F. Juries Getting Smarter, and Stingier." *The Recorder,* June 14.

Orenstein, Susan. 2000. "What Happened at Juno." *Standard,* February 7.

Ó Riain, Seán. 2001. "Net-Working for a Living: Irish Software Developers in the Global Workplace." In *The Critical Study of Work: Labor, Technology, and Global Production,* ed. Rick Baldor, Charles Koeber, and Philip Kraft, 258–82. Philadelphia: Temple University Press.

O'Shaughnessy, K.C.; David I. Levine; and Peter Cappelli. 2000. "Changes in Managerial Pay Structures 1986–1992 and Rising Returns to Skill." National Bureau of Economic Research Working Paper 7730, June.

Osterman, Paul. 1999. *Securing Prosperity: The American Labor Market: How It Has Changed and What to Do About It.* Princeton, NJ: Princeton University Press.

————, ed. 1996. *Broken Ladders: Managerial Careers in the New Economy.* New York: Oxford University Press.

Osterman, Paul; Thomas A. Kochan; Richard Locke; and Michael J. Piore. 2001. *Working in America: A Blueprint for the New Labor Market.* Cambridge, MA: MIT Press.

Oyer, Paul, and Scott Schaefer. 2002. "Why Do Some Firms Give Stock Options to All Employees?: An Empirical Examination of Alternative Theories." Stanford Graduate School of Business Research Paper No. 1772. gobi.stanford.edu/Research Papers/Library/RP1772.pdf.

Packard, David. 1995. *The HP Way: How Bill Hewlett and I Built Our Company.* New York: Harper Business.

Pakes, Ariél, and Shmuel Nitzan. 1983. "Optimum Contracts for Research Personnel, Research Employment, and the Establishment of 'Rival' Enterprises." *Journal of Labor Economics* 1: 345–65.

Pandya, Sachin S. 1999. "Retrofitting Unemployment Insurance to Cover Temporary Workers." *Yale Law & Policy Review* 17: 907–47.

Parden, Robert J. 1981. "The Manager's Role and the High Mobility of Technical Specialists in the Santa Clara Valley." *IEEE Transactions on Engineering Management* EM-28(1): 2–8.

Park, Edward J.W. 1999. "Racial Ideology and Hiring Decisions in Silicon Valley." *Qualitative Sociology* 22: 223–33.

Pearce, Jone L. 1993. "Toward an Organizational Behavior of Contract Laborers: Their Psychological Involvement and Effects on Employee Co-Workers." *Academy of Management Journal* 36(5): 1082–96.

Pender, Kathleen. 1992. "Job Agency Will Settle Bias Lawsuits." *San Francisco Chronicle,* June 17, B3.

Peters, Thomas J., and Robert H. Waterman, Jr. 1982. *In Search of Excellence: Lessons from America's Best Run Companies.* New York: Harper and Row.

Pfeffer, Jeffrey. 2001. "What's Wrong with Management Practices in Silicon Valley? A Lot." *MIT Sloan Management Review* 42(3): 101–102.

Pitti, Stephen J. 2003. *The Devil in Silicon Valley: Northern California, Race, and Mexican Americans.* Princeton, NJ: Princeton University Press.

Piven, Frances F., and Richard A. Cloward. 1977. *Poor People's Movements: Why They Succeed, How They Fail.* New York: Pantheon.

Podolny, Joel M., and James N. Baron. 1997. "Resources and Relationships: Social Networks and Mobility in the Workplace." *American Sociological Review* 62: 673–93.

Polanyi, Michael. 1962. *Personal Knowledge: Towards a Post-Critical Philosophy.* Chicago: University of Chicago Press.

Poletti, Therese. 2001. "The HP Way Hits a Rough Patch." *San Jose Mercury News,* January 31.

Posner, Eric A., and George G. Triantis. 2001. "Covenants Not to Compete from an Incomplete Contracts Perspective." University of Chicago Law and Economics, Olin Working Paper 137.

Powell, Walter W. 1996. "Inter-Organizational Collaboration in the Biotechnology Industry." *Journal of Institutional and Theoretical Economics* 152: 197–215.

PR Newswire. 2002. "SEMI Survey Affirms Broad Employee Participation in Stock Option Plans." (September 27). Available on Lexis news file.

Pratt, John S., and Peter Dosik. 1997. "Whose Idea Is It? Company Sues Ex-Employee." *National Law Journal* 20, October 20.

Putnam, Robert D. 2000. *Bowling Alone: The Collapse and Revival of American Community.* New York: Simon and Schuster.

Rai, Saritha. 2002. "Harassment Suit in U.S. Shifts India's Work Culture." *New York Times,* September 6, W1.

Rivlin, Gary. 2000a. "Busting the Myth of the Meritocracy." *Standard,* February 28.

———. 2000b. "Cleaning Up In Silicon Valley." *Standard,* April 24.

Roemer, John. 2001. "Should Tech Workers Unite?" *Standard,* January 23.

Rønde, Thomas. 2001. "Trade Secrets and Information Sharing." *Journal of Economics and Management Strategy* 10(3): 391–417.

Rogers, Everett M., and Judith K. Larsen. 1984. *Silicon Valley Fever: Growth of High-Technology Culture.* New York: Basic Books.

Romer, Paul M. 1986. "Increasing Returns and Long Run Growth." *Journal of Political Economy* 94: 1002–37.

———.1990a. "Capital, Labor, and Productivity." *Brookings Papers on Economic Activity: Microeconomics* 1990: 337–67.

———. 1990b. "Endogenous Technological Change." *Journal of Political Economy* 98: S71–S102.

———. 1993. "Implementing a National Technology Strategy with Self-Organizing Industry Investment Boards." *Brookings Papers on Economic Activity: Microeconomics* 1993(2): 345–99.

———. 1994. "The Origins of Endogenous Growth." *Journal of Economic Perspectives* 8: 3–22.

Rose, Stephen J. 1995. "Declining Job Security and the Professionalization of Opportunity." National Commission for Employment Policy, Research Report No. 95-004.

Rosen, Sherwin. 1981. "The Economics of Superstars." *American Economic Review* 71(5): 845–58.

Rosenberg, Geanne. 1997. "An Idea Not Yet Born, But a Custody Fight." *New York Times,* September 8, D3.

Rubin, Paul H., and Peter Shedd. 1981. "Human Capital and Covenants Not to Compete." *Journal of Legal Studies* 10: 93–110.

Rutherglen, George. 1995. "From Race to Age: the Expanding Scope of Employment Discrimination Law." *Journal of Legal Studies* 24: 491–521.

Ryle, Gilbert. 1949. *The Concept of Mind.* New York: Barnes and Noble.

Ryskamp, John. n.d. "The Changing Nature of the H-1B Computer Professional." http: //papers.ssrn.com/paper.taf?abstract_id=239903.

Saint-Paul, Gilles. 1999. "On the Distribution of Income and Worker Assignment under Intra-firm Spillovers, with an Application to Ideas and Networks." www.cepr.org (Discussion Paper 2290) and www.econ.upf.es/deehome/what/wpapers/postscripts/417.pdf.

Saxenian, AnnaLee. 1994. *Regional Advantage: Culture and Competition in Silicon Valley and Route 128.* Cambridge, MA: Harvard University Press.

———. 1999a. *Silicon Valley's New Immigrant Entrepreneurs.* San Francisco: Public Policy Institute of California.

———. 1999b. "Comment on Kenney and von Burg, 'Technology, Entrepreneurship and Path Dependence: Industrial Clustering in Silicon Valley and Route 128.'" *Industrial and Corporate Change* 8(1): 105–109.

Schor, Juliet. 1991. *The Overworked American: the Unexpected Decline of Leisure.* New York: Basic Books.

Schultz, Vicki. 1990. "Telling Stories About Women and Work: Judicial Interpretation of Sex Segregation in the Workplace in Title VII Cases Raising the Lack of Interest Argument." *Harvard Law Review* 103: 1750–1843.

Schumpeter, Joseph. 1942. *Capitalism, Socialism, and Democracy.* New York: Harper.

Schwab, Stewart J. 1993. "Life-Cycle Justice: Accommodating Just Cause and Employment at Will." *Michigan Law Review* 92: 8–62.

Scully, Maureen. 1997. "Managing the Legitimacy of Controversial Issues: The Role of Gay Employee Groups in the Adoption of Domestic Partner Benefits." Paper presented at the Industrial Relations Research Association Meeting, Spring. New York.

Sennett, Richard. 1998. *The Corrosion of Character: The Personal Consequences of Work in the New Capitalism.* New York: Norton.

Shapiro, Carl, and Joseph E. Stiglitz. 1984. "Equilibrium Unemployment as a Worker Discipline Device." *American Economic Review* 74(3): 433–44.

Shapiro, Carl, and Hal R. Varian. 1999. *Information Rules: A Strategic Guide to the Network Economy.* Boston: Harvard Business School Press.

Sharpe, Richard. 2001. "'Globalization': The Next Tactic in the Fifty-Year Struggle of Labor and Capital in Software Production." In *The Critical Study of Work: Labor, Technology, and Global Production,* ed. Rich Baldoz, Charles Koeber, and Philip Kraft, 215–35. Philadelphia: Temple University Press.

Shell, Karl. 1966. "Toward a Theory of Inventive Activity and Capital Accumulation." *American Economics Review Papers and Proceedings* 56: 62–68.

———. 1967. "A Model of Inventive Activity and Capital Accumulation." In *Essays on the Theory of Optimal Economic Growth,* ed. Karl Shell. Cambridge, MA: MIT Press.

———. 1973. "Inventive Activity, Industrial Organization and Economic Growth." In *Models of Economic Growth,* ed. James A. Mirrlees and Nicholas H. Stern, 77–96. New York: Wiley.

Shockley-Zalabak, Pamela; and Sandra Buffington Burmester. 2001. *The Power of Networked Teams: Creating a Business Within a Business at Hewlett-Packard in Colorado Springs.* New York: Oxford University Press.

Shreve, Jenn. 2000. "The Paper Padlock." *The Industry Standard.* thestandard.com/article/0,1902,12994,000html.

Shuchman, Philip. 1979. *Problems of Knowledge in Legal Scholarship.* West Hartford: University of Connecticut Law School Press.

Siegel, Lenny. 1998. "New Chips in Old Skins: Work and Labor and Silicon Valley." In *Global Productions: Labor in the Making of the "Information Society,"* ed. Gerald Sussman and John A Lent, 91–110. Cresskill, NJ: Hampton Press.

Silverstein, Eileen; and Peter Goselin. 1996. "Intentionally Impermanent Employment and the Paradox of Productivity." *Stetson Law Review* 26: 1–52.

Sitkin, Sim B. 1986. "Secrecy in Organizations: Determinants of Secrecy Behavior among Engineers in Three Silicon Valley Semiconductor Firms." Ph.D. dissertation, Graduate School of Business, Stanford University.

Slind-Flor, Victoria. 1993. "More Trade Secrets Wars." *National Law Journal,* March 22, 1.

Smith, Douglas K., and Robert C. Alexander. 1988. *Fumbling the Future: How Xerox Invented, Then Ignored, the First Personal Computer.* New York: Morrow.

Smith, Ethan. 2000. "Labor Pains for the Internet Economy." *Standard,* October 20.

Smith, Stephen C. 1988. "On the Incidence of Profit and Equity Sharing: Theory and an Application to the High Tech Sector." *Journal of Economic Behavior and Organization* 19: 45–58.

Smith, Vicki. 2001. *Crossing the Great Divide: Worker Risk and Opportunity in the New Economy.* Ithaca, NY: ILR Press.

Solomon, Karen. 2000. "Girls' Night Out: Women Executives Network on Their Own Terms." *Standard,* August 7.

Solow, Robert M. 1956. "A Contribution to the Theory of Economic Growth." *Quarterly Journal of Economics* 70: 65–94.

Southwick, Karen. 1999. *Silicon Gold Rush: The Next Generation of High-Tech Stars Rewrites the Rules of Business.* New York: Wiley.

Spence, Michael. 1984. "Cost Reduction, Competition, and Industry Performance." *Econometrica* 52: 101–21.

Stabile, Susan J. 1999. "Motivating Executives: Does Performance-Based Compensation Positively Affect Managerial Performance?" *University of Pennsylvania Journal of Labor and Employment Law* 2: 227–85.

Steffy, Loren. 2000. "A Lawsuit for Your Thoughts." *Chicago Sun-Times,* October 1, 42.

Stewart, James B., ed. 1997. *African Americans and Post-Industrial Labor Markets.* New Brunswick, NJ: Transaction.

Stone, Katherine Van Wezel. 1991. "Employees as Stakeholders Under State Nonshareholder Constituency Statutes." *Stetson Law Review* 21: 45–72.

———. 2001. "The New Psychological Contract: Implications of the Changing Workplace for Labor and Employment Law." *UCLA Law Review* 48: 519–661.

Storper, Michael, and Robert Salais. 1997. *Worlds of Production: The Action Frameworks of the Economy.* Cambridge, MA: Harvard University Press.

Strauss, Will. 2000. "Forward Thinking." *Electronic Engineering Times,* July 17.

Sturgeon, Timothy J. 2000. "How Silicon Valley Came to Be." In *Understanding Silicon Valley: The Anatomy of an Entrepreneurial Region,* ed. Martin Kenney, 15–47. Stanford, CA: Stanford University Press.

Sturm, Susan. 2001. "Second Generation Employment Discrimination: A Structural Approach." *Columbia Law Review* 101: 458–568.

Suggs, Robert E. 1991. "Racial Discrimination in Business Transactions." *Hastings Law Journal:* 1257–1323.

Sundaram, Viji. 2001. "A Tech Worker's Tale of H-1B Exploitation." *India-West.*

Supiot, Alain. 1999. *Au-delà de l'emploi: transformations du travail et devinir du droit du travail en Europe.* Paris: Flammarion.

Sussman, Gerald, and John A. Lent. 1998. *Global Productions: Labor in the Making of the "Information Society."* Cresskill, NJ: Hampton Press.

Swann, G.M. Peter; Martha Prevezer; and David Stout, eds. 1998. *The Dynamics of Industrial Clustering: International Comparisons in Computing and Biotechnology.* Oxford: Oxford University Press.

Swinnerton, Kenneth A., and Howard Wial. 1995. "Is Job Stability Declining in the U.S. Economy?" *Industrial and Labor Relations Review* 48: 293–304.

Teuke, Molly Rose. 1999. "Dice Clicks!" www.cpuniverse.com/newsite/archives/1999/may/dice.html.

Thaler, Richard H. 1992. *The Winner's Curse: Paradoxes and Anomalies of Economic Life.* New York: Free Press.

Thorne, Mister. 2002. "Age Bias Persists in Silicon Valley." *Wall Street Journal,* August 26. www.careerjournal.com.

U.S. Bureau of Labor Statistics. 2001. "Contingent and Alternative Employment Arrangements." USDL 01-153. http: //www.bls.gov/news.release/conemp.nro.htm.

U.S. Department of Commerce. Bureau of the Census. 2000a. *Educational Attainment in the United States: Detailed Tables* (March). 222.census.gov/population/www/socdemo/education/p20–536.html.

————. 2000b. "Profile of General Demographic Characteristics." http: //censtats.census.gov/data/CA/05006085.pdf.

————. 2002. "California County Shows Biggest Percentage Increase in Jobs and Payroll." www.census.gov/Press-Release/www/2002/cb02–76.html (May 30, 2002).

————. Technology Administration, Office of Technology Policy. 1999. *The Digital Workforce: Building Infotech Skills at the Speed of Innovation.* www.ta.doc.gov/Reports/TechPolicy/digital.pdf.

U.S. Department of Labor. 1999a. *Employee Benefits in Small Private Establishments, 1996.* Bulletin 2507. Washington, DC: U.S. Government Printing Office.

————. 1999b. *Employee Benefits in Medium and Large Private Establishments, 1997.* Bulletin 2517.

U.S. Economic Report of the President. 2001. w3.access.gpo.gov/usbudget/fy2002/pdf/2001_erp.pdf.

U.S. General Accounting Office. 2000. "H-1B Foreign Workers: Better Controls Needed to Help Employers and Protect Workers." (September 7). www.gao.gov/new.items/he00157.pdf.

Vaas, Lisa. 2002. "CWA Calls for Repeal of H1-B Program." *e week,* June 28.

Valletta, Rob. 2002. "On the Move: California Employment Law and High-Tech Development." *Federal Reserve Bank of San Francisco Economic Letter.* No. 2002-24, August 16.

Varian, Hal R. 2002. "Economic Scene: Productivity and Profitability: An Odd Couple in an Odd Recession." *New York Times,* June 6, C2.

Virgin, Bill. 2000. "Microsoft Settles 'Permatemp' Suits: Two $97 Million Cases Reshape Employment for Temps Nationwide." *Seattle Post-Intelligencer,* December 13, A1.

von Hippel, Eric. 1988. *The Sources of Innovation.* New York: Oxford University Press.

Wachter, Michael L., and George M. Cohen. 1988. "The Law and Economics of Collective Bargaining: An Introduction and Application to the Problems of Subcontracting, Partial Closure, and Relocation." *University of Pennsylvania Law Review* 136: 1349–1417.

Wallace, Patricia. 1999. *The Psychology of the Internet.* Cambridge, UK: Cambridge University Press.

Weiler, Paul C. 1990. *Governing the Workplace: The Future of Labor and Employment Law.* Cambridge, MA: Harvard University Press.

Weinberg, Neal. 1998. "Career Crisis: Feeding Frenzy for Java-savvy Whiz Kids Leaves 40-Something IT Pros High and Dry." *Network World,* September 14.

Weiss, Andrew. 1980. "Job Queues and Layoffs in Labor Markets with Flexible Wages." *Journal of Political Economy* 88(3): 526–38.

Whaley, Susan Street. 1999. "The Inevitable Disaster of Inevitable Disclosure." *University of Cincinnati Law Review* 67: 809–857.

White, Harrison C. 2002. *Markets from Networks: Socioeconomic Models of Production.* Princeton: Princeton University Press.

Wial, Howard. 1993. "The Emerging Organizational Structure of Unionism in Low-Wage Services." *Rutgers Law Review* 45: 671–738.

Wilkins, David B., and G. Mitu Gulati. 1996. "Why Are There So Few Black Lawyers in Corporate Law Firms?: An Institutional Analysis." *California Law Review* 84: 493–625.

William M. Mercer Inc. 2002 "Tech Firms Continue to Refine Compensation Programs." July 12 Press Release. www.mercerhr.com/pressrelease/details.jhtml?idContent=1062030.

Williamson, Oliver E. 1985. *The Economic Institutions of Capitalism: Firms, Markets, Relational Contracting.* New York: Free Press.

Wilms, Wellford W. 1996. *Restoring Prosperity: How Workers and Managers Are Forging a New Culture of Cooperation.* New York: Times Business.

Winch, Peter. 1958. *The Idea of a Social Science and Its Relation to Philosophy.* London: Routledge and Kegan Paul.

Wolff, Edward N. 2002. *Retirement Insecurity: The Income Shortfalls Awaiting the Soon-to-Retire.* Washington, DC: Economic Policy Institute.

Women of Silicon Valley. 2001. *Unfinished Business: Women in the Silicon Valley Economy.* www.womenofsv.org.

Wood, Jason S. 2000. "A Comparison of the Enforceability of Covenants Not to Compete and Recent Economic Histories of Four High Technology Regions." *Virginia Journal of Law and Technology* 5: 14–43.

Worth, Erica. 1995. "In Defense of Targeted ERIPs: Understanding the Interaction of Life-Cycle Employment and Early Retirement Incentive Plans." *Texas Law Review* 74: 411–45.

Wysocki, Bernard, Jr. 1996. "Flying Solo: High-Tech Nomads Write New Program for Future of Work." *Wall Street Journal,* August 19, A1.

Yablon, Charles M. 1999. "Bonus Questions: Executive Compensation in the Era of Pay for Performance." *Notre Dame Law Review* 75: 271–308.

Zell, Deone. 1997. *Changing by Design: Organizational Innovation at Hewlett-Packard.* Ithaca, NY: ILR Press.

Zhou, Yu. 1996. "Inter-firm Linkages, Ethnic Networks, and Territorial Agglomeration: Chinese Computer Firms in Los Angeles." *Papers in Regional Science* 75(3): 265–91.

Zlolniski, Christian. 1994. "The Informal Economy in an Advanced Industrialized Society: Mexican Immigrant Labor in Silicon Valley." *Yale Law Journal* 103: 2305–35.

Zucker, Lynne G.; Michael R. Darby; and Jeff Armstrong. 1998. "Geographically Localized Knowledge: Spillovers or Markets?" *Economic Inquiry* 36: 65–86.

INDEX

ABOUT THE AUTHOR

Alan Hyde is professor and Sidney Reitman Scholar at Rutgers University School of Law in Newark. He has also been a visiting professor of labor law, employment law, and legal theory at Yale, Columbia, New York University, University of Michigan, and Cardozo law schools. His books include *Bodies of Law* (1997), and *Cases and Materials on Labor Law* (2d ed., 1982, with Summers and Wellington). His law review publications include work on the sociology of comparative labor legislation, employee ownership, democratic collective bargaining, new forms of employee organization, labor relations under government contract, legitimation, and transnational application of U.S. employment statutes. His current research includes legal and policy issues raised by short-term employment, such as intellectual property disputes between employers and employees, temporary and contracted labor, new labor market intermediaries, the redefinition of discrimination, and ethical and philosophical issues raised by labor mobility. He frequently represents the Association for Union Democracy and the American Civil Liberties Union in labor and employment litigation.